International Energy and Resources Law and Policy Series

European Community Energy Law
Selected Topics

Editors

General Editor

Professor Thomas W. Wälde, *Executive Director, Centre for Petroleum & Mineral Law & Policy (CPMLP), University of Dundee, UK*

Editoral Working Committee
(All of the Centre for Petroleum & Mineral Law & Policy)

Ayesha Dias, *Senior Research Fellow*
David Mac Dougall, *Lecturer*
James Gunderson, *Honorary Lecturer; General Counsel, Schlumberger Electricity Management*
James Otto, *Senior Lecturer*
Professor Paul Stevens

Consulting Editors

Dr. Emilio J. Cárdenas, *Ambassador, Permanent Representative of Argentina to the United Nations, New York, USA*
Dr. Istvan Dobozi, *Technical Department, Energy Division, The World Bank, New York, USA*
Dr. Fereidun Fesharaki, *Director, Program on Resources, East-West Center, Honolulu, Hawaii, USA*
Professor William F. Fox, *Columbus School of Law, Catholic University of America, Washington DC, USA*
Professor Rosalyn Higgins, QC, *London School of Economics, London, UK*
Dr. Kamal Hossain, *Dr. Kamal Hossain and Associates, Dhaka, Bangladesh*
Philippe Kahn, *Director, CREDIMI, Université de Bourgogne, Dijon, France*
Dr. Amanda Niode Katili, *Agency for the Assessment and Application of Technology, Jakarta, Indonesia*
Professor Eugene M. Khartukov, *Ministry of Foreign Affairs, Moscow, CIS*
Professor Alain Lapointe, *Director, Oil & Gas Company Management Programme, Centre d'Etudes en Administration Internationale, Ecole des Hautes Etudes Commerciales, Université de Montréal, Quebec, Canada*
Dr. Ole Anders Lindseth, *Director General, Oil & Gas Department, Royal Ministry of Industry and Energy, Oslo, Norway*

International Energy and Resources Law and Policy Series

European Community Energy Law
Selected Topics

Editors
David S. Mac Dougall
and
Thomas W. Wälde

Graham & Trotman/Martinus Nijhoff
Members of the Kluwer Academic Publishers Group
LONDON/DORDRECHT/BOSTON

Graham & Trotman Limited
Sterling House
66 Wilton Road
London SW1V 1DE
UK

Kluwer Academic Publishers Group
101 Philip Drive
Assinippi Park
Norwell, MA 02061
USA

ISBN 1-85333-962-8
Series ISBN 1-85333-796-X

© Centre for Petroleum & Mineral Law & Policy,
Dundee University, Dundee, DD1 4HN, 1994
First Published in 1994

British Library Cataloguing in Publication Data is available

Library of Congress Cataloging-in-Publication Data

European Community energy law: selected topics/editors, David S.
  Mac Dougall and Thomas W. Wälde.
    p.   cm.—(International energy and resources law and policy
  series
    Includes index.
    ISBN 1-85333-962-8
  1. Energy industries—Law and legislation—European Economic
  Community countries. 2. Public utilities—Law and legislation—
  European Economic Community countries. 3. Energy policy—European
  Eonomic Community countries. I. MacDougall, David S. II. Wälde,
  Thomas W. III. Series
  KJE6848.E93 1994
  346.404'67915—dc20   93–47941
  [344.06467915]   CIP

Typeset in 10/11pt Times by Concept Typesetting Ltd., Salisbury, Wilts.
Printed and bound in Great Britain by Hartnolls Ltd., Bodmin, Cornwall.

Contents

SECTION 2: EUROPEAN ENERGY LEGISLATION

Preface

This book arose out of the Centre for Petroleum and Mineral Law and Policy's 1992 Summer Courses on 'European Integration in 1992 and its Impact on Energy Industries' and 'Recent Developments and Concepts of United Kingdom Energy Law'. The success of these courses, the interest generated by the participants, the quality of the presentations, and the dearth of authoritative texts on the expanding field of European Community energy law encouraged the Centre to produce a compilation of key works in this growing and vital field.

The works included in this text, with the exception of Chapters 7 and 20, have been derived by their respective authors from the presentations given by or on behalf of the authors at the above noted Centre courses. Chapter 20 on Derivative Financing arose out of the author's presentation on the same topic at the Centre's 'International Oil and Gas Policies' course also held in the summer of 1992; and Chapter 7 on the EC Directives on the Transit of Gas and Electricity, which summarises an earlier publication in the German language, was kindly provided by the authors for use in this text.

Due to the swiftly changing nature of EC energy law it must be noted that although the chapters contained herein are current to at least the summer of 1992, and every effort has been made to update them as close as possible to the publication date, events have in some instances overtaken the status, particularly of proposed legislation, noted in the text.

The actual status of a body of law that can be termed 'European Community Energy Law' is in itself unclear, primarily because it has only been relatively recently that the Community has put its mind to fuller regulatory control of the Community energy sector as a whole. As such, the approach of this text is to look at selected topics, in certain key energy areas, which are of current interest. Section 1 deals with current and emerging Community policy with respect to the Community energy sector; Section 2 with current and proposed EC legislation of particular relevance to the energy sector; Section 3 with EC environmental law and its potential impact on the energy sector; Section 4 with commercial issues relevant in particular to the oil and gas industries; and Section 5 with current issues in energy financing.

The focus of the text is primarily on the oil and gas industry, and less so on Community regulation of the EC electricity industry which has already been thoroughly covered by a monograph prepared by one of the contributing authors to this text. Due to the Centre's location in the United Kingdom, and the importance of the UK Continental Shelf (UKCS) to the EC oil and gas industry, the UK example has been used by various contributors, including where appropriate reference to domestic law, to highlight key issues. A broader EC and international focus has however been maintained wherever possible and many of the issues of relevance to the UKCS are similarly relevant throughout the Community as well as within an international context.

It is hoped that this book will serve as a key reference for anyone interested in the issues of current relevance to the EC energy sector, as well as providing the international energy audience an insight into the approach to energy sector regulation currently being taken by the Community, in that many of the issues affecting European energy industries are indicative of situations in other jurisdictions, particularly within the oil and gas sector.

Many of the contributors have gone beyond a description of the current and proposed regulatory regime, critically to analyse Community energy regulation, thus hopefully providing the reader with a deeper insight into the ongoing debate over the future course of energy regulation in the Community and the issues of greatest relevance.

David Mac Dougall

Foreword

The Community is at an important crossroads in its evolution towards closer union. December 31 1992 was a historic day for the Community since it marked the completion of the Single Market for practically all sectors, a fundamental objective of the Treaty of Rome. In the coming years, the Maastricht Treaty on European Union will pose fresh challenges but also opens up new horizons for the European Community. In these developments, it is my firm conviction that a Community dimension for energy is essential.

The development of a cohesive and broadly acceptable energy policy at Community level was one of my major responsibilities as Commissioner in the European Commission. This was not always an easy task since in the energy sector important political and economic interests are at stake and this inevitably militates in favour of keeping the *status quo*. In this context, it is vital therefore that the options facing us are examined in an objective and open way before changes are decided upon. There is no doubt that the centrepiece of this debate which is still continuing is the completion of the internal energy market.

In working towards open and transparent energy markets the Commission was not motivated by ideological reasoning. We must always bear in mind that energy accounts for a significant proportion of the Community's GDP – similar to that of agriculture – and in a number of industrial sectors is a major cost element. It is therefore of considerable importance to the competitiveness of our industry and ultimately the economic well-being of our citizens that its energy supplies are provided in the most economic way, without of course damaging security of supply or with adverse environmental effect. An integrated energy market would reduce energy costs and allow advantage to be taken of the complementarities of the Community's energy industries; increase trade in energy products between member states; and make an important contribution to security of supply.

During my tenure as Commissioner responsible for energy, progress was made in opening up the energy markets and removing existing obstacles. Important work was done on public procurement in the energy equipment sector, on tax structures and standardisation of energy equipment and products and towards the liberalisation of electricity and gas markets by opening up national networks to the transit of gas and electricity and with a significant improvement in price transparency.

However, Commission proposals that would significantly remould the closed and often monopolistic nature of the gas and electricity industries in many member states by allowing new entrants into the industry and a limited opening of networks to certain eligible consumers and distributors have met, and are still meeting, opposition.

The goals being set are certainly ambitious and this may explain the reluctance of the Energy Council to reach firm conclusions on Commission proposals. However, the debate is still very much alive and there is a general recognition that the present situation cannot continue – the forces for change are too strong. Work is continuing to see if the Commission draft proposals can be adapted to take account of certain criticisms without watering down the fundamental thrust of the policy – opening up and making more competitive the gas and electricity sectors.

Although the internal market occupied much of my time, an issue that has had perhaps an even higher profile is the relation between energy and the environment and in particular the problem of global climate change. The Community has already made a commitment to stabilise emissions of carbon dioxide, one of the major greenhouse gases, at 1990 levels by the year 2000. It will be a challenge to bring together the various elements – technological, fiscal, economic, trade – in order to achieve a coherent response to this challenge. A contribution has already been made by putting in place innovative energy technology programmes such as Altener and SAVE. The more controversial responses such as an energy/CO_2 tax which would have far-reaching effects not only internally but also with our trading partners and energy suppliers need further evaluation. A convincing case must be made not only for the Community, but if our initiatives are to have an impact at a global level, in respect of other major industrial economies.

The Community, with its important worldwide economic, trading and political links, cannot ignore the external dimension of its energy policy – it is still dependent on imports for half its energy supply. Commission analysis shows this dependence is likely to increase in the long-term. The Community therefore has a vital interest in developing a framework where its energy security is assured. This can be achieved to some extent by developing co-operative relations with energy suppliers, such as the Gulf and southern Mediterranean countries. In this context the Community has also been an active supporter of strengthening links between producers and consumers of energy through intensified dialogue.

On our own doorstep the new democracies of eastern and central Europe and the republics of the former USSR are also looking towards a common energy future with the Community. As they adjust to becoming market economies, the Community – through its co-operation programmes such as PHARE and TACIS, and through its efforts to establish a pan-Europe energy agreement, the European Energy Charter Treaty – is contributing to this transition.

We also cannot ignore the developing countries; Commission analysis shows that in the next century their economic development will lead to their having a major influence on world energy markets and so indirectly on the Community. We must make efforts to ensure that our energy model and the associated technology become an essential component of their energy strategies.

In the short term the below trend level of economic activity and plentiful energy supplies could perhaps lead to complacency and a tendency to put energy matters lower down the political agenda. However, the issues with which I lived during my tenure at the Commission will in my view still need to be addressed at the Community level particularly as it moves towards closer economic and political union.

Antonio Cardoso e Cunha

List of Contributors

Julian P. Armstrong is General Counsel, Esso UK plc.

David Aron is Managing Director of Petroleum Development Consultants Ltd.

David Brock is a Partner and Head of the Environmental Law Group of London solicitors Herbert Smith. He specialises in Planning Law.

Antonio Cardoso e Cunha former Commissioner (responsible for energy) of the European Communities.

Galina Carroll is Economic Assistant, Economics and Statistics, UK Department of Trade and Industry.

Dr. Fraser Davidson is a Senior Lecturer, Department of Law, University of Dundee.

Hew Dundas is Legal Manager, Cairn Energy PLC.

Professor David Edward is a Judge of the Court of Justice of the European Communities.

James L. Gunderson is General Counsel, Schlumberger Electricity Management.

Leigh Hancher is Professor of Public Economic Law at Erasmus University, Rotterdam.

Adrian Hill is Corporate Legal Adviser, Upstream for Conoco (UK) Ltd.

Gareth Jones is a Partner and member of the Energy Group of London solicitors Nabarro Nathanson.

David S. Mac Dougall is a Solicitor and Lecturer on Energy Law, Centre for Petroleum and Mineral Law and Policy, University of Dundee.

Denzil Millichap is a member of the Planning and Environmental Law Unit of London solicitors Linklaters & Paines.

Eoin O'Shea is Director of the Legal Department of Credit Suisse Financial Products.

Dr. Johann-Christian Pielow is Akademischer Rat at the Institut für Berg- und Energierecht der Ruhr-Universität Bochum.

Sidney A. Price is Senior Economic Adviser, UK Department of Trade and Industry.

Colin T. Reid is a Senior Lecturer, Department of Law, University of Dundee; and a Council Member, United Kingdom Environmental Law Association.

William Robinson, formerly a Research Associate of the European Law Institute, University of Durham, is a temporary Legal Secretary at the Court of Justice of the European Communities.

Charles Robson is a Solicitor with the London firm Lovell White Durrant.

Clive J.V. Robson is a Partner of London solicitors Slaughter and May.

Drs. Martha M. Roggenkamp is a Research Fellow, Internationaal Instituut voor Energierecht, Rijksuniversiteit Leiden.

John R. Salter is a Partner of London solicitors Denton Hall Burgin & Warrens.

Mark Saunders is a Partner of London solicitors Nabarro Nathanson.

Dr. Georges Schneider is Portfolio Development Manager of Shell Petroleum Development Co of Nigeria Ltd.

Michael Stanger is a Partner of London solicitors Lovell White Durrant.

Michael P.G. Taylor is a Partner and Head of the Energy and Natural Resources Group of London solicitors Norton Rose.

Prof. Dr. Peter J. Tettinger is Chairholder of Public Law of the Faculty of Law, and Executive Director of the Institut für Berg- und Energierecht der Ruhr-Universität Bochum.

Tom Winsor is a Partner and member of the Energy and Natural Resources Group of London solicitors Denton Hall Burgin & Warrens.

Dr. Norbert Zimmermann is a Research Fellow at the Lehrstuhl für Offentliches Recht der Ruhr-Universität Bochum.

Acknowledgements

Chapter 13 of this volume, *Acreage Portfolio Management*, is derived from a paper prepared by the author for presentation at the SPE Oil & Gas Economics, Finance and Management Conference held in London, April 28–29 1992 and for which copyright is held by the Society of Petroleum Engineers as follows: Copyright 1992, Society of Petroleum Engineers, Inc.

Chapter 6 of this volume, *Third Party Access to Gas and Electricity Transmission Systems in the Community: Third Party Access – Your Flexible Friend?*, is derived by the author from an earlier version first published in 1993 in the *Journal of Energy and Natural Resources Law*, Vol.11, No.1, at pp.27–35.

Introduction

European Community Energy Law in Perspective

David S. Mac Dougall

1.0 EUROPEAN COMMUNITY ENERGY LAW?

As noted in the Preface one of the difficulties faced in preparing a work on 'European Community Energy Law' is the task of defining what this phrase encompasses. The founding Treaties[1] of the European Communities aimed to create a common market[2] in which there would be a free flow of goods, services, labour and capital. Since the inception of the European Economic Community in 1957 progress has been steadily made towards this goal, so that today a majority of sectors within the Community are free or virtually free of any significant barriers to intra-Community trade. The Single European Act which came into force in 1987 had as its main goal the speeding up of this process, setting December 31 1992 as the date by which the internal market[3] was to be complete, a process which to a large degree has been achieved.

In its 1988 Working Document[4] the Commission of the European Communities highlighted the creation of an Internal Energy Market as one of the specific goals in the establishment of the larger common market. Prior to this time there was no clear Community policy regarding the energy sector, energy not being specifically

---

1. The Treaty of Rome, 1957, establishing the European Economic Community (EEC Treaty); the Treaty of Rome, 1957, establishing the European Atomic Energy Community (EAEC) (Euratom Treaty); and the Treaty of Paris, 1951, establishing the European Coal and Steel Community (ECSC Treaty).
2. As opposed to merely a more limited free trade area or customs union.
3. Art. 8A EEC Treaty, added by Art.14 of the Single European Act, states in part that '[t]he internal market shall comprise an area without internal frontiers in which the free movement of goods, persons, services and capital is ensured...'
4. COM(88) 238 Final.

mentioned in the EEC Treaty.[5] The policy approach of the Commission is clearly set out by the former Commissioner responsible for energy matters, Antonio Cardoso e Cunha, in Chapter 1. The current approach is based on three stages of liberalisation of the Community energy market: Stage 1 consisted of a Directive on price transparency for gas and electricity,[6] and two separate Directives on the transit of gas[7] and electricity;[8] Stage 2 consists of proposals for the adoption of common rules for the internal markets in electricity and gas,[9] and is currently ongoinging;[10] and Stage 3 is to consist of a further extension and completion of the liberalisation of the electricity and gas markets, based on the experience acquired during the second Stage.

However, for various reasons, the Stage 2 Commission proposals have met resistance within the Council of Ministers and the future of EC energy policy is at the moment unclear. Along with the resistance of certain EC member states (including Spain, Italy, France, Greece, Luxembourg and the Netherlands) to acceptance of the Stage 2 proposals in their original form (particularly the concept of third party access to gas and electricity transmission systems), the debate over which is thoroughly canvassed in Chapter 6 of this text, a report[11] prepared by the Section for Energy, Nuclear Questions and Research of the Economic and Social Committee of the European Communities (ESC) only partially supported the proposals[12] and on November 17 1993 the European Parliament gave its opinion on the proposals, calling for several hundred amendments.

As noted it was not until the 1988 Working Document that the Commission actually focused particularly on the energy sector, a sector which has been notably

industries, respectively, but do not provide the basis for any coherent Community energy policy. See notes 20 and 21 infra in respect of the role of these treaties.

6. Council Directive 90/377/EEC, OJ L185/16, July 17 1990; concerning a Community procedure to improve the transparency of gas and electricity prices charged to industrial end users.

7. Council Directive 91/296/EEC, OJ L147/37, June 12 1991; on the transit of natural gas through grids.

8. Council Directive 90/547/EEC, OJ L313/30, Nov. 13 1990; on the transit of electricity through transmission grids.

9. COM(91) 548 Final; Proposal for a Council Directive concerning common rules for the internal market in electricity, and the Proposal for a Council Directive concerning common rules for the internal market in natural gas, OJ C65/14, Mar. 14 1992.

10. The Commission's original proposals consist in part of the following key concepts: 1) the elimination of exclusive rights of production, transportation and distribution; 2) the 'unbundling' of vertically integrated enterprises including a separation of accounts; and 3) limited third party access for certain large energy consumers.

11. ENE/202, Opinion of the Economic and Social Committee on the Proposal for a Council Directive concerning common rules for the internal market in electricity and the Proposal for a Council Directive concerning common rules for the internal market in natural gas, Brussels, Jan. 27 1993, Mr. Gafo Fernandez Rapporteur.

12. In particular ECS, ibid., supported the application of 'commercial criteria' as a future guideline for the electricity and gas sectors (para.2.1.7), the liberalisation introduced in the generation stage and the gradual deregulation of the transmission and distribution stages (para.2.1.7), the liberalisation of the construction of power stations, LNG facilities and electricity/gas transmission or distribution lines (paras. 2.5.2 and 4.6), the principle of accounting transparency and the unbundling of accounts (paras 2.6.1 and 4.10), and the safeguard clauses and procedures for consultation (paras 2.10.1 and 2.10.5, respectively).

It specifically rejected the plans and deadlines for the introduction of the third party access system as provided in the Directives (para.4.7, see also para.2.9.7 where it states that it does not rule out third party access at some future date).

13. See in particular Case 202/88 *French Republic v Commission* [1991] ECR I-1223 (Telecoms);

slow to liberalise. The Commission proposals are geared to an opening up of the EC energy market and the fostering of greater competition on a Community-wide basis. These proposals are not being put forward to foster competition merely for competition's sake but to ensure comparable prices, for comparable classes of consumers, and adequate supply, throughout the Community. The energy sector is not alone in its slow pace of liberalisation, the same slow rate being witnessed particularly in other utility sectors such as telecommunications. The Commission, bolstered in part by recent European Court of Justice (ECJ) decisions,[13] has targeted the telecommunications sector as well and has been quite successful in increasing liberalisation. The energy sector is however even more politicised, but drawing by analogy on recent EC legislation, and supporting case law, particularly in the telecommunications sector, there is clearly precedent for the opening up of monopolised and politicised sectors of the Community, though at a much slower rate than that of less vital market sectors.

Clearly the energy sector is a special case[14] due to its importance to the economic well-being, and security, of the Community. It is this 'strategic' importance that has led the liberalisation of this sector of the Community to lag behind. Questions of sovereignty and control over natural resources, particularly as this impacts on the issue of security of supply, exacerbated by the oil price shocks of the 1970s and 1980s, and the varying structural/organisational nature of the energy sector within each of the member states, makes it particularly difficult to reach compromises acceptable to all parties. Furthermore, the economic and political strength of the industry participants, more often than not monopolies with strong government ties, allows for intense opposition to be mounted when proposals are seen by the industry players who are affected as detrimental to their long-standing dominant positions.

Thus, at present, 'European Community Energy Law' can be seen to comprise essentially two main facets: 1) that specific law that has been passed into or proposed as Community legislation within the ambit of the Internal Energy Market programme (and the limited ECJ decisions dealing specifically with energy matters[15]); and 2) the general law of the Community as set down in the Treaties, Community legislation, and case law of the ECJ, which although not directly or specifically aimed at the energy sector is binding upon it as general Community law.[16]

One must not lose sight of the fact that although there is a particular Community programme under way with respect to the energy sector, this sector is no less a part of the overall economy of the Community, and at all times subject to Community

Case 260/89 *ERT v Dimotiki*, Judgment of June 18 1991 [1991] ECR I-2925; Case 18/88 *RTT v GB-Inno*, Judgment of Dec. 13 1991, [1991] ECR I-5941; and Case 311/84 *CBEM-Telemarketing v CLT and IPB* [1985] ECR 3261 (Telemarketing). For a discussion of these and related cases as they may impact on the development of the internal energy market see L. Hancher and P. Armin Trepte, 'Competition and the Internal Energy Market' [1992] 4 ECLR 149. See also Cases C271, C281 and C289/90, *Spain, Belgium and Italy v Commission* [1992] ECR I-5833. For a discussion of the judgment see P. Armin Trepte [1992] 4 *Utilities Law Review* 165.

14. For a discussion of whether the energy market should be treated as a special case under the EEC Treaty rules see Chapter 2.

15. See Chapter 2, particularly notes 3–5 and accompanying text, for a discussion of various decisions of the ECJ and Court of First Instance regarding the energy industries.

16. For example, see Chapter 8 regarding the application of EC law to employment offshore.

law. However, one of the key reasons for a distinct energy programme is the realisation that the energy sector, for the reasons noted above, is unique, and that a slower, more gradual and more targeted approach is essential. Unlike most other sectors of the Community economy the Commission has rarely attempted to use the general powers available to it to legislate, propose legislation, or bring actions before the ECJ, involving the energy sector; despite in many cases existing breaches of general Community law. In particular, many of the existing arrangements for the supply of energy within member states could be found to be in violation of the competition law provisions of the Treaties.

If the member states are unable to formulate a fuller EC energy policy it may be possible for the Commission to utilise its enforcement powers under Community competition law to open up the energy market.[17] The EC Competition Commissioner, Karel Van Miert, had threatened to take France, Italy, Denmark, Ireland, Spain and the Netherlands to the ECJ for maintaining monopolies on the import and export of electricity and gas and on electricity transit, in contravention of the EEC Treaty,[18] despite resistance to act hastily in this regard from Energy Commissioner Matutes. In the event the Commission has decided to proceed to the ECJ with the infringement proceedings. This is particularly important in light of member state opposition to the Commission liberalisation programme.

2.0 EC ENERGY REGULATION

Despite the current impasse on the direction of EC energy policy, there is already in place a significant body of EC legislation directly applicable to the energy sector. In particular, the Directives on price transparency and electricity and gas transit noted above.

There is also legislation in place which directly impacts on the production, supply and use of oil and natural gas;[19] control of certain aspects of the Community nuclear

17. See Hancher, op. cit., supra note 13, and Chapter 2 this volume, particularly 4.2.2, for discussion of the application of EC competition law to the energy sector.

18. Cameron Markby Hewitt, *European Newsletter*, May 1993, p.31. Reasoned Opinions were sent to the relevant member states by the Commission in Nov. 1992.

19. See in part Council Directive 68/414/EEC, OJ L308, Dec. 23 1968 (as amended by Directive 72/425/EEC, OJ L291, Dec. 28 1972) imposing an obligation on member states to maintain minimum oil stocks; Council Regulation 1055/72, OJ L120, May 25 1972 on notifying the Commission of imports of crude oil or natural gas; Council Regulation 1056/72, OJ L120, May 25 1972 (as amended by Regulations 1215/76, OJ L140, May 28 1976 and 3025/77, OJ L358, Dec. 31 1977) on notifying the Commission of investment projects of interest to the Community in the petroleum, natural gas and electricity sectors; Council Directive 73/238 EEC, OJ L228, Aug.16 1973 on measures to mitigate the effects of difficulties in the supply of crude oil and petroleum products; Council Regulation 338/75, OJ L145, Feb. 19 1975 on notifying the Commission of exports of crude oil and natural gas to third countries; Council Directive 75/339/EEC, OJ L153, June 13 1975 obliging the member states to maintain minimum stocks of fossil fuel at thermal power stations; Council Directive 75/405/EEC, OJ L178, July 9 1975 concerning the restriction of the use of petroleum products in power stations; Council Directive 76/491/EEC, OJ L140, May 28 1976 regarding a Community procedure for information and consultation on the prices of crude oil and petroleum products; Council Dec. 77/186/EEC, OJ L61, March 5 1977 (as amended by Dec. 79/879/EEC, OJ L270, Oct. 27 1979) on the exporting of crude oil and petroleum products from one member state to another in the event of supply difficulties; and Council Dec. 77/706/EEC, OJ L292, Nov. 16 1977 on the setting of a Community target for a reduction in the consumption of primary sources of energy in the event of difficulties in the supply of crude oil and petroleum products.

energy industry;[20] regulation of the Community coal industry;[21] energy and the environment;[22] and procurement in the energy sector.[23]

Key proposed legislation includes the controversial proposals concerning the common rules for the internal market in electricity and natural gas noted above (see Chapter 6 for a fuller discussion of the ongoing debate over third party access in particular); and a proposal for a Council Directive on the conditions for granting and using authorisations for the prospection, exploration and extraction of hydrocarbons,[24] on which a common position was adopted by the Energy Council on December 10 1993.

For a fuller discussion of the Utilities, Services and Licensing Directives see Chapter 4 and the subsequent Commentary. For a description of the application of the Remedies Directive see Chapter 5.

As noted, the second facet of EC energy law is the application of the general law of the Community. The importance of Community competition law as a means of furthering the creation of the internal energy market has already been mentioned. However, numerous other areas of Community law have a large impact on the Community energy industries. The specific importance of the regulation of the environment by the Community requires further elaboration and as such is discussed below. A fuller discussion of the application of other areas of general Community law to the energy sector is beyond the scope of this chapter, but it is useful to note the following areas in which Community regulation will have a direct effect on the Community energy industries: 1) health and safety (particularly with respect to the offshore oil and gas and nuclear industries);[25] 2) technological developments[26] and conformity measures; 3) work with dangerous substances;[27] and 4) employment.[28]

20. In particular the Euratom Treaty, which concentrates primarily on safety and co-operation. See also in part Council Regulation (EAEC) No.4, OJ 17, Oct. 6 1958 defining the investment projects to be communicated to the Commission in accordance with Art. 41 of the Euratom Treaty; and Commission Regulation (Euratom) No.2014/76, OJ L221, Aug. 14 1976 on the support of projects concerning uranium prospecting programmes within the territories of the member states.

21. See in particular the ECSC Treaty which concentrates on trade and modernisation of production.

22. See in particular Council Dec. 91/565/EEC, OJ L307/34, Nov. 8 1991 concerning the promotion of energy efficiency in the Community (the SAVE programme); and Proposal for a Council Directive to limit carbon dioxide emissions by improving energy efficiency (SAVE programme) OJ C179/8, July 16 1992 and Proposal for a Council Decision concerning the promotion of renewable energy sources in the Community (Altener Programme) OJ C179/4, July 16 1992, each of which were approved at the Energy Council of June 25 1993.

23. See particularly Council Directive 93/38/EEC, OJ L199/84 Aug. 9 1993 on the procurement procedures of entities operating in the water, energy, transport and telecommunications sectors (the 'Utilities' Directive) and the associated Council Directive 92/13/EEC, OJ L76/14, Mar. 23 1992 co-ordinating the laws, regulations and administrative procedures relating to the application of Community rules on the procurement procedures of entities operating in the water, energy, transport and telecommunications sectors (the 'Remedies' Directive).

24. Original Proposal: OJ C139/12, June 2 1992 (the 'Licensing' Directive).

25. See Chapter 8, 3.0, for a discussion of the application of EC law with respect to offshore health and safety. In particular 3.3.3 dealing with Directive 92/91 concerning minimum requirements for improving the health and safety protection of workers in the mineral extracting industries through drilling.

26. With respect to direct Community involvement in the promotion of energy related technology see Council Regulation (EEC) No.2008/90, OJ L185/1, July 17 1990 concerning the promotion of energy technology in Europe (Thermie Programme). See also the Commission's mid-term review of the Thermie Programme (COM(93)642).

27. On Nov. 11 1993 the Council adopted a common position on a Directive on explosive atmospheres which will affect the oil industry.

28. For a description of relevant Community legislation (adopted and proposed) covering these areas as regards the EC offshore see: T. Hollobone, and J. Mirzoeff, *The European Community and its Offshore Oil and Gas Legislation* (T. A. Hollobone & Co, 1992). See also Chapter 8, this volume, regarding the impact of EC law on employment offshore.

3.0 EC ENVIRONMENTAL LAW

As previously mentioned another vital component of 'European Community Energy Law' is the development of a growing body of 'European Community Environmental Law'. Chapters 9–11 of this text canvass this area of EC law from, respectively, the following points of view: 1) past, present and future development of EC environmental policy and regulation; 2) the role of the ECJ in environmental protection; and 3) the impact of EC environmental law on a specific member state regime, the United Kingdom. Again one can see the two key streams of EC Energy Law at work: 1) specific programmes aimed at the energy sector;[29] and 2) general EC law as it is applicable to all sectors equally.

With respect to specific action the focus is to a large degree on conservation of energy, energy efficiency,[30] the promotion of innovative energy technologies,[31] and the encouragement of the use of renewable/alternative energy sources.[32] Pollution control measures referable to the energy industry are also in place.[33]

The most controversial Commission proposal is that for a combined energy/CO2 tax[34] to reduce CO2 emissions and help security of supply. (See Chapter 1, 4.0, for a discussion of the Commission proposal.)

It is interesting to note that the ECS Opinion on the 'common rules' proposals particularly states its concern 'over the lack of any reference to the implications of these proposals for the environment' and encourages the Commission to study ways of developing the concepts of competition and liberalisation in the energy sector so as not to detract in any way from the requirements of environmental protection.[35]

With respect to EC environmental law generally, there has been an awakening in the Community, as elsewhere, to the need for greater protection of the overall environment, and since the 1972 UN Conference on the Environment, held in Stockholm, there has been a significant development of a body of EC environmental regulation, along with a growing body of ECJ case law in the environmental sphere, which will undoubtedly impact on the energy sector.[36] (See Chapters 9–11.)

29. The first statement of Community energy policy which addressed environmental problems in a global way was COM(89) 369 Final, Feb. 8 1990 'Communication from the Commission to the Council on Energy and the Environment'.

30. Particularly the SAVE Programme (Specific Actions for Vigorous Energy Efficiency), op. cit., supra note 22.

31. Particularly the Thermie Programme, supra note 26.

32. Particularly the Altener Programme for renewable energies, op. cit., supra note 22.

33. In particular Directive 88/609/EEC, OJ 1988 L336/1 on emission standards for large combustion installations; and Directive 84/360/EEC, OJ 1984 L188/20 on air pollution from major industrial plants (including certain thermal plant).

34. See SEC(91) 1744 Final, Oct. 14 1991 and COM(92) 246 Final, June 1 1992: 'A Community Strategy to limit carbon dioxide emissions and to improve energy efficiency', particularly at COM(92) p.3, para.7. The tax as initially proposed would apply in equal proportions: 50 per cent as a tax on all non-renewable energy sources, and 50 per cent based on the carbon content of the energy source.

35. Supra note 11 at p.14, para.2.11.1.

36. See in particular Council Directive 85/337/EEC, June 27 1985 on the assessment of the effects of certain public and private projects on the environment, which requires environmental assessment for certain classes of projects including projects in the extractive and energy industries; and the Commission's Fifth Action Programme on the Environment [OJ 93/C 138/1] entitled 'Towards Sustainability' which gives priority in part to the fields of: sustainable management of natural resources; integrated pollution control and waste management; and reduction in consumption of non-renewable energy.

4.0 MEMBER STATE ENERGY REGULATION/EXTERNAL IMPACT AND COMMUNITY ENLARGEMENT

Two other key areas impact on, without actually coming under the umbrella of, 'European Community Energy Law': 1) internal member state regulation of national energy industries; and 2) the role of a larger Europe, outside the Community, as it impacts on the EC energy regime.

4.1 Member State Energy Regulation

With respect to the first issue it is clear that EC Energy Law, as with EC law in all sectors, is only a portion of the law applicable within the member states. Despite the ever-increasing body of EC law, such law is limited to the purposes proposed in the Treaties – essentially the liberalisation of trade and movement of factors of production[37] – and the vast majority of law applicable in the member states is each respective state's own national body of law. Thus, although in the author's opinion, national member state law impacting on the energy sector is not a component of 'European Community Energy Law' *per se*, the interaction of the two systems is critical.[38] In the energy sector an excellent example of this interaction is the ability for member states to apply for partial exemption from the full scope of the provisions of the Utilities Directive where they can prove that certain alternative conditions are satisfied. See Chapter 4 for a fuller discussion of the Utilities Directive in general and the S.3 exemption in particular.

Two points are vital to keep in mind when analysing the relationship between national and EC law in any sphere: 1) it has long been established that Community law is supreme when directly effective within the member states[39] and more recently that national law must conform to Community law or be read in light of such law;[40] and 2) the recent development of the concept of 'subsidiarity'[41] will lead the Community in future to delegate greater powers to legislate, even in areas of Community legal competence, where not exclusive to the Community, to the individual member states, where the objectives of the proposed action can be sufficiently achieved by the member states.[42]

37. Although the impact of the Treaty on European Union, Feb. 7 1992 (the Maastricht Treaty) will be to extend the competences of the Community. Notably with respect to Community economic and monetary policy.

38. A key finding of the ECS Opinion on the proposed 'common rules' Directives for gas and electricity was that it would be difficult to achieve the Community-wide organisational changes proposed for these sectors without such action being preceded by a 'proper alignment' of national energy policies. Supra note 11 at p.5, para.2.1.5; p.14, para 2.9.7; and p.19, para.4.8.

39. See for example Case 26/62 *NV Algemene Transport – en Expeditie Onderneming Van Gend ed Loos v Nederlandse Administratie der Belastingen* [1963] ECR 1; and Case 6/64 *Costa v Ente Nazionale per l'Energia Elettrica (ENEL)* [1964] ECR 585 which actually dealt with the Italian electricity industry.

40. See Case 14/83 *Colson v Land Nordrhein-Westfalen* [1986] 2 CMLR 430; and Case 106/89 *Marleasing SA v La Comercial Internacional de Alimentacion SA* [1992] 1 CMLR 305.

41. See Art. 3b Maastricht Treaty.

42. See Chapter 2, 3.1, for a discussion of the subsidiarity principle and its potential impact on the energy market. Certain aspects of Community competition law have been specifically noted as ripe for the axe of subsidiarity (*eg* a change in the threshold allowing Community action regarding merger control under Council Regulation (EEC) 4064/89).

In its Opinion on the 'common rules' proposals the ECS noted that it believed the proposed Directives must clearly state that security of supply is primarily the responsibility of the distributors of natural gas and electricity and this responsibility must be underpinned by proper institutional arrangments in each member state in accordance with the principle of subsidiarity, and in accordance with such principle security of supply should be guaranteed by the states themselves, combined with necessary Community level co-ordination.[43]

4.2 External Impact and Community Enlargement

With respect to the external dimension, the recent changes in the political and economic climate of eastern Europe and the former Soviet Union have opened up vast energy reserves on the doorstep of the Community. Along with many of the non-EC western European countries, the countries of eastern Europe and the former Soviet Union are looking to foster greater links with the Community – with the potential for some becoming members at a later date. Although the future role of expansion for the EC is not totally clear any desire to allow new member states must be considered when proposing legislation which may directly affect future membership decisions.[44]

In the sphere of energy this is particularly critical, and the Community has recognised the importance of a stable energy sector within a larger European context. In December 1991 the European Energy Charter[45] was signed[46] and a treaty[47] based on the principles set-out therein is under ongoing negotiation. Furthermore, there also exist various Association Agreements between the Community and several countries of eastern Europe.

The issue of energy regulation as an impediment to future expansion of the EC is not an abstract proposition as is made clear by the Norwegian debate over potential membership. Of crucial importance to a Norwegian decision is the EC law that impacts on Norway's vital North Sea petroleum industry. Such issues as EC regulation of licensing procedures (the Licensing Directive) and a more competitive EC procurement regime (the Utilities Directive) are delicate issues in the state-dominated Norwegian petroleum sector.[48] However, as with the European Energy

43. Supra note 11, p.6, paras 2.2.2, 2.2.3.

44. One commentator has noted that 'any new gas policy for Europe will be seriously incomplete unless it takes into account the potential future role of Russian gas' (R.J. Pierce, 'Experiences with Natural Gas Regulation and Competition in the US Federal System: Lessons for Europe', in *Natural Gas in the Internal Market: A Review of Energy Policy* (ed. Ernst J. Mestmacker) (London Graham & Trotman, 1993, p.138).

45. The Charter sets out certain basic principles on the development of energy trade, co-operation in the energy field, energy efficiency and environmental protection. It also provides for the negotiation of a Basic Agreement (now to be a treaty) and related Protocols. For a brief discussion of the Charter see P. Cameron, 'The European Energy Charter: A Magna Carta for Energy?' [1991] 7 OGLTR 207.

46. By 48 country representatives, including the 12 EC member states, all the countries of western Europe, seven eastern European countries, the three Baltic republics, 12 republics of the former Soviet Union, the United States, Japan, Canada and Australia, and by representatives of the European Community and the Interstate Economic Committee.

47. Version 6, Dec. 20 1993, Draft Treaty, Energy Charter Treaty.

48. The ECS Opinion on the 'common rules' Directives, supra note 11, p.15, para.2.11.5, also recommends an assessment of the application of the proposed Directives on the new European Economic Area, in light of the fact that this new bloc will bring new competition factors into play in the European market.

Charter, the EC has continued to move in a positive direction with the creation of the European Economic Area (EEA)[49] between the EC and the European Free Trade Association (EFTA) countries of which Norway is one.[50]

A similar concern is also addressed by the ECS Opinion on the 'common rules' proposals, with respect to the Commonwealth of Independent States (CIS) and central and eastern Europe. In general the European Energy Charter is perceived as a positive development and as such ECS has stated its concern over the potential harmful effects of the proposed Directives on the possibility of new supplies of natural gas from the CIS or the need for short-term electricity supplies to central and eastern Europe to offset closure of their own facilities for environmental or nuclear safety grounds.[51]

It is also important to note that the Community's heavy reliance on imported energy (particularly oil) makes it crucial that any EC energy policy take account of potential impacts on the larger international stage. An example of an international impact of EC energy policy is the OPEC backlash to any notion of the introduction of a carbon tax. The Community itself is unwilling to impose such a tax, which would be to its competitive detriment, if similar charges are not imposed in other OECD countries. (See Chapter 1, 3.0, for a fuller discussion of the external impact of EC energy policy.)

5.0 RECENT DEVELOPMENTS

Although the EEC Treaty does not make specific reference to the energy sector the Community has clearly shown that it considers regulation of this 'strategic' sector as especially important, although final agreement on what form this regulation will take will be difficult to reach.

One area of interest is the new Title XII on 'Trans-European Networks' added to the EEC Treaty, by the Maastricht Treaty. The provisions of the new Title provide in part that 'the Community shall contribute to the establishment and development of trans-European networks in the areas of transport, telecommunications and energy infrastructures' [Article 129b(1)] and that '[w]ithin the framework of a system of open and competitive markets, action by the Community shall aim at promoting the interconnection and interoperability of national networks as well as access to such networks' [Article 129b(2)].

Furthermore, relying on the new Article 129c(1), which provides in part for the establishment of guidelines for the objectives in the sphere of trans-European networks (which guidlines are to identify projects of common interest), the Commission has issued a 'Proposal for a Council Regulation introducing a declara-

49. Agreement on the European Economic Area, May 2 1992. The aim of the Agreement is 'to promote a continuous and balanced strengthening of trade and economic relations between the Contracting Parties' [Art. 1(1)]. The association is to entail the free movement of goods, services, persons and capital; a system to ensure competition is not distorted; and closer co-operation in other fields such as research and development, the environment, education and social policy [Article 1(2)].

50. The other EFTA countries are Austria, Sweden, Finland, Switzerland, Iceland and Liechtenstein. The Swiss however voted against joining the EEA and they and consequently Liechtenstein remain outside the Agreement.

51. Supra note 11, p.15, paras 2.11.2–2.11.4.

tion of European interest to facilitate the establishment of trans-European networks in the areas mentioned by the Maastricht Treaty'.[52] Such a Declaration of European Interest acts as 'an instrument for the implementation of guidelines established by the Council' and 'gives the Commission a powerful instrument to plan, co-ordinate and implement major investment decisions'.[53]

Article 129c(2) further provides, in part, for inter-member state co-ordination of 'the policies pursued at national level which may have a significant impact on the achievement' of the proposed objectives, and 129c(3) allows for co-operation 'with third countries to promote projects of mutual interest and to ensure the inter-operability of networks'.

The new approach to trans-European networks highlights the Commission's more active intervention in the utilities (including energy) sectors; interventionism which is likely to continue in one form or another for some time.

6.0 COMMERCIAL CONCERNS

Despite the growth in pure EC energy regulation, this is a very young field, and much will be done in the future. It is also a field that requires an understanding of other areas of concern, as already noted particularly the environment. Furthermore, it is also a highly developed commercial sphere of industry which requires and generates vast quantities of money. As such, any discussion of energy regulation requires an analysis of key legal/commercial concerns, notably financing issues, facing the industry, as commercial factors play as vital a role, if not more so, than political factors in most energy developments.

Section I.B. ('Financing of Trans-European Networks') of the Explanatory Memorandum of the Commission Proposal for a declaration of European interest (DEI) for trans-European network projects[54] highlights the importance of private sector financing for the emergence of such large-scale infrastructure networks and the DEIs are to be aimed at projects which, in part, can attract private investment.[55]

In its Opinion on the 'common rules' proposals the ECS has endorsed the introduction of 'commercial criteria' as a future guideline for the gas and electricity sectors. It is, however, interesting to note the ECS's conclusion that such guidelines must maintain necessary links with the 'public interest obligations' of these sectors, notably security of supply.[56] The author agrees with the ECS conclusion that a balance must be struck between competition, decisions based on commercial criteria, and the public service obligations; not just with respect to the 'common

---

52. COM(92) 15 Final, Feb. 24 1992.

53. Ernst J. Mestmacker, 'Energy Policy for Natural Gas in the Internal Market – An Overview', in *Natural Gas in the Internal Market*, supra note 44, pp.5, 6. Mestmacker provides a good review of the potential importance of the Maastricht Treaty provisions, pp.4–7. See also Y. Smeers, 'Aims and Means of European Energy Policy in the Light of the Completion of the Internal Market', in *Natural Gas in the Internal Market* (above), p.39, section 7.1.4, for a discussion of trans-European networks.

54. Supra note 52.

55. Ibid., section I.C.13; and see also p.14 the Proposed Regulation on a Declaration of European Interest to Facilitate the Establishment of a Trans-European Network in the Electricity and Gas Domains and the annex thereto.

56. Supra note 11, pp.6, 8, paras 2.1.7, 2.5.1. See also pp.6, 8, paras 2.2.6, 2.4.2 regarding the interaction of economic and political considerations.

rules' proposals but for EC energy regulation in general. The recently revised Commission proposals on 'common rules' make a number of concessions to the public service concept. Thus, as noted, the economic/commercial and socio-political aspects of EC energy regulation must be analysed together to reach viable conclusions for the present and future regulation of the EC energy industries. (See Chapters 13–18 for consideration of selected key commercial issues and agreements within the oil and gas industry; and Chapters 19–21 with respect to energy financing.)

An excellent example of the interaction between commercial concerns and Community energy policy can be seen in the debate over third party access in the gas industry. The enormous costs involved in developing the transmission infra-structure for a gas grid, and in bringing on stream gas developments, have led to the conclusion of long-term take-or-pay contracts for the sale/purchase of gas. It is argued by opponents of third party access that such contracts, and the monopoly rent currently enjoyed by EC transmission companies, is required to justify the sunk costs of the infrastructure and that 'free-riders' on such infrastructure, under a third party access regime, and a change in the contractural arrangements of the industry, will prevent additional new investment, the development of new gas fields and reduce demand growth.[57]

The Community itself is highly active in assisting in financing the energy sector. In 1991 the Community's financial institution, the European Investment Bank, loaned ECU 2.7bn to the energy sector for projects primarily involving the development of indigenous resources; promotion of the efficient use of energy; and the diversification of natural gas imports.[58]

7.0 CONCLUSIONS

As noted above it is the author's belief that there now exists a body of 'European Community Energy Law' separate from, though clearly affected by, national member state energy regulation. Thus, the following text does not aim to deal with specific member state energy regulation, with the exception of some greater focus on the UK oil and gas regime generally as an example for the wider EC/ International oil and gas industry; rather, the aim is initially to discuss the current energy policy framework of the Community; then to deal specifically with certain key existing and proposed EC legislation directly aimed at the energy sector; to highlight key aspects of EC environmental regulation as an area of EC law with a potentially strong impact on the energy sector; to discuss in detail some of the key commercial concerns of the oil and gas industry (particularly within the UK but in such a manner as to allow for extrapolation to the broader EC/International oil and gas industry); and finally to highlight some of the key issues involved in the continuing search for the vast sums of money required to keep the energy industry alive.

---

57. For a fuller discussion of this issue see J. Stern, 'The Prospects for Third Party Access in European Gas Markets', in *Natural Gas in the Internal Market*, supra note 44, p.183 particularly pp.192–5. Regulatory changes in the US gas regime have in the past played havoc with long-term take-or-pay contracts and the Community must seek to avoid the problems encountered within the US gas industry. (See Pierce, supra note 44, for a discussion of lessons to be learned from US gas regulation.)

58. *The European Investment Bank – The European Community's financial institution*, (1992), p.6.

Section 1

European Energy Policy

Chapter 1

Energy Policy – The European Community Dimension

Antonio Cardoso e Cunha

1.0 INTRODUCTION

This Chapter will highlight the major issues facing the European Community in the energy field and the implications for European energy policy. It focuses on four major themes:

- the Community's internal energy market;
- energy security and the external dimension of energy policy;
- the relation between energy and the environment; and
- energy technology and innovation.

2.0 THE INTERNAL ENERGY MARKET

In an increasingly competitive world it was recognised early on by the policy makers that if the Community's industry was to deal effectively with international competition and benefit from attractive and secure energy supply conditions there would have to be a more integrated and competitive Community energy market.

However, this issue was only fully addressed in the second half of the 1980s when it was recognised that energy could not be isolated from mainstream developments in the Community, notably the commitment to achieve a Single Market. An integrated energy market would reduce costs particularly for energy intensive industries, allow advantage to be taken of the complementarities of the Community's energy industry, increase trade in energy products between member states and so make an important contribution to the security of supply. The dramatic turn of events in central and eastern Europe and in the former USSR, where the spectacular failure of their centrally planned economies was a major factor in inducing changes, reinforces the case for a market-based competitive system in the EC.

Since 1988, when the obstacles to the achievement of this objective were first identified, the Community has made excellent progress. However, it has to be recognised that there still exists a formidable challenge in securing the goal of free and competitive markets in energy and it is clear that not all obstacles can be removed overnight. Given the complex and varying nature of the energy markets in each member state it will take time for existing structures to adapt. This is born out by the experience in the UK where, in recent years, radical measures in relation to its energy industries were adopted.

The challenge faced is best illustrated by the situation in the electricity and gas sectors on which the latest Commission proposals based in part upon Article 100A of the Single Act focus. There are few areas in most member states of the Community where state monopolies have such a dominance and which are subject to the same level of government intervention on price structures or business behaviour.

The first steps in establishing free and competitive markets in these sectors were taken in 1991 with the adoption of Directives on 'Price Transparency' and 'Transit'. Under the first measure – Price Transparency Directive, adopted in 1991 – industrial consumers now have access to aggregate data on charges made by gas and electricity utilities to all categories of customers throughout the Community, thus giving them the tools to negotiate more effectively their contracts with suppliers.

The Transit Directives create opportunities for gas and electricity to trade more effectively across the Community even if there is a third grid between grid operators establishing a contract. For instance, an entity in the energy sector in Spain wishing to buy electricity from a counterpart in Germany has, under certain conditions, notably maintaining the reliability of the grid, the right to utilise the grid system in France to realise its trade.

Despite this progress in opening up markets one has to recognise that this was only a first step; numerous obstacles still remain to real integration in these energy sectors. If we take electricity for instance we find that new entrants cannot enter the market both as regards production or transmission, nor can customers choose their supplier, often because of the monopoly structure of the industry. For historic reasons, energy markets in the Community are compartmentalised and vested interests often block economically justified trade within the Community.

For the second phase of liberalisation it was necessary therefore to have far-reaching proposals for these sectors. These were approved by the Commission in January 1992 and submitted to the Council of Ministers. These are based in part upon Article 100A brought in by the Single Act. This provides the legal base for progressively establishing the internal market of Article 8A. Article 100A also offers a great advantage for progress in that the proposals based on it need a qualified majority of the Council, rather than unanimity, to reach the status of Directives. The involvement of the European Parliament has more recently been extended by the new Co-Decision Procedure (Article 189b of the EC Treaty) introduced by the Treaty of European Union (Maastricht). [See Chapter 6, 7.1, for a full discussion of the Co-Decision Procedure as it relates to the 'common rules' proposals.] If adopted the proposals would progressively allow large industrial energy consumers to have a choice in their purchase of electricity and gas and to open up investment in production and transport to new independent operators.[1]

1. Following the Opinion of the Economic and Social Committee (ENE/202) and the European Parliament's Opinion of Nov. 17 1993, the Commission, on Dec. 8 1993, adopted a substantially amended proposal for the 'common rules' directives.

First, production and transportation would be open to new entrants on a non-discriminatory basis. Second, vertically integrated electricity undertakings would, from an accounting standpoint, be required to unbundle their various components – generation, supply and distribution – without necessarily changing ownership structures and independence of management at least at the administrative level must be guaranteed. In this way one would hope it would become apparent where cross-subsidising is taking place and also reveal if some users and/or producers have unfair advantages.

Furthermore, the concept of third party access (TPA) is to be introduced on a limited basis. Transmission and distribution companies will be obliged to offer negotiated access to their network, within the limits of available transmission and distribution capacity, to certain eligible consumers or distributors at reasonable rates. (For a more in-depth discussion of the proposals on TPA see Chapter 6 and Chapter 7)

If adopted these proposals would begin to create opportunities for large energy consumers and distributors above a certain size to buy gas and electricity on a competitive basis throughout the Community. On the basis of criteria proposed by the Commission it is estimated that, in a first phase, about 500 large industrial undertakings in energy intensive sectors such as cement, aluminium, steel, etc. would benefit and that as far as distributors are concerned about 100 would be eligible. Suitable mechanisms will ensure that neither the less developed regions nor disadvantaged social classes will suffer unduly from this opening up of the market.

Great care is to be taken to avoid the introduction of new bureaucratic rigidities. In the second phase, member states will be able to choose the model and the organisation that best fits their specific situation in line with the principle of subsidiarity, as long as the principles in the Treaty of Rome which are the foundation of the internal market are respected.

On the basis of experience in the working of this innovative system, the access provisions should be reviewed in 1996[2] to ensure completely free and open markets in these important energy sectors by the end of this decade.

It is clear that the issues at stake often touch matters of a sensitive and strategic nature; not everyone is pleased and there is strong resistance to change by well-established structures in this sector. These proposals are undergoing a rigorous and far-reaching debate not only in the Council of Ministers, but also in the European Parliament. Nor can we neglect the importance of continuing consultations with industry. Nevertheless, the author firmly believes that the path chosen, albeit now already significantly modified, is the most feasible option after intense consultations and discussion with all concerned; with fair consideration of the interests of producers and consumers the proposals, albeit ambitious, are firmly on the rails of practicability.

Although the proposals on the Internal Energy Market for electricity and gas are taking up a considerable amount of time as they pass through the Community institutional process; this is only one of the Commission's objectives, which is also active in applying Single Market principles to other energy sectors.

2. The hold-up in the Commission's second stage proposals will necessitate a longer time frame for energy market liberalisation than at first envisaged. The transitional provision for 'common rules' is now set to end on Dec. 1 1998 at the earliest.

In coal there is a commitment to limiting state subsidies by a rigorous application of the rules of the Treaty. The aim is to allow financial support only if it improves the competitiveness of the Community coal industry or in the case of new production, economic viability if fulfilled. Of course one must recognise that social imperatives cannot be swept away overnight. In fact, pressures for change will arise when the Commission proposals are adopted since they would make transparent the link between higher electricity prices and subsidies to coal in some member states.

In the oil sector the intent is to make sure that a competitive framework is the norm in the granting of production and exploration licences and so end the current situation of privilege for national undertakings and discrimination against entrepreneurs from other member states. (For a more in-depth discussion of the Community legislation regarding Licensing see Chapter 4 and the following commentary.)

A more rational choice of plant in all energy sectors has been possible with public procurement subject to Community rules. Progress has also been achieved on norms and standards–technical matters which are vital to the smooth running of the internal market.

The above concerns the policy approach but what is also interesting is the way in which the great questions of competition are enshrined in Community law right across the whole range of industry and commerce. This implies that in energy matters one must frequently be attuned to what is proving legally possible in other sectors, where jurisprudence is accumulating and giving ever-more positive signals for future action by the Commission.

Commission interest in the jurisprudence of Community competition law, in particular Articles 37 and 90(2), is all the more marked because the approach to the internal energy market is only partly reliant upon bringing in new legislation. Where obstacles to competition exist, the Commission naturally looks to see whether these can be abolished by reference to the existing law before trying to frame new legislation to deal with them. Apart from the correctness of principle in using the existing Treaty powers to the full, this is normally much easier than seeking new legislation because it does not involve the co-operation of the Council of Ministers.

3.0 THE EXTERNAL DIMENSION

The appeal of what is trying to be achieved in the Community is demonstrated by the increasing willingness of other European countries to become more closely associated with our efforts. For instance, under the European Economic Area agreement, the countries of the European Free Trade Association (EFTA) (absent Switzerland and Liechtenstein) will take on board most of the Community's legislation. The upshot will be that as regards energy, these countries will be adopting practically all the current legislation as well as being committed to future developments without being members as such of the Community.

Of course, in a longer perspective, many EFTA countries wish to become members in order to ensure that they have a more effective say in the shaping of the new Europe. In fact, the Community is already in the process of examining requests for accession from various EFTA states and accession negotiations with Austria, Finland, and Sweden are now complete.

Not too far in the future, once they have found their feet, the new democracies of eastern and central Europe are also likely to be knocking on our door in order to be more closely associated with the Community's development. It would not be too fanciful to say, therefore, that what the Commission is trying to achieve as regards a single energy market could eventually have a much wider application beyond the existing Community of Twelve.

In many respects the process of integration in Europe, and this is particularly true of the energy sector, is unique. It requires sovereign states adopting mutual obligations which often touch on matters of a sensitive and strategic nature. This shows that even where decision making at local level – or subsidiarity – should be resorted to where it is more efficient there is still a need in some areas for Community action.

This need for Community action at Community level is reinforced by other challenges in the energy field, notably:

— the growing need to improve security of supply, and
— the need for common action to solve global environmental problems.

As regards supply security, the Community's vulnerability in the supply of energy, particularly oil, has increased since 1986. Having become the largest importer of energy in the world, the Community must still cover almost half of its energy requirements by means of imports and in a longer-term perspective this dependence is likely to increase. There is a danger therefore, particularly in the case of oil, that the Community could become unduly dependent on a limited number of countries or even a single producing region whose political stability leaves much to be desired.

It is at the Community level that we need to address the problem of security of supply, given that the Community is one of the main players on the international energy scene. It is to this end that the Commission has approved a report that examines the possibility of increasing the effectiveness of our existing crisis measures and also ways in which we can mobilise existing oil stocks more efficiently and if needed establish additional ones. The accession of the Community to the IEA must be seen in this context. On the external front, the Community is actively promoting increased dialogue and co-operation between producers and consumers since it is thought this will introduce further elements of stability and predictability in the market.

It must be emphasised that, for the Community, international co-operation is not just a matter of efforts to bind together the rich market-orientated economies of Europe with the oil-rich states. It has always been aware of the need for intensified co-operation with the developing world and more recently with the countries of central and eastern Europe and the former USSR as a result of the fundamental political and economic changes under way in these countries.

A key objective of the Community is to find a way of integrating these newly emerging democracies into Europe and the energy issue offers an excellent opportunity. It was in this context that the European Community launched its 1990 initiative for a European Energy Charter, which after a year of intensive negotiation was signed at The Hague on December 16 1991 by about 50 countries.

The central idea of the Charter is to find a political framework in which East–West co-operation can develop in the energy sector with a view to expanding trade in energy; making the optimum use of energy; obtaining adequate environmental protection and promoting the transfer of technology and investment.

Since the Charter has been signed, intensive work has been under way on the framing of a Basic Agreement (or Treaty) designed to give practical effect to the Charter. This Agreement aims to set out the instruments and mechanisms as regards co-ordinated legislation, mining rights, taxation, treatment of investment and free trade, so that practical effects can be given to the Charter. This is not an easy task since it needs to address horizontal provisions larger than energy. For the Community the implementing agreements can in no way affect obligations in other international agreements such as the GATT. The emphasis needs to be put on the notion of co-operation on the one hand and the creation of favourable conditions for the investors on the other. In a nutshell mutual advantage must prevail.

Once the Basic Agreement is signed rapid progress can then be made in a number of sectoral protocols: hydrocarbons, energy efficiency, etc. These specific agreements are essential to maintain the impetus provided by the Charter. They will also provide an opportunity to identify priorities in a number of branches of the energy sector, and to propose guidelines for the countries in the process of restructuring. Above all, they will help to give concrete shape to the political intentions expressed in the Charter.[3]

Outside this framework the Community has for a long time been providing substantial financial assistance for the PECO (east and central European) countries energy sector through the PHARE Programme and, more recently, to the new republics of the former USSR in order to help them reform and restructure their energy sectors.

This assistance, usually in the form of grants, is intended to encourage progress towards a market economy and pave the way for investment from both public and private sectors. In 1991, the energy part of the PHARE Programme provided +/- 5 mio ECUs for each country. For the former USSR, 115 mio ECUs out of 400 mio ECUs of technical assistance aid was allocated to energy. Some of this technical assistance will contribute to continuing production of hydrocarbons, essential for EC economies, but a large part is earmarked for improvements in the safety of their energy operations, particularly the nuclear sector. We must accept that without this help the Community could face the consequences of an energy crisis in these new transitional democracies.

4.0 ENVIRONMENT/TECHNOLOGY

In the Community public opinion ranks the environment, which has a dimension well beyond the Community or even the European continent, as one of the most important issues we face.

There has been considerable focus on the proposals made by the Commission to address the issue of CO_2 emissions and the associated problem of global warming.

---

3. As of Dec. 20 1993 the Draft Energy Charter treaty was put in its sixth version. For an overview of the Commission's position see COM(93) 542 Final, Nov. 4 1993, 'The European Energy Charter: Fresh impetus from the European Community'.

The Community is currently committed to stabilising its CO_2 emissions by the year 2000 at the 1990 level. How does the Commission propose to achieve this goal?

The Commission strategy has many facets. It recognises the importance that energy technology can play in this field and intends to strengthen and broaden its existing programmes, such as Thermie, Altener and SAVE, within the Community, and take steps to transfer this know-how to the countries of central and eastern Europe and the developing countries. These programmes focus on innovative energy technology, energy efficiency and alternative energy sources.

However, it is the element in the Commission's strategy advocating the use of fiscal means, a carbon/energy tax, that has attracted most attention and which warrants some particular attention.

It is generally recognised in the environmental field that wherever possible the principle of the polluter pays should apply. Consequently, in the Commission proposal, the carbon element of the tax would penalise fuels with high emissions of CO_2, a major contributor to global warming.

The level of the tax, which will be a minimum level that could be increased by the member states wishing to do so, was originally proposed to be US\$3 on January 1 1993 to be increased by \$1 a year up to US\$10 in 2000. The principle of revenue neutrality, that is to say the tax should not result in an overall increase in statutory contributions and charges, should be respected.

Consumers throughout the Community would receive a signal that would encourage a change in their economic behaviour. It would reinforce the energy efficiency measures that are an essential part of our strategy and also improve the security of the Community's energy supply.

A major cause of concern is the fear that the tax could jeopardise the international competitive position of industry in the Community. Therefore, the imposition of tax has been made subject to the condition that other OECD countries – leaving alone developing countries which should have more leeway – take actions resulting in a similar financial charge as the one resulting from the measures foreseen in the Community strategy. Furthermore, reductions or exemptions from the tax for companies with high energy consumption and operating on the world market are, under certain conditions, foreseen. Finally, in this context, reductions on tax payments are possible for all industries for investments in energy efficiency or in emissions reduction in the Community as well as in the third countries over a period of three years.[4]

A monitoring mechanism to follow up the national implementation plans and programmes of the member states as well as the efficiency of the Community measures has been included in the strategy proposal. Apart from the CO_2 emissions, it would also cover other greenhouse gas emissions as well as the equitable sharing of the burdens resulting from the implementation of the strategy between the member states. Indeed, with regard to the latter, financial assistance to member

4. Despite pressure from six member states to attempt to force progress on the CO_2/energy tax issue, the proposal remains blocked in the Council. During the latter half of 1993, the Belgian presidency and the Commission presented various compromises including a reduction in value of the tax, but to no avail. However, the proposal remains open to further discussion and evidence that the Community will be hard pressed to meet its CO_2 stabilisation targets for the year 2000 may well take the issue back to the top of the agenda in the near future.

states that would have difficulties in financing the required investments to adapt to the new situation is foreseen.[5]

Finally, it is important to mention in this context the Convention on Climate Change signed in Rio during the UNCED by the Community and its member states. Although the commitments reflected in this convention are not as far-going as the Community should like, they are going in the right direction. In a formal declaration, the Community desired a prompt start to the implementation of the Convention and reiterated the necessity of re-enforcement of the commitments entered into by, *inter alia*, the adoption of an additional Protocol. It is clear that this issue will remain at the top of the political agenda.[6]

5.0 CONCLUSION

In conclusion it is useful to note the likely future path of EC energy policy in the post-Maastricht period. The increasing importance attached to decision making at local level – subsidiarity – is already a feature of many Commission proposals. However, in respecting this principle the Community should not throw the baby out with the bath water – we still need a coherent and sound energy policy at Community level. The existing Treaty and the Single Act already provide the basis or inspiration for many of the Internal Market and environmental proposals and actions at Community level. Even in the new Treaty, which does hardly mention energy, there are (such as environment and trans-European networks) new possibilities for positive action. Whatever the outcome of the Maastricht Treaty the author is convinced that the European energy dimension will need to remain centre stage if the Community is to meet all the challenges it faces in a rapidly changing world.

5. The Council has now formally adopted a decision on a CO_2 monitoring mechanism (OJ L167, July 9 1993).

6. On Dec. 15 1993 the Environment Council adopted the Decision to ratify the UN Climate Change Convention.

Chapter 2

European Energy Law, Changing Concepts and Pervasive Principles

Leigh Hancher

1.0 INTRODUCTION

After three decades of relative inactivity, the Commission of the European Communities has since 1988, pursued an active interest in the European energy sector, and in particular in the markets for electricity and gas. Yet despite a concerted effort to open up these markets to more competition in an attempt to create an internal European energy market, the Commission has not succeeded in reaching its desired goals. Entrenched resistance from a number of member states, as well as their national utilities would appear to have combined with a generally inauspicious political and economic climate to frustrate the greater part of the Commission's plans.

Yet the Commission's plans are firmly rooted in concepts and principles which are basic to the ideal of the common or 'single' European market. Furthermore, these concepts and principles have been applied to virtually every other sector of the European economy, from insurance, to transport and telecommunications, and even to the provision of funeral services. What makes the energy sector so different? Is there a case to be made that energy is somehow special and should be exempted from the basic principles of Community law on free movement and competition? Can the energy market only be considered in the light of these traditional fundamental principles? What role could and should new concepts which are now becoming a feature of European law, including the concept of subsidiarity, play in shaping the future of the European energy market? In the following paragraphs, I shall try to provide an answer to some of these questions.

2.0 FROM BASIC PRINCIPLES TO BASIC ASSUMPTIONS

It is of course well known that the Treaty of Rome makes no express provision for the adoption of a common energy policy, similar to that provided for agriculture and transport. The Treaty on European Union – hereafter the Maastricht Treaty –makes passing mention of energy matters in the new Article 3T. It is possible, but not necessarily probable, that the Treaty may be further amended to include a specific article on a common energy policy when it is next considered for revision in 1996. Certainly, the European Parliament has recommended that a separate chapter on energy should be included in the revised Treaty.[1]

The absence of specific Treaty provisions dealing with energy matters has generated considerable debate as to the applicability of a number of Treaty provisions to the energy sector. It has never been seriously argued that the basic rules on the customs union (Articles 9–12), free movement of goods and services (Articles 30–37; Articles 56–59) as well as the rules on competition (Articles 85–94) do not apply to the energy sector.[2] Indeed, one of the most famous cases in Community law – Case 6/64 *Costa v Enel*[3] – concerned the nationalisation of the Italian electricity industry. The European Court of Justice has since ruled on the application of these rules to the oil and gas sectors on a number of occasions.[4] More recently, the Court of First Instance has handed down a number of rulings applying the competition rules to the electricity sector.[5]

Academic and political debate on the application of the Treaty rules to the energy sector has centred on two particular issues. First, the competence of the Commission to enact secondary legislation to regulate member states' energy markets. Second, the extent to which some special provision should be made for energy goods and services in the context of a 'market-orientated' approach to energy regulation. These two issues are in a sense interconnected, in that there is some debate over who should have competence to decide upon this latter issue. The paper shall examine the debate over the competence question first, and then turn to what in my opinion is the more complex issue of reconciling a market-based approach to energy issues with the more traditional public service-based approaches to energy provision.

3.0 COMPETENCE

In its Working Document on the Internal Energy Market, published in May 1988[6] the Commission intimated that it would consider adopting secondary legislation, based on Article 100A EEC, in order to deal with a number of matters. These included the accomplishment of the provisions concerning energy set out in the

1. See the Introduction to the Report prepared by M.C. Desema, rapporteur to the Committee on Energy, Research and Technology, Apr. 14 1993, P/E 203.946/rev.
2. For a more detailed discussion of the content and scope of these basic rules, see, *eg* Hancher *EC Electricity Law* (London: Chancery Law Publishing, 1992).
3. [1964] ECR 585.
4. For oil and petroleum products see: Case 72/83 *Campus Oil* [1984] ECR 2727; Case C347/88 *Commission v Greece* [1990] ECR 4747; Case 266/81 *SIOT* [1983] ECR 731; Case 174/84 *Bulk Oil v Sun* [1986] ECR 539. For gas, see Cases 169/84 *Cofaz I* [1986] ECR 391 and Case C169/84 *Cofaz II* [1992] CMLR 177; and Cases 67, 68 and 76/84 *Gebroeders van der Kooy* [1988] ECR 219.
5. Case T39/90 *SEP v Commission*; T-16/91 *Rendo v Commission* judgment of Nov. 8 1992 [1992] ECR II-2417; an appeal is pending in both cases. On the SEP case, see now the Opinion of Advocate General Jacobs, Case C36/92 P, Dec. 15 1993.
6. COM(88) 238 Final, May 2 1988.

Commission's White Paper on the Internal Market of 1985,[7] and where necessary the adoption of specific legislation to deal with other obstacles to the internal energy market. The Commission stated that the 'Community on the basis of Article 100A, can apply the necessary judicial instruments for the reconciling of the objectives of free circulation and the constraints of security of supply.'[8]

It is perhaps remarkable to observe that until this point in time, neither Article 100A nor the related Article 100 EEC had been used as a basis for legislation on energy matters. Many of the Community measures adopted in the 1970s dealt with specific matters such as emergency supply sharing mechanisms, and obligations to notify the Commission on certain matters. These measures were based on either Article 108 or Article 213 EEC. Between 1990 and 1991 the Council adopted three Directives on the transit of electricity[9], and gas[10] and on price transparency for electricity and gas.[11] The first and second of these measures took Article 100A as their legal basis, while the third took Article 213. In September 1990 the Council also adopted Council Directive 90/531[12] on the procurement procedures of entities operating in the water, energy, transport and telecommunications sectors. This Directive is based on Article 57(2), Article 66, Article 100A and Article 113 EEC.[13]

Prior to the adoption of the two transit Directives, it was contended by a number of national utilities that the Community had no legal powers to propose measures to regulate national energy markets. No express provision for energy markets was made in the Treaty itself, and Article 100A could not be interpreted to give the Community power to propose harmonising measures unless some national rules already existed in this field. The Commission maintained that as the completion of the internal energy market formed an essential part of the overall internal market exercise, it was competent to propose, and the Council to adopt the relevant directives on the basis of Article 100A. The choice of legal basis was never challenged before the Court of Justice and the two directives have now entered into force.

The question of the Community's legislative competence has been raised once more in the context of the Commission's more recent proposals on completing the internal market for gas and electricity.[14] These proposals are more ambitious than the earlier transit directives, and have been described by the Commission as the 'second step' towards creating the internal energy market for gas and electricity. They are based on the following objectives:

– the introduction of competition in electricity generation and in gas and electricity transmission;
– the separation or 'unbundling' of various functions performed by vertically integrated companies;
– the introduction of a limited degree of third party access.[15]

7. COM(85) 310 Final May 1985.
8. At para.30 of COM(88) 238.
9. Council Directive 90/547, OJ L313/30 1990.
10. Council Directive 91/269, OJ L147/37 1991.
11. Council Directive 90/377, OJ L185/16 1990.
12. OJ L297/1 1990.
13. For a more detailed discussion of these various measures as they affect the electricity markets, see *EC Electricity Law*, supra note 2.
14. COM(91) 548 Final.
15. The content of the two Draft Directives is analysed extensively in Chapters 6 and 7.

As regards the production of hydrocarbons, a proposal for a Directive on the conditions for granting and using authorisations for the prospecting, exploration and extraction of hydrocarbons was presented to the Council on May 11 1992.[16] Its objectives are to ensure undertakings equal access to oil and gas resources and free movement of these products between member states.

All three sets of proposals are based *inter alia* on Article 100A. Interestingly, the draft proposals on the common rules for completing the internal market for electricity and gas were preceded by two separate sets of proposals, prepared by the Commission services in 1991. It was originally envisaged that the Commission would adopt two Directives based on Article 90(3) EEC, requiring member states to withdraw exclusive rights to import, export, produce, supply and market electricity and gas respectively. These draft Directives would be complemented by two Council Directives, based on Article 100A, introducing certain common rules for the regulation of these two markets. This approach essentially mirrored that already taken in the field of telecommunications.[17] Two Commission Directives, based on Article 90(3) had been adopted requiring the withdrawal of exclusive rights to supply respectively, telecommunications goods[18] and services.[19]

The Commission's power to adopt both these measures was subsequently challenged by several member states, but confirmed in both cases by the Court of Justice.[20] Although the Court's rulings would appear to have given the 'green light' to the Commission to adopt future measures based on Article 90(3), the Commission has indicated that for political reasons it will base energy market liberalisation measures on Article 100A. One issue which might deserve further consideration is whether the Commission may base measures requiring the withdrawal of exclusive rights to import or export or otherwise transport and supply energy on Article 100A. Is it not constrained by the wording of the Treaty to use Article 90(3) if it wishes to achieve these goals?

Article 90(3) imposes a duty on the Commission to ensure that the provisions of Article 90(1) and (2) are applied. This could be interpreted to mean that the Commission must base its action on this Article. The Court of Justice has never been required to rule directly on this point. In its case law on Article 90(3) it has stated that the fact that the Council is also competent to adopt certain measures, for example, in the field of state aids, does not preclude the Commission from adopting similar measures to deal with problems expressly pertaining to the types of undertakings falling within the scope of Article 90(1).[21] The Court has not however indicated that the Commission is obliged to use this procedure.

The actual wording of the 1992 proposals effectively side-steps this issue by not making any *explicit* reference to the requirement to withdraw exclusive rights. This is merely implicit in the member states' obligations to ensure fair and equal access to electricity generation, and to gas and electricity supply. In the meantime the

16. OJ C139/12 1992. A common position on the amended draft was agreed at the Energy Council on Dec. 10 1993. For a fuller discussion of the 'Licensing Directive' see Chapter 4.

17. For a short overview of this policy, see J. Naftel, 'The Natural Death of a Natural Monopoly' [1993] 14 ECLR 105.

18. Directive 88/301, OJ L131/73 1988.

19. Directive 90/388, OJ L192/10 1990.

20. Cases C202/88 *France v Commission*, judgment of Mar. 19 1991, [1991] ECR I-1223, and Cases C271, C281 and C289/90 *Spain, Italy and Belgium v Commission*, judgment of Nov. 17 1992, [1992] ECR I-5833.

Commission has begun infringement proceedings against six member states, on the basis of Article 169 EEC, requiring the removal of import and export monopolies for electricity and gas. Nevertheless the closing recital of each of the 1992 Draft proposals notes that 'the Commission reserves the right to make use of all its powers conferred on it by the Treaty as and when appropriate'. Thus future recourse to Article 90(3) is not entirely precluded.

The present proposals, based on Articles 57(2), 66 and 100A, have once more provoked some controversy over the competence issue. This time, however, an additional factor has been brought into play, namely the impact of the scope of the principle of subsidiarity, now enshrined in Article 3b of the Treaty of Union.

3.1 The Subsidiarity Principle

The new Article 3b EC provides that the Community shall act within the limits of the powers conferred upon it by the amended EEC Treaty[22] and of the objectives assigned to it therein. In the areas which do not fall within its exclusive jurisdiction, the Community shall take action in accordance with the principle of subsidiarity only if and in so far as the objectives of the proposed action cannot be sufficiently achieved by the member states and can therefore by reason of the scale or effects of proposed action, be better achieved by the Community. Any action by the Community shall not go beyond that which is necessary to achieve the objectives of the Treaty.

The introduction of this new troublesome and ill-defined concept into the Treaty constitutional framework is already the subject of a growing body of literature.[23] The statement published at the conclusion of the Edinburgh summit on the application by the Council of the Subsidiarity Principle is intended to substantiate the rather nebulous concepts set out in Article 3b.[24] The Council is to incorporate a subsidiarity test in its examination of the Commission's proposals. It is probably safe to assume that the principle of subsidiarity should not be understood as a demarcation rule.[25] Even if it was, it could not be interpreted to debar the Community from adopting common rules in the electricity and gas sector.

3.1.1 Subsidiarity and the Energy Market

There are clearly a number of approaches to interpreting the application of the subsidiarity principle to the Community energy market. In the explanatory memorandum accompanying its original proposals published in February 1992, but drawn up prior to the finalisation of the relevant new Treaty Article 3b at Maastricht

21. See Joined Cases 188-90/80, *France Italy and the United Kingdom v Commission* [1982] ECR 2545. See also Case C202/88, *France v Commission*, ibid.

22. Titles III and IV of the Treaty of European Union amending the European Coal and Steel Community ('ECSC') and Euratom Treaties do not provide for the insertion of a provision similar to Art. 3b.

23. See generally, M. Wilke and H. Wallace, *Subsidiarity: Approaches to Power Sharing in the Community*, London (1990); A. Adonis and A. Tyrie, *Subsidiarity*, London: IEA (1990).

24. Annex 1 to Part A of the Conclusions of the Edinburgh European Council, *Agence Europe* No. 5878 bis.

25. N. Emilou, 'Subsidiarity: An Effective Barrier Against "the Enterprise of Ambition",' [1992] ELRev 383.

in December 1992, the Commission took a particular approach to the subsidiarity issue. The principle was described as one of four general principles informing its entire approach to the gradual liberalisation of the energy market. Subsidiarity required that the Community must not impose rigid mechanisms, but rather should define a framework enabling member states to opt for the system best suited to their natural resources, the state of their industry and their energy policies.

Thus the member states should remain free to determine, in an objective and non-discriminatory manner, the criteria for the granting of licences for the construction of power stations, cables and pipelines. In the case of electricity, they can also specify the criteria for dispatching power stations. They may also continue to regulate all aspects of electricity and gas tariffs for all final customers not eligible for third party access or not opting for it. This includes the possibility of tariff equalisation at national level. The member states remain free to determine the extent and nature of the rights and obligations of firms supplying gas and electricity, in particular their public service obligations. They may also continue to grant distribution companies exclusive supply rights, and to impose the obligation to connect and supply all the final consumers not eligible for third party access. Finally, each member state is left to choose the manner in which the directives are to be implemented, that is either by a regulatory authority or through the general mechanisms of national competition law.

In the view of Mr. Claude Desema, the European Parliament's rapporteur on the 1992 package of directives, subsidiarity must constitute the guiding principle with regard to both harmonisation and liberalisation: '[I]n other words, member states will retain exclusive responsibility for rules and provisions that are not laid down in these or subsequent directives'.[26] The European Parliament has taken issue with the very approach to market liberalisation set out in the Commission's original proposals. In its view the Commission should place an emphasis on harmonisation over and above liberalisation, the latter being conditional on the former. In particular it advocates that further harmonising measures are necessary on essential matters such as environmental protection requirements, the rules governing taxation on production, transmission and distribution of electricity and natural gas, the rules on transparency of costs and the definition of public service obligations and implementing rules. Any further development of the energy system towards further integration and thus towards further liberalisation will necessarily be linked to the implementation of a common energy policy, based on provisions to be inserted into the Treaty on European Union when it is revised in 1996. In the meantime, and until progress on harmonising measures is secured, member states should be free to organize their energy markets as they see fit, subject to the minimum rules laid down in the amended version of the present proposals.

It remains to be seen whether the Council is prepared to adopt any of the many far-reaching amendments to the Commission's present proposals put forward by the Parliament. The Commission has indicated in the amended version of its proposals, published in Feb. 1994, that it is prepared to accept a greater emphasis on national utilities' public service obligations but not to the extent that this would result in exclusive monopoly rights. The Commission has also indicated that it is willing to consider a system which will require member states to facilitate 'negotiated' third

26. Draft Report, PE 203.946, para.8.

party access. Network owners will not be mandated to make their free capacity available to newcomers. Finally, the Commission has relaxed its unbundling requirements.

In its Opinion on the two proposals, the Economic and Social Committee (ECS), also considered the application of the subsidiarity principle. It took a slightly different view, and it has linked the concept of security of supply with that of subsidiarity. It observed:

Security of supply is not seriously considered in the proposed Directives. It is not included in the list of definitions in Article 2. . . . This is a grave defect in these Directives; it must be clearly stated that such security of supply is primarily the responsibility of the distributors of natural gas and electricity and this responsibility must be underpinned by proper institutional arrangements in each Member State, in accordance with the principle of subsidiarity.

According to the principle of subsidiarity this security of supply shall be guaranteed by the States themselves, combined with the necessary Community-level co-ordination (paras. 2.2.2–2.2.3).

In the remainder of its report, the ECS goes on to criticise the two draft directives for failing to provide member states with sufficient guidance on what security of supply means and how it should be guaranteed in a Community context. Nevertheless it considers as excessive the powers delegated to the Commission to deal with crises situations (para.2.10.3). The Opinion concludes by supporting the Commission proposals in limited respects only, and in particular rejects the plans for the introduction of TPA. It too calls for greater emphasis to be placed on an alternative approach, based on harmonisation of environmental rules and the development of a balanced and gradual approach to common commercial criteria and common concepts of security and quality of supply.[27]

The majority of the member states would appear resolutely opposed to conceding any explicit competence to the Community in energy policy matters, either now or on any subsequent revision to the Treaty on European Union. It has been reported that the Belgian presidency, which took over the position from Denmark in the second half of 1993, would have liked to begin the groundwork for Council agreement on the broad guidelines for a Community energy policy. It is advocated that if the Commission's energy liberalisation plans were put into an energy policy framework, as opposed simply to an internal market one, then proposals would have to take into account supply-side, as well as demand-side measures, the former being left to the market at present. The Energy Commissioner, Mr. Abel Matutes, made a similar call for agreement on a common energy policy framework.[28] Any attempt by the Commission to introduce a legally binding agreement on energy policy will in all likelihood be resisted by the UK, Germany and the Netherlands, in particular, who stress that energy policy remains the responsibility of member states.[29]

The operation of the principle of subsidiarity in relation to energy policy matters is therefore very differently conceived by the Commission, the member states, and the European Parliament. Whereas the Commission assumes it has competence to enact energy-market related legislation, it must observe certain criteria in the implementation of that legislation. The member states dispute the Commission's

27. OJ C73/31 1993.
28. See Commission of the EC, DGXVII, *Energy in Europe, Annual Energy Review*, (1993).
29. See *EC Energy Monthly*, June 1993, no.54, pp.9–11.

right to intervene in energy policy matters at all, while the Parliament seems to assume that the principle requires that the Commission should only assume competence for matters relating to energy market liberalisation if and when the relevant national rules have been harmonised. Until this point in time, the member states retain exclusive competence to organise their national markets as they choose.

These different interpretations of the concept of subsidiarity are certainly of considerable relevance to the essentially *political* aspects of the debate over the desirability of Community intervention in energy market matters. They would appear to be of somewhat less relevance to the legal limitations, if any, which the principle of subsidiarity imposes on Community legislative competence in the energy sector.[30]

4.0 SHOULD ENERGY BE TREATED AS A SPECIAL CASE UNDER THE TREATY OF ROME?

Turning now to the second main issue with which this chapter set out to deal – the question of whether energy should be seen as a special case under the Treaty rules – it should be recalled that here we are dealing with Treaty articles which the Commission has autonomous powers to enforce: secondary legislation is not required. Subsidiarity, as discussed in the preceding analysis, is primarily concerned with legislative competence. It should also be noted that the titles dealing with free movement of goods and services as well as those governing competition are now grouped under the same Part Three of the EEC Treaty as amended by the Treaty of European Union, under the heading 'Community Policies', which covers Articles 9–136A inclusive.

4.1 Is the Energy Market a Special Case?

Attempts by some of the member states to have the energy market excluded from the internal market exercise entirely on the basis of its special features have so far failed to cut much ice. Nevertheless the argument that the basic principles of Community law must somehow be attenuated or otherwise adjusted to take account of certain specific features of energy supply is frequently made. Indeed the Commission itself has been prepared to fashion some special pleadings for the energy sector. This is equally true of DGIV, the Competition Directorate as of DGXVII, the Energy Directorate. While the latter has claimed that the special nature of the Community's energy sector requires a special gradual or staged approach to market liberalisation, the former has also been reluctant to apply the competition rules in undiluted form to the energy sector.

It is a well-established principle of Community law, that so long as the Community has not enacted harmonising legislation the member states retain temporary powers in certain situations to impose restrictions on the import and

---

30. The question of the justiciability of Art. 3b EC and the problems of applying the tests of 'necessity' and 'effectiveness' which it appears to contain are discussed in Mckenzie Stuart, 'A Busted Flush' in Curtin and O'Keefe (eds), *Essays in Honour of Justice O'Higgins* (1992). See also, Emilou, supra note 25.

export of goods and services. This temporary competence is not of course to be attributed in any way to the principle of subsidiarity but arises from the original schema of the Treaty of Rome. The Treaty articles on free movement and competition take precedence over national law, and in the event of conflict the doctrine of supremacy dictates that the latter must be set aside,[31] unless one of the exemptions contained in the Treaty can be invoked. Such restrictions on the operation of the basic principles must satisfy the requirements of the relevant Treaty Articles – Articles 36 (goods) and Article 56 (services); they must be objectively justifiable and proportionate to the end sought, and they must not result in an arbitrary restriction on trade. Where restrictions result from so-called 'indistinctly applicable measures', *ie* national rules applying to both imports and domestic products or services alike, the Court of Justice has devised a number of 'mandatory requirements' which may be relied upon by member states to justify such measures which none the less hinder trade. Once again the measure in question must be objectively justifiable and must be proportionate.

In competition policy the dividing line between national and Community competence is rather different. The key question is whether a particular agreement or restrictive practice effects inter state trade. Community competition law applies only when the interstate criterion is fulfilled. If there is no inter state trade effect, then national competition law should apply. As the jurisprudence of the Court of Justice and the Commission's decision-making practice makes clear, it is often possible to identify an effect on trade between member states even where the practices or agreements in question appear to be confined to one member state alone. As the Commission's decision concerning the arrangements made between Scottish Nuclear and the two Scottish electricity companies indicates, Article 85 may apply as long as there is a *probability* that inter-state trade may be effected.[32]

Although the provisions on the free movement of goods and services and on competition share a common purpose – the promotion of market integration – the tests developed and applied by the Court for the application of Articles 30 and 59 on the one hand, and for the competition rules on the other, are slightly different. Articles 30 and 59 are not subject to the so-called *de minimis* rule, for example, whereas Articles 85 and 86 are. Articles 30 and 59 cannot be invoked by nationals of a member state to deal with a purely internal situation or to contest reverse discrimination, whereas Articles 85 and 86 may well be deployed by nationals if particular arrangements potentially restrict inter state trade. In Case C41/90 *Hofner*[33] for example, the German measures at issue were alleged to breach Article 59 as well as Article 86 in conjunction with Article 90(1). The measure in question conferred a monopoly on the German Labour Office to recruit and place senior executives in certain branches of German industry. Given that the monopoly extended over the entire national territory, it met the 'substantial part of the common market' test contained in Article 86. Furthermore there was a potential effect on

31. On the potential conflict between the doctrine of supremacy and that of subsidiarity, see Cass, 'Subsidiarity – the word that saves Maastricht', [1992] 29 CMLRev 1129 at 1131.

32. Dec. 91/329 Apr. 30 1991, OJ L178/31 1991. In its subsequent Decision relating to the privatisation agreements in Northern Ireland, however, the Commission concluded that given the isolated position of the province, there was no inter state trade effect – OJ C92/5 1992. See further on the issue of interstate trade in electricity, the Opinion of Advocate General Darmon in Case C393/92, *Almelo*, Feb. 8 1994.

33. Loc. cit., note 40.

trade between the member states because employment activities undertaken by private firms may include nationals of other member states or may be conducted on their territory. It should be noted that in *Hofner*, neither the Court nor the Advocate General found that Article 59 had been breached, however, as no evidence had been put forward that freedom to provide services within the Community had been hindered.

4.2 The Treaty Exemptions and Energy Matters

If a special case is to be made out for energy, this must be substantiated on the basis of the relevant Treaty exemptions. In this context it should be borne in mind that the exemptions set in Articles 36 and 56 apply only to national measures. Arrangements between undertakings must be considered under Article 85(3). Nevertheless in certain situations national measures may also be incompatible with Articles 85 and 86, in conjunction with Articles 3f and 5.[34] As far as Article 86 – the abuse of a dominant position is concerned – the Treaty provides no express exemption. If the provision is found to apply, the only possible 'escape clause' is Article 90(2), discussed below. It should be stressed that whereas Article 36 makes express mention of public security, no such terminology is to be found in Article 85(3). This is an important distinction, as will be explained below.

4.2.1 Free Movement of Goods

The Court has examined the scope of the public policy and public security exemptions to the principle of free movement of goods, set out in Article 36 in Case 72/83 *Campus Oil*[35] and concluded that as long as the Community had not adopted harmonising legislation to the extent that the member states had an 'unconditional guarantee' that supply of petroleum and crude oil products would be maintained in the event of shortages on the world market, the member state in question, Ireland, remained competent to enact and enforce measures designed to secure a minimum supply of petroleum products at all times. The *Campus Oil* judgment has been the subject of considerable critical commentary and the precise scope of the public security exemption remains to be fully clarified. In the more recent Case C347/88 *Commission v Greece*,[36] the Court dismissed the Greek government's contention that restrictions on the import of petroleum products were justified in the interests of public security. The Greek government had in this particular case failed to demonstrate that in the absence of exclusive import rights reserved to national refineries, the latter would not be able to market their products at a competitive price. The Court did not however reject the defence as a matter of principle.

The continued uncertainty surrounding the scope of the public security exemption has undoubtedly added fuel to fire the debate on the question of competence in energy policy matters. The *Campus Oil* judgment is frequently invoked as 'cover' for a variety of national restrictive measures pertaining to the energy

---

34. See the Court's ruling in Case 13/77 *Inno v ATAB* [1977] ECR 2115.
35. Op. cit., supra note 4.
36. [1990] ECR I-4747.

market. As already noted, the Commission has initiated infringement proceedings under Article 169 against several member states in respect of statutory measures restricting import and export of electricity and gas. The Commission contends that these measures are in breach of Articles 30, 34 and 37 of the Treaty. This will provide the Court with a welcome opportunity to shed further light on the vexed issue of public security in the context of Article 36.[37]

In the specific context of electricity and gas supply, the security of supply debate has taken on an extra twist. In order to maintain overall security it is not sufficient to ensure access to primary fuel markets; in addition *continuity* of supply to certain classes of consumer must be guaranteed. This in turn means that member states remain competent to determine the organisation of the supply of these fuels. In particular, it is contended that a certain type of organisation is necessary firstly, to ensure an adequate investment in new plant and transmission capacity to meet public demand on request, and secondly, to ensure supplies at reasonable and fair prices. These various elements are usually brought under the heading of the 'public service' obligations incumbent on national electricity and gas utilities. In return for fulfilling these obligations, national utilities usually enjoy an extensive range of exclusive or monopoly rights to import and/or produce, transmit and distribute the fuels in question. The introduction of market liberalisation or competition in any form is seen by critics of the Commission's proposed draft directives as undermining the capacity of firms to fulfil their public service obligations.[38] This in turn raises issues concerning the application of the Treaty's competition rules.

4.2.2 The Competition Provisions

As already indicated, the competition provisions of the Treaty may be relevant to the energy market in two situations. Firstly, agreements between undertakings – especially long-term supply contracts – may well be caught by Article 85(1) and must therefore be notified to the Commission for exemption under Article 85(3). Secondly, certain types of national measures may also be affected by the Treaty competition provisions – usually because they confer monopoly rights on certain undertakings to supply energy. It should be stressed that the Competition Directorate – DGIV – has taken a clear position on the application of the competition rules to the energy sector. Its 22nd Report on Competition, published in May 1993[39] restates its commitment to its previously declared policy of liberalising the energy market.[40] The Report also addresses the need for security of supply and the issue of public service obligations. It concludes that the application of the competition rules will make for better security of supply, by increasing the number of suppliers on the market, and that public service obligations can be met in a way compatible with the

37. It should be noted that there remains some doubt as to whether the exemptions set out in Art. 36 are applicable to Art. 37 – which deals with the requirement to adjust state monopolies. The Court declined to rule on this issue in Case C347/88 *Commission v Greece*, ibid. Nevertheless its recent jurisprudence would seem to suggest that Art. 37 is no more than a particular application of Art. 30 and therefore that Art. 36 is relevant.

38. See further Advocate General Darmon in Case C393/92, *Almelo*, op. cit., supra note 32.

39. COM(93) 162 Final.

40. See also its 19th, 20th and 21st Reports on Competition Policy, published in 1990, 1991 and 1992 respectively.

Treaty. Furthermore 'both these concepts have in any event to be looked at in a Community context rather than a purely national one'.

4.2.2.1 The Jurisprudence of the Court   A fundamental question to which no clear answer has emerged is whether current national approaches to the organisation of electricity and gas supply are in fact compatible with the Treaty's provisions on competition law. Although the Court of Justice has not yet been asked to rule on the compatibility of electricity production monopolies, or gas or electricity supply monopolies[41] with the provisions of Articles 85, 86 in conjunction with Article 90 EEC, its recent case law suggests that where exclusive rights conferred by national measures restrict competition, then such rights are prima facie in breach of Articles 86 and 90(1).[42] It is only in the event that such restrictions can be justified, either under the mandatory requirements, or in accordance with the provisions of Articles 36 or 56 (see above) or alternatively, in accordance with Article 90(2) that exclusive rights may be permitted to subsist. The exemption contained in Article 90(2) only applies in so far as the application of the Treaty rules would obstruct the performance, in law or in fact, of the particular tasks assigned to the enterprises in question.

The Court of Justice has always interpreted this exemption narrowly, and so far it has usually declined to apply Article 90(2) in a positive sense, and exempt the contested exclusive rights from the scope of Community law. Its ruling in *Corbeau*, discussed below, is the first occasion where the Court recognised that the conditions for exemption may have been satisfied. Nevertheless the question of whether exclusive rights to transmit and distribute electricity can be justified as essential to the discharge of public service functions by electricity and gas utilities remains an open one. In this context it may be noted that the majority of cases involving Article 90(2) have come to the Court by way of Article 177 references from national courts. The Court has usually indicated that it is for these courts to apply the exemption, both positively and negatively, although it has given some indication of the sort of arguments which would be unacceptable. These have included contentions that profit levels would fall or that the mere exposure to competition would threaten the status quo.[43] In the two cases on Article 90(2) which potentially involved arguments directly related to the provision of public service-related tasks, Case C202/88 *France v Commission* (the telecommunications equipment directive case) and Joined Cases C271, 281 and 289/90 *Spain, Belgium and Italy v Commission* (the telecommunications services directive case), the application of Article 90(2) was not at issue.[44] The Commission had in fact made provision in the relevant directives to safeguard the public service element of telecommunications provision by demarcating 'reserved' and 'competitive' services. The former remained the legitimate

41. It should be noted however that a case has recently been referred to the Court of Justice involving several Netherlands electricity concerns by the District Court of Arnhem. The referring court has sought guidance, *inter alia*, on the application of Art. 90(2) to a series of exclusive purchasing agreements which are alleged to be in breach of Art. 85(1) – Case C393/92 *Almelo*. For a short discussion of the background to this litigation, see Hancher (1993) 2 *Utilities Law Review* 79. In his opinion of Feb. 8 1994, the Advocate General has argued that the Article 90(2) exemption should be available.

42 Cases C41/90 *Hofner* [1991] ECR I-1979; Case C260/89 ERT [1991] ECR I-2925, Case C 179/90 *Porto di Genoa* [1991] ECR I-5889, Case C18/88 *RTT v Inno-Atab* [1991] ECR I-5941.

43. Case C179/90 *Port di Genoa*, op. cit., ibid.; Case C288/89 *Commissariat voor het Media* [1991] ECR I-4007.

44. Judgment of Dec. 19 1992.

preserve of national telecommunications monopolies. The Court implicitly endorsed this line of demarcation in each case.

Nevertheless in a very recent ruling in Case C320/91 *Corbeau* the Court handed down a very interesting ruling on the application of Articles 86 in conjunction with 90(1) and 90(2) to the provision of postal services.[45] The criminal court of Liege had referred several questions to the Court in connection with proceedings brought against a certain Mr. Corbeau, who had started up his own postal service in the town of Liege in Belgium. Mr. Corbeau was prosecuted for having infringed the exclusive rights of the Belgian postal authorities. The Belgian judge asked the Court of Justice for clarification on the application of Articles 86, 90 and in particular on the potential application of Article 90(2) to the provision of postal services. The Court's reply is exceedingly terse on the question of whether the conferral of an exclusive right to collect, transport and distribute mail amounts to a breach of Articles 86 and Article 90(1); it seems to assume without further detailed argument that this is the case.

The Court then goes on to investigate the relationship between Articles 90(1) and 90(2) in the light of the present case, and in particular to examine the question of the extent to which a restriction on competition from other potential operators is necessary to permit the holder of the exclusive right to accomplish his public service mission, *and in particular to benefit from economically acceptable conditions.* In this latter respect the Court focused on the question of subsidising loss-making activities from more profitable ones and ruled that where this was necessary to ensure the provision of the public service then freedom of entry into the market for the more profitable services (cherry-picking or cream-skimming) could be forbidden. Where, however, certain types of 'value-added' services were offered which were not part of the public service tasks but which were designed to meet the requirements of a certain class of users, and were indeed not provided by the traditional postal service the situation might be otherwise. Much depended on whether these 'value-added' services by their very nature or by the fact that their geographical scope was limited, actually threatened the economic equilibrium of the public service provider. It is for the national court to investigate whether the services in question meet these various criteria. Case C320/91 *Corbeau* offers for the first time some general pointers on how national judges should apply these criteria. It remains to be seen whether similar criteria can be adapted to suit the peculiarities of the energy market. In the Opinion of Advocate General Darmon in Case C393/92, the supply of electricity can be exempted on essentially similar grounds. It is certainly noteworthy that in the postal sector, unlike telecommunications, neither the Commission nor the Council have arrived at a satisfactory dividing line between basic and value-added services. In the Commission's oral submissions in *Corbeau* it in fact seemed to ask the Court to refrain from ruling on where that dividing line might lie.

4.2.2.2 Commission Decisions The Commission has in fact had a number of opportunities to consider the application of the competition rules to the electricity and gas markets. In one case – *IJsselcentrale* – its decision was subject to the Court of First Instance, whose ruling in Case T-16/91 *Rendo v Commission*[46] is now in turn under appeal to the Court of Justice.[47] While I do not wish to undertake a detailed analysis of these various decisions here, it is worth considering the manner

45. Judgment of the full court May 19 1993 [1993] ECR I-2533.
46. Judgment of Nov. 8 1992, [1992] ECR II-2417.
47. Registered as Case C19/93 *Rendo v Commission*.

in which the Commission has dealt with arguments justifying restrictions on competition as necessary to guarantee security of supply.

The Commission has now considered the application of the EEC competition rules, and issued a definitive decision in respect of three separate sets of agreements.[48] In two cases – *Scottish Nuclear*[49] and the *'Jahrhundertvertrag'* – the agreements in question were notified to it in accordance with Regulation 17/62. The *IJsselcentrale* decision[50] arose out of a complaint made to the Commission, and the arrangements at issue had never in fact been notified to the Commission. It should be emphasised that in each of these cases the Commission was dealing with agreements between undertakings, even although in the German and Scottish cases, the governments in question had actively supported if not actually required the conclusion of the agreements at issue. In *IJsselcentrale* the situation was slightly more complex. The complaint, lodged in 1988, concerned agreements made between the Netherlands grid company SEP and the production companies. In 1989 however an Electricity Law was adopted in the Netherlands which effectively put the contested agreements on a statutory footing. Thus the restrictions on import and supply with which the Netherlands complainants were faced arose from a mixture of statutory provision and contractual agreements. I will deal with the three decisions in chronological order.

In *IJsselcentrale* the Commission examined the scope of the public security exemption in relation to the contractual arrangements between the SEP and the production companies. The agreement in question – the OVS – precluded any party other than the SEP from importing electricity. The subsequent Electricity Act made an express derogation from this import monopoly for very large users importing for their own use as opposed to public supply. Distributors, however, are not permitted to import electricity for the purpose of public supply (Article 34 of the 1989 Law). As the agreements had never been notified, Article 85(3) could not apply. In dealing with the application of the only possible exemption – Article 90(2) – the Commission drew a distinction between non-public and public supply (see paras 39 *et seq* and paras 49 *et seq* respectively). In respect of the former – non-public supply – the Commission concluded that the application of the competition rules did not frustrate the performance of SEP's assigned tasks. Hence the exemption provided in Article 90(2) could not apply. In respect of public supply, however, the Commission ruled that the ban imposed on imports with a view to public supply was now laid down in Article 34 of the Electricity Law:

The present proceedings is a proceeding under Regulation 17, and the Commission will not pass judgment here on the question whether such restriction of imports is justified for the purposes of Article 90(2). To do so would anticipate the question whether the new Law is itself compatible with the Treaty, and that is outside the scope of the present proceedings. (para.50)

The distributors appealed to the Court of First Instance, claiming *inter alia* that the Commission had failed to exercise its discretion in a proper way in that it had

48. It should be noted that the Commission has never published a definitive decision in respect of the various agreements notified to it in connection with the privatisation of the electricity industry in England and Wales. It has recently indicated its intention to grant an exemption to the renewed contracts between the generators and the coal companies and between the RECs and the generators. OJ C15/15, 1994.

49. Dec. 91/329, Apr. 30 1991.

50. Dec. 91/50, OJ L28/32 1991.

refused to consider the application of Article 90(2) to public supply both before and after the 1989 law had entered into force. It should be noted that the distribution companies lodged their appeal on March 14 1991. On March 20 1991 the Commission announced its intention to commence Article 169 proceedings against the Netherlands in respect of Article 34 of the Electricity Law. In Case T16/91 the Court of First Instance found for the Commission. The Court ruled firstly that the complaint in respect of the Commission's failure to examine and give a ruling on the situation under the OVS before the 1989 Law came into effect was inadmissible – the Commission had only dealt with the situation after 1989 in its Decision. As regards this period, the complaint was admissible, but nevertheless failed on substantive grounds. The Commission had in fact exercised its discretion properly, and was entitled to refuse to apply Article 90(2) to restrictions on imports destined for public supply, and instead to initiate separate infringement procedures.[51]

One is tempted to conclude that in *IJsselcentrale* the Commission side-stepped a politically sensitive decision. After all the Netherlands Electricity Act had introduced some element of competition in comparison with the prevailing situation in most of the member states. To condemn what was at least a step in the right direction would surely have been unwise. Unfortunately, however, this meant that the Commission totally ignored the impact of the restrictions the contractual agreements at issue had on electricity imports destined for public supply.[52] Given that the Act merely confirmed the contractual agreements, to condemn the latter would have inevitable consequences for the former.

In the *Scottish Nuclear* decision the Commission was required to rule on the compatibility of a series of agreements which obliged Scottish Power and Scottish Hydro-Electric to purchase all the electricity generated by Scottish Nuclear on a take-or-pay basis at a fixed price (see paras 19–25 of the Decision for a full description). The Commission considered that the agreements in question restricted competition in three ways; the arrangements involved an exclusive sales and purchasing agreement and a price fixing agreement. However, in its view, the conditions for exemption under Article 85(3) were met. In particular the agreement allows for the long-term planning that is required for reliable production ensuring security of supply and an independent energy supply market. It ensures that the nuclear stations function at full capacity and improves electricity generation and distribution in Scotland. Consumers will benefit from the gradual introduction of competition, replacing a previous monopolistic system.

The Commission's decision on the '*Jahrhundertvertrag*', adopted in late December 1992[53] concerns a series of agreements by which the German electricity generating utilities and industrial producers of electricity (auto-generators) have undertaken to purchase a specific amount of German coal up to 1995 for the purpose of generating electricity. The agreements provide that the electricity supply companies must make annual minimum purchases of one-fifth less 15 per cent of the total amount specified for a five year period. Prices are fixed in accordance with the price for power station coal set by the Federal Minister for Economic Affairs under the Third Electricity From Coal Law 1974. The electricity generating companies and the auto-generators in turn receive a state subsidy to compensate for the

51. For further analysis, see Hancher in *Utilities Law Review* 4 (1992), p.160.
52. It is in fact these very contracts which are at issue in Case C393/92, *Almelo*.
53. OJ L50/14 1993.

obligation to purchase domestic or Community coal.[54] The conditions governing the grant of state aid via the compensatory payments system are dealt with in a series of Commission decisions adopted pursuant to Decision 2064/86/ECSC.[55]

The electricity companies maintained, that the agreements at issue were essential elements of a member state's strategy for safeguarding energy and as such do not fall under the competition rules of either the EEC or ECSC Treaties, and furthermore that the application of the EEC competition rules is precluded by Article 90(2)EEC (see para.19 of the Decision). The Commission was of a different view. The agreements amounted to exclusive purchasing agreements which restrict competition among the electricity supply companies for primary energy sources such as natural gas, oil and nuclear. As such interstate trade in all fuels was undoubtedly affected, even if there was very little intra-Community trade in coal. Nor is the application of Article 85(1) precluded by Article 90(2). In principle the competition rules apply unless their application prevents the companies concerned from fulfilling particular tasks assigned to them. In this case it was not evident that the basic security of public electricity supply is ensured only by the notified agreement. Furthermore, in accordance with the second sentence of Article 90(2), the development of trade must not be affected to such an extent as would be contrary to the interests of the Community. Compliance with Article 90(2) 'cannot be judged against purely national criteria' (at para.29) and hence ultimately left to the discretion of the member states. The need for national measures must therefore be measured against Community criteria.

At first reading the Commission's analysis in the German case appears infinitely superior to its earlier reasoning in *Scottish Nuclear*. In the latter no account whatsoever was taken of competition from other primary fuels and the negative effects of the exclusive purchasing agreements sanctioned in that decision on competing fuels except in so far as low prices might put independent generators at a disadvantage. Further the Commission appeared to contradict itself by at one point stating that there was over-capacity in the nuclear industry and then going on to justify the agreements as necessary to ensure full capacity output. Nevertheless the Commission did rule that a 30 year agreement went a little too far even in the light of its own generous interpretation of the security and continuity arguments, and required that the life of the contracts be restricted to 15 years.

In both the German and the Scottish cases the Commission has also managed to interpret the exclusive purchasing agreements at issue in such a way that they benefit consumers, as is required if an Article 85(3) exemption is to be granted. In addition, agreements must contribute to improving production or distribution of goods and must not impose disproportionate or unnecessary restrictions on competition. Of course in both the Scottish and German cases the arrangements involved resulted in final consumers paying a far higher price for their electricity than might otherwise have been the case. Yet the Commission reasoned that in both cases security of supply was enhanced and that consumers have a high degree of interest in a secure supply of energy. The issue of the price to be paid for such security is not further dealt with in either Decision.

54. In fact of course no Community coal is imported, and the compensation is calculated according to the difference between domestic and world prices. Imports of third-country coal are restricted and subject to a system of import licences.
55. OJ L177/1 1986.

Once again it would seem that the Commission's reasoning in both the German and Netherlands cases was heavily influenced by the political sensitivity of the issues in hand. While it cannot be denied that competition policy is inherently political, the regrettable result is that on all the occasions so far presented to it the Commission has effectively ducked the issue, and granted exemption on the basis of highly dubious legal reasoning. Thus, even although the Commission repeatedly claims that the concept of public security must be given a Community and not a national content, it has itself consistently failed to flesh out what that Community content might be, and has instead dressed up national interests as Community ones. Certainly in its recent notice concerning the Pego power plant in Portugal,[56] it has indicated that it will ensure that competition in the independent sector is promoted. However, the Commission essentially vindicated an existing national scheme which is designed to ensure the gradual introduction of competition into the national ESI. The Commission's approach to state aid to the energy sector has been equally disappointing.[57]

5.0 CONCLUSION

This chapter has attempted to demonstrate that the concept of an internal energy market is firmly grounded in the fundamental principles of free movement and competition. This is not to deny that should the Community's attempts to promote market liberalisation eventually succeed, that this will lead to considerable change and indeed uncertainty in what have been traditionally stable, and until recently, very insular nationally orientated markets. Change in the energy market is of course already under way but so far it is proceeding along lines dictated by the existing players in the market. The European Commission's plans for imposing its own vision of how the Community's electricity and gas markets should evolve have not proved popular. The Commission has now recognised that its 1992 legislative proposals have little chance of being adopted in the Council in their present form. The version of the draft Directives published in 1994 makes a number of important concessions, in particular to the public service concept and to the continuing authority of the member states to flesh out and apply this vague and ill-defined idea. These developments still leave open the question of whether or not the Commission will make use of its autonomous powers to enforce the Treaty competition rules. The Commission has now commenced infringement proceedings against six member states in the Court of Justice. The security of supply argument is the ever-present ghost at the banquet, and although the Commission appears to insist that this does not necessarily make energy a special case, I have tried to argue that in its decision-making practice it has so far tended to bow to national interests. It has yet to fulfil its promise of imparting a genuinely Community input into the concept of security of supply. Until this happens, the debate over the potential for a single European energy market is likely to generate a considerable amount of heat, but very little light.

56. OJ C365/12, 1993.
57. See further, L. Hancher, 'State Aids and Energy' in Harden (ed.) *State Aid Community Law and Policy*, Band 4 Schriftenreihe der Europeaische Rechtsakademie Trier (1993).

Chapter 3

A United Kingdom Perspective on European Energy Policy

S.A. Price and G. Carroll[1]

1.0 INTRODUCTION

Energy issues have once again entered the spotlight with much interest centred on the European Commission's proposals for an internal energy market. Many member states have argued publicly against these proposals with the UK being the only country offering strong support for them. However, certain countries do appear to accept the *principle* of the introduction of greater competition. So long after the Treaty of Rome with its support for competition and the subsequent advance of the Single European Market in other sectors, the lack of a free internal market in gas and electricity is an anachronism.

Given the UK Government's pursuit of increased competition in the home market, it is of interest to set out a UK perspective in the context of the European energy market. This Chapter covers the main issues on the energy agenda, the main priorities as seen by the UK and will set out in some detail the principal arguments in the debate on the internal energy market with particular reference to gas. In order to appreciate the UK perspective on European energy issues it is important to understand what has taken place in the UK over the past several years. The following section provides a brief history of energy production and consumption. Section 3.0 outlines UK energy objectives. In section 4.0, the key European energy issues are outlined and discussed.

2.0 BACKGROUND

2.1 Production

Figure 1 shows that there has been a dramatic change in UK energy production in the past 25 years from a virtual dependency on coal to a more diverse energy base. Coal

1. The opinions expressed in this chapter are entirely personal to the authors.

Figure 1. UK production of primary fuels, 1965 to 1992

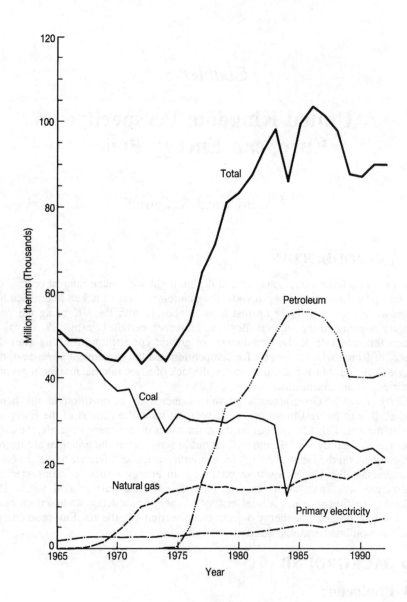

accounted for over 95 per cent of total UK production of primary fuels in 1965. Since then there has been a substantial decline in coal production, with a large dip in the mid-1980s due to the miners' strike. Gas was first discovered in the United Kingdom Continental Shelf (UKCS) in the West Sole field in 1965 and was quickly followed by other major discoveries in the southern basin. However, following the purchase of gas from Norway, UK production declined in the first half of the 1980s. Towards the end of the decade, gas production recovered and is set to increase rapidly in order to replace declining imports and to meet the increase in domestic demand.

Oil was first discovered in the North Sea in 1969 and production grew rapidly in the 1970s. At the end of 1975 just over 1.5m tonnes of oil had been produced from the Argyll and Forties fields. By 1980, production had exceeded 80m tonnes and the UK had achieved net self-sufficiency in oil. Annual output peaked in 1985 at 127.5m tonnes and was declining gradually until the tragic accident at *Piper Alpha* on July 6 1988. Production fell to 92m tonnes in 1989 and has remained around this level as major refurbishment and additional safety features involving lengthy shutdowns to existing facilities have been installed. Since 1960, there has been steady growth in the production of nuclear power due to the construction of new reactors and improved performance. By 1992 the shares in total production of primary fuels were: petroleum 45 per cent, coal 24 per cent, natural gas 22 per cent, and nuclear and hydro together 9 per cent.

2.2 Consumption

Figure 2 indicates that consumption of primary fuels has also shown a dramatic change. Coal consumption has been in steady decline since the 1960s and demand has moved from households to power generation. Coal burning displaced a significant amount of heavy fuel oil in the latter market. Petroleum consumption grew rapidly through the 1960s and early 1970s until 1974 when oil prices increased fourfold. Since then, petroleum consumption has followed much the same downward pattern as coal, although in recent years there have been signs of growing petroleum consumption mainly through transport use. There has been steady growth in the use of nuclear power.

Energy consumption, including secondary fuels such as electricity and refined petroleum products is ultimately dependent on demand by final users. In 1960, consumption of coal and other solid fuels accounted for over 60 per cent of final consumption. However, this share has declined steadily; firstly when the level of petroleum consumption increased and secondly from 1973 as natural gas usage grew at the expense of both solid fuels and petroleum consumption. In the early 1970s, British Gas Corporation embarked upon a major expansion of the domestic transmission grid and by the end of that decade, gas consumption exceeded 15b therms. Gas consumption continued to grow throughout the 1980s but at a reduced rate as gas prices were increased substantially in the early to mid-1980s. This was largely a catching-up process with the tenfold increase in oil prices which had occurred in the previous decade. Electricity demand has grown steadily since 1960, though since 1973 the average growth has been about 1.5 per cent per annum compared with over 6 per cent per annum between 1960 and 1973. The relative shares in total final consumption have changed substantially with solid fuels falling from over 60 per cent in 1960 to less than 9 per cent in 1992, gas increasing from

Figure 2. Inland consumption of primary fuels, and equivalents for energy use, 1960 to 1992

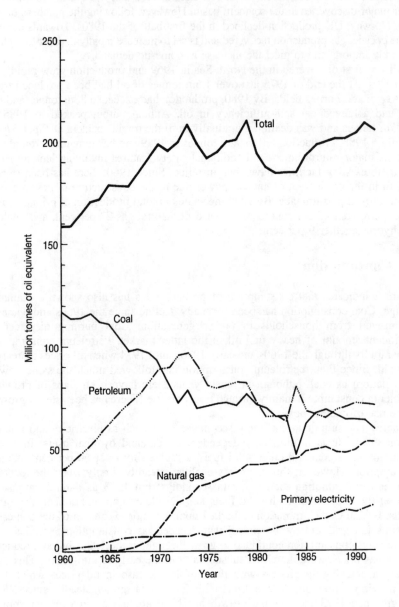

6 per cent to 32 per cent, electricity from 7 per cent to 16 per cent and petroleum increasing from 25 per cent to 43 per cent.

3.0 ENERGY OBJECTIVES

In the 1970s, the UK energy sector was largely state-owned, significantly subsidised and was effectively shielded from competitive forces. After the election of a new administration in 1979, a new policy of commitment to develop greater competition in all sectors of the energy industry emerged. This was based on the firm conviction that competition and private ownership tied to an effective regulatory regime, provide the key to meeting the needs of consumers at lowest cost.

The gas market gives an interesting example of this policy in action. On privatisation of British Gas, the tariff market (less than 25,000 therms per annum), was subject to regulation by the Office of Gas Supply (OFGAS). The contract market (over 25,000 therms per annum) was subject to normal competition law. The Gas Act 1986 also provided for third party access to the British Gas System. However, although contract customers in the industrial and commercial sectors could take gas from other suppliers, British Gas effectively remained the only supplier to this market. In 1988, following complaints from consumers, the Office of Fair Trading (OFT) referred British Gas to the Monopolies and Mergers Commission (MMC). The MMC found that extensive discrimination had developed in pricing by British Gas of gas to contract customers and recommended remedies including the active encouragement of competition. When the OFT reviewed progress on this in 1990 it found that British Gas still enjoyed 90 per cent of the total contract market. As a result a number of further steps were taken to stimulate the development of competition. These included an undertaking from British Gas to reduce its share of the contract market to around 40 per cent during 1994; the release of further supplies of gas to competitors of British Gas and the reduction of the British Gas monopoly of the tariff market from 25,000 to 2,500 therms per annum. There are now encouraging signs that competition is developing. As a result, the first company to compete with British Gas in the non-tariff market began operations on March 1 1990. By January 1 1994, there were 56 companies, licensed by OFGAS as suppliers offering competition to British Gas in the non-tariff market. The independent companies had captured some 36 per cent of this market.

In essence, the aim of the Government's energy policy is to ensure secure, diverse and sustainable supplies of energy in the forms that people and business want and at competitive prices. This aim needs to be pursued in the context of the Government's economic policy as a whole, of other Government policies, especially on health, safety and the environment and of the United Kingdom's European Community and other international commitments. The Government firmly believes that its aim will be achieved most fully through the mechanisms of the market. The UK energy scene has undergone major structural changes over the past two decades with significant shifts in the relative shares of primary fuels in both production and consumption and a new direction in energy policy. It is widely acknowledged that the UK has an open and liberalised energy regime and it is this openness which provides the basis for understanding the UK's view towards the major current policy issues in Europe.

4.0 THE KEY EUROPEAN ISSUES

Given the policy of increased liberalisation and competition it is hardly surprising that the UK supports the principle of an internal energy market in Europe. However, it is curious that so many years after the Treaty of Rome the energy sector lags behind others in achieving Single Market objectives and that gas and electricity are not yet freely traded within an internal market in Europe. The reasons for this are, we believe, twofold. Unlike many other products, gas and electricity involve considerable natural monopoly at the transmission and distribution stage, which inevitably led to various forms of regulation. Secondly, following on from the regulatory aspect and due to the fact that these fuels played an important social and economic role in regional development – governments became directly involved.

The European Commission set out an agenda for the creation of an Internal Market in electricity and gas involving the gradual introduction of market liberalisation. The proposals fell into three phases. The first involved three directives; a price transparency directive and two transit directives (for electricity and natural gas). The transit directives allow for one grid company to obtain transit across another grid to a third grid company across Community frontiers. However, they provide no general right of access by anyone other than the grid companies. These directives were the subject of much discussion before being enforced by member states, perhaps as they were seen as the first step towards third party access. (For a discussion of the legal competence of the Community to propose measures to regulate national energy markets see Chapter 2.) The Commission's proposed second phase involved a number of measures. They were the abolition of exclusive rights, a non-discriminatory licensing system for the construction and operation of pipelines, electricity grids, power stations and LNG facilities, the introduction of Third Party Access (TPA) for the very largest size of consumer and distribution companies and unbundling of transmission, accounts and services within vertically integrated undertakings. The third phase, originally intended to come into force in 1996, involves extending the eligibility of TPA.

These proposals, particularly TPA, have been the subject of considerable controversy within governments and industry. The UK Government strongly supports the principles of these directives and believes that the Commission has correctly identified TPA as a necessary condition for the creation of an open and competitive energy market in Europe. Using the natural gas market as an illustrative example, the principal arguments raised against the introduction of market liberalisation, and TPA in particular, are given below.

4.1 European Electricity and Gas Markets are Efficient; TPA is Not Necessary

There is no question that the gas industry both in Continental Europe and the UK has been highly successful over the past several decades in developing supplies of gas and in increasing the share of gas to consumers in final markets. However, in the absence of real competition, it is more difficult to establish whether the industry was operating at least cost. Two features of the European market stand out. The first is the wide variation in final selling prices to customers of similar characteristics between member states. One would expect a range of prices to be charged reflecting different cost structures, but the differences observed in the market between consumers of similar size and countries often with contiguous borders are far wider than would appear justified by any differences in transportation and trading costs.

Secondly, and with few exceptions, there is no gas-to-gas competition within EC markets. Regional and national gas monopolies price industrial gas at 'oil equivalent pricing', that is the price of the next best alternative. This approach may have had some validity during the initial build up of natural gas when it was displacing oil supplies. But for established monopoly gas producers, it conveys enormous market power and leaves gas producers open to considerable political manipulation in favour of particular sectors or consumer interests. Gas and electricity are, we believe, not being bought and sold on a level playing field within a single European market.

4.2 TPA Will Threaten Security of Supply

This argument contains two separate strands. One is that producers will not develop their gas resources without the security of long-term whole-field life contracts being in place and the transmission and distribution companies will not be able to offer such large and costly contracts without the security of monopoly. The second strand is that a monopoly buyer is essential to counter the power of the producers who would otherwise demand and obtain higher prices for their gas.

It must be made absolutely clear that TPA is not an end in itself but a means to competition. If the current situation is fully meeting all the needs of consumers nothing will change by the introduction of TPA. It is difficult to envisage a realistic situation in which new entrants successfully enter the market in competition with the incumbent monopolist and damage the interests of the very consumers on which their success depends.

We should also treat with extreme scepticism any claim that a monopoly is necessary because future investment needs are large. There are many other industries operating under competitive conditions which face similar risks and large indivisible investments. There is also no reason to believe that monopolisation and cartelisation of buying interests create lower purchase (and hence consumer) prices over the longer term. There is a danger that the unchallenged beliefs of such consortia may lead to costly mistakes. This happened in the early 1970s when the prevailing mood amongst the limited number of European gas buyers was of future scarcity of gas supplies resulting in a number of high-cost contracts being entered into. The end result is unlikely to be in the best interests of the consumer.

4.3 TPA Will Lead to a Complex Regulatory Regime and Stifle Investment

Opponents of TPA argue that a regulatory regime similar to that in the US will develop in Europe if TPA is introduced. They fail to appreciate the specific factors that gave rise to the EC proposals. The UK believes that with a clear TPA framework established across the EC, detailed regulation to ensure fair play can be left to the member states.

4.4   Surrender of Benefits of Commercial Foresight; Free Riders

Third Party Access, as envisaged in the EC proposals, is a very modest step compared to UK (and some EC member states') competition law. The directives provide for pipeline/grid owners to charge a transit fee related to both long-term costs and a rate of return on the service provided. It will allow pipeline owners to maximise their return by ensuring as much capacity as possible is taken up. There is no obligation on them to permit access if all capacity can be accounted for, while at the same time earnings on the pipeline may be improved if there is any spare capacity. The fact that TPA had to be enshrined in an EC directive rather than being introduced openly and voluntarily by those involved suggests that the real concern could be in protecting their secure markets rather than trying to use their pipelines/ grids efficiently. (For further discussion of the issue of Third Party Access see Chapters 6 and 7.)

5.0 CONCLUSION

Over the past two decades, the UK energy scene has undergone major structural changes with significant shifts in the relative shares of primary fuels in both production and consumption. A new direction for energy policy emerged and was instrumental in shaping the changing structure of the energy industry. Given its policy of increased liberalisation and competition it is hardly surprising that the UK supports the principles of the internal market for energy in Europe.

Although there has been some agreement on certain energy measures proposed by the Commission, there was no common ground in relation to the central competition issue of TPA. These differences of opinion between member states led EC Ministers at the Energy Council in November 1992 to invite the Commission to consider modifying its original proposals. The Commission presented the modified proposals to the Energy Council in December 1993 which reflected the views of the European Parliament. There are three main differences between the original and modified proposals. Firstly, TPA has been replaced by 'negotiated' TPA whereby very large consumers and distribution companies can negotiate access with the network operator. The network operator may refuse access on certain grounds but member states are to appoint an independent authority to settle disputes. Secondly, unbundling is limited to separation of accounts plus, in the case of electricity, administrative independence of the transmission system operator. Thirdly, for electricity only, a tendering procedure has been introduced as an alternative to licensing. It has become apparent from the initial negotiation of the modified proposals that even these diluted measures go far beyond what several member states are prepared to accept.

Hence, despite the proposals for an internal market for energy in Europe being the subject of several discussions involving all 12 member states and the Commission, major differences of opinion remain. As a result, the establishment of an internal market comprising of, in the words of the Treaty, 'an area without internal frontiers in which the free movement of goods, persons, services and capital is ensured' appears to be sadly lacking in the energy sector compared to other sectors. We believe, as noted, there are two main reasons for this.

Unlike other goods, gas and electricity involve considerable natural monopoly at the transmission and distribution stage, which inevitably led to various forms of regulation. Secondly, following on from the regulatory aspect and due to the fact that these fuels played an important social and economic role in regional development – governments became directly involved. To conclude, although electricity and gas are not yet freely traded within an internal market in Europe, we feel there has been some progress towards this goal. This will continue, particularly as consumers become aware of the benefits involved.

Section 2

European Energy Legislation

Chapter 4

The Impact of European Community Law on the United Kingdom Upstream Oil and Gas Industry: Directives on Services and Licensing

Hew R. Dundas

1.0 INTRODUCTION[1]

1.1 General

The main legislative provisions implementing the Single European Market in UK law should have been in place by June 30 1992 and effective on or before January 1 1993, in accordance with the UK's obligations under the Treaty of Rome and the Single European Act.[2] Provisions of some EC Directives will have a significant effect on the placing of services contracts through requiring them to be placed only after a competitive tendering process as provided for in the Directives. Further, member states' regimes for award of licences for hydrocarbon exploration and exploitation have been brought within the 'single market' umbrella and will now be subject to a Directive; compliance with this may cause significant problems. This Chapter[3] examines the relevant EC Directives from a UK viewpoint.

---

1. This Chapter is derived from research originally carried out (and subsequently considerably revised and expanded) by the author in his capacity as BRINDEX representative on the E&P Forum Legal and Insurance Committee, and he wishes to record his appreciation of the support of all three organisations and of his employer Cairn Energy PLC. The opinions expressed in this Chapter are those of the author personally and may not be those of any or all of Cairn Energy PLC, BRINDEX, nor the E&P Forum.
2. To be referred to hereinafter as 'the Treaty' and 'SEA' respectively.
3. This Chapter should be taken neither as an exhaustive survey of EC or UK law in this area, nor as a detailed procedural manual for procurement post-Jan. 1 1993. However, the law as stated herein, as it relates to the UK, is current as at Jan. 13 1994.

1.2 The Problems

In late 1991 it became apparent that the scope of the draft Services Directive[4] was potentially incompatible with the functioning of relevant markets; particular difficulties were seen with insurance and financial services. A concerted oil industry lobbying effort[5] was organised to try to change the draft. Further, in 1992 it became apparent that the Directive covering licensing, although superficially innocuous, contained elements raising fundamental questions.

2.0 THE UTILITIES DIRECTIVES[6, 7]

2.1 Origins

Public procurement amounts to about 15 per cent of Community GDP, with around half of this in the utilities sectors, but less than 5 per cent of public authority contracts are awarded to foreign suppliers in all major member states. The Treaty states that 'Quantitative restrictions on imports and all measures having equivalent effect shall . . . be prohibited between member states[8] and that '. . . restrictions on freedom to provide services . . . shall be progressively abolished'.[9] In the Commission's view, the procurement procedures of public undertakings did not satisfy the requirements of Articles 30 and 59 and were a distortion of the free market. The Procurement Directives were intended to redress this distortion and to open up such procurement to competition within the EC; however, their effectiveness has been limited until recent amendments.[10] The Commission envisage substantial annual savings[11] through introduction of competitive public procurement.

The early Directives addressed 'the State, regional or local authorities, bodies governed by public law, or associations formed by one or several such authorities

---

4. 'Proposal for a Council Directive on the Service Procurement Procedures of Entities Operating in the Water, Energy, Transport and Telecommunications Sectors CCO/91/08 and CC/91/07 issued Feb. 1 1991. Note that, whereas the final version of the Directive was published (COM(91) 347 OJ C337/1) as an amending text to the Utilities Directive 90/531/EEC; a consolidated directive 93/38/EEC was issued dated June 14 1993 (OJ L199/84 Aug. 9 1993), hereinafter referred to as the 'Utilities Services Directive'. This Chapter's references are to the later document.

5. Led by the E&P Forum.

6. The Public Works Directive 71/305 July 26 1971 and the Public Supply Directive 77/62 dated Dec. 21 1976, each as subsequently amended, together with associated Directives are hereinafter referred to as the 'Procurement Directives'; refer also to note 10 below. Directive 90/531/EEC and associated Directives are hereinafter referred to as the 'Utilities Directive'.

7. The topic of Utilities Directives in particular has been comprehensively aired recently; refer [1989/90] 1 OGLTR 8 and [1990] 10 OGLTR 344 for general summaries of the Directives, refer also to the article by the author in [1991] 6 OGLTR 171–176, based on an earlier and simplified version of this Chapter. Other relevant articles can be found at [1992] 9/10 OGLTR 269 (Remedies) and [1993] 9/10 OGLTR 329 (Commission Decision on UK derogation). Refer also to the newly published journal *Public Procurement Law Review*. A major text is *Public Procurement in the EC* by Peter Armin Trepte (CCH Europe).

8. Art. 30.

9. Art. 59.

10. Public Works Directive, as most recently amended by 89/440/EEC and replaced by 93/37/EEC and Public Supply as amended by 88/295/EEC and replaced by 93/36/EEC.

11. A study estimates potential annual savings as 17.2bn ECU (1989 prices); refer 'Study of the Cost of Non-Europe' in *European Economy* No.35 Mar. 1988.

or bodies governed by public law'. It became clear to the Commission that these Directives were not creating the intended effect, and three broad categories of omission came to be recognised: first, the target base was too narrowly drawn by the definition of 'contracting authority' in terms of governance by public law, and that there existed classes of entities (typically in the utilities sector) which were not so included, but whose origins and activities bore some of the hallmarks of a public undertaking; second, while works and supply contracts were addressed, contracts for services[12] were not; and third, there were inadequate means of enforcement of the provisions of the Directives.

2.2 Introduction and Legal Basis of the Utilities Services Directive

The nature of the legal basis for promulgation of Directives has been considered by the European Court of Justice[13] and the Utilities Services Directive (in its first recital) relies on Articles 57(2), 66, 100A and 113 of the Treaty.[14] The utilities sectors were excluded from the early Procurement Directives principally on the grounds that some such entities were governed by public law, some by private law and therefore that the latter were not directly within the Commission's jurisdiction. The Utilities Services Directive[15] consequently recognises that the entities which are required to be addressed must be identified other than by reference to their legal status.

2.3 Outline of the Utilities Services Directive

The Directive distinguishes between, first, entities which possess some special or exclusive right granted by Government[16] *ie* such entities as might thereby be subject, directly[17] or indirectly[18] to some degree of governmental control, and, second, those which do not, in contrast to the previous approach which merely distinguished conventionally between the public and private sectors.

The earlier Utilities Directive was adopted by the Council of Ministers on September 17 1990, and it is mandatory on member states to have adopted implementing legislation before July 1 1992 to come into force no later than January 1 1993, but there

12. A separate EC programme is intended to free the provision of financial services across the Community.

13. Case C300/89: *Commission v Council* (June 11 1991); the *Titanium Dioxide* case.

14. Art. 57(2): last sentence only, referring to the qualified majority; this is as amended by Art. 6(7) SEA; Art. 66: this introduces by reference Arts 55 to 58. Art. 100A: essentially the 'single market' Article, added by Art. 18 SEA; refer to S. Crosby 'The Single Market and the Rule of Law' [1991] 16 ELRev 451 for a stimulating discussion of the applicability of Art. 100A. Art. 113: which introduces Chapter 4 'Commercial Policy' of Title II 'Economic Policy' of Part 3 of the Treaty 'Policy of the Community', in which Chapter Art. 113 appears.

15. At Recital 9.

16. Art. 2(1)(b).

17. For example, through a requirement such as was in contention in the *Du Pont* case; refer to text at note 26 below.

18. A UK example here could be argued to be the award of UKCS production licences up to the Ninth Round, where the evaluation of licence applications took into account the applicant's support of UK industry through its giving (euphemistically) 'full and fair opportunity' to UK suppliers; the latter was enforced by the Offshore Supplies Office and was clearly discriminatory in effect (refer note 53 infra).

are extended deadlines for the legislation to come into force for Spain (January 1 1996), and Portugal and Greece (each January 1 1998).

The underlying principles of the Utilities Services Directive are set out in a preamble thereto; these provide (in part) that the 'rules to be applied by the entities concerned should establish a framework for sound commercial practice and leave a maximum of flexibility' but 'as a counterpart for such flexibility . . . a minimum level of transparency must be ensured . . .' In addition the Directive recognises that there may be 'alternative arrangements which will achieve the same objective of opening up procurement'.[19]

The Directive states[20] that it applies to contracting entities which ' . . . have as one of their activities any of those referred to in [Article 2(2)] or any combination thereof'; and 'operate on the basis of special or exclusive rights granted by a competent authority of a Member State', where 'relevant activities' are defined as including 'the exploitation of a geographical area for the purpose of exploring for or extracting oil, gas . . .'[21] and where 'special or exclusive rights' means 'rights deriving from authorisations granted by a competent authority of the Member State concerned . . . having as their result the reservation for one or more entities of the exploitation of an activity defined in [Article 2(2)]'.[22]

The upstream oil and gas sector is thus brought into the scope of the Utilities Directives through the grant (to use the UK example) 'to the Licensee of *exclusive licence and liberty* . . . to search and bore for, and get, petroleum . . .'[23]

The main provisions of the Utilities Services Directive regarding contracting procedures are as follows: first, it will apply to contracts exceeding ECU 5m for works contracts and ECU 400,000 for supply or services contracts; second, there must be no discrimination between bidders for the contracts; third, the bidding procedure must be either 'open' or 'restricted' to invited (*eg* prequalified) bidders or 'negotiated' where purchasers negotiate with one or more suppliers of their own choice; in the 'restricted' case (b) the prequalification system must be open, non-discriminatory and transparent, and the 'negotiated' case may be applied only in limited circumstances, generally where open bidding is impossible or wholly impracticable;[24] fourth, contracts must be awarded to the lowest bid, or to the 'most economically advantageous' bid;[25] and fifth, there are a number of reporting obligations.

Such case law as exists relevant to the Utilities Directives indicates the way in which the courts may interpret their function: typical are the *Du Pont* case,[26] where Italian legislation obliged local authorities to obtain at least 30 per cent of supplies from companies in the Mezzogiorno region, and the *Dundalk* case,[27] where there

19. Recitals 45, 46 and 16 respectively.
20. Art. 2(1)(b); of course, it applies much more widely than drawn here, *ie* to the whole 'utilities' sector; consideration of the complete definition of what entities are included is outside the scope of this Chapter.
21. Art. 2(2)(b)(i); note how this excludes the downstream sector.
22. Art. 2(3).
23. The language originated in the Petroleum (Production) Regulations 1935 and is currently given in the Petroleum (Production) (Seaward Areas) Regulations 1988 ('the 1988 Regulations') Schedule 4, Model Clause 2.
24. Refer below for definitions and further discussion of bidding procedures.
25. Art. 34 which includes a number of criteria for the latter case.
26. Case C21/88 *Du Pont de Nemours Italiana SpA v Unita Sanitaria Locale No.2 di Carrara* [1990] ECR 1-889; [1991] 3 CMLR 25.
27. Case C45/87 *Commission v Ireland* [1988] ECR 4929; [1989] 1 CMLR 225.

was an effective 'buy Irish' requirement, each of which were held to be discriminatory and in contravention of Article 30 of the Treaty.

2.4 Structure of the Utilities Services Directive[28]

This is written largely as an amendment of the original Utilities Directive stating that 'the rules on the award of service contracts should be as close as possible to the rules on works and supply contracts . . . '.[29] The original proposal for dealing with services stated that it '. . . foresees provisions which are as similar as possible to those of [the Utilities Directive] . . .'[30] and that '[it] shall apply to contracting entities within the meaning of [the Utilities Directive]'.[31]

The Directive is structured[32] so that every contract awarded by a contracting entity is *either* a works contract *or* a supply contract *or* a services contract *or* is specifically excluded and it has a number of exclusions comparable to those in the earlier Utilities Directive. The general threshold for the energy sector is set at ECU 400,000 to be consistent with that for supply contracts[33] and the procedural regime is broadly the same as for works and supply contracts under the Utilities Directive; however, in contrast, there is a two-tier regime, whereby certain services[34] are subject to a minimal regime only; however, the partial exemption applicable to certain services may be temporary only, since 'it is necessary to obtain precise information on cross-frontier exchanges [in these areas] before foreseeing the full application of the Directive'.[35] The contract award criteria are largely as in the Utilities Directive but with two provisos covering the cases of either possible prejudice to national laws or regulations on the remuneration of certain services[36] or award of contracts to public authorities whose bid is (or may be) influenced by public funds.[37]

The terminology of the three approaches to tendering permitted by the Directive[38] is crucial; 'open procedures' are those where all interested suppliers or contractors may submit tenders, 'restricted procedures' are those where only candidates invited (*ie* prequalified) by the contracting entity may submit tenders and 'negotiated procedures' are those where the contracting entity consults suppliers or contractors of its choice and negotiates the terms of the contract with one or more of them.

Consideration of the detailed provisions of the Directive is outwith the scope of this Chapter, but some special aspects require mention. First, the Directive does not

28. All references in this section are to Council Directive 93/38/EEC 'Co-ordinating the Procurement Procedures of Entities Operating in the Water, Energy, Transport and Telecommunications Sectors' unless otherwise stated; refer also to note 4 supra.

29. The services elements of the Utilities Services Directive were originally adopted as a separate text, the final form being published as (COM(91) 347 Final SYN 361 OJ C337/1 Dec. 1 1991 as amended by COM(92) 292 Final SYN 361 OJ C188/21 July 25 1992); this was by way of an amendment to the Utilities Directive 90/531/EEC, although the early draft was a stand-alone document; refer note 4 supra.

30. Explanatory Memorandum to the Services Directive ('EM') para.1.

31. Art. 2.

32. Art. 1(4).

33. Art. 14(1)(a).

34. These are listed in Annex XVIB; refer to text at note 44 below for comment.

35. Recital 33.

36. Art. 34(1).

37. Art. 34 (final paragraph).

38. Art. 20(1); the procedures are defined in Arts 1(7)(a), 1(7)(b) and 1(7)(c) respectively.

apply to service contracts awarded in relation to activities *either*[39] not covered by the definition in Article 2(2) of the Utilities Directive *or* taking place outwith the EC. Contracting entities may choose any one of the three bidding procedures provided a call for competition has been made;[40] however, prequalification procedures are required to be on the basis of objective rules and criteria which are required to be made available to interested parties on demand, but broadly the rules governing prequalification are consistent with those governing contract awards;[41] selection of candidates for tendering in restricted or negotiated procedures must also be by objective criteria. Contracts may be awarded only on the basis of *either*[42] the most 'economically advantageous' tender *or* the lowest price, where in the former case, the tender documents have to state the criteria, in descending order of importance, which will be applied in assessing the award, and the minimum requirements to be met in the event that variation to the overall requirements is permitted.[43]

The Directive contains two lists of categories of services,[44] and the two-tier regime provides that certain services are subject only to a minimal regime, and then possibly only temporarily. This minimal regime requires only adherence to the Directive's provisions concerning technical specifications[45] and publication of notices.[46] All financial-type services are subject to the full regime of the Directive[47] and it would appear that the Commission is satisfied that the temporary suspension appropriate to certain services need not apply to insurance contracts.

While insurance contracts are highlighted as causing particular difficulty in view of the unique nature of the oil and gas insurance markets, it should be noted that such contracts are not the only ones affecting the upstream oil and gas sector and giving rise to anticipated difficulties consequent on this Directive;[48] the full regime applies to (to quote only two examples) auditing, where there are many similarities with the insurance client/broker relationship and where tendering could be equally disruptive, and banking and investment services where remunerated by fees, commissions, etc; it appears that upstream oil and gas companies need not put out their current account banking business to tender, but will have to do so for purchase of currencies, provision of loan facilities, and provision of merchant banking and stockbroking services.

2.5 Remedies Directive[49]

The early Directives lacked 'teeth' in that the mechanisms for enforcement were inadequate. A Remedies Directive[50] was finalised in 1992, but its scope and details

39. Art. 6(1).
40. In accordance with Art. 21.
41. Art. 30.
42. Arts 34(1)(a) and 34(1)(b) respectively.
43. Art. 34(3).
44. Respectively Annex XVIA and Annex XVIB.
45. Art. 18.
46. Art. 24.
47. Arts 18 to 37 inclusive.
48. Refer also to section 2.8 below regarding the impact of the Utilities Services Directive.
49. Refer to Griffiths, 'Public Procurement: the EC's Review Procedures' [1991] 2 PLC 19 and Gormley, 'The New System of Remedies in Procurement by the Utilities' [1992] 1 PPLR, 259.
50. Directive 92/13 EEC, OJ L76/14 1992; the original proposal was COM(90) 297 (Final), OJ C216/8 1990, and amended in COM(91) 158 (Final) OJ C179/18 1991.

are outwith the purposes of this Chapter but are covered in full in Chapter 5. For the present, it should only be noted that the Remedies Directive may make the award of contracts a litigious area, with dissatisfied bidders allowed legal redress against the contracting entity.

2.6 Current Status of the Utilities Services Directives in the UK

Regulations passed by Statutory Instrument and effective January 13 1993 gave direct effect to the provisions of the Utilities Directive in UK law[51] irrespective of the UK's then stated intention to apply under Article 3(1) for exemption of certain activities, as set out below, in view of their applicability to a wider class of entity that is covered by that exemption. Consequent on the UK's obtaining exemption under Article 3 (see below), these regulations were amended in December 1993.[52]

2.7 Utilities Services Directive: Article 3 Exemption

There are two main reasons why oil and gas companies were brought under a Directive aimed in essence at public procurement: first, state-controlled national oil companies in some member states are assumed to adopt (or, at least, be in a position to adopt) discriminatory procurement practices by virtue of such state control; and second, some member states have used the licensing system as a means of indirect discrimination in relation to procurement practices, the UK being an example.[53]

Article 3(1) of the Directive therefore provides that member states may request the Commission to provide that certain exploitation activities[54]

shall not be considered to be an activity [as] defined[55]... and that entities shall not be considered as operating under special or exclusive rights[56]

provided certain alternative conditions are satisfied.[57] These alternative conditions are phrased both in terms of licensing regulations and in terms of procurement transparency; the former appears to be met by the proposed Licensing Directive, discussed below.

These 'alternative conditions' require that licence applications be part of an open process, that technical and financial capabilities of applicants be established prior to evaluation of competing applications, that licences be granted on the basis of objective criteria established and published in advance of submission of applica-

51. The Regulations were made under Section 2(2) European Communities Act 1972 and apply throughout the UK.

52. The Utilities Supply and Works Contracts (Amendment) Regulations 1993, which came into force on Jan. 13 1994.

53. Refer to note 18 supra; in the years 1987–1991 the UK shares of UKCS orders for Goods and Services were 87 per cent, 84 per cent, 81 per cent, 77 per cent and 78 per cent respectively; the generally downward trend relating rather less to any increased Euro-openness of the UKCS than to the upturn in the UK offshore supplies markets over that period, leading to exhausting of UK capacity (source: Department of Energy Brown Books for 1989, 1991 and 1992 pp. 89, 87 and 99 respectively).

54. Exploring for, or extracting, oil, gas, coal or other solid fuels; however, the UK sought exemptions under Art. 3 only in relation to oil and gas.

55. In Art. 2(2)(b)(i); refer to preceding note.

56. Within the meaning of Art.2(3)(b); refer also to text related to note 22 supra. The extract is from Art. 3(1).

57. These conditions are set out in detail in Arts 3(1)(a) to 3(1)(e).

tions, and that licence regulations be published in advance and applied thereafter non-discriminatorily and non-selectively; finally no requirement for information on procurement intentions may form part of the application process.[58]

Exemption from the Directive under Article 3(1) is by no means the end of the oil and gas companies' obligations under the Directive: such exemption does not remove the obligation[59a] on member states to ensure, whether through the licence regulations or otherwise, that contracting entities:

observe the principles of non-discrimination and competitive procurement . . . in particular as regards the information . . . [made] available to undertakings concerning its procurement intentions.

The Directive makes no specific provisions covering the foregoing obligations, and the onus will be on member states in presenting their application for exemption under Article 3(1) to demonstrate both that its licensing regulations meet the criteria established in Article 3(1) of the Directive and outlined above, and that its licensing regulations, or other measures, meet the obligations established in Article 3(2). It is understood that the Department of Trade and Industry was satisfied that the then licensing regime on the UKCS met the requirements of the Directive, but that the Commission could not agree in view of the element of Ministerial discretion contained in the regulations. Accordingly, the UK's application for exemption under Article 3 was initially refused.

However, after extensive negotiation, the Commission Decision of July 14 1993,[59b] granted the UK an exemption under Article 3 in its oil and gas industry for a one-year period from July 15 1993, provided that certain UK legislation and regulations were amended (as set out in an annex to the Decision) before April 15 1994. As at mid-March 1994 these amendments had not been made and, following France's failure to implement similar amendments before a comparable deadline, followed by the Commission's stating that no second temporary exemption would be considered, suggests that the UK may be in danger of losing the exemption completely. Grant of such temporary exemptions has raised doubts in authoritative quarters.[59c]

2.8 Impact of the Utilities Services Directive

The upstream oil and gas industry represents itself as being open to competition and being non-discriminatory, although it is clear that the extent to which such a claim can be justified varies across the EC. In so far as such a claim is indeed valid, then the provisions of the Directive, in themselves, may be of no substantive impact, requiring principally a reorganising of procurement procedures to comply with the new set of rules. In so far as such a claim is not valid, then the impact will clearly be correspondingly greater.

In those member states where oil industry procurement is already broadly open and non-discriminatory, there will, however, be areas where opening up procurement in line with the Directive will indeed cause problems, perhaps significant; the case of insurance has already been highlighted above, but other possible difficult

58. Per Art. 3(1)(e), other than as specifically to meet the objectives of Art. 36 of the Treaty.
59a. Art. 3(2)(a).
59b. Decision 93/425/EEC OJ L196/55, Aug. 5 1993.
59c. Refer [1993] 9/10 OGLTR at 329 for a penetrating review of the Decision by Professor Hancher.

areas include computer services, where companies may wish to negotiate a worldwide network on common equipment where the circumstances governing the worldwide procurement may not be compatible with the 'EC-only' concept of the Directive-induced tender, and several areas of financial services, including merchant banking advice on corporate acquisitions and auditing, where worldwide factors may (as with computers) prove incompatible with EC-only circumstances and these two themes (incompatibility of integrated worldwide contracts with the EC-only Directive, and types of contracts not normally tendered) recur in other service sectors.

It is submitted that, in general, compliance with the provisions of the Directive will have relatively minor substantive impact on the industry, although some service sectors (particularly insurance) will be seriously affected and this may necessitate changes, perhaps significant, in market practices. It is further submitted that a more substantive impact on the industry will derive from the associated Remedies Directive, since it introduces a wholly novel element, at least into UK practice.

3.0 THE LICENSING DIRECTIVE[60]

3.1 Introduction

The completion of the internal market, the process which started with the 1985 White Paper,[61] was itself due for completion by the end of 1992. The internal market has been defined[62] as 'an area without internal frontiers in which the free movement of goods, persons and capital is ensured', and the Commission's view is that this is no less applicable to the energy market, since the importance of energy to the EC's economy is such that completion of the internal market, in the absence of an integrated energy market, is hardly conceivable. On the narrower front which this chapter addresses, the Commission sees the Directive as an integral part of the process leading to completion of the internal market, since the activities of exploration for, and exploitation of, hydrocarbon resources are governed by restrictions and regulations in the various member states of differing degrees to the extent of incompatibility with the concept of the internal market. The consequences of this Commission view are widespread and fundamental to the future of the energy industries in the EC,[63] but are generally outwith the scope of this Chapter (see Chapter 6 for a more in-depth discussion of third party access in particular). The Commission's particular interest in the hydrocarbon industries derives largely from the EC's producing only 26 per cent of its oil, and 62 per cent of its gas consumptions.[64]

The Directive accordingly sets out to harmonise the conditions attaching to upstream activities across member states while allowing them to retain due rights

60. A final draft of the Directive was issued (reference 11231/93) in March 1994 reflecting the common position adopted by the Energy Council on Dec. 10 1993; all references hereunder are to this document unless otherwise specified. The key term used throughout the Directive is 'authorisations' but this Chapter generally refers to 'licences', the equivalent, and more familiar, UK term.
61. 'Completing the Internal Energy Market'; COM(85) 310 Final, June 14 1985.
62. Art. 8a of the Treaty, inserted by Art. 13 SEA.
63. Including electricity and gas transit, price transparency and third party access.
64. Para. 4 of the explanatory memorandum accompanying the first draft of the Directive.

and responsibilities for administration of their hydrocarbon resources in a manner consistent with their individual legal structures. It is recognised that the outlook for significant new hydrocarbon discoveries is limited, and that the bulk of EC hydrocarbon production in the future will come from existing licences, hence the scope for application of the Directive is also limited; however, the Commission envisages advanced exploration technologies as playing significant roles in future licences.

Particular concerns of the Commission in relation to licensing included:

- privileges granted to state-controlled entities, whether by reservation of acreage on an exclusive basis,[65] or by mandatory inclusion of such an entity in licence groups;[66]
- application of different regulations to state-controlled entities than to private ones, principally through exemptions from laws or regulations;[67]
- use of the licensing system as an indirect restriction of competition among suppliers, as has been discussed above;[68]
- use of the licensing system to control the final destination of the production,[69] deemed thereby to restrict competition; and
- the position in relation to authorisations issued prior to the Directive becoming effective, particularly since these will generally be the most prospective.

The Commission's prime objectives in issuing such a Directive included:

- the establishing of a single 'market' in authorisations by giving equal access thereto by EC entities and on a common and harmonised basis;
- removal of anti-competitive restrictions still extant in the licensing regimes of some EC member states while still permitting restrictions demonstrably necessary in the context of optimum exploitation of the resources; and
- limitation of the restrictive effect of previously granted authorisations; this last was the most contentious of all the provisions in early drafts of the Directive and will be discussed further below.

The Directive lays down general principles which underlie it, including the retention of member states' sovereign rights over their hydrocarbon resources, including the rights both to long-term management and short-term administration thereof.[70a] It allows individual member states freedom to select the method of detailed implementation of the general principles laid down as a framework by the Directive. The approach of the Directive is to be consistent with that derived for the Utilities Directive[70b] rather than that adopted for the electricity industry. Member states'

65. As is the case in parts of the Italian onshore, reserved for AGIP; refer also Ninth Recital to the Directive and Art. 7.

66. Typically the 'recommended' inclusion of the National Coal Board or British Gas Corporation as party to 2nd and 3rd Round, and the mandatory inclusion of BNOC/BGC in UKCS 5th and 6th Round, UK licence groups, and the imposition of the Participation Agreement whereby BNOC became entitled to acquire 51 per cent of production.

67. Typically BNOC was initially exempted from Petroleum Revenue Tax (PRT) and, under the Petroleum (Production) Regulations 1976 (SI 1976/1129), Regulation 6(6), BNOC and BGC were exempted from the rule restricting licence applications to invited ones.

68. Refer to notes 18 and 53 supra.

69. For example Model Clause 30(1) of the 1988 Regulations; in this context refer to Daintith and Willoughby *UK Oil & Gas Law* at paras 5–371 and 1–1013.

70a. Fourth Recital and Art. 2(1).

70b. Thereby cross-referring to Art. 2(2)(b)(i) of the Utilities Directive – refer to text following note 20 supra.; refer also to Twelfth Recital to the Directive.

systems for award of authorisations must be based on transparent and non-discriminatory procedures, open to all (EC) entities, and where the bases of award will be through application of objective criteria, published in advance, and their licence regulations may be based only on ensuring proper exploitation, on standards related to the environment, health, safety, national defence and security, and on a royalty system.

The UK Government broadly approves the Directive but is understood to be looking for some amendments; the comments below on the interface of the Model Clauses and the Directive will indicate areas where there may be differences and the initial rejection of the UK's application for exemption under Article 3 of the Utilities Directive indicates that there are unresolved differences between the Directive and the UK licensing regulations.

3.2 Analysis of the Directive

The legal basis for the Directive is stated as being derived from Articles 57(2 (first sentence)), 66 and 100A of the Treaty.[71] It focuses on 'authorisations', which mean 'any law, regulation, administrative or contractual provision or instrument issued thereunder by which the competent authorities of a member state entitle an entity to exercise, on its own behalf and at its own risk, the exclusive right to prospect or explore for or produce hydrocarbons in a geographical area'.[72]

The main general provisions of the Directive are that:

- access by entities to the relevant activities must be non-discriminatory, but such access by any third country-controlled entity may be refused on grounds of defence and national security,[73] typically, the requirements that applicants be incorporated in the relevant member state or maintain a place of business there, are no longer to be permitted;
- such activities may be restricted or prohibited on a limited range of grounds, including defence and national security, health, environmental protection, safety or resource management;[74] note that these provisions limit the activities which may be carried out and do not directly impinge on the award procedure;
- award procedures must be open and appropriately publicised (including OJ notification);[75]
- acreage must be delimited in such a way as to maximise efficient exploration/ exploitation, and durations of authorisations must be no longer than is necessary to permit appropriate activity to be carried out, with appropriately relevant surrender requirements;[76] this introduces a number of elements designed to enhance 'competition', ie through eliminating the licensing of large blocks of acreage which may accordingly remain unexplored for many years, as has been

---

71. Preamble to the Directive; however, since Art. 57(2) refers to self-employed persons, the relevance in this context is not clear to the author. Further, Art. 66 is a sweep-up for Art. 59–65 on Services, the relevance of which is no less unclear. Early drafts of the Directive referred also to Art. 113 of the Treaty, which reference was removed following political difficulty within the Commission.
72. Art. 1(3).
73. Art. 2; early drafts required prior notification of such exchanges to the Commission.
74. Art. 6(2).
75. Art. 3(1), 3(2).
76. Art. 4.

the case in some early UKCS licences; further, there is an implied 'fallow block' requirement to free 'graveyard acreage';
- award criteria may include the technical and financial status of the applicant(s), their proposals for exploitation, their record under other authorisations and (if appropriate) price offered in an auction;[77a] by implication, these are the only criteria permitted to be employed, although the language is flexible; applicants who are unsuccessful are entitled to be informed of the reasons therefor;[77b]
- there are provisions[78] designed both to minimise state interference and to improve the tie-back to the Utilities Directive, through requiring that licence regulations are justified by the necessity for proper exploitation of the licence area as constrained by Article 3; specifically, state use of licence regulations to compel entities to reveal their procurement intentions is prohibited.[79]

3.3 Expropriation and Retroactive Application

While much of the Directive does no more than codify the better practices[80a] of the leading EC hydrocarbon-producing states it did in early drafts contain two inter-linked themes considered unacceptable by the industry, those of expropriation and retroactive application. These concepts appear in several forms[80b]:

- while the Commission considered that the 'exclusive right' to exploit an area should be fair compensation for the risks inherent in such exploitation, undue prolonging of such exclusive right (eg for an unlimited duration) led to over-compensation, and the Commission envisaged such a situation being 'remedied' and the licensee being compensated (if necessary);
- the Commission proposed that entities holding existing authorisations granted under regimes not compliant with the provisions of the Directive should be released from any conditions and obligations contrary to said provisions, being compensated if necessary;
- the Commission proposed that where an entity held an authorisation on January 1 1993 granted under conditions which precluded applications from other entities, the member state must grant new authorisations in respect of those parts of the licence area which had not then been exploited;[81] payment of compensation was envisaged; and
- the draft Directive provided that its Article 7 (which effectively governs the shape of licence regulations) should apply to authorisations granted before January 1 1993.

77a. Art. 5(1); the award criteria require to be published in the OJ.

77b. Art. 5(5).

78. Art. 6(1).

79. Art. 6 (final para.); there is an exception in so far as may be necessary to meet the objectives of Art. 36 of the Treaty.

80a. Typically, current discussions between the Department of Trade and Industry (DTI) and the United Kingdom Offshore Operators' Association (UKOOA) are reconsidering some aspects of the existing Regulations with a view to tailoring them to reflect more accurately the UKCS in the 1990s, eg with regard to fallow acreage, part-blocks, frontier acreage, out-of-round applications and such matters.

80b. Contained in COM92(110) Final.

81. 'Exploitation' as used throughout the drafts of the Directive was rather a wider term than customary English usage, and included what would normally be distinguished as 'exploration' activities.

The Commission's rationale in introducing such controversial provisions apparently derived from its assessment that, with the North Sea being a mature area in hydrocarbon exploration terms, the best and the majority of the acreage would have already been awarded and on licence terms that may stretch well into the next century, leading to the conclusion that the Directive will have little material effect unless its scope of application is retroactive.

Concerted opposition by the oil and gas industry, and by all member states with significant hydrocarbon reserves, led to material changes in the form of the Directive before its adoption as a Common Position in December 1993. However, the main principles of the argument are of such significance that they merit coverage in this Chapter.

It is submitted that it was indeed an essential principle to resist the imposition of retroactive and/or expropriatory legislation. It is, however, submitted[82] that, not-withstanding the fundamental nature of the aforesaid general principle, some of the industry's concerns over such retroactive application may perhaps have been overstated:

- in the UK, licence terms for the first four rounds of UKCS licensing were unilaterally and retroactively amended, and for no compensation, in 1975;[83] while the industry's response at the time was strongly critical of such amendments, no actual substantive counter-action was taken and ultimately all companies accept-ed the changes;
- while Article 7 of the draft Directive was retroactive, its applicability was limited since Article 7(1) refered to Article 6(2) which covers publication of licence conditions and award criteria and the retroactive application thereof is a physical impossibility and since Article 7(2) places limitations on member states' abilities to use the licensing regulations for indirect purposes, particularly influencing procurement activity; the author envisages, perhaps controversially, no particular difficulty under either heading; and
- Article 8 applied only where both the licence award was non-competitive and the licence area had not been exploited, and, given general industry concerns, at least in the UKCS, over 'fallow blocks' and 'graveyard acreage' the latter rationale was difficult to counter.[84a]

Notwithstanding these misgivings, and the industry's case, the final form of the Directive is broadly acceptable to the industry. It is not retroactive[84b], its imple-mentation into national legislation automatically qualifies it for an exemption under Article 3 of the Utilities Servies Directive,[84c] it provides for a 'Chinese wall' to be

---

82. With no little trepidation on the part of the author.

83. Petroleum and Submarine Pipe-Lines Act 1975 Section 18 and Part II of Schedule 2 to that Act, which amended all existing UKCS licences; refer to Daintith and Willoughby op. cit., supra note 69 (at paras 1-223, 3-080) for an excellent discussion of this unprecedented move. Some interesting historical insight is given by Cameron, *Property Rights and Sovereign Rights: The Case of North Sea Oil* (1983), particularly at p.125ff.

84a. However, the time limits provided by Art. 8 have been criticised by the ECOSOC Study Group as being unnecessarily rigid, envisaging the possible consequences of litigation, grave disruption to operations and third country reprisal action.

84b. Eleventh Recital and Art. 11.

84c. Twelfth Recital and Art. 12.

created in cases where a member state-controlled entity participates in licensing,[84d] and it provides relief for Denmark from the requirements to abolish exclusive rights[84e].

Overall, the oil and gas industry can be well satisfied with the final outcome since the advantage gained through automatic exemption under Article 3 of the Utilities Services Directive is likely significantly to outweigh any loss of freedom in obtaining licences consequent on the [Licencing] Directive's provisions. In addition, many oil and gas companies may find opportunities opening up in jurisdictions other than their own, which opportunities may be much more restricted at present.

3.4 Implications for the Utilities Services Directive

The question arises over what effect the implementation into national law of the provisions of the Licensing Directive will have in relation to the Utilities Services Directive. The mechanism provided in the Licensing Directive[85] is that once it has been implemented into national legislation, the requirements of Article 3(1) of the Utilities Directive shall be considered to be satisfied; the requirements of Articles 3(2) and 3(3), however, remain and therefore the Directive will not be the 'saving grace' it was at one time assumed (or rather hoped) to be.

3.5 Implications for UKCS Licensing

Whereas up to the UKCS Ninth Round at least, compliance with the Directive might have caused difficulties for the UK, recent changes, particularly introduced by the 1988 Regulations have broadly brought the UK into line with the Directive and few problems are envisaged in implementing its provisions. The 1988 Regulations may demonstrate the general compatibility thereof with the Directive: Regulation 4 provides that 'any person may apply in accordance with these regulations'; this satisfies Articles 2(2) and 3(1) of the Directive requiring open non-discriminatory access. Further, Regulation 7(1)(a) provides that applications shall be for one or more blocks as shown on a master map; Article 4(a) places restrictions on the areas to be licensed, with a view to preventing awards of unreasonably large areas, and it is understood that the UKCS block system is acceptable to the Commission.

In contrast, the criteria governing applications for licences (these criteria are conventionally published as Departmental guidelines) will require amendment for licensing rounds subsequent to implementation of the Directive, and certain aspects of the Model Clauses require amendment[86]; typical of the amendments required:

• Model Clause 30(1) requires the landing in the UK of all petroleum won and saved from the licensed area, other than as consented to by the Minister;[87] and

---

84d. Art. 6(3); it is understood that these provisions are primarily aimed at Norway's subsequent entry into the EC with consequential effects on Statoil. The provision with regard to Norway is of particular interest, but detailed consideration thereof is outside the scope of this Chapter.

84e. Fourteenth Recital and Art. 13; abolition of such rights is given by Art. 7.

85. Art. 12 adding a new Art. 3(5) to the Utilities Directive.

86. Refer Commission Decision 93/425/EEC discussed in section 2.7 above.

87. Refer also to Daintith and Willoughby op. cit., supra note 69, paras 5-371 and 1-013.

- Model Clause 42(1)(g) makes it a licence revocation offence for the licensee to cease to have its 'central management and control' in the UK, and this is principally because such determines the licensee's tax residence;[88] however, provisions of this nature may not only be incompatible with Article 2(1) of the Directive but may also contravene Articles 52 and 59 of the Treaty.

3.6 Impact of the Licensing Directive on the UKCS

It is submitted that the impact on the UKCS will be limited, both since the existing 1988 Regulations are broadly compatible with the provisions of the Directive, and since the greater part of the UKCS, at least the more prospective part, has already been licensed, hence, unless the retroactive element of the Directive is ascertained to contain hidden teeth, the relevance to future licensing activity is muted. It is further submitted that the Directive is more of a governmental concern than an industry one since it is aimed at licensing regulations rather than at the activities of individual companies.

There are two broadly positive aspects of the Directive which may assist UKCS explorers; first, some elements of governmental control through the Model Clauses will be removed, *eg* the requirement to land petroleum in the UK and, second, UK-based companies may find more opportunities becoming available in those countries with a relatively undeveloped licensing system, *eg* Spain, Italy and Greece; further, should Norway enter the EC, the imposition of the Directive upon the existing highly restrictive Norwegian regime will significantly open up possibilities on the Norwegian Continental Shelf.

4.0 CONCLUSIONS

Industry procurement practices (across all member states) and member state licensing regulations (with some more affected than others) will require amendment to comply with the new regulations. Particular concerns remain over application of the Remedies Directive and over implementation of the 'Chinese Walls' implied by the Licensing Directive in circumstances of State participation inherent in the Licensing Directive. However, the Directives will involve no substantive changes of principle, rather will necessitate amendments to the fine details of practical procedures.

The oil and gas industry, despite strong resistance to individual aspects of these Directives, will, it is submitted, ultimately see a net benefit therefrom, given the opening up of procurement (with advantages to the buyer as well as the seller) and of licensing particularly in jurisdictions previously partly closed.

The author submits that the oil and gas industry should be reasonably satisfied with the completion of the Internal Energy Market, at least insofar as it relates to the Utilities Services Directive and the Licensing Directive.

---

88. Refer to comment in Daintith and Willoughby, ibid., at para.5-380.

The Directives on 'Utilities' and 'Licensing': How Do They Affect Netherlands Petroleum Legislation?

Commentary to Chapter 4

Martha M. Roggenkamp

1.0 INTRODUCTION

Chapter 4 describes the origin and status of the Directive on public procurement in the utilities sector (hereinafter 'Utilities Directive')[1] and the proposed Directive on the conditions for granting and using authorizations for the prospection, exploration and production of hydrocarbons (hereinafter 'Licensing Directive')[2] as well as their possible implications for the petroleum industry on the UK continental shelf. These Directives stem from the action programme with regard to the establishment of an internal energy market presented by the Commission in 1988.[3] The actions envisaged in this document, *inter alia*, refer to the application of the White Paper of 1985 which includes the opening up of public procurement and the application of existing Community law in the energy sector, as well as the adoption of specific measures in the field of energy. The Licensing Directive as described in the preceding Chapter can be considered to be such a specific measure. Prior to this proposed Directive other measures concerning the establishment of the internal energy market have been adopted, i.e. the Directive governing price transparency[4] and the so-called transit Directives.[5] These were followed by proposals for the

1. See Council Directive 90/531/EEC and the new Council Directive 93/38/EEC of June 14 1993 co-ordinating the procurement procedures of entities operating in the water, energy, transport and telecommunications sector.

2. COM(92) 110 final SYN 412 submitted by the Commission on May 11 1992. The Council has issued a Common Position on Dec. 16 1993 (reference 11231/93).

3. The Internal Energy Market, COM(88) 238 final of May 2 1988. See the Commission's working document on the internal energy market, in: Energy in Europe, Commission of the European Community, DG XVII, 1988.

4. OJ L185 of July 17 1990.

5. Electricity Transit Directive, OJ L313 of Nov. 13 1990; Gas Transit Directive, OJ L147 of June 12 1991.

second phase of the completion of the internal market in natural gas and electricity. The latter proposals aim at a gradual integration of the gas and electricity markets through, for example, the introduction of a limited system of third party access (hereinafter TPA).[6] A Directive concerning upstream licensing together with the gas transit Directive and a possible system of TPA which would apply to the downstream aspects of the gas industry, would, for instance, have the effect of regulating the gas industry from wellhead to consumer.

With respect to the effects of the Utilities and Licensing Directives on exploration and production of petroleum on the UK continental shelf, the author concludes in Chapter 4 that the implications for UK licensing are limited as the existing national regulations more or less have been brought into line with the provisions of the Directives. Although the Netherlands government also broadly approves the principles of the Directives, this commentary will further examine the implications of the public procurement Directive for petroleum licensing in the Netherlands as well as the possible implications of the proposed Licensing Directive for Netherlands petroleum legislation in its entirety. There are a number of reasons for examining the situation in the Netherlands. Firstly, the Netherlands is, after all, the largest gas producer in the European Union (EU), and its system like most countries in the world, is characterised by a high degree of state participation. Discrimination in favour of state entities fits rather uneasily with the assumption of competition on which the Directives are based. Secondly, it is interesting to note that at the moment the Directives were drafted, compliance with the Directives would have caused significant difficulties for the Netherlands. Important parts of the Netherlands petroleum regime would not have complied with the principles of these Directives. This is particularly true for the regime governing onshore petroleum exploration and production which, by contrast to the offshore petroleum regime, is based on legislation established in the last century.[7] Hence, it is not surprising that until some amendments were made to the onshore mining legislation last year, important parts of the Netherlands petroleum regime would not have followed the principle that member state's licensing regimes should be transparent, non-discriminatory and open to all (EU) entities and that objective criteria for licensing should be published in advance.

2.0 THE UTILITIES DIRECTIVE: THE IMPLICATIONS FOR PETROLEUM LICENSING

2.1 General

The background, legal basis and scope of the Directive on public procurement has been thoroughly examined in Chapter 4. The importance of this Directive for the oil

6. Proposal for a Council Directive concerning common rules for the internal market in gas (COM(91) 548 final SYN 385) and Proposal for a Council Directive concerning common rules for the internal market in electricity (COM(91) 548 final SYN 384). An amended proposal for a European Parliament and Council Directive has been issued in December 1993 in order to meet the opposition from the industry and member states (COM(93) 643 final COD 384/385). For a more in-depth discussion of these proposals see Chapters 6 and 7.

7. The legal basis for the exploitation of hydrocarbons onshore is the 'Lio concernant les Mines, les Minières et les Carrières' of April 21 1810. This originally Napoleonic Act governs the production of the above three sets of minerals. The production of oil and gas is, for practical reasons, grouped under the category of 'Mines'. Exploratory drilling is governed by an Exploration Act of May 3 1967, Staatsblad 258.

and gas industry results from the fact that it also applies to public undertakings and companies having a special or exclusive right to explore and exploit oil and gas in a certain geographical area. In addition, the Licensing Directive establishes a direct link with the Utilities Directive.[8] The reasons for bringing oil and gas companies under this Directive are twofold. Firstly, a state may treat state-controlled national oil companies different from other companies. Secondly, a licensing system can be used as a means of indirect discrimination in relation to procurement practices. A clear example of such practice is, for example, to be found in Article 54 of the Norwegian Petroleum Act of 1985 which states that '... competitive Norwegian suppliers shall be given genuine opportunities to secure orders for deliveries of goods and services'.

Basically, the Utilities Directive assumes that the general principles and procedures with regard to public procurement, as established in the Directive, apply. However, a member state may request an exemption under Article 3(1) if certain conditions are fulfilled. In general, a member state has to prove that the award of licences is already based on procedures which are open, transparent and non-discriminatory. If an exemption is granted under Article 3(1), member states have to ensure that the parallel mechanism of Article 3(2) is then put in place. Hence, in order to apply for an exemption a member state has not only to demonstrate that its licensing criteria meet the criteria of Article 3(1), but also that the existing procurement regime meets the obligations established under Article 3(2) of the Utilities Directive. The procurement criteria enterprises have to meet have recently been established by the European Commission.[9] Member states have to ensure that enterprises awarding contracts with a value of between ECU 400,000 and 5 million, communicate to the Commission within 48 hours of the award of the contract specified information about the contract such as its nature, duration and value.[10]

2.2 Article 3 Exemption in the Netherlands

2.2.1 Netherlands Petroleum Regime before the Exemption of Article 3

The Netherlands authorities applied for an exemption under Article 3(1) of the Utilities Directive in 1991. In order to acquire such an exemption, the then existing system of licensing needed to be open, transparent and non-discriminatory. However, when assessing the onshore and offshore petroleum licensing regimes, it was obvious that these systems at that time did not always meet the above requirements. Particularly, the onshore licensing regime did not agree entirely with the assumptions of the Directive. This is not so surprising if one keeps in mind the background and origins of the system. It consists of several pieces of legislation which have been designed to provide temporary solutions and quite often also to give the companies the necessary financial security in relation to their investments. As a consequence a system has been developed which has virtually no elements of true competition. Although exploration and production onshore *is* based on a system of licensing, these licences are not granted by way of bidding rounds, but succeed each other more or less automatically. Seismic surveys, for example, can be regulated by way

---

8. See Art. 13 of the Licensing Directive as published in the Common Position of Dec. 1993.
9. Commission Decision 93/327, OJ 1993, L129/25.
10. The information required is listed in an annex to Commission Decision 93/327/EEC.

of the grant of a 'declaration of priority for geophysical prospecting' which is a written pledge from the Minister of Economic Affairs to the effect that a drilling licence will be considered and decided upon with priority. This system is based on an agreement entered into by the Minister of Economic Affairs and the NOGEPA (Netherlands Oil and Gas Exploration and Production Association) in 1982. Consequently, the companies who are members of this association received preferential treatment when applying for a so-called priority declaration. The holders of a priority declaration would as a result of the above agreement, in general, always be awarded a drilling licence. Since concessions for the production of oil and gas will normally always be granted to the holder of a drilling licence, as long as the licensee has carried out the number of drillings required in the licence, competition is also lacking in the last stage of licensing. Hence, it is not surprising that the onshore licensing regime as described above was considered to be non-competitive and discriminatory.

Furthermore, it can be noted that the system was not transparent. Most of the conditions were not published beforehand. As a result of the fact that the applicable mining laws did not contain many licensing criteria, more detailed conditions were in practice attached to each concession or licence individually. The conditions might differ from concession to concession. However, in practice, the criteria published under the Continental Shelf Mining Act (CS Mining Act) were also included in the onshore concessions and drilling licences.[11]

2.2.2 The Situation after the Exemption

As a result of the negotiations between the Commission and the Netherlands authorities, the above system has been changed so that it should meet the requirements of the Utilities Directive. By Royal Decree of July 19 1993[12] the original agreement between the government and NOGEPA regarding the award of a 'declaration of priority for geophysical prospecting' has been changed in a way that the procedure is now open to all (EU) entities. Although this new arrangement certainly is an improvement in that it is not limited to a specific group of oil companies, it could be argued that these changes do not make the whole system more competitive. In effect, the onshore licensing system is in practice still based on the assumption 'first come, first served'. Nevertheless, it seems that these new provisions will comply with the provisions in Article 3 of the proposed Licensing Directive, i.e. that authorisations may be granted without initiating special procedures as long as the acreage is available on a permanent basis.

In addition, another Royal Decree was issued on the same date. This Decree contains rules with regard to 'applications for and financial obligations under drilling licences and concessions'. The provisions of this Decree can be considered as a codification of established legal practice. In the absence of legal requirements with regard to conditions and requirements for onshore drilling licences and concessions, the Minister of Economic Affairs (and the Crown) fell back on the conditions used offshore since 1967. Although this method was widely acknowledged in the Netherlands, it has never been officially published. The publication of

11. The mining legislation offshore consists of the Continental Shelf Mining Act of 1965 (Staatsblad 428) as implemented by, *inter alia*, two Royal Decrees governing the exploration and production of hydrocarbons: Decrees of Jan. 25 1967 (Staatsblad 24) and Feb. 6 1976 (Staatsblad 102).

12. Staatscourant 136, July 21 1993.

this Decree is therefore a step forwards to greater transparency of the onshore petroleum regime. On the basis of the ongoing discussions between the Netherlands government and the Commission and the above-mentioned amendments to the onshore petroleum licensing regime, the Netherlands government was granted in December 1993 an exemption under Article 3(1) of the Utilities Directive.[13]

In its Decision the Commission has not referred to the petroleum licensing regime offshore. The implications of the proposed Directive for the offshore regime are limited indeed. The procedure according to which licences are granted is basically non-discriminatory and transparent. Exploration licences, for example, are awarded in rounds which are 'open' periods of three months during which applications for one or more blocks (or part-blocks) can be made.[14] In the period January–April 1992 the eighth round of applications was held. The conditions according to which licences will be awarded are generally transparent as they are to be found in the Royal Decrees of 1967/1976 implementing the CS Mining Act.[15]

However, there is one aspect of offshore petroleum licensing which basically can be considered as being non-transparent, i.e. the stage in which the holder of a drilling licence applies for a production licence. Contrary to other licensing regimes in the North Sea, exploration and production are not covered by one licence. The fact that for exploration and production two separate licences must be applied for is one of the specific features of the Netherlands offshore petroleum regime. A production licence is granted 'automatically' when under the exploration licence an economically exploitable quantity of minerals has been discovered. Since the CS Mining Act and the Decrees implementing it do not define this term, it is the Minister who finally decides about the grant. In practice, this has been dependent on several aspects such as the possibility to connect the field with the existing infrastructure, the price of oil and the rate of the dollar. This means that the procedures governing the award of a production licence are not transparent. Furthermore, there is no specific period of time within which a production licence has to be granted. Although this situation is not directly covered by the provisions of the Utilities Directive or the proposed Licensing Directive, it could be argued that these applications for production licences, which are kept on file indefinitely, should be surrendered after a specific period of time.

2.2.3 Some Concluding Remarks

As a result of the exemption granted under Article 3(1) of the Utilities Directive, the alternative regime of Article 3(2) entered into force. From this it might be concluded that the existing procurement procedures are considered to be open and non-discriminatory. It is interesting to note, however, that government and the oil and gas industry within the policy programme of the Ministry of Economic Affairs 'Toeleveren en Uitbesteden' (Supply and Farm out), recently have established a

13. Commission Decision of Dec. 10 1993 establishing that the exploitation of geographical areas for the purpose of exploring for and extracting oil and gas does not constitute in the Netherlands an activity defined in Art. 2(2)(b)(i) of Council Directive 90/531/EEC and that entities carrying on such an activity are not to be considered in the Netherlands as operating under special or exclusive rights within the meaning of Art. 2(3)(b) of the Directive, 93/676/EC, OJ 1993, L316/41.

14. Art. 5 CS Mining Act.

15. Decree of Feb. 7 1967, Staatsblad 75, most recently amended on June 16 1981, Staatsblad 379.

standard fabrication contract for the petroleum industry.[16] The reason for issuing such a standard contract was twofold. Firstly, a large number of different standard contracts were used by the petroleum industry. Therefore the criteria for procurement were considered to be non-transparent. Consequently, Netherlands contractors and subcontractors in practice often decided not to submit a tender. It was considered that the establishment of a general standard contract would lead to more transparency and competition. In addition, it would improve the position of Netherlands suppliers.[17] Whereas the establishment of this standard contract is broadly in line with the principles of the Directive as it improves transparency and competition, it could be argued that the reasons for making this standard contract might be contrary to the spirit of the Directive.

3.0 THE LICENSING DIRECTIVE

3.1 General

The proposed Licensing Directive is an important component of the establishment of the Internal Energy Market. The Directive lays down common rules for the production of hydrocarbons. Hence, it aims at the harmonisation of the conditions according to which upstream petroleum licences can be awarded in the EU. The licensing procedures should therefore be transparent, objective and open to all interested (EU) entities. As well, the award of licences should be non-discriminatory and based on pre-established criteria which are published in advance. However, member states retain their rights with regard to the management of the resources and allocation of areas open for exploitation. At the urgent request of member states and industry, the issue of sovereignty received more emphasis in the text of the Common Position of December 1993. The Licensing Directive also establishes a close link with the Utilities Directive. When member states have satisfied the requirements of the Licensing Directive, the alternative regime provided for in the public procurement Directive applies directly. Member states are only required to demonstrate that their procurement regime is transparent and non-discriminatory. On the other hand, from the fact that a member state has been granted an exemption under Article 3(1) of the Utilities Directive it cannot be concluded that the state's licensing regime automatically meets all requirements of the Licensing Directive.[18] In addition to the requirements regarding the licensing regime, the Licensing Directive contains some other additional conditions with which the upstream petroleum legislation should comply.

3.2 Implications for Petroleum Licensing in the Netherlands

The present text of the Licensing Directive might have some implications for the Netherlands. These will probably be less compared to the implications the original

16. The Standard Construction/Modification/Maintenance Contract for the energy and offshore sector in the Netherlands was officially presented on Feb. 15 1993.

17. Cf. the preface of this standard contract where the reasons for drafting the contract have been outlined by the chairman of the drafting committee.

18. Despite the amendments made to the onshore mining regime in order to make the licensing procedures transparent and non-discriminatory, compliance of this new system with the Licensing Directive is not guaranteed.

text of the Directive would have had. Especially the original clauses regarding retroactivity and expropriation as discussed in Chapter 4 would have had serious implications for the petroleum industry in the Netherlands. These provisions which are deleted in the common position, would, for example, have affected most of the onshore concessions which have been awarded in the 1960s and 1970s. Until 1989 the onshore concessions, including the Groningen concession which was granted on May 30 1963, were awarded for an unlimited period of time, i.e. in perpetuity.[19] Under the first draft of the Licensing Directive, new authorisations had to be awarded for those areas which had been previously licensed for indefinite periods of time and which, furthermore, had not yet been developed. It is not suprising that the oil and gas industry in the Netherlands regarded this aspect of the Directive as unacceptable. Besides, such retroactive and expropriatory application would be contrary to the principles of Netherlands petroleum law. When, for example, in 1976 the existing criteria for the exploration and exploitation of oil and gas offshore were replaced by a new set of conditions, the issue of retroactivity was discussed. The petroleum industry successfully opposed the idea that production licences could be awarded under the regime of the Royal Decree of 1976 whereas exploration had taken place under the 'old' regime of the Royal Decree of 1967. Such a system would have had a retroactive effect and, subsequently, withhold from industry the required certainty about the licence obligations.

Compared to the first draft of the Directive the provisions with regard to state participation have also been changed. In fact, the text of Article 7 of the Directive has been extremely modified. Under the first draft Directive, state participants could only act as 'sleeping partners' because member states should not be involved, directly or indirectly, in ongoing procurement activities. However, due to amendment, *inter alia* suggested by the European Parliament, the proposed system of state participation has been liberalised.[20] States are entitled to participate as long as participation takes place on the basis of transparent, objective and non-discriminatory principles. This means that states may participate as long as such participation does not put the other participants (i.e. the oil and gas companies) under undue pressure. Consequently, states shall not take part in decision making, nor shall they have information regarding sources of procurement for entities, or exercise majority voting rights. Neither shall they prevent management decisions from being taken on the basis of normal commercial principles.[21] On the other hand, the state participant will be granted the opportunity to oppose certain decisions taken by the licensee such as those regarding depletion policy and the financial interest of the state.

Although the Netherlands government now broadly approves of the proposed Directive, one could argue that the present system of state participation still does not agree with the principles of the proposed Licensing Directive. In the Netherlands, state participation is restricted to participation in the production of oil and gas. The state is not taking part in the production activities directly, but through a company called Energie Beheer Nederland BV (EBN) of which the state holds all the shares but which is managed by the private company and former state participant

19. Since 1989 concessions are granted for a limited period of time, usually some 40 years. See Act of June 30 1988, Staatsblad 327.
20. Report A3-0355/92 European Parliament, Nov. 6 1992.
21. Energy in Europe, No. 22, Dec. 1993, p.32.

DSM.[22] According to the CS Mining Act (Article 11, para. 2) the Minister may require participation of the state when a production licence is granted. According to the government White Papers, the state would only participate in the case of a reasonable-sized discovery; in practice it has nearly always participated. Nevertheless, theoretically a private oil company (or a group of companies) does not know with any certainty before a production licence is granted whether the state will participate or not. In case the state decides to participate a limited (private) liability company has to be established in which the state and the licence holders take part with a maximum of 50 per cent each.[23] In order to avoid all profits being taxed in the Netherlands, the companies in general make use of an alternative regime. In addition to the legally required establishment of a limited (private) liability company, a cost company is established which works directly and for the risk of the shareholders. So, whereas the limited (private) liability company is still solely responsible for the management of the production operations in the Netherlands, the profits of these activities are not necessarily taxed in the Netherlands. Under this alternative regime the approval of the general meeting of shareholders with a majority of votes is required for a number of decisions such as the annual investment and financing plan, the conclusion of long-term loans and the activities and acquisitions not included in the annual investment and financing plan exceeding the amount of 250,000 guilders.[24] This means that the state participant, in theory, has the power to obstruct any of the above decisions. Although the state participant in practice is acting as a sleeping partner and therefore does not use it powers under the above regulation, one could go as far as to say that the present system of state participation is not completely in line with the principles of state participation as outlined in the Directive.

Finally, there are two other aspects of the current licensing system which, as in the UK, may need to be amended: 1) the requirement that the operator should have an office in the Netherlands[25] and 2) the requirement that all gas produced and consumed in the Netherlands should be landed in the Netherlands and sold to the NV Nederlandse Gasunie.[26] The latter requirement constitutes an important part of the present Netherlands gas policy. The offshore legislation, in accordance with the conditions used onshore after the award of the onshore Groningen concession, requires that all gas used in the Netherlands is to be supplied to the NV Nederlandse Gasunie.[27] Under the provisions of the Licensing Directive it could be argued that this provision is not justified exclusively by the need to ensure proper exploitation of the geographical area for which a licence is requested.[28] It can be noted that this provision dealing with the disposal of gas is also contrary to Article 34 of the

22. State participation in the petroleum industry has always been taken care of by the state-owned NV Nederlandse Staatsmijnen or NV DSM. After NV DSM was (partly) privatised in 1989, state participation was transferred to EBN. In the present system, economic and legal ownership has been separated.

23. Under the Royal Decree of 1967 the state can take a share of 40 per cent in the production of gas only. However, under the Royal Decree of 1976 this has been changed in a way that the state takes a share of 50 per cent in the production of oil and gas.

24. Art. 2 of Art. IV Royal Decree 1976.

25. Art. 18 of Art. II Royal Decrees 1967 and 1976.

26. Arts 24 and 25 of Art. III Royal Decrees 1967 and 1976.

27. Art. 25 of Art. III Royal Decrees 1967 and 1976.

28. Cf. Art. 6, para. 1 Licensing Directive.

EEC Treaty, i.e. quantitive restrictions to export. However, until now no attempts have been made to repeal this clause.[29] Such an encroachment on the present system of licensing would, however, affect the whole gas supply policy of the Netherlands. A change of this policy, as we have seen with regard to the transit and TPA debates, seems to be unacceptable for the Netherlands government.

4.0 CONCLUSION

Although Netherlands authorities have always claimed that the upstream licensing regime consists of transparent, competitive and non-discriminatory procedures, the above has shown that basically this was only the case for the regime offshore. However, as from 1993 when amendments were made to the regime governing onshore petroleum licensing, this system has more or less been brought in line with the principles used offshore. Nevertheless, as a result of the fact that the criteria are published beforehand, the number of legal provisions governing onshore exploration and exploitation has increased once more. In general a growth in regulation does not enhance the transparency of the legal system as a whole. Perhaps these recent developments will take us a step forward to a full revision of the onshore mining legislation which, since 1813, has a provisional status until further measures are taken.

From the above it can also be concluded that compliance with the criteria of Article 3(1) of the Utilities Directive, will not necessarily lead to compliance with the provisions of the Licensing Directive. Be that as it may, the impact of the latter Directive on the present system of petroleum legislation will presumably be limited. It could affect the provisions on state participation and the landing of gas. Changes in the latter provisions would also be of importance with regard to the establishment of an internal gas market. However, strong opposition of the Netherlands government can be expected to any such changes. Not only is the government a strong advocate of the present structure of the European gas market, but also the above landing provisions constitute one of the few legal instruments for the government to influence the Netherlands gas sector.

29. An attempt was made in 1975 when the company Placid directly entered into a sales agreement with some German buyers. The Netherlands government was strongly opposed to this agreement and used its powers under Art. 25 of Art. III Royal Decree 1967 according to which Placid was forced to land the gas produced in the Netherlands. Although a complaint was launched by Placid and the European Commission started to review the case, the parties reached a compromise.

Chapter 5

The EC Remedies Directive

Julian P. Armstrong[1]

1.0 INTRODUCTION

The purpose of this Chapter is to introduce the Remedies Directive which was issued by the Council of Ministers on February 25 1992. The Chapter will deal with:

- The legislative background to the Directive.
- An outline of the provisions of the Directive.
- A discussion of the new grounds for legal action introduced by the Directive.
- The procedure to be followed by, and the remedies available to, a plaintiff seeking to rely on the Directive before the courts of the United Kingdom.
- A few issues of tactics and timing which appear likely to be relevant following the introduction of implementing legislation in the United Kingdom.

2.0 LEGISLATIVE BACKGROUND TO THE DIRECTIVE

This section will place the Remedies Directive in its legislative context, and explain briefly why the Commission thought it necessary to legislate on this topic.

The first pertinent piece of legislation was the Public Works Directive 71/305 of July 26 1971 as subsequently amended and then repealed and replaced by Council Directive 93/37 of June 14 1993. This was followed in 1977 by the Public Supplies Directive 77/62 of December 21 1976 as subsequently amended and then repealed and replaced by Council Directive 93/36 of June 14 1993 which is to be implemented by June 14 1994. The purpose of these two Directives was to deal with the purchasing practices of government authorities, typically national, regional and local authorities, and including universities, schools, hospitals, scientific research

1. The views expressed in this chapter are personal to the author.

facilities and non-military suppliers for the armed forces. The intention of the Directives was to secure non-discriminatory purchasing practices on the part of such governmental authorities. The Directives were based on Articles 30–36 of the Rome Treaty which deal with government-inspired restrictions on interstate trade.

In the United Kingdom, the Government did not implement the Directives in legislation, but sent a circular to all those affected.

Perhaps compliance with the Public Works Directive was not as widespread as the Commission had hoped, because the 1977 Directive considerably tightened up the compliance aspect. However, even this attempt at encouraging compliance was itself eventually seen as inadequate, and in December 1989 Council Directive 89/665 setting out rules for ensuring compliance in the public sector was issued. This Directive led to the issue in the United Kingdom of the Public Works Contracts Regulations and the Public Supply Contracts Regulations of 1991 (respectively the 'Public Works Regulations' and 'Public Supply Regulations').

On September 17 1990, Council Directive 90/531 was issued. By this Directive the principles of non-discrimination governing public procurement, which had existed in the public sector since the Directives of 1970, were extended to those bodies which had 'monopolistic or special rights derived from the Government'. This includes the holders of exclusive oil and gas production licences. However, it also includes other industries such as gas, electricity and telecommunications – hence the general title of 'Utilities Directive'.

The Utilities Directive initially covered 'works' and 'supplies' (construction projects on the one hand and the procurement of goods on the other). On June 14 1993 the initial Utilities Directive was repealed and replaced by Council Directive 93/38, which Directive incorporated 'services' within its ambit, and which will catch, *inter alia*, insurance services.

The Utilities Directive setting out the obligations of the utilities in the area of procurement is complemented, in the same way as the Public Sector Directives were complemented by the Compliance Directive in 1989, by the Remedies Directive, which was issued as Council Directive 92/13/EEC on February 25 1992. Implementation of both the Utilities Directive and the Remedies Directive in UK law is by way of 'The Utilities Supply and Works Contracts Regulations 1992', which came into force on January 13 1993 ('1992 Utilities Regulations').

3.0 OUTLINE OF THE REMEDIES DIRECTIVE

3.1 Review Body

The Remedies Directive requires each member state to set up a procedure which will enable decisions on procurement by entities caught by the Utilities Directive to be reviewed effectively. The 'review body' must be able:

(i) to take interim measures to correct an alleged infringement or prevent injury to the interests concerned, including suspension of the procedure for an award of a contract; and/or

(ii) to order 'dissuasive payments' *ie* payments designed to encourage contracting entities to comply with the law or remove discriminatory specifications etc; and

(iii) to set aside decisions taken unlawfully *eg* remove discriminatory technical, economic or financial specifications from tender or contract documents; or

(iv) to award damages – but the member state will have the option (see para.6 of the Directive) to make damages the only remedy once the procurement contract has been concluded.

The latter option was taken up both in the Public Works and Public Supply Regulations, and in the 1992 Utilities Regulations.

3.2 Attestation

The Directive requires a procedure to be available to contracting entities under which their contracting procedures may be 'attested'. Attestation would lead to a certificate that the 'practices and procedures (of the contracting entity) are in conformity with Community law concerning the award of contracts and the national rules implementing that law'.

Attestors would have to be independent and objective, and have relevant qualifications and experience, but the details for the system are to be worked out by each member state. The 1992 Utilities Regulations do not include any specific arrangements for attestation.

3.3 Corrective Mechanism

In addition to the remedies made available to individuals, the Directive also requires that the Commission be able to intervene whenever it considers that a 'clear and manifest infringement of Community provisions in the field of procurement has been committed'. The Commission may only intervene prior to the conclusion of the procurement contract. The Commission will notify its view to the member state, which then has 30 days to reply, either that the infringement has been corrected or giving an explanation as to why it has not, or informing the Commission that judicial proceedings have been started, which may include interlocutory proceedings.

3.4 Conciliation

Finally there is provision in the Directive for Commission-sponsored conciliation. This procedure, which is entirely voluntary, is open to any person who 'has an interest' in obtaining a particular contract within the scope of the Directive. The conciliation procedure can be terminated by either party at any time.

If both parties are willing to engage in conciliation, the Commission will appoint a conciliator, and each of the parties will appoint their own conciliator: the issue is to be the correct application of Community law. The purpose of the conciliation will be to reach agreement between the parties which is in accordance with Community law. Conciliation may be initiated even during judicial proceedings, although the impact of taking such a step on the proceedings themselves is not dealt with, and would be a matter for agreement between the parties.

3.5 Future Review

The Commission is to review the working of the Remedies Directive no later than four years after the date of its application, *ie* January 1 1997.

4.0 GROUNDS FOR COMPLAINT

The purpose of the Directive is to give new causes of action and also to lay down procedures for enforcement. The principal ground of complaint will be that the defendant has 'infringed Community law in the field of procurement' as regards:

– contract award procedures within the scope of Directive 90/531/EEC (now Directive 93/38 EEC);
– compliance with Article 3(2)(a) of the Utilities Directive where relevant (this is the Article which deals with the 'opting out' regime for upstream contracts, under which the UK Government as well as France and the Netherlands, received exemptions with respect to their extractive oil and gas sector (see Chapter 4 and the commentary thereto for a further discussion of the UK and Netherlands exemptions, respectively)); or
– national rules implementing that law.

In the case of the opted-out regime, the ground of complaint will be failure to comply 'with the principles of open and non-discriminatory purchasing'.

The wording of this section of the Directive is reasonably self-explanatory; however there are two comments which can be made:

1. The legislation we are dealing with is a Directive, not a Regulation, and yet the Directive speaks of a right to complain about breach of 'any enforceable Community obligation'. There seems to be something odd in this, in that if a Community obligation which is relevant is enforceable, the plaintiff will have the right to enforce it without reference to the Remedies Directive: if it is not enforceable then it is in any event not relevant.
2. The potential impact of the UK Government Article 3 exemption, currently due to expire on July 15 1994 – with permanent extension dependent on the Commission's review of the provisions to be enacted by the Government to fully align itself with the requirements of Article 3, to opt out of the Utilities Directive for the oil and gas business is interesting: instead of complying with detailed procedures, the offshore operators will need to comply with principles which will be set out either in the licences themselves or 'in other appropriate measures'. These principles would be designed to ensure that the operators 'observe the principles of non-discrimination and competitive procurement . . . in particular as regards the information which the entity makes available to undertakings covering its procurement intentions'. The legislative/regulatory changes required by the Commission as a condition for agreeing to the UK permanently opting out are set out in the Annex to Commission Decision 93/425/EEC, July 14 1993, and were to be notified as adopted to the Commission no later than April 15 1994.

5.0   PROCEDURE AND REMEDIES

5.1 Reviewing Authority

The Directive leaves open the nature of the 'reviewing authority'. The only requirement is that there should be a possibility of judicial review of the reviewing authority's decisions, and the possibility of referral of cases of doubt to the European Court of Justice. In the 1992 Utilities Regulations the UK opted for the High Court as its 'reviewing authority', as it did when implementing the Compliance Directive.

5.2   Cause of Action

The cause of action in UK terms will be breach of a statutory duty 'owed by the purchasing entity to the plaintiff'. This would put the proceedings on a similar footing to a number of other actions based on EEC law, *eg* private actions under Article 85 or actions against the state on the basis of the decision of the European Court of Justice in joined cases *Francovich v Republic of Italy*, Cases C6/90 and C9/90, [1993] 2 CMLR 66.

5.3 Pre-conditions for Action

First, proceedings must be brought promptly and in any event within three months of the date when the grounds for complaint arose, unless the court extends that period. Second, the plaintiff will have to give prior notice to the defendant (Regulation 30(4)(a) of the 1992 Utilities Regulations). Third, the plaintiff will have to show that he 'has an interest in obtaining a particular contract'. A well-established main contractor would presumably have no difficulty with this if he could satisfy a court that he had the necessary technical/financial/management expertise to be considered for a particular contract. However, it might be more problematic for a subcontractor who expected to be included in a project execution proposal to demonstrate that he had such an interest.

The plaintiff must show that he risks being harmed or has been harmed by the alleged infringement. If he is seeking interlocutory relief the challenge will be to establish a nexus between the harm done to him and the infringement, and then show, as explained below, that the damage is so overwhelming that an injunction rather than damages is the only appropriate remedy.

Finally, if the plaintiff is prepared to limit the damages which he seeks to the costs to him of preparing a tender, then the only requirement will be for him to show that the infringement adversely affected his chance of being awarded the contract. This is of a somewhat different standard to that applying for the other more significant remedies of injunction, etc.

5.4   Remedies

The remedies available to a plaintiff with evidence to support his complaint are as follows:

1. The Court could order the contracting entity to stop its contract award procedure, either temporarily, pending a further decision on the lawfulness of what had been done, or permanently, forcing the contracting entity to go back and start again, presumably on the grounds that there was some irreversible flaw in what had been done already.
2. The Court could order the contracting entity to do something which would enable it to comply with its obligations either under the Directive or under the implementing law. Such an order could be temporary pending trial, or permanent at trial.
3. The Court could award damages to the plaintiff. Attractive as this may sound, there are significant issues on the measure of the damages which a plaintiff could hope to recover. If breach of the Regulations is regarded as a tort (breach of statutory duty) then presumably the rules for assessing damages in tort would apply. This would mean that the plaintiff would not be able to recover loss of anticipated profit on the contract which he did not win, but would be limited to the expenditure (if any) thrown away on a bid which was not properly handled by the contracting entity. It is noteworthy that subsection 8 of Section 19 of the Local Government Act 1988 provides quite specifically that where a tenderer sues a local authority for failure to comply with a compulsory tendering procedure contained in that Act 'the damages shall be limited to damages in respect of expenditure reasonably incurred by him for the purpose of submitting the tender'. There is no equivalent provision in the 1992 Utilities Regulations, but it may be that the effect will, in the end, be the same.

5.5 Dissuasive Payments

The UK Government has decided *not* to adopt the remedy of 'dissuasive payments' which are described in Article 2(1)(c) of the Directive. The purpose of dissuasive payments, as understood from the Treasury, was to provide the equivalence of an injunction; the dissuasive payments option was introduced into the Directive because Germany, in the course of negotiations on the Directive, said that injunctions could not be ordered against the bodies to be subject to the new Directive: it was then agreed that in order to ensure that an equally effective remedy was available, there should be the option for the courts to order punitive sanctions in the form of payments of money against any utility which acted in contravention of a court order. In the United Kingdom the Treasury canvassed views on dissuasive payments, while making it clear that it did not support this option. The United Kingdom Offshore Operators' Association also came out against dissuasive payments. They have not appeared in the final Regulations.

5.6 Forum

The issue also arises of what might be the 'forum' in which an action against a UK offshore operator should be mounted. The scenario might be that a disappointed contractor from another EEC state wanted to sue a UK operator in the (possibly more friendly) courts of his own state. Under normal circumstances, this would probably not run for the following reasons. The action would be between private parties: on the basis that it was an action in tort for breach of statutory duty, it would be a 'civil and commercial matter' which, in turn, would mean that the forum had to be determined under the Brussels Convention of 1968 on Jurisdiction and the Enforcement of Judgments in Civil and Commercial Matters under the Civil Jurisdiction and Judgments Act 1982. The basic principle of the Convention is that the correct forum for an action against a corporation is the place of incorporation (domicile) of the corporation. None of the exceptions to that basic principle appears likely to apply to the case of a contractor suing an operator working on the United Kingdom Continental Shelf (UKCS). It is therefore a reasonable conclusion that an action against a UKCS operator incorporated or otherwise domiciled in the United Kingdom would have to be brought before the English (or conceivably the Scottish) courts.

6.0 TIMING AND TACTICS

Finally this Chapter deals with three issues which could arise in the course of litigation relying on the 1992 Utilities Regulations, implementing the Remedies Directive: the first two are issues of timing, and the third one of tactics.

6.1 Timing

The first timing issue arises because the action will have to put in issue the 'award procedures' of the contracting entity, normally in relation to a particular contract. There is obviously some ambiguity about when the 'award procedure' actually starts, although it is arguable that it starts when the contracting entity invites contractors to express an interest in a project: it could, however, also operate at the earlier stage of establishing a list of qualified contractors.

The second timing issue is that, once the contract has been 'concluded' with another contractor, the remedies of the contractor are limited to damages. There are two points here, first, when is a contract actually 'concluded', given that the normal pattern is expression of intent, followed by commercial agreement, followed by execution of a lengthy contract document? The second point is that the impact of this constraint on the contracting procedures is likely to be that they become noticeably less leisurely!

6.2 Tactics

There may well be tactical issues, given that decisions in cases brought under the implementing regulations are likely to adopt the principles followed generally by the UK courts when considering the grant of interlocutory injunctions. It is probably no exaggeration to say that from a practical standpoint this is the heart of the whole topic because it is here that the battle for commercial leverage will occur: if the plaintiff can stop a project in its tracks he will have the leverage given to him by the massive time pressure on the operator to help him in his negotiations; if he is unable to stop the project, then he may very well (see above) be left with nothing more than a claim for the expenses of tendering for the contract. It is not necessary to examine in detail here the application to this situation of the principles laid down by Lord Diplock in the House of Lords in *American Cyanamid v Ethicon* 1975 1 All E.R. 504, but one or two comments may be helpful:

1. The rules on injunctions laid down in *Cyanamid* are primarily designed to preserve the *status quo* pending trial of the central issue. Quite apart from the specific points considered below, if the court thinks that the grant of an injunction will have the effect of deciding the case, this may be enough to persuade it not to grant the injunction.

2. The principles on which the court makes a decision to grant or not to grant an injunction, and their possible relevance to the scenario considered here, are as follows:

    (a) Is there a serious issue to be tried? It seems likely that the court would examine the relevance of the nexus between the alleged infringement of procedure (and this Directive is primarily about procurement *procedures*) and the harm alleged to be suffered by the contractor.

    (b) Are damages an adequate remedy to the plaintiff? – Is it sufficient to allow the defendant to continue with his contract procedure and leave the plaintiff to his remedy in damages: given that the only remedy available to the plaintiff (if I am right on the measure of damages – see above) is likely to be the expenses thrown away on tendering. This may work either to the advantage of the plaintiff (he can argue that damages would be so trivial that he ought to be granted an injunction – and the opportunity to obtain the profit on the contract) or to the advantage of the defendant (the measure of damages being an indication of the value set by the rules of tort on the plaintiff's claim, to be set against the immense disruption to the defendant's project if the injunction is granted).

    (c) There must be a credible undertaking by the plaintiff to pay damages to the defendant if he loses; there would also be an issue of whether the defendant himself would be adequately compensated in damages if the injunction turns out at trial to have been unjustified.

    (d) The court will then look at the balance of convenience, the position of each party, and whether what the defendant is proposing is a new activity or the continuation of an existing one. It is noteworthy here that para.4 of the Directive does in terms require the Court to engage in a balancing exercise before granting interlocutory remedies, although it is also noticeable that the UK Government has chosen to regard para.4 as being equivalent in all respects to the common law principles on which the UK courts operate.

Chapter 6

Third Party Access to Gas and Electricity Transmission Systems in The Community

Third Party Access – Your Flexible Friend?

J.R. Salter[*]

1.0 INTRODUCTION

'To take the opening up of the market first, the key is the abolition of national frontiers and the free circulation referred to in the EEC Treaty. In other words, this implies the removal of obstacles to trade and the creation of healthy competition both between products and undertakings. The Commission has chosen to give priority in this area of increased trade to the cases of gas and electricity, which, being carried by networks, have up till now enjoyed a considerable amount of national protection.'[1]

The European Commission's proposals for the creation of an internal market for electricity and gas involve a gradual liberalisation of the internal energy market, consisting of three phases. In the first phase, three directives were introduced; one was a directive on price transparency in electricity and gas, taking effect from July 1 1991; the other two were transit directives, which took effect respectively for electricity from July 1 1991, and for gas from June 1 1992. The second phase consists of a number of measures. These are the abolition of exclusive rights; a non-discriminatory licensing system for the construction of pipelines; the introduction of limited third party access for the very largest size of electricity and gas consumer and 'unbundling' of transmission and services within vertically integrated under-takings. These provisions are embodied in two draft proposals concerning common

[*]The author is indebted to and has relied substantially upon research material provided by Nisha Arora of his firm in the preparation of this chapter, and is grateful to his partner, Michael Brothwood, for his comments.

1. *The Internal Energy Market*, Antonio Cardoso e Cunha, *Journal of Energy and Natural Resources Law*, Vol.9, No.4, p.291.

rules for the internal market in gas and electricity respectively, submitted by the EC Commission to the Council of Ministers in February 1992.[2] The proposals will be discussed in detail below. Finally, the third phase, which is intended to come into force in 1996, involves extending the eligibility of third party access.[3]

Whilst there has been unanimous support from the member states and the gas and electricity industry for increased competition and liberalisation of the internal energy market, support has not been unqualified. Many of the member states, their major gas and electricity companies and major oil and gas producers are strongly opposed to the introduction of Third Party Access (TPA) as a part of the liberalisation process, and it is this issue which is holding up progress on the discussion of the latest Commission proposals in the Council of Ministers. Indeed, the discussions have, at times, become so unproductive, that an official from one large member state described them as 'a dialogue of the deaf'.

The question which this Chapter must address is why the issue of third party access has proved to be such a sticking point in the Community's proposals for liberalisation of the internal energy market. It will also consider the various reactions to TPA by the member states and electricity and gas companies in the Community. Before such issues are tackled, it is necessary to understand what really lies behind the concept of TPA and how it would affect the Community's gas and electricity markets and industries. Brief mention will also be made of the introduction of TPA in the UK.

2.0 THIRD PARTY ACCESS IN THE GAS AND ELECTRICITY INDUSTRIES

Third party access would allow producers, eligible consumers, local distribution companies and other suppliers to have the right to be offered access to the gas or electricity network by transmission and distribution companies. It is important to distinguish the concept of TPA from that of transit of natural gas or electricity across Community networks; further, TPA should be distinguished from the concept of 'common carrier', the former denoting a service provided on a 'first come-first served' basis, in contrast to the latter, wherein a service is provided on a 'pro rata' basis.

Whilst differences in the gas and electricity industries and markets mean that the TPA regime will be implemented differently in respect of gas and electricity, the philosophy and objectives behind liberalisation of gas and electricity and the use of TPA as an instrument in this liberalisation, remains the same for both sectors. Both industries are dominated by monopolies in the form either of state-owned entities or by private sector entities endowed with public utility status. Because of this it is often difficult to attribute a cause to the distortion of competition, in that it could be as a result of state action, company policy or a culmination of the two.

---

2. COM(91) 548, OJ C65/04 and C65/05, Mar. 14 1992. These proposals were amended by the Commission on Dec. 8 1993, taking into account some of the proposals contained in the Opinions of the European Parliament on the two draft Directives.

3. Oxford Energy Forum, Aug. 1992, p.13.

It was evident that the former Energy Commissioner Mr. Cardoso, was determined to remove the obstacles between member states' markets for electricity and gas, in order to proceed along the road to a liberalised and single energy market. It was also evident that Mr. Cardoso saw TPA as playing an integral part in the attack on anti-competitive practices and trade barriers in the Community's energy market.

Reaction of the member states to TPA in the Community has been divided. The Continental countries, eager to guard the interests of their well-ordered and (often) state-owned power monopolies, have objections to the proposals. On the other hand, the UK, with its privatised industries, supports them; in between, are Mr. Cardoso's Portugal, where the industry is partly privatised, and smaller countries such as Denmark which have given qualified support.[4] During the Belgian presidency at a working lunch of the EC Energy Ministers on December 10 1993, the Commission's amended proposals (submitted on December 8) were discussed among ministers then present. The Council President 'showed some reluctance . . . asking for more time to examine the texts before expressing a view on their merit.'[5]

3.0 THIRD PARTY ACCESS IN THE UNITED KINGDOM

Third party access is no stranger to the UK; both the Gas Act 1986 and the Electricity Act 1989, which established regulations for the newly privatised industries, provided for the concept of TPA.

Section 19 of the Gas Act 1986 allows for the acquisition of rights by third parties to use pipelines belonging to public gas suppliers. With the active support of OFGAS, quite significant quantities of natural gas have been carried under transportation agreements negotiated against the background of Section 19 of that Act. However, supervisory bodies have been concerned by British Gas' considerable advantages over its competitors in the gas market which derive from its size and its complete control over its 'very comprehensive infrastructure'. In March 1992, British Gas and the Office of Fair Trading (OFT) reached agreement on the form of undertakings to be given by British Gas, pursuant to negotiations over an OFT Report of the industrial and commercial market for gas of October 1991. Important for the effective implementation of third party access in the UK was the undertaking which provided that British Gas would split its transmission and storage division from its marketing activity by forming a separate pipeline division within the company from October 1992, which would publish separate accounts for 1993 and be in full operation by January 1 1994. The pipeline division to thus deal at arm's length with the gas trading arm of British Gas and refrain from discriminating between British Gas and other shippers. Regulation was to be by OFGAS under new powers provided under the Competition and Service Utilities Act 1992. Section 38 of that Act extends the powers and duties of the Secretary of State and of the Director General of Gas Supply beyond the powers and duties originally prescribed under the Gas Act.[6] With the making of the references regarding British Gas to the

---

4. 'Single Market Stalemate', *Financial Times*, May 14 1992.
5. As reported in 'Europe', Dec. 13–14 1993, No.6128 (n.s.).
6. 'Increasing Competition for British Gas?', Charlotte Villiers, *Utilities Law Review*, Spring 1992, p.7.

Monopolies and Mergers Commission (MMC) on July 31 1992, both the Directors General of Gas Supply and Fair Trading announced they no longer regarded the undertakings on transportation and storage as in force. British Gas however still regard separation as decided policy and following the Government's decision of December 21 1993 on the MMC's reports, full internal separation is required along the lines recommended by the MMC.

In the case of the UK electricity industry, Section 7(2) of the Electricity Act 1989 allows for conditions to be included in the licences granted under Section 3 of the Act for the generation, transmission or supply of electricity. One of the conditions which may be included makes provision for TPA to be granted by the licence holder. Both the transmission licence granted to National Grid Company (NGC) and the public electricity supplier licences, granted to the regional electricity companies, contain requirements for third party access under their 'use of system' provisions, which, in turn, provide for 'use of system' agreements. National Grid's requirement to offer TPA is in respect of use of its transmission system, whereas the regional electricity companies are required to offer terms for connection to their distribution system.

4.0 THIRD PARTY ACCESS AND THE EUROPEAN COMMUNITY

The Commission's working document on the internal energy market of May 1988[7] provided the basis for future action. It established what would be the obstacles to the establishment of an internal energy market, and pointed to the diverse nature of that market. The main concerns were with the electricity and gas sectors, whose transmission and distribution systems rely on a particular network infrastructure. These industries had developed on a national basis rather than on an international one, thereby impeding intra-Community trade.

The Community realised that the economic importance of the electricity and natural gas industries in the EC necessitated the improvement of production and supply efficiency. It urged that a more efficient, integrated and competitive energy market would have a positive effect on the structure of the Community's electricity and gas industry, allowing for new entrants, more diversity of fields and technologies and an increase in the trade of energy products between member states and thereby a higher level of security of supply. Further, removing the barriers to intra-Community trade would allow electricity and gas users, whether small or large, to enjoy the benefits of a more competitive market including more freedom of choice and reduced price disparities between member states. The Community laid out three main objectives for the internal market for gas and electricity, namely:

(a) Free movement of products, ensuring that electricity and natural gas can be moved both within and between member states in response to demand.
(b) Improved security of supply, by way of the opening-up of gas and electricity markets leading to a more flexible and broadly based supply, which, in turn, would lead to a higher level of security of supply.

7. COM(88) 238.

(c) Improving competitiveness, by way of using resources in the most efficient manner so that all consumers, large or small, would be able to reap the benefits of greater efficiency, which is particularly important for energy intensive industries competing in the world market.

Further, the completion of the internal energy market would also yield benefits in other policy areas such as environmental protection.[8]

As outlined in the introduction to this Chapter, the EC's agenda for an internal energy market consists of three phases. The first stage was completed by the approval by the Council of the transit directives for electricity and natural gas respectively. The transit directive for electricity[9] provides that each high voltage transmission utility shall facilitate power exchanges between other utilities through its grid, provided that transmission or reliability is not affected. The directive is designed to promote and maximise power exchanges between grids at European level. In the natural gas sector the gas transit directive[10] is also designed to maximise and facilitate gas exchanges across non-neighbouring gas transmission utilities. Further, the June 1990 Council Directive on price transparency[11] provides that electricity and gas utilities shall supply to the Statistical Office the rates they charge to all major industrial consumers on the understanding that published aggregate figures will respect confidentiality.

The second phase of the internal energy programme is manifested in the two proposals for directives for the internal market in natural gas and electricity, which were submitted by the EC Commission to the Council of Ministers on February 24 1992, containing provisions, *inter alia*, establishing limited third party access rights to electricity and gas networks in the Community.[12] Whilst the introduction of third party access in the Community is so near, it is also very far, and the proposals have kindled heated debates on its pros and cons.

4.1 The Provisions of the 1992 Proposals

The proposals find their legal base in Articles 57(2), 66 and 100A of the EC Treaty. This provides for a political dialogue with the Council and European Parliament under the co-operation procedure, and also enables consultations with other interested parties to be pursued. Further, it allows for approval of the proposals by way of qualified majority. Whilst the proposals vary in certain respects due to the differing natures of the gas and electricity industries and markets, they do contain certain common provisions, to which discussion will be addressed.

4.2 Objectives

The proposals contain numerous 'recitals', outlining the Commission's objectives and principles of gradual liberalisation tempered by the concept of subsidiarity, the creation of a transparent and non-discriminatory system for granting licences, the concept of unbundling, and the introduction of third party access on a limited basis.

---

8. See further the author's section on 'Environment and Consumers' in *Law of the European Communities Service*, (London: Butterworths, updated 1994).
9. OJ L313/30, Nov. 13 1990.
10. OJ L147/37, June 12 1991.
11. OJ L185/16, July 17 1990.
12. See note 2 supra, and accompanying text.

4.3 Provisions

Article 3 urges member states to ensure that their companies are operated on 'commercial principles'. The implementation of a clause as equivocal as this is bound to vary greatly amongst the member states as a result of their widely differing interpretations of 'commercial principles'. Further, to ensure the implementation of a market-based industry, member states are precluded from influencing or regulating prices or tariffs to customers of gas or electricity that is transported and supplied by way of TPA. However, in the case of those customers who are not eligible for access to the transmission and distribution system, member states are allowed to retain the power to regulate all aspects of gas or electricity tariffs.[13]

This dichotomous approach reflects the Commission's desire to liberalise the internal energy market, without treading on the toes of the member states. Indeed, the presence of the subsidiarity principle, allowing for the detailed implementation of principles to be left to the individual member states, was not present in the earlier draft of the proposals and has been incorporated into these proposals as a result of political expediency.

Article 4 provides a requirement for member states to allow third parties to construct or operate electricity or gas facilities in their territories. Member states are required to lay down criteria to be met by the undertaking applying for a licence to build or operate those facilities; these criteria must be objective and non-discriminatory. Member states may refuse or defer the grant of a licence if the transmission or distribution requirements concerned can be satisfied by the existing transmission and distribution capacities available in the interconnected system at a reasonable and equitable price. Both proposals allow member states to ensure that producers and suppliers established in their territory are able to supply their own premises, subsidiaries and affiliate companies and customers through a direct line. A direct line involves a line linking one or more customers with a point of supply without using the interconnected grid system; because the same producers have the right to supply their own affiliates in *any* member state, using other lines, the provision could lead to interstate battles.[14]

Articles 6(2) and 7(2) of the gas and electricity proposals respectively provide for the implementation of TPA in the Community. However, unlike the previous drafts, the 1992 draft proposals introduce a threshold of eligible customers who may participate in the access to the relevant networks. The number of industrial market players will be severely limited by this rule; however, if the member state does not wish to operate a lower threshold it is not obliged to do so: Britain for example, has a substantially lower threshold.

Chapter 3 of the proposals deals with transmission system operation. The practicality of operation will differ according to the technical features of each of the sectors. Whereas, in the electricity sector, storage is impossible and therefore, a precise matching of supply and demand is necessary, in the natural gas sector storage is possible and the pipelines can vary pressure so that there is scope for variation of supply and demand in the operation of the grids. This means that central control of the grid is not needed for technical reasons and that any grid operator can be responsible for the safe and reliable operation of its own pipelines provided that

13. *Gas Matters*, Jan. 30 1992, p.19.
14. *Gas Matters*, Jan. 30 1992, p.21.

the appropriate arrangements between the grid operators are made. However, whilst it is not necessary to create a transmission system operator, for the distribution of natural gas a system operator is foreseen because, at distribution level, no parallel grid is possible in practice and the distribution company is therefore responsible for the distribution area. In the electricity sector, where supply and demand must be matched, the existence of a network operator, who ensures that the technical quality of the required service is maintained and that supplies are reliable, is essential. The proposals require the provision of sufficient data to customers and the publication of technical rules concerning design and operational requirements.

Chapter 4 of the proposals outlines the operational requirements of distribution companies and requires the distribution system operator to maintain a secure, reliable and efficient distribution system and to provide sufficient information to facilitate use of the system by third parties.

Chapter 5 of the proposals contains important provisions concerning 'unbundling'. This requires the separation of the management and accounting of production, transmission and distribution operations in vertically integrated undertakings. This is essential in order to ensure transparency of operations and is therefore important for the efficacy of implementation of competition principles and policies. These requirements are substantially the same as those contained in the transportation undertaking given by British Gas in March 1992, and as required by the Government's decision on the latest MMC references mentioned above.

Chapter 6, containing final provisions, outlines procedures for dealing with sudden crises in the energy market. Finally, the Chapter allows member states to establish their own dispute resolution procedure on which parties can settle disputes or matters covered by the directives. Again, this dispute resolution procedure clause leaves the member states with a wide degree of discretion, appealing to their demands for the maintenance of subsidiarity in both principle and practice. However, whether it is either feasible or expedient to leave dispute resolution and enforcement totally in the hands of the individual member states is questionable.

The 1992 proposals have experienced substantial dilution since the earlier drafts, allowing greater discretion to member states by emphasising the subsidiarity principle, and introducing thresholds which limit the implementation of TPA. Whilst the draft directives, in their 1992 form, would provide an important step on the path to an internal energy market, it is evident that the political opposition of many of the member states has led to very much weaker proposals than first envisaged. Despite this compromise, the 1992 proposals faced substantial opposition, which, during 1992–1993 showed no signs of abating. The question we must now turn to is why TPA has become such a sticking point.

5.0 THIRD PARTY ACCESS – PROS AND CONS

The advantages and disadvantages of TPA have been debated in the European Community extensively in recent years. The idea of introducing a third party access system into the Community was first suggested in the draft proposals on the transit of gas and electricity in 1989.[15] Indeed, the proposal concerning the transit of natural

15. Proposal for a Council Directive on the Transit of Natural Gas Through the Major Systems, COM(89) 334, Sep. 6 1989, and proposal for a Council Directive on the Transit of Electricity Through Transmission Grids, COM(89) 336, Sep. 29 1989.

gas outlined the advantages and disadvantages of TPA and revealed the intention of establishing committees on the subject.

It is in these Consultative Committee reports that the pros and cons of TPA are debated. The reports were produced by the Commission in May 1991, after the Committees had met at monthly intervals for a year and a half. Reports were produced, from two professional and two member state committees on electricity and natural gas respectively. Further, position statements of certain participants were annexed to them. Whilst it is clear that the Commission has taken into consideration the reservations of some of the member states and professional bodies on the committees, it is also evident that, despite the fact that both member states' committees for electricity and natural gas concluded that the general consensus was against the introduction of a system of TPA, the Commission was determined to go ahead with it, hoping that a watered down version would appease the opposition.

For every positive aspect put forward for the TPA case, there are counter arguments against the introduction of the system. The main points of debate centre on three issues, namely, the effects on prices, the effects on competition and efficiency, and the effects on security of supply.

5.1 The Effect of Third Party Access on Prices

Proponents of TPA argue that its introduction would allow the possibility of lower purchase prices by the presence of fiercer competition. They argue that this would come from more efficient utilisation of the gas grid or electricity network, and that both small and large consumers will have a greater choice of supply and the ability to negotiate terms according to their needs. These benefits may well be achieved if the current buyers' market conditions persist.

Whilst the Commission has anticipated that the 'buyers' market situation would remain for the next 10–15 years, sceptics of the system say otherwise. They believe that TPA is unlikely to lead to lower prices and that if, as they expect, increase in demand changes the growing market into a sellers market, this could lead to higher prices. Third Party Access would lead to a situation of fragmentation of demand and the 'bidding-up' of prices by buyers clamouring for additional volumes. In the case of the electricity sector, costs and prices may well increase due to difficulties with management of multiple contracts, the reduction of the possibilities for optimisation exchanges between the electricity companies and the increase in distances which the energy supplied would have to travel.

5.2 Increased Competition and Efficiency and the Erosion of Monopoly Profits

Proponents of TPA argue that the current state of affairs involving the presence of monopolies and the absence of competition encourages inefficiency and proves detrimental to the consumer. Moreover, the competitive climate resulting from TPA would favour the entry of new investors and independent producers and would accelerate investments. Further, TPA would lead to a closer relationship of prices with costs, which would reduce the risk of discriminatory cross-subsidies between consumer types, thereby leading to a more rational price structure which would be more favourable to general economic development. Cross-subsidisation would also be reduced through unbundling, which in their view, TPA would require.

In contrast, opponents of TPA argue that the Community's energy market is naturally both oligopolistic and oligopsonistic. They claim that the present industries are sufficiently efficient and that TPA would not have a particularly beneficial effect as it would not produce a truly competitive market. Moreover, the intended regulation of the industries could have the effect of fragmenting demand during a period of tight supply, thereby shifting market power towards non-Community suppliers. This would promote regionalisation and would be contrary to the objectives of the internal market policy. Moreover, there would be the risk that TPA would introduce an element of uncertainty in an increased competitive environment, thereby dissuading investors. Further, the risk of cross-subsidisation would be increased because integrated companies or distributors might try to hold on to their larger consumers by cutting prices to them and charging franchise customers more, a situation which would be difficult, if not impossible, to control.

5.3 Security of Supply

Those in favour of TPA argue that it would enable new suppliers to enter the market, offering both reliability and security of supply. In the case of current contractual commitments, transitional arrangements could be introduced in order to avoid parties breaching their obligations. A TPA regime would provide consumers with the opportunity to negotiate the reliability of supply they need, thereby ensuring that resources are allocated sufficiently to those consumers who need a high level of supply security and are prepared to pay for it. Such a regime would also provide clear market signals for new investment and encourage the use of lower cost alternatives.

Those opposed to TPA are concerned that it would jeopardise security of supply. The present situation, with its monopolies and its ability to aggregate consumer demand and provide 'take or pay' guarantees in long-term contracts means that supply can be secure and reliable, reducing investment risks. Transitional arrangements would not be sufficient to overcome the problem of the disappearance of long-term 'take or pay' obligations in contracts. Such a situation would discourage new suppliers developing projects to supply the European market, thereby creating an even tighter market, increasing demand and raising prices.

6.0   RECENT DEVELOPMENTS

6.1 Energy Council Policy Debate – November 30 1992

On November 30 1992 the Energy Council held a policy debate on the proposals for Directives concerning common rules for the internal market in electricity and natural gas. The Council confirmed the importance it attaches to the completion of the internal energy market. It stated that energy is a vital component in the economy of the Community and the energy sector in all of its aspects must become part of the Single Market. The Council thought it essential to work towards more open, transparent, efficient and competitive electricity and gas markets, while bearing in mind the specificities of electricity and natural gas and the different situations in member states. The Council also noted that reservations had been expressed about important elements of the Commission's proposals, notably about those concerning TPA. The Council invited the Commission to consider modifications to its proposals in the light of the Council's discussions and of the Opinion of the European Parliament, with the aim of achieving more competition in the internal energy markets. The Commission was asked to present a revised text to the next Energy Council meeting due to take place some time during the Danish presidency, but in the event did not do so until December 8 1993.

6.2 Competition

On December 1 1992, the internal energy market and the rules of competition were discussed between the European Parliament Committee on Energy, Research and Technology and Sir Leon Brittan, Commisioner for External Relations. Sir Leon stressed that the integration of the energy sector into the internal market could be a gradual process bearing in mind the need for security of supply and the principle of energy being a public service. He called for the removal of barriers hindering trade and for transparency to allow prices to be set through free competition. More particularly he expressed support for the introduction of TPA, not agreeing with the arguments against TPA, namely that the level of investments will fall causing prices to rise and discontinuance of supply. He stated that the contrary would happen so that in a competitive environment producers would be forced to keep costs as low as possible. On the other hand, the European Parliament Energy Committee warned against having competition just for the sake of competition, stressing that the energy sector, more particularly the gas industry, was a special case. Furthermore, in the draft opinion on the energy market prepared by Mr. Desama, he stated that there is little possibility of developing a common energy policy before 1996.

6.3 Debate During 1992–93

The issue of TPA was not exactly earmarked as a priority under the Danish and some of the following presidencies. As far as the liberalisation of electricity and gas markets is concerned, the deadlock following the Energy Council's decision on December 30 1992 has not prevented presidencies pressing ahead in those areas where there is common ground among the member states, namely opening up competition in electricity production and establishing new electricity and gas networks.[16] During 1993 the European Parliament voted in favour of the report of the EP's Committee on Energy, Research and Technology (CERT) chaired by Claude Desama and the EP opinion was given on November 17 1993. The Report

16. See Leigh Hancher and Peter-Armin Trepte 'Competition and the Internal Energy Market', [1992] 4 ECLR 149.

recommended several hundred amendments to the Commission's 1991 proposals which are aimed at making them more acceptable to member states. The Report emphasised the need for harmonisation in the gas and electricity sectors before liberalisation. This would necessitate the creation of common rules for production, transport and distribution in the electricity sector; and storage, transport and distribution in the gas sector. The Report also suggested that harmonisation should be introduced gradually with a transition period. The Report left open the question of TPA to power networks after the end of the transition period which was proposed to be December 1998. One suggestion made is that access to the grid should be open to independent and 'self' producers, as well as producers from outside the area covered by the grid, as a means of avoiding abuses of dominant positions. The question of exemptions from TPA for end-user customers was raised in the European Parliament. In answer to a question about the extent to which the Commission would draw upon the example of USA law and exempt end-users from TPA, Mr. Abel Matutes, the EC Energy Commissioner, replied that US legislation goes beyond the Community Directive on Transit, which covers only exchanges between transmission companies. In the United States the opening up of the market concerns both the producers and the distributors connected to the transmission grids. It was nevertheless accepted that the Energy Policy Act of 1992 in the USA had been studied in depth and is being considered in internal discussions at Commission level. Towards the end of 1993 Mr. Matutes indicated that the Commission was moving closer to an acceptance of negotiated, as opposed to mandatory, introduction of TPA to gas and electricity networks.[17] In the event, on December 8 1993 the Commission adopted an amended proposal for a Council Directive concerning common rules for the internal market in electricity and an amended proposal for a Council Directive concerning common rules for the internal market in natural gas.[18]

7.0 THE 1993 PROPOSALS

The Commission did not incorporate amendments suggested by the European Parliament[19] relating to the imposition of an obligation upon the member states to set up gas and electricity authorities, on the establishment of a link between the initial stage of harmonisation and the final stage of liberalisation and relating to the monopoly of distribution companies. So far as TPA is concerned, for the original provisions on regulated access, there have been substituted provisions relating to negotiated access supported by arbitration provisions to take effect in the event of difficulties arising in either negotiations of access or the implementation of negotiated arrangements. Rules relating to the operation of transmission and distribution grids have been simplified and a specific chapter is now devoted to the question of access to grids. In presenting the proposals the Commission emphasised that account was also being taken of six principles recommended by the Council

17. See Denton-Hall's Brussels Newsletters for Oct. and Dec. 1993.
18. Not yet published in the OJ.
19. EP Opinion was given on Nov. 17 1993.

regarding the objective to secure continuity of supplies, the desire to achieve environmental protection, the desire to protect small consumers, the desire to achieve transparency and a non-discriminatory approach, the recognition of differences that exist between existing national systems and the giving of effect to transitional provisions. The transitional provision now proposed is set to begin on July 1 1994 ending on December 1 1998 at the earliest. Thus the revised proposals of December 8 1993 differ substantially from the original proposals of February 24 1992 and from the EP opinion of November 17 1993. They are divided into seven chapters which do not directly relate to the original proposals or to the EP's opinion.

7.1 Co-Decision

The proposals find their legal base, like the 1992 proposals, in Articles 57(2), 66 and 100A of the EC Treaty. The Parliament's review of the common position of the Council is, however, being undertaken under the new procedure introduced by the Treaty of European Union known as the Co-Decision Procedure which is contained in Article 189b of the EC Treaty. This new procedure substantially increases the role of Parliament in the legislative process as it provides for a conciliation procedure in cases where the Parliament proposes amendments to the Council's common position at the Second Reading Stage. If the Parliament proposes amendments to the text by an absolute majority of its component members, then the amended text is to be forwarded to the Council and to the Commission who are required to deliver an opinion on those amendments.[20] If the Council does not approve the amended text, the President of the Council, in agreement with the EP President, is obliged forthwith to convene a meeting of a body known as the Conciliation Committee.[21] The Conciliation Committee is composed of the members of the Council or their representatives and an equal number of EP representatives. The task of the Committee is to reach agreement on a joint text by a qualified majority of the members of the Council or their representatives and by a majority of EP representatives. The Commission is required to take part in the Conciliation Committee's proceedings and to take all necessary initiatives with a view to reconciling the position of the Parliament and the Council. The Commission may alter its proposals so long as the Council has not adopted the proposal. If a joint text is approved by the Conciliation Committee then the text is passed to the Parliament and to the Council who must adopt it within six weeks or the proposal fails. If a joint text is not approved, then the proposal is deemed not to have been adopted unless the Council confirms its original common position within six weeks and Parliament fails to veto that confirmation by an absolute majority of its members within six weeks of the Council's confirmation.

7.2 Objectives

With regard to scope and definitions, the 1993 proposals introduced precise definitions of 'independent producers' 'auto-producers' and 'large-scale industrial

20. Art. 189b(2)(d).
21. Art. 189b(3).

consumers'. The EP proposed definitions of 'fair price' and 'general interest' are excluded. The recitals outlining the Commission's objectives have been substantially amended.

7.3 Provisions

Member states may, as far as Community law allows, impose public service obligations on undertakings operating in the natural gas or electricity sectors as regards the security, regularity, quality and price of supplies.[22] The recommendation contained in the EP's opinion[23] was that the member state's obligations in the two sectors should be set out.

Chapter 3 of the proposals is now headed 'Storage and Transport' and contains most of the original provisions relating to transmission system operation for the gas sector but those for the electricity sector have been amended. Member states must authorise the construction on their territory of new production and transmission capacity on the basis of objective, transparent and non-discriminatory criteria and open tender procedures. Member states are to be responsible for defining the criteria of the dispatch and for the use of inter-connectors. Transmission system operators must be independent from other activities related to the electricity sector.

Chapter 4 of the proposals outlines operation of the distribution system and provides for member states to be able to define the rights and public service obligations assigned to distribution companies. This is in addition to their being able to do this in relation to the rights and obligations of their customers.

Chapter 5 still deals with unbundling but the unbundling of management is no longer required save that the independence of the network manager must be guaranteed at least at administrative levels. The separation of accounting of production, transmission and distribution operations for both gas and electricity including gas storage remain.

A new Chapter 6 is introduced establishing third party rights for negotiated access to the networks by production and transmission or transportation companies from all the member states, by a large-scale industrial consumer (defined as a final customer whose consumption, in the case of electricity, exceeds 100 GWh per year or a lower quantity to be specified by the member state, or, in the case of gas, an individual consumer whose consumption exceeds 25,000,000m^3 per year or such lower figure as may be specified by the member state), by distribution companies and by auto-producers (defined in terms of electricity as independent producers who produce electricity essentially for their own use). An independent producer is a producer who does not carry out electricity transmission or distribution functions on the territory covered by the network where he is established. Member states are obliged to designate a competent authority, who must be independent of the parties, to settle disputes relating to the contracts and negotiations in question. Recourse to this authority may be had without prejudice to the exercise of rights of appeal to Community law.

Chapter 7 deals with final provisions similar to the 1992 proposals but with an implementation date of July 1 1994 as recommended by Parliament.

22. Art. 3.2 of the revised proposals.
23. Supra note 19.

7.4 Energy Council Informal Debate

The 1993 proposals were presented to the Energy Council by the Commission two days after the Commission had adopted them, namely on Friday December 10 1993, for an exchange of views. The discussion was informal. The Committee of Permanent Representatives (COREPER) have been instructed to examine the revised proposals so that formal consideration can take place at the Energy Council meeting presently scheduled under the current Greek presidency to take place on May 25 1994.

8.0 CONCLUSION

Supporters of TPA cite the UK and the US as examples of countries where the system has worked. However, such a comparison cannot be sustained because there are major differences between the industries in the US and UK, on the one hand, and continental Europe on the other. Although its implementation in the US and the UK may provide some comfort to the sceptics, it is not a sufficient basis on which to introduce a new regime of TPA into the Community, in which there is a very finely balanced electricity and gas market and industry existing already.

Those opposed to TPA do not oppose the idea of increased competition, liberalisation and the removal of intra-Community trade barriers. However, they believe that these objectives can be achieved by other means, such as more convergence in fiscal, environmental and accounting policies, the abolition of import and export monopolies and by strengthening the existing market-related framework. Further, the competition rules which are already in the EC Treaty should be sufficient to ensure efficient market-related structures and performance. They believe that in an environment which presents such significant differences in fiscal and organisational aspects of the electricity and gas industries, in which there is increasing dependence on supplies not subject to the same legal and political regime, and in which there is a tightening market environment, the introduction of TPA would prove to be too great a gamble to take.

However, despite the cries of opposition, it seems that the Commission, supported by the major industrial users, remains determined to pursue the introduction of a TPA regime as part of the achievement of an internal energy market in the Community. By basing such a regime on minimum regulation, subsidiarity, and a gradual approach to liberalisation, they hope to be able to appease the voices of dissent.

Whether a TPA regime is introduced in the Community remains to be seen. However, if a third party access system is introduced, even in a compromised form, it will be a watershed from which the European energy market and the electricity and gas industries of the Community may, perhaps, never be able to return.

Chapter 7

The Directives on Transit of Gas and Electricity

Considerations Regarding the Juridical Limits of the Realisation of the Internal Market in the Energy Sector

Peter J. Tettinger, Johann-Christian Pielow, Norbert Zimmermann

1.0 INTRODUCTION

As part of the process of creating a Single Market within the European Economic Community, the European Commission in 1989 put forward proposals for gas and electricity transit in the Community. The drafts of the Directives on the transit of gas[1] and electricity[2] were placed within the overall context of the Commission's move towards completing the internal market by 1992 and were to be understood as measures of law approximation. They were meant to guarantee the fulfilment of the aims established in the working document 'The Internal Energy Market' (COM(88) 238). This document focuses specifically on the implementation of the 1985 White Paper and the application of Community law in the energy sector. It does not attempt to prescribe solutions but presents a comprehensive inventory of possible barriers to trade in each major form of energy, including natural gas and electricity, and identifies the priority areas for action to remove the most significant barriers. In agreement with the situation of the electricity sector the working document identifies the following priorities in the case of natural gas: (a) greater price transparency for non-tariff sales; (b) harmonisation of taxation on energy; (c) increased interconnection and integrated operation of the European gas pipeline

---

1. OJ C247/6, Sep. 28 1989 (gas).
2. OJ C8/4, July 20 1989 (electricity).

network; and (d) the possibility of 'common carrier' third party access to the grid in return for a reasonable carriage charge – either for other gas transmission and distribution undertakings only or for industrial customers as well.

The Commission therefore put forward proposals for gas and electricity transit based upon Article 100A brought in by the Single European Act. Both these draft Directives 'provide for Member States to respect the right of transit through networks on their territory'.[3] Networks under this obligation are to negotiate the terms of contracts of at least one year's duration in the case of electricity and without any limits for gas.

The following Chapter summarizes the central theses of a publication in the German language which was concerned with a study of the draft Directives on transit.[4] Meanwhile the European Community has adopted these Directives,[5] made it clear that the regulations were restricted to procedural questions in the case of transit request,[6] and that they should not establish an existing transit obligation. For this the Commission looked forward to other regulations.

Commission proposals have given rise to a lively debate, as a first discussion at the beginning of April 1991 proved that member states support in principle the idea of a Single Market for energy. But the Commission's proposals in detail have met considerable opposition[7] that was not entirely unexpected since most changes to the status quo take time to digest. In accordance with the announcement of then EC Commissioner Cardoso e Cunha, which introduced the second stage of creating the Single Market for energy including the system of Third Party Access (TPA), the two new proposals[8] distinguish three elements: (1) Creating a system of non-discrimination and transparency; (2) 'Unbundling' – the separation of production, transmission and supply with respect to management and accounting; (3) Limited introduction of TPA to the transmission facilities. The modified Commission proposals, presented to the Energy Council in December 1993, limit 'unbundling' to a separation of accounts as long as administrative independence is maintained, and provide for third party access to be on a 'negotiated' basis.

These Commission objectives in basic positions pose questions similar to those in the 1991 study. It bears mentioning, that since the Conference of Maastricht of February 7 1992 the member states of the EEC decided to change the content of the EC Treaty in several respects. With respect to the energy sector Articles 3, 3B and 129B–129D are especially important.[9] Therein the member states at first declared that in areas which do not fall within its exclusive competence, the Community shall

3. A.C. e Cunha, 'The Internal Energy Market', *Journal of Energy and Natural Resources Law* 1991, p.291. L. Hancher, 'Energy and the environment: striking a balance?' [1989], CMLR 475 ff.

4. U. Hüffer, K. Ipsen, and P.-J. Tettinger, 'Die Transitrichtlinien für Gas und Elektrizität', *Bochumer Beitrge zum Berg- und Energierecht*, Vol. 14, 1991.

5. Council Directive of Oct. 1990 on the the transit of electricity through grids (90/547/EEC, OJ L313/30 1990); Council Directive of May 1991 on the transit of natural gas through grids (91/296/EEC, OJ L147/37 1991).

6. See L. Eckert, 'Die Erdgastransitrichtlinie', in F.S. Börner, 1992, p.525.

7. See *eg* R. Scholz and St. Lange, *Europäischer Binnenmarkt und Energiepolitik,* (1992); L. Eckert, 'Die Vorschläge der EG-Kommission zu "Third Party Access"' in *der Gaswirtschaft*, (RdE 1992), p.56 ff; H.P. Hermann, *Die Konzeption der EG-Kommission zur Ordnung des europäischen Strommarktes*, (RdE 1992), p.96 ff; D. Kuhnt, *Aktuelle Rechtsfragen der Energiewirtschaft*, (RdE 1992), p.125 ff.

8. See COM(91) 548 Final SYN 384–385, Feb. 21 1992, which contains the original proposals for Council directives establishing common regulations for the Single Market in electricity and gas.

9. See Treaty on European Union and Final Act, Maastricht, Feb. 7, 1992, (International Legal Materials 1992), p.247 ff – reproduced Appendix V.

take action in accordance with the principle of subsidiarity, only so far as the objectives of the proposed action cannot be sufficiently achieved by member states and can therefore, by reason of the scale or effects of the proposed action, be better achieved by the Community (Article 3B). Further changes to the Treaty noted in Title XII 'Trans-European networks' are in accordance with the aims of a Single Market for energy. The central theme of these is noted in Article 129B(2): 'Within the framework of a system of open and competive markets, action by the Community shall aim at promoting the interconnection and interoperability of national networks as well as access to such networks. It shall take account in particular of the need to link island, landlocked and peripheral regions with the central regions of the Community.' In order to achieve these objectives the Community shall at first establish a series of guidelines covering the objectives, priorities and broad lines of measures envisaged in the sphere of trans-European networks. These guidelines shall be adopted by the Council. Second, the Community has the right to implement any measures that may prove necessary to ensure the interoperability of the networks, in particular in the field of technical standardisation. Member states shall, in liaison with the Community, co-ordinate among themselves the policies pursued at national level which may have a significant impact on the achievement of the objectives mentioned above. The following text will help to review the legal pre-conditions of European Community intervention in the energy sector.

2.0 BASIC CONSIDERATIONS REGARDING THE COMPETENCES OF THE EUROPEAN COMMUNITIES

2.1 Dogmatic Basic Positions in Regard to European Community Law

2.1.1 The Legal Nature of Primary and Secondary Community Law

Scope of action of the EC bodies exists only within the framework of primary Community law as laid down in the treaties establishing the European Community (ECSC Treaty, EAEC Treaty and EEC Treaty) and as modified by the Single European Act and the Treaty on European Union.[10]

On the basis of these treaties the European Communities were created as 'intergovernmental institutions' because the member states transferred part of their sovereinty to the Community ('common autonomous view') without, however, completely losing possibilities of influence, ie the member states continue to have sovereign rights over the treaties.[11] The European Communities differ from traditional international organisations because of the rights granted to them to maintain an independent jurisdiction with binding enforcement as far as the member states are concerned. Their sovereign jurisdiction is not to be understood as a unique static

10. See eg H.P. Ipsen, *Europäisches Gemeinschaftsrecht*, (1972), p.64 and BVerfGE 22, 293 (296); P. Pescatore, 'Die Gemeinschaftsverträge als Verfassungsrecht', in *Festschrift für Kutscher*, (1981), p.319 ff.

11. See H.P. Ipsen, op. cit., p.193 f; Schweitzer and Hummer, *Europarecht*, (3rd ed., 1990), p.60.

act; the German Constitutional Court has rather held that it is a community *sui generis* in the process of advancing integration.[12]

2.1.2 The Relation Between EC Law and National (Constitutional) Law

The Community has its own autonomous legal order[13] composed of the primary Community law of the founding treaties and the secondary law deriving from it, established by the Community's bodies; in its totality the latter takes precedence over the national laws of the member states.[14]

This opinion was developed by the European Court of Justice and has been confirmed by the German Constitutional Court with reference to Article 24BL (Basic Law). Referring to the precedence of European law, the German Court – after initial hesitation[15] – now assumes in the context of the relationship between European law and national (constitutional) law that an examination of the Community's law-making acts in regard to national constitutional law is no longer to occur ('Solange II').[16]

2.1.3 Methods of Interpreting European Community Law

Starting from the methods of interpretation customary in international law according to the Vienna Convention on the Laws of Contract, the European Court of Justice has developed further methods of its own for the interpretation of Community law.[17]

(a) The following principle applies for primary Community law: in an objective textual approach the content of a legal rule is to be determined on the basis of its exact wording. Because of the functional link between the procedural instruments and the aims of the founding treaties a teleological interpretation is to be used in the second place. On account of the frequently vague wording of the treaties' provisions, the latter method has advanced to the predominant method of analysing Community law.[18] In addition, actual principles of applying the law have to be taken into consideration, which have been developed by the court in a process of continuous legal rulings.[19] These consist of the principle of the Community's ability

12. BVerfGE 22, 293 (296); 37, 271 (278).
13. See H.P. Ipsen, op. cit., p.63.
14. Court of Justice of the European Communities, Dec. July 15 1964 Case 6/64 *Costa v ENEL [1964]* ECR 1251 (1269).
15. BVerfGE 37, 271 ff ('Solange I'); BVerfGE 53, 187 ff ('Vielleicht-Beschluss').
16. BVerfGE 73, 339 (387).
17. Cf. W. Bernhardt, 'Zur Auslegung des europäischen Gemeinschaftsrechts', in *Festschrift für R. Kutscher*, (1981), p.17 ff; A. Bleckmann, 'Teleologie und dynamische Auslegung des europäischen Gemeinschaftsrechts, in Europarecht (EuR) 1979, p.239 ff; A. Bleckmann, 'Zu den Auslegungsmethoden des Europäischen Gerichtshofs, in *Neue Juristische Wochenschrift (NJW)* (1982), p.1177 ff; U. Everling, 'Rechtsanwendungs- und Auslegungsgrundstze des Gerichtshofs der Europäischen Gemeinschaften', in Kruse (ed.), *Zölle, Verbrauchssteuern, Europäisches Marktordnungsrecht,* (1988), p.51 ff; F. Degan, 'Procédés d'interpretation tirés de la jurisprudence de la Cour de Justice des Communautés européennes – Exposé comparatif avec la jurisprudence de la Cour international de Justice', in *Revue Trimestrielle de Droit Européen,* (1966), p.189 ff.
18. See A. Bleckmann, *NJW* 1981, p.1178 and the within (notes 7 and 9) cited Decisions of the Court of Justice.
19. See in this context the former judge of the Court of Justice, U. Everling, op. cit., p.59.

to function, the principle of the uniformity of interpretation and application of Community law, and the principle of securing the Common Market;[20] these principles have in the final analysis led to rulings of the European Court which have been in favour of the Community.[21]

(b) Secondary Community law is preferably to be interpreted by means of the subjective approach; the intention of the author of a secondary regulation, which is the primary consideration in this approach, is to be determined mainly with reference to the stated reasoning accompanying that regulation.[22] The teleological approach is also to be granted particular importance since in addition it is necessary to interpret the regulation in conformity with the primary law.[23]

2.2 The Network of Competences of the European Communities: The Independence of the System of Legal Acts in Community Law

2.2.1 The Principle of Individual Authorisation Limited by Contract – Limits of the Community's Competence

The autonomous structure of the European Communities and of their legal system implies that the Community bodies have an original competence for action, ie that they are independent of the sovereign power of the member states. This of course cannot mean that the EC bodies have an overriding competence. The competences, which are at any rate limited by the transfer of individual sovereign rights, follow rather the principle of limited individual authorisation. Accordingly, the Community bodies are only competent to act in so far as the treaties expressly grant them powers to carry out particular measures. Competences extending beyond these limits, which would in fact constitute the ability to establish a new law or be a kind of 'super competence', are not provided for in Community law.[24] The competences of the EC bodies are additionally limited because they are functionally orientated on the basis of the treaties' objectives and because they are meant to realise these objectives in each individual case. In this context the dynamic character of the Community is to be taken into consideration, which in some special cases may justify a Community-wide regulation of previously not included areas.[25]

20. Especially with respect to the last criterion see Court of Justice of the European Communities, Case 15/81, *Gaston Schul v Inspecteur der invoerrechte an accijnzen* [1982], ECR p.1409 (1431 f, note 33).

21. Cf. U. Everling, op. cit., pp.61, 66.

22. Cf. Court of Justice of the European Communities, Case 29/69, *Erich Stauder v Stadt Ulm Sozialamt* [1969], ECR 419 (425); A. Bleckmann, supra note 18, p.1178; U. Everling, op. cit., p.59 f.

23. Cf. A. Bleckmann, supra note 18, p.1179.

24. This rule can be deduced from Art. 4 (1) EEC Treaty, 3 (1) EAEC Treaty, 8, 20 and 26 ECSC Treaty. See Beutler, Bieber, Pipkorn and Streil, *Die Europäische Gemeinschaft – Rechtsordnung und Politik*, (3rd ed. 1987, p.75); E. Grabitz (ed.), *Kommentar zum EWG-Vertrag*, 1989, Art. 189 note 2; Schweitzer and Hummer, op. cit. p.108; H.P. Ipsen, op. cit., p.425 ff.

25. See for instance Court of Justice of the European Communities, Case 43/75, *G. Defrenne v SABENA* [1976], ECR 455 (472 ff); Case 91/79 *Detergents* [1980], ECR 1099 (1106); Case 52/79, *Debauve* [1980], ECR 833 (865 f); in this context BVerfGE 75, 223 (242).

2.2.2 The Normative Instruments for Action at the Disposal of the EC Bodies

The Community's legal instruments comprise, according to Article 189 of the EEC Treaty, the immediately applicable regulation, the directive which is to be transformed by the member states into national law and which is only in exceptional cases immediately effective,[26] and the right to take individual decisions. The choice and form of the concrete acts of lawmaking have to be in accordance with the general legal principles developed in Community law as they are recognised as basic rights as well as for the requirements of the rule of law – namely legality, certainty, specificity, and reasonableness.[27]

3.0 THE LEGALITY OF THE COMMISSION'S PROPOSALS CONCERNING THE INTERNAL ENERGY MARKET

3.1 Provisions of the Primary Law

3.1.1 The Requirements of Article 100A EEC Treaty

The drafts of the directives on the transit of gas and electricity were to be understood as measures of law approximation on the basis of Article 100A EEC Treaty, all the requirements of which must be met.

In the context of establishing the Single European Act (SEA) Article 100A EEC Treaty was inserted in order to simplify the procedure of approximation in its formal and material requirements, so that the envisaged objective of an 'internal market' could be reached more quickly. In view of the sphere of application of this provision, Article 100, which had been employed as the authority for approximation prior to the establishment of the SEA, is only to be applied as a subsidiary regulation.

Article 100A, however, is only applicable if more specific basic authorities do not apply (*eg* Article 63, para.2 in connection with Article 59; Article 66 in connection with Article 57, para.2; Article 87, para.1; Article 101 as well as Article 103, para. 4 EEC Treaty), which was not the case for the drafts of the directives as proposed.[28]

Approximation of laws can only be understood in the sense of an alignment of national regulations while decreasing or abolishing the differences existing among

---

26. See Court of Justice, Case 9/70, *I. Grad v Finanzamt Traunstein* [1970], ECR 825 (825 f); Case 41/74, *A. Duyn v Home Office* [1974], ECR 1337 (1348); Case 79/83, *D. Harz v Deutsche Tradax* [1984], ECR 1921 (1938 ff.); Case 222/84, *M. Johnston v Chief Constable of the Royal Ulster Constabulary* [1986], ECR 1651 (1691); concerning directives without favouring effect cf. Case 152/84, *Marshall v Southampton and South-West Hampshire Area Health Authority* [1986], ECR 723 ff; Case 14/86, *Pretore di Salo v X* [1987], ECR 2545 (2570); Case 103/88, *Fratelli Constanzo SpA*, Decision of June 22 1989, published in *Europarecht (EuR)* 1990, p.156.

27. Cf. E. Grabitz (ed.), op. cit., Art.189 note 40; I.L. Pernice, ibid., Art. 164 notes 88 ff.

28. Cf. B. Langeheine, in Grabitz (ed.), op.cit., Art. 100A note 15; see in this context Court of Justice, Case 68/86, *United Kingdom/Council*, Decision of Feb. 23 1988, published in *Europarecht (EuR)* (1988), p.290.

the member states. Thus a prerequisite for any approximation process is the existence of a particular law in at least one of the member states.[29]

This analysis, which was already valid for Article 100 EEC Treaty, has not changed with the adoption of the SEA and the insertion of Article 100A EEC Treaty. In particular the sphere in which approximation is applied has not been enlarged by the introduction of the objective to create an internal market, since the concept of the internal market is to a large extent identical with the previously authoritative term 'common market'.[30]

The instrument of approximation is consequently limited because it presupposes a minimum of a particular national law which is to be harmonised in the interest of a functioning internal market. It functions primarily in a reactive sense and may not be abused as an instrument to introduce totally new, independent community concepts. Besides, any initiative to approximate national laws is of course dependent upon the general principles of Community law, particularly those of reasonableness and basic rights.[31]

A measure of approximation according to Article 100A EEC Treaty can only be adopted if it is certain that the matter to be regulated is subject to the EEC Treaty. It is true that the general provisions of this Treaty are by principle applicable to all areas of the economy because of the universal character of the Treaty. The creation of an 'internal energy market' intended in the drafts of the directives can only be assigned to the Treaty's sphere of application if it is clear that the member states intended to invest the Community with the competence to develop a Community-wide energy policy of its own.

A more detailed examination, which also takes into consideration the historical development of Community law, raises considerable objections. In the past 'energy policy' had always been regarded as a sphere of regulation pertaining only to the member states. This was not even changed after the adoption of the European Economic Area (EEA), which may indeed have opened up further areas of policy (*eg* in environmental protection), but which does not cover the development of an energy policy of the Community's own. The evaluation of other political agreements and measures of the EC bodies leads to the same result. Thus it must be concluded that the EEC Treaty, although providing instruments for the fragmentary regulation of particular aspects of energy policy,[32] does not authorise the establishment of a new comprehensive concept of 'European energy policy'.

A further important limitation of the approximation instrument follows from its functional link with the objectives of the Treaty inherent in it as a whole. This is

29. Cf. A. Bleckmann, *Europarecht*, (5th ed. 1990), p.612; H.C. Eiden, *Die Rechtsangleichung nach Art. 100 des EWG-Vertrags*, (1984), p.18; Schweitzer and Hummer, op. cit., p.348; furthermore W. Schmeder, *Die Rechtsangleichung als Integrationsmittel der Europischen Gemeinschaft*, (1978), p.19.

30. See the definition of the Common Market made by the Court of Justice within Case 15/81, *Gaston Schul v Inspecteur der invoerrechten en accijnzen* [1982], ECR p.1409 (1431 f).

31. Cf. P.-C. Müller-Graff, 'Die Rechtsangleichung zur Verwirklichung des Binnenmarkts', in *Europarecht (EuR)* (1989), p.128; B. Langeheine, in Grabitz (ed.), op. cit., Art. 100A note 8. On the effect of the basic principle as a base for the interpretation of the Treaty see for instance Court of Justice, case 6/72, *Europemballage Corp. and Continental Can Co. v Commission* [1973], ECR 215 (244).

32. Cf. within the context of other fields of action Court of Justice, Case 45/85, *Verband der Sachversicherer v Commission* [1987], ECR 405 (451); Cases 209–213/84, *Ministère Public v L. Asjes a.o.* [1986], ECR 1425 ff; Case 167/73, *Commission v France* [1974], ECR 359 (370).

expressed in Article 100A EEC Treaty, which makes reference to the objectives of Article 8A ('establishment of an internal market'), and also in Article 3 – particularly subpara.h – EEC Treaty. Central directives and limitations thus result from the regulations of the Treaty concerning the basic freedoms of the Common Market, the implementation of which is the objective of the Treaty as a whole. Legal steps by the Community bodies taken in the process of approximation must consequently be suitable and necessary in order to enforce these basic freedoms. Conversely approximation is not permissible if it is at variance with the basic freedoms of the Treaty, but also if it brings about situations which are not demanded by the basic freedoms and which therefore exceed the objectives of the EEC Treaty.[33]

3.1.2 The Commission's Proposals in the Context of the EEC's Rulings on Competition

For want of an exception pursuant to para.103 ff of the Law Against Restraints on Competition, the rules on competition as laid down in Article 85 ff EEC Treaty apply in principle for the sector of public utilities as well.[34]

Article 87 EEC Treaty does not grant Community bodies any competence to further develop the law; the transit directives for gas and electricity would thus only be valid on the basis of this provision if they were explicitly covered by Articles 85, 86 EEC Treaty.[35]

Article 85 EEC does not apply – either in fact or in legal consequence; for rejecting a transit application does not constitute a concerted practice and the statement of nullification contained in Article 85 para.2 EEC Treaty cannot create an obligation to transit.[36]

Consequently Article 86 EEC Treaty is decisive. In this context the question is crucial as to whether the transit market presumed by the Commission exists at all. This cannot be decided in general terms. Rather the particular characteristics of the gas, or electricity, sector must be examined separately.

3.1.3 Requirements of Further Contractual Law and of General Legal Principles

The obligation to state reasons laid down in Article 190 EEC Treaty requires that directives shall state the reasons on which they are based. To ascertain if the reasons accompanying the regulations, directives and decisions are sufficient, it is indispensable that they be theoretically connected with the measure adopted. Following

33. See H.C. Taschner, in vd.Groeben, Thiesing and Ehlermann (eds.), *Handbuch des Europäischen Rechts*, Art. 100 note 28; P.-C. Müller-Graff, op. cit, p.107(121f); earlier H.P. Ipsen, op.cit., p.196 ff.

34. See for instance B.E. Niederleithinger, in Lukes (ed.), *Ein EWG-Binnenmarkt für Elektrizität – Realität oder Utopie*, (1988), pp.63, 66 ff; furthermore S. Klaue, in *Festschrift für Lukes*, (1989), p.408; D.Kuhnt, op. cit., p.411(417) with more detailed references in note 18. The Court of Justice postulated this principle for the field of assurances: Case 45/85, *Verband der Sachversicherer v Commission* [1987], ECR 405 (451).

35. See Court of Justice, cit.; furthermore Schröter, in v.d.Groeben, v.Boeckh, Thiesing and Ehlermann, *Kommentar zum EWG-Vertrag*, (3rd ed. 1983), Art. 87 note 2 f; I. Pernice, in Grabitz (ed.), op. cit., Art. 87 note 2; Gleiss and Hirsch, *Kommentar zum EWG-Kartellrecht*, 3rd ed. 1978, Art. 87 note 2. Of a different opinion: Smit and Herzog, *The Law of the EEC,* (1976), No. 87.05 and 87.06; A. Deringer, *Das Wettbewerbsrecht der EWG*, p.162 ff; Art. 87 note 13.

36. Cf. Koch, in Grabitz (ed.), op. cit., Art. 85 note 18. As to the relation between Art. 85 and Art. 86 EEC Treaty cf. Court of Justice, Case 6/72 *Continental Can* [1973], ECR 215 (245 f).

pertinent court rulings, a lack of reason is, however, only legally relevant in cases where the legal step taken would have had a more favourable outcome for the plaintiff, provided a correct reason had been given, or in cases where an error in substance is concealed by the formal error.[37]

In contrast to the Basic Law of the Federal Republic of Germany there is no provision in the Community treaties which expressly establishes the validity of the rule of law for all the bodies of the Community.[38] However, the European Court of Justice has developed and continuously applied principles relating to the rule of law as general legal principles inherent to the law of the Community. Among these are on the one hand the basic rights governing procedure, and on the other hand, further basic requirements relating to the rule of law such as the principle of legal certainty and the principle of reasonableness. The principle of legal certainty requires that a burdening regulation be worded clearly so that the party involved can unambiguously recognise the duties imposed upon him and his rights and can thus comply accordingly. As to its content and scope the principle of reasonableness corresponds to the prohibition of excess valid in German law. Any Community measure has to serve a legitimate objective, ie one provided for in the founding treaties. The means used has to be suitable and necessary, in order to attain this objective, and the regulation has to appear appropriate.[39]

Secondary Community law furthermore may not violate guarantees covered by the basic rights. Even though a consistent written catalogue of basic rights does not exist in the legal system of the European Communities today, there is – in view of the continuous rulings of the European Court of Justice – an inventory of basic rights.[40] The Court in its function as a guardian of the law endeavours to guarantee the compliance with these basic rights and their preservation. The determination of the

37. Case 24/62, *Bundesrepublik Deutschland v Commission* [1963] ECR 145 f. (notes 3 and 4); E. Grabitz, op.cit., Art. 190, note 6.

38. Case 1/73, *Westzucker GmbH v Einfuhr und Vorratsstelle für Zucker* [1973] ECR 723 (729); joined Cases 17 and 20/61, *Klöckner and Hoesch v Hohe Behörde* [1962] ECR 653 (686); Case 281/84, *Zuckerfabrik Bedburg v Council and Commission* [1987] ECR 41 (94). See generally H. Lecheler, *Der Europäische Gerichtshof und die allgemeinen Rechtsgrundsätze*, 1971, p.3 ff; Schweitzer and Hummer, *Europarecht*, 2nd ed. 1985, p.187.

39. See Case 44/79, *Hauer v Land Rhineland-Pfalz* [1979] ECR 3727 (3748); Case 4/73, *Nold v Commission* [1974] ECR 491 (508); joined Cases 351/85 and 360/85, *Dillinger Hüttenwerke a.o. v Commission* [1987] ECR 3639 (3669 ff); Case 281/84, *Zuckerfabrik Bedburg a.o. v Council and Commission* [1987] ECR 41 (94); Case 56/86, *Société pour l'eportation des sucres v OBEA ECR* [1987] 1423 (1449). H. Kutscher, 'Zum Grundsatz der Verhältnismässigkeit im Recht der Europäischen Gemeinschaften', in *Deutsche Sektion der internationalen Juristenkommission (Hrsg), Der Grundsatz der Verhältnismässigkeit in europäischen Rechtsordnungen*, (1985), p.89(94f).

40. See generally Hüffer, Ipsen, Tettinger, op.cit., p.147; further Case 29/69, *Stauder v Stadt Ulm* [1969] ECR 419 (425), Case 424, 425/85, 257/85 and 40/86 (cited in EuGRZ 1989, S. 190); Case 130/75, *Vivien Prais v Council* [1976] ECR 1589 (1599); Case 175/73, *Gewerkschaftsbund, Denise Massa a.o. v Council* [1974] ECR 917 (925); Case 44/79, *Hauer v Land Rhineland-Pfalz* [1979] ECR 3727 (3728, 3744); Case 240/83, *Procureur de la Republique v ADBHU* [1985] ECR 531 (548); Case 59/83, *SA Biovilac v EEC* [1984] ECR 4057 (4058); Case 230/78, *SpA Eridania v Minister für Landwirtschaft und Forsten a.o.* [1979] ECR 2749 (2750); Case 116/82, *Bundesrepublik Deutschland v Commission* [1986] ECR 2519 (2545); Case 234/85, *Keller v Einfuhr- und Vorratsstelle für Futtermittel und Getreide* [1986] ECR 2897 (2912); Case 136/79, *National Panasonic v Commission* [1980] ECR 2033 (2034); Case 85/76, *Hoffmann-La Roche v Commission* [1979] ECR 461 (511); Case 7/72, *Boehringer v Commission* [1972] ECR 1281 (1290); Case 32/62, *Alvis v Council* [1963] ECR 107 (123); Cases 42 and 49/59, *SNUPAT v Hohe Behörde* [1961] ECR 107 (169); generally Schweitzer and Hummer, op. cit., supra note 11, p.216.

contents of the basic rights protected is mainly achieved by way of evaluating and comparing national laws.[41] The basis for the court's rulings can be found in those regulations of Community law which are pertinent to the basic rights – such as Article 7 EEC Treaty. The declaration on basic rights and basic freedoms adopted by the European Parliament on April 12, 1989[42] is to be applied. The stipulations of the Convention for the Protection of Human Rights and Fundamental Freedoms, which have been recognised by all the member states, also have effect as basic rights.[43]

A yardstick for the drafts of the directives under consideration is above all to be found in the basic rights of property,[44] and freedom of trade and business,[45] as well as in the basic right of non-discrimination.[46] These basic rights of the Community, however, do not take unlimited precedence. They are rather to be seen in regard to the social function of the protected activity (of the protected right), *ie* they must be incorporated into the structure and objectives of the Community.[47] The principles of reasonableness and of preserving essence are emphasised as strict limitations for any encroachments on basic rights. Furthermore the concept has been recognised that no such measures can be accepted which are not compatible with the basic rights recognised by the constitutions of the member states.

3.2 Consequences in Regard to the Directive on the Transit of Natural Gas

An examination of the Draft Directive of September 1989 concerning the transit of natural gas on the basis of the above-mentioned legal principles of Community law led to serious objections.

41. Court of Justice of the European Communities, Sep. 21 1989, joined Cases 46/87 and 227/88, *Höchst v Commission* [1989] – not yet reported; with it U. Everling, 'Brauchen wir "Solange III"?, Zu den Forderungen nach Revision der Rechtsprechung des Bundesverfassungsgerichts', *Europarecht EuR* (1990), p.195 (208 f). Case 4/73, *Nold v Commission* [1974] ECR 491 (507); Case 44/79, *Hauer v Land Rheinland-Pfalz* [1979] ECR 3727 (3744).

42. See B. Beutler, 'Die Grundrechtserklärung des Europischen Parlaments', EuGRZ 1989, p.187. Earlier, concerning the statement of the European Parliament in 1977, Case 222/84, *M. Johnston v Chief Constable of the Royal Ulster Constabulary* [1986] ECR 1663 (1682).

43. See Case 4/73, *Nold v Commission* [1974] ECR 491 (507); Case 44/79, *Hauer v Land Rhineland-Pfalz* [1979] ECR 3727 (3744); joined Cases 41, 121 and 796/79, *Testa v Bundesanstalt für Arbeit* [1980] ECR 1979 (1996).

44. Case 44/79, *Hauer v Land Rheinland-Pfalz* [1979] ECR 3727 (3728, note 4); Case 232/81, *Commerciale Olio v Commission* [1984] ECR 3900 (3911); Case 265/87, *Schräder v Hauptzollamt Gronau* [1989] July 11 1989, S. 12.

45. Case 11/70, *Internationale Handelsgesellschaft v Einfuhr- und Vorratsstelle für Futtermittel und Getreide* [1970] ECR 1125 (1134 f); Case 25/70, *Köster v Einfuhr- und Vorratsstelle für Futtermittel und Getreide* [1970] ECR 1161 (1175 f); Case 4/73, *Nold v Commission* [1974] ECR 491 (507). See R. Streinz, *Bundesverfassungsgerichtlicher Grundrechtsschutz und Europäisches Gemeinschaftsrecht*, (1989), p.404; C.O. Lenz, in Case 240/83, *Procureur de la Republique v ADBHU* [1985] ECR 531 (533 f).

46. For instance Case 78/82, *Commission v Italien* [1983] ECR 1956; Case 181/82, *Roussel v The Netherlands* [1983] ECR 3849 (3851 ff); EuGH, joined Cases 117/76, 16/77, *Albert Ruckdeschel & Co a.o. v Hauptzollamt St. Annen* and joined Cases 124/76 and 20/77, *S.A. Moulins et Huilieries de Pont-a-Mousson a.o. v Office national interprofessionel des cereales* [1977] ECR 1753 (1812 ff); Case 245/81, *Edeka-Zentrale v Bundesrepublik Deutschland* [1982] ECR 2745 (2745 ff.); Case 11/74, *L'Union des Minotiers de la Champagne v French Government* [1974] ECR 877 (891).

47. Case 11/70, *Internationale Handelsgesellschaft v Einfuhr- und Vorratsstelle für Getreide und Futtermittel* [1970] ECR 1125 (1135); Case 4/73, *Nold v Commission* [1974] ECR 491 (507).

3.2.1 The Scope of Possibilities for Interpretation in Regard to Individual Wordings in the Directive

Initial objections arose when evaluating the wording of the Directive on the basis of the requirement of specificity which follows from the principle of the rule of law.[48] It was not possible exactly to determine what the concept of 'natural gas transit' means. Further interpretation problems arose with the term 'high pressure system' if one considers the gas companies which will be affected by the Directive; and finally there were problems concerning the Commission's rights of intervention in case a transit agreement could not be reached.

3.2.2 The Incompatibility Between the Objectives of 'Transit Right' or 'Transit Obligation' with the Community Law Regulations of the EEC Treaty

The draft Directives were not compatible with the central objectives of the Treaty focused on the realisation of the basic freedoms. It is true that the objective of establishing a common market or an internal market for gas can be derived from the basic freedoms of visible trade or freedom of services.[49] Especially in view of the degree of liberalisation, which has in the meantime been attained in this area,[50] one may not infer from these basic freedoms[51] any regulation providing for the introduction or effectuation of a transit obligation that would bind the current pipeline owners. The reason is that there are no trade barriers caused by the sovereign actions of the member states. To the extent that private companies have the effect of creating trade barriers, the EC bodies have to rely primarily on the instruments of the European Law on Competition,[52] which in turn is limited by the legal status of the individual which is protected as a basic right.

The envisaged measure of approximating the law consequently went beyond the objectives of the EEC Treaty and thus proved to be not in conformity with Community law.[53]

48. On this principle see Court of Justice, for instance Case 1/73, *Westzucker GmbH v Einfuhr- und Vorratsstelle für Zucker* [1973], ECR 723 (729); joined Cases 17 and 20/61, *Klöckner and Hoesch* [1962], ECR 653 (686); Case 281/84, *Zuckerfabrik Bedburg a.o. v Council and Commission* [1987], ECR 41 (94); Case 116/82, *Commission v Bundesrepublik Deutschland* [1986], ECR 2519 (2526). Especially to the requirement of specificity see Court of Justice, case 29/69, *Stauder v Stadt Ulm* [1969], ECR 419 (425); B.Beutler, 'Grundrechtsschutz' in v.d.Groeben, v.Boeckh,Thiesing and Ehlermann (eds), op. cit., supra note 35, Vol. 2, notes 10 ff.

49. On the nature of gas as a 'good' in the sense of the EEC Treaty see C.D.Ehlermann, 'Die rechtlichen Instrumentarien zur Verwirklichung eines Gemeinsamen Marktes nach dem EWG-Vertrag', in Lukes (ed.), *Ein EWG-Binnenmarkt für Elektrizität – Realität oder Utopie*, (1988), p.38; C. Stewing, *Gasdurchleitung nach Europäischem Recht*, (1989), p.202 with note 9. See the definition of 'good' made by the Court of Justice, Case 7/68, *Commission v Italy* [1968], ECR 633 (642).

50. See the communication of the Commisson 'Die Vollendung des Binnenmarktes für Erdgas', COM(89)334 Final July 12 1989, p.6 note 10.

51. On the requirements of Art. 30 EEC Treaty see Court of Justice, for instance Case 8/74, *Dassonville* [1974], ECR 837 (852); Case 88-90/75, *SABAM a.o. v Minister für Industrie, Handel u. Handwerk a.o.* [1976], ECR 323 (340); Case 120/78, *Rewe v Bundesmonopolverwaltung für Branntwein ('Cassis de Dijon')* [1979], ECR 649 (660 ff); Case 220/81, *Robertson* [1982], ECR 2349 (2360).

52. Cf. for instance C. Stewing, op. cit., p.207 with more detailed references in note 26.

53. On the requirement that EC activities serve the principal aims of the Treaty see E. Steindorff, *Grenzen der EG-Kompetenzen*, (1990), p.86. In fact, the prescriptions about liberty of goods and services also bind EC bodies, see H. Matthies, in Grabitz (ed.), op. cit., Art. 30 note 41; W. Roth, 'Die Harmonisierung des Dienstleistungsrechts in der EWG', in *Europarecht (EuR)* (1987), p.9 f.

3.2.3 Authorisation of the Commission to Approximate the Law Pursuant to Article 100A EEC Treaty.

In addition there were considerable doubts as to whether the pre-conditions for the application of Article 100A EEC Treaty are given.

In particular the points of reference necessary for a process of approximation[54] are not given in the legal systems of the member states. The envisaged Directive thus turned out to be an attempt at establishing an overriding Community concept for the regulation of energy which in its entirety is incompatible with the system of competence as outlined in the EEC Treaty.

An additional inspection of the Directive in view of the requirement of reasonableness[55] leads to the conclusion that the EC bodies, in preparing the individual measures now adopted, have neglected to approximate the extremely heterogeneous legal and technical structures in the energy sector of individual member states.[56]

The consequences which will result from the implementation of the Directives (above all for competition within the Community) give rise to serious doubts as to whether the Directive is the suitable way to realise the objectives of the EEC Treaty.[57]

3.2.4 Rules on Competition and the Natural Gas Directive

An accusation of abuse pursuant to Article 86 EEC Treaty can only be made in connection with a firm's power in a particular market.[58] Any serious examination of a case of abuse thus presupposes the demarcation of the relevant market.

A factually relevant market in the context of Article 86 EEC Treaty is only to be determined according to the concept of a market based upon demand.[59] It is consequently crucial what service the market partner (*ie* the party interested in the transit) demands or what service he could demand as an alternative.[60]

This service does not consist in making available an empty pipeline nor in the transportation of a specifiable quantity of gas, but rather because of the inevitable connection in the combined feeding-in and extraction of the same quantity and an equivalent quality of gas.[61]

---

54. See note 20 supra.

55. Cf. Court of Justice, *Hauer v Land Rheinland-Pfalz* [1979], ECR 3727 (3748); Case 4/73, *Nold v Commission* [1974], ECR 491 (508); Cases 351 and 360/85, *Dillinger Hüttenwerke a.o. v Commission* [1987], ECR 3639 (3669 ff).

56. On those methodologic matters see R. Zweigert, 'Grundsatzfragen der europäischen Rechtsangleichung', in *Festschrift für H.Dölle*, 1952, Vol.2, p.40; W. Schmeder, op. cit. supra note 29, p.17 with more detailed references.

57. On this requirement see Court of Justice, Case 281/84, *Zuckerfabrik Bedburg a.o. v Council and Commission* [1987], ECR 41 (94); Case 56/86 *Société pour l'exportation des sucres v OBEA* [1987], ECR 1423 (1449); Case 154/78, *Valsabbia a.o. v Commission* [1980], ECR 907 (1025 ff.).

58. Koch, in Grabitz (ed.), op. cit., Art. 86 note 1; Langen, Niederleithinger, Ritter and Schmidt, *Kommentar zum Kartellgesetz*, 6th ed. 1982, §22 GWB note EG 80; V. Emmerich, *Kartellrecht*, (6th ed. 1991), p.570 with further references to the jurisdiction (note 3).

59. See communication of the Commission COM(89) 334 Final, pp.6, 13.

60. Cf. Court of Justice, Case 85/76, *Hoffmann La Roche-Vitamine* [1979], ECR 461 (516 f).

61. See Immenga and Klaue, *Kommentar zum GWB*, (1981), § 103 GWB note 75; C. Stewing, op. cit., p.18.

Operations such as similar or dissimilar tie-in transactions or the construction and operation of pipelines by enterprises in the Community may be disregarded as services which establish a market because of their particular structure.[62]

Disregarding the operations discussed under para.4, there is neither a contractual practice nor a marketable capacity for the combined feeding-in and extracting of gas of a similar quantity and an equivalent quality. The overriding consideration here is the securing of a safe and economical gas supply, the quality of which remains constant.[63]

Since there is no factually relevant market, a further examination pursuant to Article 86 EEC Treaty is superfluous, especially the examination as to abuses.[64] Such considerations can only have subsidiary character.

The assumption of abuse would imply an obligation to contract which is at the expense of the owner of the pipeline while his competitor would be favoured. There is no precedence for this in the rulings of the European Court of Justice.[65]

Even a required comprehensive weighing of interests[66] will not lead to a situation of abuse, the reason simply being that the pipeline owner would be obliged to construct new pipelines for lack of capacity. This, however, is a measure which potential competitors can quite easily adopt themselves, as current examples show.

On the whole it is obvious that Article 86 EEC (and thus Article 87 also) have not been put into practice. The so-called 'common carrier' – or Third Party Access – model initially under discussion would not be supported by the wording and content of these provisions either.

---

62. Cf. B. Börner, in *Probleme der 4. Novelle zum GWB*, (Veröffentlichungen des Instituts für Energierecht an der Universität zu Köln), Vol.48 (1981), pp.77, 92; see in this context Court of Justice, Case 48/69, *ICI* [1972], ECR p.619 (665); Case 52/69, *Ciba-Geigy* [1972], ECR 787 (838); Case 53/69, *Sandoz* [1972], ECR 845 (849).

63. See Bramkamp, Ritzmann and Richter, 'Die energie- und gaswirtschaftliche Entwicklung im Jahr 1987', in *Die Entwicklung der Gaswirtschaft in der Bundesrepublik Deutschland im Jahre 1987*, p.387 f; W. Tegethoff, 'Novellierungsbestimmungen zum Kartellgesetz aus der Sicht der Energiewirtschaft', *FIW-Schriftenreihe Heft* 128, (1988), p.53: Weizsäcker, Schneider and Schmitt, *Erdgas im europäischen Binnenmarkt*, (1990), p.42 f.

64. On the different methods of examination, see a) Court of Justice, Case 6/72, *Continental Can* [1973], ECR 215 (244); joined Cases 6 and 7/73, *Commercial Solvents* [1974], ECR 223 (252 and 254); Case 85/76, *Hoffmann La Roche-Vitamine* [1979], ECR 461 (552 f); b) Court of Justice, Case 40ff/73, *Suiker Unie* [1975], ECR 1663 (2004); Case 27/76, *United Brands* [1978], ECR 207 (303); c) Court of Justice, Case 127/73 *SABAM* [1974], ECR 313 (316 f); Case 7/82 *Gesellschaft zur Verwertung von Leistungsschutzrechten mbh (GVL) v Commission* [1983], ECR 483 (507 ff); Case 41/83 *Italian Republic v Commission* [1985], ECR 873 (887). Furthermore: Koch, in Grabitz (ed.), op. cit., Art. 86 note 40.

65. The decisions in this context concerned other situations, see for instance joined Cases 6 and 7/73, *Commercial Solvents* [1974], ECR 223; Case 27/76, *United Brands* [1978], ECR 207; Case 77/77, *British Petrol* [1978], ECR 1513.

66. Cf. Court of Justice, Case 127/73 *SABAM* [1974], ECR 313 (316 f); Case 7/82 *Gesellschaft zur Verwertung von Leistungsschutzrechten mbh (GVL) v Commission* [1983], ECR 483 (507 ff); Case 41/83 *Italian Republic v Commission* [1985], ECR 873 (887); on the consideration of public interests within the Community Law see Case 41/83, *British Telecommunication* [1985], ECR 873 (887). Furthermore Koch, in Grabitz (ed.), op. cit., Art. 86 note 43; C. Stewing, op. cit., p.56.

3.2.5 Compatibility of the Directive with Further Contractual Law and General Legal Principles

The draft of the directive on the transit of natural gas via large networks violated the basic right of property as recognised in the Community's legal system.[67]

The obligations imposed upon the undertakings concerned to place their pipeline networks at the disposal of other companies requesting transit so that these companies can transfer gas does not affect a complete or partial revocation of positions protected by property law and thus does not result in expropriation. It does, however, clearly encroach upon the competence – equally protected by the Community's legal order – freely to decide about the use of one's own pipeline system. It is thus an encroachment upon the exercise of property rights.

Following the rulings of the European Court of Justice, such restrictions are only legal if they remain in the framework of overall social obligations, *ie* if they correspond to the general public interest and do not exceed the necessary extent.[68] The standard to be used is the degree to which the citizens of the Community are forced to rely on the use of their property. In view of the rulings of the European Court of Justice up to this point such a social obligation can only be assumed if the denial of the service would lead to a complete collapse of the existing commerce. This absolutely necessary condition of dependence is not given as the starting point upon which the drafts of the directive were based. Apart from the fact that no gas supplier in a member state who desires the 'transit' of gas would be endangered in his economic existence if the transit were not granted, these suppliers will be able to go on functioning exactly as before. It is only their opportunity to extend their business position which would be restricted. In this context it must also be taken into consideration that taking advantage of this opportunity would not be the result of their own efforts, but would to a considerable extent derive from the efforts of potential competitors. Finally, it must be remembered that – at least in the Federal Republic of Germany – no one is prohibited from establishing his own pipeline system.

One must also see an infringement of the basic right of property as recognised in the Community's legal system in respect of the material requirements which the Court of Justice regarded as crucial in the *Hauer* case.[69] In contrast to the basic situation in that case the transit obligation does not simply affect one of several basic possibilities for use which can only be realised in the future; it rather affects already existing real and concrete uses which are totally based on the guarantee of personal property. Moreover, the transit obligation constitutes a positive duty to act which has immediate effects on competitors, and thus it is a serious encroachment on basic guarantees of freedom. Already rendered services are placed at the disposal of competitors without being justified by absolute necessity or a present emergency. In this context it will also be relevant if the transit obligation is standardised without a temporal limitation, in contrast to the prohibition of usage which was applied in the above-cited case.

67. See Hüffer, Ipsen and Tettinger, op. cit., p.226.
68. For instance Case 44/79, *Hauer v Land RheinlandPfalz* [1979] ECR 3727 (3746 f); U. Everling, 'Eigentumsordnung und Wirtschaftsordnung in der Europäischen Gemeinschaft', in F.S. Raiser, (1974), p.379 ff.
69. Case 44/79, *Hauer v Land Rheinland-Pfalz* [1979] ECR 3727 (3748).

The principle of equality inherent in Community law prohibits the Community's bodies from applying dissimilar conditions to equivalent transactions and equivalent conditions to dissimilar transactions.[70] The draft of the directives did not conform to the legal requirement from this standpoint either.[71]

The very fact that the member states have variant structures[72] as far as energy supplies are concerned leads to essential differences: while in most of the member states a two-track system applies, in which transportation and distribution are two separate and independent activities, the situation in the UK and France is essentially different. In these countries there is only a single organisation which takes care of the transportation and distribution of gas. In addition there is a particular structural aspect in the energy supply of the Federal Republic of Germany, where there are supra-regional, regional, and local gas supply companies. Here the transportation of gas constitutes a dependent branch of gas supplying as a whole, which – contrary to what the Commission says[73] – cannot be characterised as an independent transport function.

These commercial gas companies are rather firms which as business enterprises transport gas from the point where the supplier makes it available to the point where the customer takes control of it. Even in cases where these firms are so-called 'Community firms', they are by no means comparable to the 'transport companies' in the member states with nationalised structures.

There are also variations in respect of the different degrees of state participation[74] in the gas companies. Whereas in most of the member states the state plays a predominant role – eg in the case of nationalisation it holds a monopoly – there are specific peculiarities with regard to the Federal Republic of Germany: here the share of the energy sector under private ownership is significantly higher.

The Commission also recognises that only in the Federal Republic of Germany is there in principle competition between several companies, and it notes a market-orientation there as well as a reliance on the factors of the open market economy.[75]

These specific aspects of the situation in the Federal Republic of Germany were not given enough consideration in the directives. If the energy sector in the member states with predominantly nationalised structures were, because of the material stipulations of Article 90 para.2 EEC Treaty, to be exempted from the provisions regulating competition, this would cause a discrimination against already liberalised energy sectors. An even more serious consideration is that the gas directive would affect 29 firms in the Federal Republic of Germany, while in other member states only one or at most two companies would as a rule be involved.

70. See Case 6/71, *Rheinmühlen Düsseldorf v Einfuhr- und Vorratsstelle für Getreide und Futtermittel* [1971] ECR 823 (823 f). Concerning the constitutional law in Germany see only BVerfGE 49, 148 (165); M. Sachs, *Die Grenzen des Diskrimierungsverbots*, (1987).
71. Also D. Kuhnt, 'Übertragung von Strom nach deutschem und europäischem Recht', in *Festschrift für Lukes* (1990), p.41. Fundamentally Case 78/82, *Commission v Italy* [1983] ECR 1956; joined Cases 15 and 16/76, *France v Commission* [1979] ECR 322; A. Bleckmann, 'Das Verbot der Wettbewerbsverfläschung', in *Festschrift für Lukes* (1990), p.271 (273).
72. COM(89) 334 Final, July 12 1989, p.4.
73. COM(89) 334 Final, July 12 1989, p.5; COM(88) 238 Final, May 2 1988, p.46.
74. COM(89) 334 Final, July 12 1989, p.5.
75. COM(88) 238 Final, May 2 1988, p.46; COM(88) 174 Final, May 3 1988, pp.52, 59 (consequences); COM(89) 334 Final, July 12 1989, p.5.

The protection of individual rights is furthermore guaranteed in the Community by the absolute necessity of complying with the principle of proportionality.[76]

In view of the principle of appropriateness it must be recalled that the major objective of the Directives is the guaranteeing or even the increasing of the energy supplies available at the present time. Running counter to this goal, however, on the one hand are the predicted effects of a general transit obligation in the economic sector; and on the other hand the objections voiced about the availability of the evidence for and the distribution of 'free transit capacity'. It has also been established that the premiss laid down by the Commission itself – namely that an access of third parties (*eg* industrial clients) is to be prevented[77] – can by no means be absolutely guaranteed by the implementation of the binding provisions of the Directives.

Further proof that the Directives are inappropriate can be found in the fact that it is unlikely that the consumer gas prices will go down as hoped;[78] even the Commission itself is aware of the risk that rather a rise in prices for the small consumers could be the result.

The material and legal provisions of the Directives are moreover not 'necessary' for the attaining of the objectives set. An approximation of the diverging gas supply structures would not only correspond to the justified interest in introducing a system of free competition; it would also encroach to a far smaller extent upon the individual interests involved. In particular it must be stated that upon implementation of the Directives, those member states in which competition is already a given fact will be placed at a severe disadvantage, while those monopolistic states, which totally lack market characteristics, would hardly suffer any inconveniences.[79]

With these regulations the Commission has ultimately chosen not only a disproportionate, but even a downright counterproductive point of departure. In all vertically structured energy supply systems transit obligations have much less effect than in the context of liberal market structures. In the last analysis a discrimination of liberal market structures is caused – especially if compared with the vertically integrated state economies.[80]

3.3 Consequences for the Electricity Directive

The examination of the draft for the electricity directive also led to serious objections as to its compatibility with the provisions of the EEC Treaty.

In view of the Common Standpoint adopted by the Council of Ministers on May 21 1990,[81] some further basic modifications of the original draft were to be expected and meanwhile realised.

---

76. See Case 1/73, *Deuka v Einfuhr- und Vorratsstelle für Getreide und Futtermittel* [1973], ECR 723 (729); Case 281/84, *Zuckerfabrik Bedburg v Council and Commission* [1987], ECR 49 (94); Case 116/82, *Commission v Bundesrepublik Deutschland* [1986], ECR 2519 (2526).

77. See COM(89) 334 Final, July 12 1989, p.14 and 3.

78. Same opinion: E. Steindorff, 'Durchleitung von Gas im Binnenmarkt für Energie', *RIW* 1989, Suppl. 1 to Issue 1, p.7; H.-W. Arndt, 'Common Carrier bei Strom und Gas', *RIW* 1989, Suppl. 7 to Issue 10, p.8.

79. COM(88) 238 Final, May 2 1988, pp.43, 46; Hüffer, Ipsen and Tettinger,op. cit., p.241 ff.

80. For instance, Weizsäcker, Schneider and Schmitt, op. cit.

81. See press communication 70-G (615/90), p.5 ff.

3.3.1 The Scope of Possibilities for Interpretation as far as Individual Formulations in the Directive are Concerned

The examination on the basis of the specificity obligation[82] led to objections in the case of the electricity transit directive as well. There were interpretational uncertainties concerning the meaning of the terms 'electricity transit' and 'high voltage transmission system', even though the Common Standpoint of the Council of Ministers had cleared up a few of the doubts. What cannot be clarified beyond doubt either is the meaning of the objective pursued by the regulation,[83] namely 'improvement of the supply guarantee', especially since the opinions on these objectives are very different in the individual member states.

3.3.2 No Incorporation of a 'Transit Obligation' Concerning Electricity in the EEC Treaty

Also, it is not possible to derive from the directives of the EEC Treaty governing the establishment of free movement of goods[84] and services[85] provisions for the creation of a transit obligation for the electricity sector – while at the same time complying with the normative regulations in the member states and considering the degree of liberalisation already attained.[86] Consequently the envisaged approximation measure exceeded the regulation objectives set down in the Treaty.

3.3.3 No Authorisation of the Commission to Undertake an Approximation of Laws According to Article 100A EEC Treaty

There are also considerable doubts as to whether the material conditions laid down in Article 100A EEC Treaty[87] are fulfilled.

No regulations impeding electricity transit[88] are to be found for electricity exchange occurring between member states – at any rate as far as the situation in the Federal Republic of Germany is concerned.

The fact that the Directive is illegal was also deduced from an examination of the draft in the light of the principle of reasonableness, which must be applied in

82. Cf. *eg* I. Pernice, in Grabitz (ed.), op. cit., Art. 164 note 92 with further references to the jurisdiction of the Court of Justice.

83. On the requirement, that objectives of EC activities have to be specified as well, see *eg* R. Zweigert, 'Grundsatzfragen der Europäischen Rechtsangleichung, ihrer Schöpfung und Sicherung', in *Festschrift für Dölle*, Vol.2, 1963, p.406 f.

84. On the requirements of the principle of the free movement of goods see above (note 39) and the there cited judgments of the Court of Justice.

85. The European Court of Justice seems to understand 'electricity' as a good in the sense of Art. 30 EEC Treaty, cf. Case 6/64, *Costa v E.N.E.L.* [1964], ECR 1251 (1273). Especially on the requirements following from the principle of free movement of services see Court of Justice, Case 33/74, *van Binsbergen v Bestuur vaan de Bedrijfsvereiniging voor de Metaalnijverheid* [1974], ECR 1299 (1308 f); and Case 279/80, *A.J. Webb* [1982], ECR 3305 (3324 ff).

86. See in this context communication of the Commission, COM(89) 336 Final, July 14 1989, p.5.

87. See above 3.1.1 and the there cited literature and jurisdiction.

88. Especially on the requirement of impeding particular rights into the member states see H.C. Eiden, in Bleckmann, *Europarecht*, (5th ed. 1990), p.612; H.C. Eiden, *Die Rechtsangleichung nach Art. 100 des EWG-Vertrages*, 1984, p.18 with further references; W. Schmeder, supra note 29, op. cit., p.10; E. Steindorff, op. cit, supra note 53, p.98.

Community law as well.[89] Against the backdrop of the highly heterogeneous energy supply concepts in the individual member states[90] it is in particular not foreseeable whether the instrument of a transit obligation will be suitable to attain the objectives pursued by the directive. The 'necessity' of such a measure is also doubtful in view of the fact that electricity exchange is already being practised on a voluntary basis and on a large scale in the UCPTE alliance.[91]

3.3.4 Rules on Competition and Electricity Transit

As in the case of gas transit the question of the market is also a decisive one for electricity transit as well, if an abuse in the sense of Article 86 EEC Treaty is considered.[92]

The market demarcation necessary in this context has in turn to proceed from the service demanded by the market partner.[93] It is not easy to determine the exact nature of this problem. In the actual given context there is for technological reasons no identifiable connection between the energy fed into the system by a company and the energy extracted. Thus it is not possible to speak of a 'transit' process in a factual sense.[94]

In so far as the demand means 'transit' it should to be noted that transit means the system's operator is obliged to tolerate the feeding-in of electrical energy; in this context the feeding-in takes place because a consumer is to be supplied under the conditions of the feeding-in company instead of under the conditions of the electrical supplier responsible for making the supply of electricity available.[95] Consequently 'transit' in the sense of the Directive is only given if other requirements of the Directive are also fulfilled (transit between the large networks; at least a trilateral process, *ie* three undertakings are concerned; supplier and consumer network within the Community area; the crossing of at least one inter-Community frontier; a sales contract for electricity of at least one year).[96]

---

89. On this principle see Court of Justice, for instance Case 1/73, *Westzucker GmbH v Einfuhr- und Vorratsstelle für Zucker* [1973], ECR 723 (729); joined Cases 17 and 20/61, *Klöckner and Hoesch* [1962], ECR 653 (686); Case 281/84, *Zuckerfabrik Bedburg a.o. v Council and Commission* [1987], ECR 41 (94); Case 116/82, *Commission v Bundesrepublik* [1986], ECR 2519 (2526). Especially on the requirement of specificity see Court of Justice, Case 29/69, *Stauder v Stadt Ulm* [1969], ECR 419 (425); B. Beutler, in v.d.Groeben, v.Boeckh, Thiesing and Ehlermann (ed.), op. cit., supra note 48 notes 10 ff.

90. See for instance A.A. Schweitzer, *Der grenzüberschreitende Stromverbund in Europa*, (1984), p.77 f; especially on the characteristics and on the expected consequences in Germany: ibid., p.18 ff., p. 146 ff; E. Steindorff, op. cit., supra note 78, Suppl. 1 to Issue 1, p.1 ff.

91. See A.A. Schweitzer, op. cit., p.92 f. and 100 f.

92. Cf. Koch, in Grabitz (ed.), op. cit., Art. 86 note 1; Langen, Niederleithinger, Ritter and Schmidt, op. cit., 22 GWB note EG 80; V. Emmerich, op. cit., with references to the jurisdiction (footnote 3).

93. *Eg*, Gleiss and Hirsch, op. cit., Art. 87 note 12; H. Schröter, op. cit., Art. 86 note 29.

94. Cf. Verband der Deutschen Elektrizitätswirtschaft (VDEW) (ed.), *Der europäische Strommarkt*, (1988), p.19; W. Kiwit, *Bericht der Deutschen Verbundgesellschaft Heidelberg*, (1987), p.1 f; G. Klätte, 'Wettbewerb und EG-Binnenmarkt', in *Energiewirtschaftliche Tagesfragen (et)* (1988), p.417; D. Kuhnt, op. cit., supra note 71, p.412. Furthermore the Commission's paper 'Extension of electricity delivery within the community', p.3 No.7.

95. See Hüffer, Ipsen and Tettinger, op. cit., p.275.

96. This way of interpretation of Art. 3II whose wording concerns only the obligation of communication follows the answer of the responsible Commissioner on a written question to energy politics, cf. C190/16 (July 30 1990).

The transfer supplies which occur in practice, in particular the services rendered in the UCPTE area, typically do not fulfil the above-mentioned criteria. In addition there is no actually existing 'transit' market in the sense that alliance services on a large scale would be made available commercially for a transit with the above-mentioned characteristics.[97]

The question as to a marketable capacity for unilateral long-term transits has to be seen in a technological and economic context of electricity supply; in this context the requirement of a safe and inexpensive electricity supply is to be given particular prominence. If in the last analysis an answer is only possible after weighing all the circumstances, still one can say that the tendency will be to make available only very limited capacities.[98]

As far as in individual cases such individual capacities can be confirmed, the problem is still one of local market demarcation.[99] For Europe at least the UCPTE area is to be considered a relevant market.

In view of the geographical extent of the relevant market a dominant position cannot simply be confirmed, and if it can be confirmed, then only for essential parts of one large member state.[100]

If a market-dominant enterprise refuses to comply with a transit demand, then the question arises as to whether it has abused its market power. What was true for the gas sector is also true here: abuse would amount to an obligation to contract in favour of a potential competitor and such a legal consequence has no precedent in the rulings of the European Court of Justice.

If nevertheless an examination of abuse is regarded as appropriate,[101] those arguments have to be taken into consideration arising from the technological characteristics of electricity supply and from the double objectives of a safe and economical electricity supply.

Finally the assumption of an abuse is incompatible with the decision to place a high evaluation on private property, which is inherent in European law;[102] for the encroachment upon the electrical network would be an infringement on the central sphere of a company's freedom to carry out economic activities, and this would occur in favour of a competitor and at the same time on the grounds of the active obligation to provide support (compensatory measures in particular for providing frequencies).

The serious legal objections outlined above would increase even further, if the 'common carrier' or TPA model initially discussed were realised. This is true in view of all the reasons given, in particular, however, for private property as protected by European law because the support of a competitor would require not only

97. Cf. Hüffer, Ipsen and Tettinger, op. cit., p.275 ff; J.F. Baur, 'Sinn und Unsinn einer Energierechtsreform', in *Festschrift für Lukes*, (1989), p.253 (267); D. Kuhnt, op. cit., supra note 71 p.419 with further references in note 28.

98. Cf. Hüffer, Ipsen and Tettinger, op. cit., p.278 ff. with more references.

99. Cf. Koch, in Grabitz (ed.), op. cit., Art. 86 EWGV note 39.

100. See Court of Justice, joined Cases 40ff./73, *Suiker Unie* [1975], ECR 1663 (1696); Case 26/76, *Metro* [1977], ECR 1875 (1904); Case 27/76, *United Brands* [1978], ECR 207 (290); Case 85/76, *Hoffmann La Roche-Vitamine* [1979], ECR 461 (526 ff). Further Koch, in E. Grabitz (ed.), op. cit., Art. 86 note 24 f; H. Schröter, op. cit., Art. 86 notes 14 ff.

101. On the different methods of examination used by the Court of Justice see note 64.

102. See note 35 and Court of Justice, Case 44/79, *Hauer v Land Rheinland-Pfalz* [1979], ECR 3727 (3728).

compensatory measures but over and above this the sacrifice of one's own ability to feed in to the network. 'Negotiated' TPA may be a different matter depending, however, on how it is instituted.

Despite some difficulties[103] it is not out of the question to have recourse to Article 90, para.2 EEC Treaty, but this is not necessary. The peculiar characteristics of the energy sector must and can be done justice to in the context of Article 86 EEC Treaty alone, as has been shown.

3.3.5 Compatibility of the Directive with Other Contract Law and General Legal Principles

The obligations imposed upon the undertakings concerned to place their networks at the disposal of other companies requesting transit so that these companies can transfer electricity does not affect a complete or partial revocation of positions protected by property law and thus does not result in expropriation. It does, however, clearly encroach upon the competence – equally protected by the Community's legal order – freely to decide about the use of one's own network system. It is thus an encroachment upon the exercise of property rights.

Following the rulings of the European Court of Justice, such restrictions are only legal if they remain in the framework of overall social obligations, *ie* if they correspond to the general public interest and do not exceed the necessary extent.[104] The standard to be used is the degree to which the citizens of the Community are forced to rely on the use of their property. In view of the rulings of the European Court of Justice such a social obligation can only be assumed if the denial of the service would lead to a complete collapse of the existing commerce. This absolutely necessary condition of dependence is not given as the starting point upon which the drafts of the Directive were based. Apart from the fact that no electricity supplier in a member state who desires the 'transit' of electricity would be endangered in his economic existence if the transit were not granted, these suppliers will be able to go on functioning exactly as before. It is only their opportunity to extend their business position which would be restricted. In this context it must also be taken into consideration that taking advantage of this opportunity would not be the result of their own efforts, but would to a considerable extent derive from the efforts of potential competitors.[105] Finally it must be remembered that – at least in the Federal Republic of Germany – no one is prohibited from establishing his own network system.

One must also see an infringement of the basic right of property as recognised in the Community's legal system in respect of the material requirements which the Court of Justice regarded as crucial in the *Hauer* case.[106] In contrast to the basic situation in that case the transit obligation does not simply affect one of several basic possibilities for use which can only be realised in the future; it rather affects

---

103. Concerning the requirement of a good or service of 'public economic interest' see I. Pernice, in Grabitz (ed.), op. cit., Art. 90 note 36 f. Concerning the act of entrusting see Court of Justice, Case 127/73, *BRT v SABAM* [1974], ECR 313 No.19; and Case 172/80, *Züchner* [1981], ECR 2021 (2030).

104. *Eg,* Case 44/79, *Hauer v Land Rheinland-Pfalz* [1979] ECR 3727 (3746 f); U. Everling, supra note 68.

105. See A.A. Schweitzer, op. cit., p.179.

already existing real and concrete uses which are totally based on the guarantee of personal property. Moreover the transit obligation constitutes a positive duty to act which has immediate effects on competitors and thus it is a serious encroachment on basic guarantees of freedom. In contrast to the initial situation in the *Hauer* case this encroachment cannot even be justified as an existing situation of emergency. The Commission itself has established that the existing electricity alliance has been steadily extended beyond the national boundaries as a further logical development of the local, regional and national electricity system and has led to the growth of one of the most strongly integrated high voltage networks in the world.

The claim to equality of treatment which is also protected as one of the basic rights contains the requirement to apply similar conditions to equivalent transactions and to treat dissimilar conditions according to the peculiarity of their nature. The draft of the directive on the transit of electricity via large networks did not conform to the legal requirements from this standpoint either.

It has been determined that the structures of national electricity supplies in the Community are extremely heterogeneous. Whereas in some member states there are state-run monopolies (*eg* France and Italy), the Federal Republic of Germany is characterised[107] by undertakings under public law, mixed undertakings, and private undertakings.

This specific German situation[108] was not considered when the directive was established. If the energy sector in the member states with predominantly nation-alised structures were, because of the material stipulations of Article 90, para.2 EEC Treaty, to be exempted from the provisions regulating competition, this would mean that energy sectors with an already liberalised structure would be placed at a disadvantage. An even more serious consideration is that the electricity transit Directive would affect a large number of companies in the Federal Republic of Germany while in the other member states only one or at most two companies would as a rule be involved.

The protection of the basic rights is furthermore guaranteed in the Community by the absolute necessity for compliance with the principle of proportionality with its three components; appropriateness, necessity, and suitability.[109]

The major objective of lawmaking in the Community is the introduction of a free, unadulterated internal market for electricity, *ie* the guarantee or even the increasing of the energy supplies available at the present time.[110] Running counter to this goal, however, on the one hand are the predicted effects of a general transit obligation in the economic sector; and on the other hand the objections voiced about the availability of the evidence for and distribution of free transit capacity. In view of the objective to be reached, 'a guaranteeing of a Community-wide supply of electricity', it should further be criticised that for lack of specificity of content there are no indications as to how this objective can be reached by means of a transit obligation. Rather, the existing system, which is known to guarantee a supply of electricity, would be impaired. This system is at present characterised by the voluntary collaboration of the electricity supply companies in the form of the UCPTE.

106. Case 44/79, *Hauer v Land Rheinland-Pfalz* [1979] ECR 3727 (3748).

107. COM(88) 238 Final, May 2 1988, pp.50, 52 (note 9).

108. COM(88) 238 Final, May 2 1988, p.50.

109. See Case 1/73, *Deuka v Einfuhr- und Vorratsstelle für Getreide und Futtermittel* [1973] ECR 723 (729); Case 281/84, *Zuckerfabrik Bedburg v Council and Commission* [1987] ECR 49 (94); Case 116/82, *Commission v Bundesrepublik Deutschland* [1986] ECR 2519 (2526).

The material and legal provisions of the directive are moreover not 'necessary' for the attaining of the objective set. An approximation of the diverging energy supply structures would not only correspond to the justified interest in introducing a system of free enterprise; it would also encroach to a far lesser extent upon the individual interests concerned. In comparison, the Commission's point of approach seems counterproductive. In vertically structured energy supply systems transit obligations have a far lesser effect than in the context of liberal market structures. In the final analysis the result is thus a discrimination of liberal market structures as compared with vertically integrated state economies.

4.0 POSSIBILITIES OF LEGAL RECOURSE FOR ENTERPRISES IN THE FEDERAL REPUBLIC OF GERMANY

I. Any measure by a body of the European Community, which is intended to produce an individual legal effect – no matter what external form it takes – is open to appeal;[111] the decisive criterion for the appeal is that the plaintiff be directly and individually affected[112] by the action carried out on the basis of EC law.

To the extent that administrative agencies, whether they be agencies of the member states or agencies of the European Community, still have to put a legal provision into practice, ie to the extent that a further step must be taken to implement the provision, an immediate effect is fundamentally to be excluded. Thus, at this point, the possibility of legal recourse would not be open.

The European Court of Justice[113] has, however, affirmed the possibility of appeal in so far as – prior to the adoption of a Community measure – national authorities have stated the intention of taking a particular decision or if the means of executing the measure is as a matter of course clear and the possibility of a discretionary decision only remains as a 'purely theoretical' possibility, as when Community measures regulate situations pertaining to the individual or effectuate a direct impairment of interest without the necessary enforcements.

Cases appear possible in which – in view of the rulings of the European Court and the consenting jurisprudence – individual undertakings mentioned in the appendices of the Directives will be affected in the preliminary stages of national transformation.

II. If, after the adoption of the Directives into the German legal system, the illegality of the Directives is asserted before a German court and the court has to make a decision as to whether the transit Directive complies with the primary law as stated

110. COM(89) 336 Final, July 14 1989, p.16.
111. See joined Cases 789 and 790/79, *Calpak SpA v Commission* [1980] ECR 1949 ff (1961).
112. See W. Bernhardt, *Verfassungsprinzipien – Verfassungsgerichtsfunktionen – Verfassungsprozeßrecht im EWG-Vertrag*, (1987), p.292; Case 30/67, *Industria Molitoria a.o. v Council and Commission* [1968] ECR 174 (182); H. Wenig, in Grabitz (ed.), op. cit., Art. 173 note 53.
113. Case 62/70, *W.A. Bock v Commission* [1971] ECR 897 (908); Case 11/82, *Piraiki/Patraiki a.o. v Commission* [1985] ECR 207 (242); joined Cases 106 and 107/63, *A. Töpfer a.o. v Commission* [1965] ECR 548 (556).

in the EEC Treaty and with the general principles of Community law among which are also the basic rights, then this court can refer the question to the European Court of Justice for a decision (Article 177, para.2 EEC Treaty). If a competent court makes a decision in the final instance, then it must report the decision to the European Court of Justice.

Such an obligation to make a report to the European Court also exists if an enterprise involved objects to a decision in an individual case by a member state on the basis of a transformation provision.[114] This derives from the fact that any examination of this question implicitly comprises the problem of the legality of the transformation law as it is to be evaluated in the context of European law.

According to German law an arbitrary non-compliance with this obligation to report such decisions to the European Court is tantamount to a violation of the basic right to a 'legal judge' in the sense of Article 101, para.1, (2) Basic Law.[115]

After the Directives have been implemented, it now lies in the jurisdiction of the European Court to examine a violation of basic rights[116] and stipulations of the rule of law, using the objectives laid down in the Directives as a guideline. The basic objections raised against the Directives have to do with central issues of their content. Consequently it is in the jurisdiction of the European Court to determine whether these constitute a violation of the basic rights of Community law.

Only after such an examination can the German Constitutional Court deal with the question as to whether that ruling complies with the basic laws as they are laid down in the German constitution. In so far as the basic rights guaranteed by the German constitution are not realised through the means of legal recourse provided in Community law, the German Constitutional Court can by exception be appealed to and can, if necessary, rule that a violation of the constitution has occurred.[117]

If a legal issue centres upon questions having to do with the scope for national implementation, the national law courts' competence is increased in comparison. The German Constitutional Court would have to interpret such provisions in the light of German basic rights[118] and declare them unconstitutional if necessary.

III. If German legal bodies co-operate in establishing EC Directives, this does not constitute an exercise of German legal authority according to the opinion of the German Constitutional Court, but only a contribution to laying down a provision which can only affect private individuals after its enactment or after its implementation into German law.

---

114. See in particular: I. Pernice, 'Gemeinschaftsverfassung und Grundrechtsschutz-Grundlagen, Bestand und Perspektiven', *NJW* (1990), p.2409 (2412); R. Streinz, *Der Verfassungsstaat als Glied einer europäischen Gemeinschaft*, (DVBl. 1990), p.949 (957); R. Streinz, op. cit., supra note 4.5, pp.178 ff, 188 ff.

115. See BVerfGE 73, 339 (366 ff), 'Solange II'.

116. See P.J. Tettinger, 'Die Grundrechtsberechtigung von Energieversorgungsunternehmen im Europäischen Gemeinschaftsrecht', in *F.S. Börner*, (1992), p.625 ff.

117. BVerfG EuGRZ 1989, 339 (340).

118. BVerfG EuGRZ 1989, 339 (340); R. Scholz, in Friauf and R. Scholz (ed.), *Europarecht und Grundgesetz*, (1990), p.60; U. Everling, op. cit., supra note 41, p.212.

Chapter 8

The Impact of EC Law on Employment Offshore

Fraser Davidson

1.0 INTRODUCTION

This Chapter concerns a subject which has rarely been considered over the years, so that much of the content is conjectural. The subject is considered generally, then aspects of health and safety are particularly considered, as it is in this area that the most significant developments have occurred.

2.0 EMPLOYMENT OFFSHORE AND BRITISH EMPLOYMENT LAW

2.1 Introduction – Offshore Employment Law

As those familiar with employment offshore will know, the initial approach of Great Britain was to restrict the application of employment legislation to Great Britain itself and its territorial waters. Yet, this approach was abandoned during the 1970s, so that currently most employment legislation, including anti-discrimination legislation in the employment sphere, extends to employment for the purposes of activities connected with the exploration of the sea-bed or subsoil or the exploitation of their natural resources in designated areas of the Continental Shelf.[1] This legislation even extends to the Frigg Gas Field in the Norwegian sector of the Continental Shelf, provided certain conditions are met.[2]

1. Exceptions include the Wages Act 1986; and the Transfers of Undertakings (Protection of Employment) Regulations 1981; SI 1981/1794.
2. See *eg* the Employment Protection (Offshore Employment) Order 1976 SI 1976/500 (as amended).

2.2 British Labour Law and EC Law

2.2.1 Interpretation of Domestic Legislation

The extension of British legislation offshore involves in certain cases the indirect application of EC norms, given that some of that legislation aims to implement EC Directives.[3] It is also the case that the applicable provisions of the Treaty, together with relevant Regulations and Directives are important in the context of interpreting the provisions of British legislation. The European Court has observed[4] that

in applying national law and in particular a national law specifically introduced to implement a directive, national courts are required to interpret domestic law in the light of the wording and purpose of the directive.

Following that line, the House of Lords has in a couple of cases in the employment sphere deliberately interpreted the terms of British legislation to give effect to the intention, as interpreted by the European Court of Justice, behind the provisions of EC law which that legislation purported to implement, even though the interpretation thus arrived at seemed to be at odds with the clear words of the legislation.[5] One limitation on this approach was perhaps suggested by the case of *Duke v GEC Reliance*[6] where their Lordships held that British legislation which was enacted prior to the coming into effect of an EC Directive could not be construed in the light of that Directive. However, the soundness of that view became questionable following the decision in *Marleasing SA v Commercial Internacional de Alimentacion SA*[7] where the ECJ pointed out that

the obligation of Member States under a Directive to achieve its objects, and their duty by virtue of Article 5 of the Treaty to take all necessary steps to ensure the fulfilment of that obligation, binds all authorities of Member States, including national courts within their jurisdiction. It follows that in applying national law, whether the provisions concerned predate or postdate the Directive, the national court asked to interpret national law is bound to do so in every way possible in light of the text and the aim of the Directive to achieve the results envisaged by it . . . .

In light of the above case, the House of Lords has now accepted that[8]

it is for a United Kingdom court to construe domestic legislation in any field covered by a Community Directive so as to accord with the interpretation of the Directive as laid down by the European Court, if that can be done without distorting the meaning of the domestic legislation: this is so whether the domestic legislation came after or preceded the Directive.

---

3. *Eg* the Equal Pay (Amendment) Regulations 1983 SI 1983/1794; amend the Equal Pay Act 1970 so as to give effect to Art. 119 of the Treaty and Directive 75/117 (Equal Pay).

4. In *von Colson v Land Nordrhein-Westfalen* [1984] ECR 1891 (1909).

5. See *Pickstone v Freemans plc* [1988] IRLR 357; HL and *Litster v Forth Dry Dock & Engineering Co. Ltd.* [1989] IRLR 161; HL.

6. [1988] ICR 339.

7. [1992] 1 CMLR 305 (322).

8. Per Lord Keith in *Webb v EMO Air Cargo (UK) Ltd* [1993] IRLR 27 (32).

2.2.2 *The Application of EC Law to the Continental Shelf*

The discussion thus far has referred to EC obligations which have received effect through national legislation, which has in turn been extended offshore. But what of the more fundamental question of whether EC law in itself extends offshore? The terms of Article 227, which indicate that the Treaty shall apply to the Kingdom of X etc, seem to imply that the geographical scope of the Treaty is confined to the territory within the national boundaries of each member state. On the other hand, the view of the EC Commission, expressed over 20 years ago, is that

The exercise of the Member States of their sovereign rights for the purpose of economic activity, in particular for the exploration and exploitation of the natural resources of the continental shelf, is subject to the provisions of the Treaty. The same principle holds true for the application of national laws to economic activities engaged in by private individuals for the same purposes.[9]

Yet, the question has never been determined by the ECJ, and indeed one might suspect that member states were deliberately avoiding such determination, as in the case of *Re the Key Gibraltar Oil Drilling Rig*[10] where the National Insurance Commissioner referred the question whether an oil rig resting on the Continental Shelf of a member state was to be regarded as part of the territory of that state for the purposes of EC Social Security rules. The case was settled by the Department of Health and Social Security and the reference withdrawn.

Nevertheless, the views of the ECJ in a slightly different context are instructive. In a number of cases the ECJ has upheld the view that the Treaty applies to a member state's exclusive fisheries zone, on the basis that the Treaty applies to any geographical area over which a member state claims sovereignty or jurisdiction.[11] Thus, it would be most surprising if the ECJ were now to hold that the Treaty did not apply to the Continental Shelf. In the same way, references in certain of the provisions relating to freedom of movement of workers to the 'territory' of member states might be expected to be construed accordingly.

2.2.2.1 Direct Effect of EC Law   If EC law does extend offshore, then certain of its provisions may have an immediate importance to offshore employment. This is because they have direct effect, *ie* they confer rights upon individuals without the need to be implemented by national legislation. Among those which are significant in this context are:

Freedom of movement
Article 7 which proscribes any discrimination on grounds of nationality; Article 48(1) which establishes the right of freedom of movement for workers within the Community;[12]

9. EC Bulletin 11 (1970) p.51.
10. [1979] 1 CMLR 362.
11. See *Officier van Justitie v Kramer* [1976] ECR 1279; *Commission v Ireland* [1978] ECR 417; and *France v UK* [1979] ECR 2923.
12. This should be seen alongside Art. 48(2) which proscribes 'discrimination based on nationality between workers of member states as regards employment, remuneration and other conditions of work and employment'. Similarly, Art. 48(3) confers the right (subject to limitations justified on grounds of public policy, public security or public health) 'to accept offers of employment actually made; to move freely within the territory of Member States for this purpose; and to stay in a Member State for the purposes of employment'. See also *Kenny v National Insurance Commissioner* [1978] ECR 1489; *Van Duyn v Home Office* [1974] ECR 1337; and Regulation 1612/68.

Equal Pay

Article 119 establishes the principle that men and women should receive equal pay[13] for equal work, while Directive 75/117 (Article 1) makes it clear that 'equal work' means the same work or work to which equal value is attributed. Article 119 also embraces indirect discrimination, *ie* the universal application of an ostensibly sex neutral criterion, which in reality affects a considerably greater proportion of one sex.[14] Thus employers could be obliged to justify, for example, the differential treatment of part-time workers. Current British legislation itself discriminates against certain part-timers by effectively excluding them from most employment protection rights. Yet, the House of Lords has recently found this to be in breach of Article 119.[15]

There might then still be an argument that part-timers may be able to invoke Article 119 to claim certain statutory rights denied to them under British employment legislation. Nevertheless, the practical significance of this for employment offshore is limited. Very few women are employed offshore, and part-time working is rare.[16]

2.2.2.2 Provisions without Direct Effect   There are a number of Directives which do not have direct effect which apply in the employment sphere. It is not intended to analyse all of these. Chief among them for the purpose of this Chapter, however, is Directive No.77/187, on the Safeguarding of Employees' Rights in the Event of Transfers of Undertakings, Businesses or Parts of Businesses, (the Acquired Rights Directive) which is implemented by the Transfers of Undertakings (Protection of Employment) Regulations 1981 SI 1981/1974. This Directive aims to protect the rights of workers when the enterprise where they work is taken over, and it is undoubtedly the case that the Regulations until recently fell far short of properly implementing its terms.[17]

13. According to the European Court of Justice 'pay' embraces any consideration, whether in cash or in kind, whether immediate or future, provided the worker receives it, albeit indirectly, in respect of his employment from his employer – *Defrenne v Belgium* [1971] ECR 445 (451). Thus pension benefits (*Barber v Guardian Royal Exchange Assurance Group* [1990] IRLR 240; ECJ), sick pay (*Rinner-Kuhn v FWW Spezial-Gebaudereinigung GmbH* [1989] IRLR 493; ECJ), and even travel facilities (*Garland v British Rail Engineering Ltd* [1982] IRLR 111; ECJ) fall within the definition. Also to be regarded as 'pay' are payments which statute obliges the employer to make to the employee, such as redundancy payments, unfair dismissal compensation (*R v Secretary of State for Employment ex parte Equal Opportunities Commission* [1991] IRLR 493; DC) and paid time off work (*Arbeiterwohlfahrt der Stadt Berlin e V v Botel* [1992] IRLR 423; ECJ and cf *Hairsine v Kingston-upon-Hull CC* [1992] IRLR 211; EAT).

14. *Bilka-Kaufhaus GmbH v Weber von Hartz* [1986] ECR 3047.

15. In *R v Secretary of State for Employment ex parte Equal Opportunities Commission*, decided March 3 1994.

16. In fact, given the requirement underpinning almost all British employment protection legislation that an employee have a certain period of continuous employment, many offshore workers will be effectively excluded from employment protection rights in any case, as continuous employment is premised on the idea that the employee is employed under a contract which normally involves him working for at least 16 hours each week, the point being that many offshore workers are alternately at home or offshore for long periods, so that it is difficult to claim that they 'normally' work at least 16 hours a week. See Employment Protection (Consolidation) Act 1978 sch.13 para.4; *Corton House Ltd v Skipper* [1981] ICR 307.

17. In particular they did not apply to a transfer of an 'undertaking or part of an undertaking which is not in the nature of a commercial venture' (reg. 2(1)) – an exclusion which is not to be found in the Directive and which the UK Government ultimately accepted was not justified. The commercial venture requirement was removed by the Trade Union Reform and Employment Rights Act 1993 s.33(2).

Nevertheless, a more fundamental problem confronts the application of these Regulations in an offshore employment context. They do not extend to the Continental Shelf at all.

What happens then, when a member state fails to confer upon workers all the rights which they should enjoy under EC law, either by imperfectly implementing its obligations through legislation, or by denying particular groups of employees the benefit of that legislation? It is, of course, open to the Commission to bring enforcement proceedings against a recalcitrant member state where the provisions of EC law are not directly effective, but are the employees affected denied an individual remedy? That appeared to be the case until recently, but is probably no longer the position in light of the judgment of the ECJ in the now celebrated case of *Francovich v Italy*.[18]

In that case the Court decided that a member state could be liable in damages to a disadvantaged individual where that state had failed to implement its EC obligations, provided that three conditions are met:

(1) that the result required by the Directive includes the conferring of rights for the benefit of individuals;
(2) that the content of these rights may be determined by reference to the Directive; and
(3) that there exists a causal link between the breach of the obligation of the State and the damage suffered by the persons affected.

Thus, it is conceivable that offshore workers might still be able to gain redress for breach of EC law obligations which are not directly applicable, although their right of action would be against the state, rather than their employer. Moreover, it is surely arguable that the three conditions referred to above are applicable to the non-extension of the Transfer of Undertakings regulations to employees offshore, since the essential purpose of the Directive is to preserve the employment rights of the individual employees affected.

Of course, this argument is premised on the view that EC law does indeed extend to the Continental Shelf and in this particular context a further uncertainty must be confronted. Directive 77/187 provides under Article 1(2) that

This Directive shall apply where and in so far as the undertaking, business or part of the business to be transferred is situated within the territorial scope of the Treaty.

This wording obviously invites the conclusion that the Directive applies only to the territory which physically forms part of the member states. Yet, once again it can be suggested that the concept of the territorial scope of the Treaty is legal rather than physical so that it would embrace any territory over which the member state exercises sovereignty.

2.3 EC Law and Offshore Employment – The Future

2.3.1 The Procedural Dimension

Having suggested that the provisions of the Treaty and any provisions made thereunder apply to the Continental Shelf, and having indicated how individuals

---

18. [1992] IRLR 84.

might find a basis for action under applicable provisions, even when not directly effective, what might the EC contribute to employment rights offshore in the future? Before considering substantive rights, it is important to look briefly at procedures for introducing new employment rights in the Community.

The reason why this is important is the UK government's traditional hostility to the extension of EC employment rights. Thus one requires to know what kind of measures can be piloted through the legislative mechanisms of the Community, despite opposition from the UK. Following the Single European Act, unanimity among member states was no longer necessary to introduce certain measures, as long as they could obtain a qualified majority in terms of Article 100A of the Treaty. However, Article 100A(2) states that the principle of the qualified majority does not extend to 'the free movement of persons, nor to those relating to the rights and interests of employed persons'. In other words, measures relating to employment still require unanimity. Yet there is one major exception in that by virtue of Article 118A a qualified majority is all that is required to introduce measures 'encouraging improvements, especially in the working environment, as regards the health and safety of workers'. In other words, health and safety measures can be piloted through against the opposition of the UK.

At the Maastricht Summit the opposition of the UK to the inclusion of the Social Chapter in the Treaty meant that the other eleven member states signed a separate Social Protocol, wherein they expressed their intention to 'continue along the path laid down by the Social Charter of 1989'. The broad effect of this is that the range of issues which can be decided by qualified majority vote is greatly expanded.[19] Of course, since the UK is not bound by the Social Protocol, any attempt to introduce provisions with binding effect in the UK must continue to depend upon a sufficient basis for the introduction of those provisions being found in the EC Treaty. To put matters simply, the principle of unanimity means that the UK government can prevent any measure affecting the rights of employed persons, with which it disagrees, achieving binding force on the UK, with the single exception of measures concerning health and safety.

Accordingly, most of the provisions of the Charter of the Fundamental Social Rights of Workers have little chance of attaining legal force in the UK (unless the government is obliged to adopt such provisions as a result of domestic political misfortune), and the same is true of most other proposed measures which are founded upon Article 100.[20] As we have seen, the exception is those measures which have a health and safety dimension such as the Directive on the Protection of Women Workers During and After Pregnancy,[21] the Directive Protecting Atypical

19. Thus it will include – working conditions; information and consultation of workers; equality at work between men and women; and integration of persons excluded from the labour market. The following matters will still require unanimity – social security and social protection of workers; protection of workers where their employment contract is terminated; representation and collective defence of the interests of workers and employers; conditions of employment for third country nationals; financial contributions for the promotion of employment and job creation. Certain matters, moreover, are regarded as outwith the legislative competence of the Community – pay; the right of association; and the right to strike or impose lock-outs.

20. Eg the draft Directives on Atypical Contracts of Employment (1982 C128/2); the Working Conditions of Part-time and Temporary Workers (1990 C224/4); Distortions of Competition through the Recruitment of Part-time and Temporary Workers (1990 C224/6) and the European Works Council (1991 L39/10).

21. 1990 C281/3.

Workers in Health and Safety Matters,[22] and the Draft Directive on the Organisation of Working Time.[23] In such matters the UK is restricted to attempting to dilute the form which the measure finally adopts.[24] Finally, it is possible that the UK may have to accept some limited form of employee participation under either the draft European Company Law Statute or the draft fifth Company Law Directive, since the basis for such measures would not be Article 100 but Article 54 (Freedom of Establishment), with a qualified majority being sufficient under Article 54(2).

3.0 OFFSHORE HEALTH AND SAFETY AND EC LAW

3.1 The Existing Offshore Health and Safety Regime

The existing offshore health and safety regime has developed over several years.[25] The first attempt to legislate on health and safety matters came in s.6 of the Mineral Workings (offshore installations) Act 1971, which allows the Secretary of State to 'make regulations for the safety, health and welfare of persons on offshore installations'. Several sets of detailed regulations have been made under this section.[26] Yet, a truly comprehensive scheme was not applied to offshore employment before the provisions of the Health and Safety at Work etc Act 1974 were extended offshore.[27] The 1974 Act imposes a number of general duties relating to health and safety on employers, employees and those having control of premises. It also provides mechanisms for the creation of detailed regulations and codes of practice, and sets up its own specialised enforcement devices.

While the provisions of the 1974 Act are in general extended under the 1989 Order, the detailed regulations made under the Act are not so extended. Indeed, by virtue of s.15(9) of the Act no such regulations will apply to 'offshore installations outside Great Britain or persons at work outside Great Britain in connection with

22. 91/383.

23. COM(83)543 Final.

24. As it did with some success in relation to the Working Time Directive – see 1992 *Employment Gazette* p.325.

25. The Continental Shelf Act 1964 s.1(4) provided that the model clauses incorporated in licences under the Petroleum (Production) Act 1934 'shall include provisions for the safety, health and welfare of persons employed on operations undertaken under the authority of any licence under that Act.' However, pursuant to the new offshore health and safety regime, this provision is to be repealed from a date to be appointed by the Secretary of State – Offshore Safety Act 1992 ss.3(1)(a), 7(3), while from such a date s.3(2) of the 1992 Act allows the functions of the Secretary of State under a licence to be 'exercised without regard to safety considerations'.

26. *Eg* The Offshore Safety (Operational Safety, Health and Welfare) Regulations 1976 SI 1976/1542; The Offshore Installations (Life Saving Appliances) Regulations 1977 SI 1977/486; The Offshore Installations (Fire-Fighting Equipment) Regulations 1978 SI 1978/611; The Offshore Installations (Well Control) Regulations 1980 SI 1980/1759; The Offshore Installations (Safety Representatives and Safety Committees) Regulations 1989 SI 1989/971.

27. By the Health and Safety at Work etc Act (Application Outside Great Britain) Order 1977 SI 1977/1232 – now supplanted by The Health and Safety at Work etc Act (Application Outside Great Britain) Order 1989 SI 1989/840.

submarine cables or submarine pipelines except in so far as the regulations expressly so provide'.[28]

3.2 The Legacy of *Piper Alpha* and the Cullen Report

The *Piper Alpha* disaster of July 6–7 1988 moved the Secretary of State to exercise his powers under The Offshore Installations (Public Inquiries) Regulations[29] and appoint Lord Cullen to conduct a public inquiry into the circumstances of the accident and its cause and to report thereon together with any observations and recommendations with a view to the preservation of life and the avoidance of similar accidents in the future. The subsequent report[30] makes 106 recommendations all of which the government has accepted and promised to implement.[31] This has dramatic consequences for the offshore health and safety regime.

In health and safety matters the basic thrust of the recommendations is that 'the principal regulations in regard to offshore safety should take the form of requiring that stated objectives are to be met rather than prescribing that detailed measures are to be taken. In relation to such regulations guidance notes should give non-mandatory advice on one or more methods of achieving such objectives without prescribing any particular method as a minimum or as the measure to be taken in default of any acceptable alternative'. At the same time the report accepts 'that there will be a continuing need for some regulations which prescribe detailed measures'.[32]

Central to the new regime will be the Safety Case which the operator must submit to the Health and Safety Executive in respect of each of its installations. The Safety Case 'should be a demonstration that the hazards of the installation have been identified and assessed, and are under control and that the exposure of personnel to these hazards has been minimised'.[33] Regulations[34] have been produced to implement these recommendations. Like, the Control of Industrial Major Accident Hazard Regulations 1984,[35] 'the new offshore regime will complement rather than replace existing health and safety legislation, with which operators, owners and employers must continue to comply irrespective of whether a safety case is required, or has been accepted'.[36]

28. Regulations which make such provision include the Control of Lead at Work Regulations 1980 SI 1980/1248; The Diving Operations at Work Regulations 1981 SI 1981/399; The Asbestos (Licensing) Regulations 1983 SI 1983/1649; The Freight Containers (Safety Convention) Regulations 1984 SI 1984/18; The Asbestos (Prohibition) Regulations 1985 SI 1985/910; The Ionising Radiation Regulations 1985 SI 1985/1333; The Control of Asbestos at Work Regulations 1987 SI 1987/2115; The Offshore Installations and Pipeline Works (First Aid) Regulations 1989 SI 1989/1671; The Genetic Manipulation Regulations 1989 SI 1989/1810.

29. (1974) SI 1974/338.

30. 1990 Cm 1310.

31. H.C. Debs, Nov. 12 1990 col 329.

32. Cullen Report para. 21.67.

33. Ibid. para.17.37. The idea of the Safety case is borrowed from the Control of Industrial Major Accident Hazards Regulations 1984 SI 1984/1902, which in turn implements EC Directive 82/501.

34. Offshore Installations (Safety Case) Regulations 1992 SI 1992/2885.

35. SI 1984/1902; see also Control of Industrial Major Accident Hazards (Amendment) Regulations 1988 and 1990, SI 1988/1462, S.I. 1990/2325.

36. Health and Safety Commission – Consultative Document 41 para. 28.

Safety cases are required for various stages in the operational life of an installation,[37] and the person required to prepare the safety case must revise its contents as often as appropriate, and should any revision render the safety case materially different from that accepted by the HSE, it must be resubmitted. An updated safety case must in any event be submitted every three years (or such longer interval as the HSE may agree).[38] Operation without a safety case accepted by the HSE, or failure to operate so far as is practicable in conformity with an accepted safety case, is an offence.

The replacement of the existing health and safety structure with new 'goal-setting' regulations will obviously take some years to complete, but the foundation of this process has already been laid in the form of the Offshore Safety Act 1992. In line with the recommendations of the Cullen Report (para.22.34) responsibility for health and safety offshore has been transferred from the Department of Energy to the Health and Safety Executive, and the HSE is empowered to begin the task of reforming the existing regime by virtue of s.1(1) of the Act which adds to the general purposes of the Health and Safety at Work etc Act 1974:

(a) securing the safety, health and welfare of persons on offshore installations or engaged on pipe line works;
(b) securing the safety of such installations and preventing accidents on or near them;
(c) securing the proper construction and safe operation of pipelines and preventing damage to them; and
(d) securing the safe dismantling, removal and disposal of offshore installations and pipelines.

At the same time, The Mineral Workings (Offshore Installations) Act 1971, ss.26, 27 and 32 of The Petroleum and Submarine Pipelines Act 1975 and ss.11(2)(a) and 21–24 of The Petroleum Act 1987 (all of which relate to health and safety) are made 'existing statutory provisions' for the purposes of Part 1 of the 1974 Act. This means that the HSE is empowered to enforce them, while more importantly, they can over the course of time be replaced by regulations made under s.15 of the 1974 Act.

Finally, it can be noted that The Offshore Safety (Protection Against Victimisation) Act 1992 renders it unlawful to dismiss an employee for performing or proposing to perform the functions of a safety representative or a member of a safety

37. The concept design safety case, to be submitted by the operator of a fixed installation before commencing detailed design; the safety case submitted by the operator of a fixed installation before commencing operations; the safety case to be submitted by an operator before drilling any well from a fixed installation; the vessel safety case to be submitted by the owner of a mobile installation before the installation is moved with a view to being operated in relevant waters; the well operations safety case, for a well to be drilled (or for a suspended well to be re-entered) at a particular location from a mobile installation, to be agreed between the owner and the operator and submitted by the operator; the abandonment safety case to be submitted by the operator of a fixed installation before he commences decommissioning; the combined operations safety case, to be agreed between the operator of a fixed installation and the owner of a mobile installation before engaging in such operations, and to be submitted by the operator.

38. Sufficient details must be included in the safety case to show that: the management system is adequate to ensure that statutory health and safety requirements will be complied with in relation to the installation and connected activities; adequate arrangements have been established for the audit of the system at regular intervals; hazards with the potential to cause a major accident have been identified, their risks evaluated and measures taken to reduce the risks to persons affected by those hazards to the lowest level that is reasonably practicable.

committee under the Offshore Installations (Safety Representatives and Safety Committees) Regulations 1989[39] or under any corresponding regulations made under the 1974 Act. It is similarly made unlawful to take action short of dismissal to prevent or deter an employee from carrying out such functions or to penalise him for doing so. The remedy in the former case would be a complaint of unfair dismissal and in the latter case a similar complaint to an Industrial Tribunal under ss.146(1) and 152(1) of the Trade Union and Labour Relations (Consolidation) Act 1992. Similar protection was recently extended to onshore employees.[40]

3.3   The EC and Health and Safety

Any student of employment law could vouch for the fact that the UK Government is not well disposed towards the involvement of law in the employment relationship. Thus, given that health and safety at work is the only area where provisions can be introduced into EC law by a qualified majority (and thus against the opposition of the UK), it is likely to be this area where the most significant developments occur. Prior to 1987, several Directives were adopted in this area.[41] However, in 1987 the Commission issued its Third Action Programme concerning safety, health and hygiene at work,[42] which indicated the intention of the Commission to propose 15 new health and safety Directives, together with a large number of other recommendations. Then at the Council of Ministers in December 1988 the Commission indicated that it would recommend a further six Directives covering specific areas of industry, including Extractive Industries, while a number of other Directives related to health and safety were suggested in the Action Programme relating to the implementation of the Community Charter of the Fundamental Social Rights of Workers.[43]

This process culminated in the appearance of Directive 89/391 on the Introduction of Measures to Encourage Improvements in the Safety and Health of Workers at Work – the so-called Framework Directive, which 'contains general principles concerning the prevention of occupational risks, the protection of safety and health, the elimination of risk and accident factors, the informing, consultation, balanced participation in accordance with national laws and/or practices and training of workers and their representatives, as well as general guidelines for the implementation of the said principles' (Article 1(2)). The idea is that these 'general principles'

39. SI 1989/971.
40. Trade Union Reform and Employment Rights Act 1993 s.28 and sched. 5.
41. *Eg* Directive 77/576 on Safety Signs at Work – implemented by the Safety Signs Regulations SI 1980/1471; Directive 80/1107 on Exposure to Chemical, Physical and Biological Agents at Work – implemented by the Control of Substances Hazardous to Health Regulations 1988 SI 1988/1657; Directive 82/605 on Exposure to Metallic Lead and its Ionic Compounds – implemented by an amended Code of Practice to accompany the Control of Lead at Work Regulations SI 1980/1248; Directive 83/477 on Risks Related to Exposure to Asbestos at Work – implemented by the Asbestos (Prohibition) Regulations 1985 SI 1985/910 and the Control of Asbestos at Work Regulations 1987 SI 1987/2115; Directive 86/188 on Exposure to Noise at Work – implemented by the Noise at Work Regulations SI 1989/1790.
42. COM(87) 520 Final.
43. COM(89) 568 Final.

should be supplemented by 'daughter' Directives laying down detailed provisions on specific issues (Article 16).[44]

3.3.1 The Framework Directive

What are the general principles laid down by the Framework Directive? Without going into immense detail, it can be pointed out that employers are expected to:

- evaluate the health and safety risks involved in the equipment and material employed and the characteristics of the workplace;
- adopt necessary preventive measures which are integrated into all activities of the undertaking at every level;
- take into account a worker's health and safety capabilities before entrusting a task to that worker;
- ensure that the planning and introduction of new technologies are the subject of consultation with the workers and/or their representatives, as regards the health and safety consequences;
- ensure that only adequately instructed workers have access to areas where there is serious and specific danger.

The employer must also designate one or more workers to carry out activities related to the protection and prevention of occupational risks. Such workers must be given the requisite information, time and means to carry out this task, and must not be placed at a disadvantage because of their role. If no competent worker can be found to discharge this role, then competent external services/persons can be engaged.

The employer must also take all necessary measures for first aid, fire-fighting and the evacuation of workers. He must also obtain an assessment of safety risks and decide upon the necessary protective measures, as well as maintaining records of accidents at work and making reports thereof to the relevant authorities.

Finally, he shall ensure that workers receive all necessary information relating to health and safety, must 'consult workers and/or their representatives and allow them to take part in discussions on all questions relating to health and safety at work', and ensure that each worker receives adequate health and safety training.

3.3.2 Implementation of the Framework Directive in Britain

The response of the Health and Safety Commission to this Directive is premised on the view that 'existing health and safety law already goes a long way towards meeting the requirements of the directive'.[45] Thus their approach towards the drafting of Regulations has been informed by 'the need to dovetail the new regulations within the existing framework of health and safety law while minimising changes to existing regulations particularly the most recent'.[46] There are, therefore,

---

44. So far a number of 'daughter' Directives have appeared which have been implemented by the UK and extended offshore; see:

The Provision and Use of Work Equipment Regulations 1992, SI 1992/2932;

The Manual Handling Operations Regulations 1992, SI 1992/2793;

The Personal Protective Equipment at Work Regulations 1992, SI 1992/2966;

The Health and Safety (Display Screen Equipment) Regulations 1992, SI 1992/2792.

45. Proposals for Health and Safety (General Provisions) Regulations and Approved Code of Practice – Consultative Document 34 para.6.

46. Ibid. para. 15.

only a dozen substantive regulations in the Management of Health and Safety at Work Regulations[47] which seek to implement the Framework Directive.

Thus an employer must adequately assess the risks to anyone who might be affected by his working activities in order to identify the measures he needs to take to comply with his duties under the relevant health and safety legislation (Reg. 3).

He must introduce arrangements 'for the effective planning, organisation, control, monitoring and review of the protective and preventive measures' (Reg. 4).

He must provide appropriate health surveillance for his employees with regard to the risks identified by the assessment (Reg. 5).

He must appoint one or more competent persons to assist him in undertaking the measures necessary to ensure compliance with his statutory obligations, unless being a self-employed person he is competent to undertake 'the necessary measures' without any assistance. Competence is defined as having 'sufficient training and experience or knowledge and other qualities' to allow the person to render the necessary assistance. The employer must ensure that the numbers of such persons, the time available to them and the means at their disposal are adequate to allow them to perform their task. The persons appointed could be employees or outsiders, but in the latter case they must be given the information necessary for them to perform their role (Reg. 6).

In light of the risk assessments, he must establish procedures to be followed in the event of serious and imminent danger to employees. Such procedures must indicate the circumstances in which employees would stop work and proceed to a place of safety (Reg. 7).

In light of the risk assessments, he must provide employees with relevant and comprehensible information on health and safety risks, protective and preventive measures and emergency procedures and the identities of those responsible for implementing them (Reg. 8).

Where employees of two or more employers[48] work together on the same premises, the employers must co-operate on health and safety matters and co-ordinate protective and preventive measures, while each employer shall inform the others of the risks to their employees arising from 'the conduct by him of his undertaking' (Reg. 9).

Similar information must be provided by an employer in whose undertaking the employees of other employers are working, as well as information as to the measures taken by that employer to comply with his duties towards those employees. Similarly, such an employer must provide such employees with appropriate instructions regarding health and safety risks arising from his conduct of his undertaking. Finally, such an employer must inform other employers and their employees of the person(s) responsible for implementing evacuation procedures (Reg. 10).

Before entrusting an employee with any health and safety task, an employer must take into account that individual's health and safety capabilities. He must also ensure that all employees receive (during working hours) adequate health and safety training – on recruitment and if exposed to new or increased risks on transfer or change of responsibilities, or on the introduction of new equipment or new systems of work or new technology. Such training must be repeated periodically if necessary and adapted to take account of new or changed risks (Reg. 11).

47. 1992 SI 1992/2051.
48. An employer includes a self-employed person for this purpose.

For their part, employees must make proper use of any machinery, equipment, dangerous substance, transport equipment, means of production or safety device. Each employee must inform his employer or safety representative of anything which might be a serious danger to health and safety, or a shortcoming in the employer's health and safety arrangements (Reg. 12).

Finally, the Safety Representatives and Safety Committee Regulations 1977[49] are modified to oblige employers to consult safety representatives on the kind of matters mentioned above, the introduction of any measure at the workplace which may substantially affect the health and safety of the employees represented; his arrangements for appointing competent persons to assist him in terms of Reg. 6, or nominating persons to implement evacuation procedures; any health and safety information he requires to provide to the employees represented; (he must also provide reasonable facilities and assistance to safety representatives to allow them to carry out their functions) the planning and organisation of any health and safety training he requires to provide to the represented employees; and the health and safety consequences for the represented employees of the planned introduction of new technology (Reg 17. and Schedule).

It is intended that these Regulations apply offshore (Reg. 16).

3.3.3 The Directive Concerning Minimum Requirements for Improving the Safety and Health Protection of Workers in the Mineral-Extracting Industries through Drilling

Although the Cullen Report seems to indicate the way forward for the offshore health and safety regime, it is impossible to ignore the EC dimension. We have seen that the Framework Directive in that it lays down broad duties can be accommodated within the existing health and safety regime with a minimum of substantive changes, but what of the more specific 'daughter' directives, and in particular the Extractive Industries Directive[50]? What are the requirements of that directive, and to what extent are they reconcilable with the planned new regime?

The Directive was proposed because 'the extractive industries are higher than average risk activities', while 'the oil and gas sector of these industries is deemed to be of particular importance for introducing improvements in the protection of the safety and health of workers'. It envisages a great many obligations being imposed on employers. Thus Article 3 (General Obligations) states

(1) To safeguard the safety and health of workers, the employer shall take necessary measures to ensure that:
   (a) workplaces are designed, constructed, equipped, commissioned, operated and maintained in such a way that workers can perform the work assigned to them without endangering their safety and/or health and/or those of other workers;
   (b) the operation of workplaces when workers are present takes place under the supervision of a person in charge;
   (c) work involving a special risk is entrusted only to competent staff and carried out in accordance with the instructions given;
   (d) all safety instructions are comprehensible to the workers concerned;
   (e) appropriate first aid facilities are provided;
   (f) any relevant safety drills are performed at regular intervals.
(2) The employer shall ensure that a document concerning safety and health, hereinafter referred to as 'safety and health document', covering the relevant requirements laid

49. SI 1977/500.
50. Directive 92/91.

down in Articles 6, 9 and 10 of Directive 89/391/EEC (the Framework Directive), is drawn up and kept up to date.

The safety and health document shall demonstrate in particular:

– that the risks incurred by the workers at the workplace have been determined and assessed;
– that adequate measures have been taken to attain the aims of this Directive;
– that the design, use and maintenance of the workplace and of the equipment are safe.

The safety and health document must be drawn up prior to the commencement of work and be revised if the workplace has undergone major changes, extensions or conversions.

(3) Where workers from several undertakings are present at the same workplace, each employer shall be responsible for all matters under his control.

The employer who, in accordance with national laws and/or practices, is in charge of the workplace, shall co-ordinate the implementation of measures concerning the safety and health of the workers and shall state, in his safety and health document, the aim of that co-ordination and the measures and procedures for implementing it.

The co-ordination shall not affect the responsibility of individual employers as provided for in Directive 89/191/EEC.

(4) The employer shall without delay report any serious and/or fatal occupational accidents and situations of serious danger to the competent authorities.

If necessary, the employer shall update the safety and health document recording measures taken to avoid any repetition.

Similarly, the other Articles impose detailed obligations on employers with regard to a considerable range of issues.[51] Moreover, the Annex prescribes even more detailed requirements which will represent minima in respect of 'workplaces used for the first time' after the date on which the Directive is brought into effect (Article 10.1) and workplaces which 'undergo changes, extensions and/or conversions' after that date (Article 10.3), while Article 10(2) demands that workplaces already in use must satisfy the minimum requirements of the Annex as soon as possible and no later than five years after that date.[52] Under Article 12(1) member states are allowed 24 months from its adoption to implement the Directive.

51. *Ie* protection against fire, explosions and health endangering atmospheres (Art. 4); escape and rescue facilities (Art. 5); communication, warning and alarm systems (Art. 6); provision of health and safety information to workers (Art. 7); health surveillance (Art. 8); consultation of workers and workers' participation in health and safety (Art. 9).

52. The minimum requirements in the Annex are divided into common minimum requirements (Part A), and special minimum requirements applicable to the onshore sector (Part B) and the offshore sector (Part C). Under Part A these requirements concern such matters as the stability and solidity of workplaces (para.1), organisation and supervision (para.2), mechanical and electrical equipment and plant (para.3), the maintenance of plant and equipment in general and safety equipment in particular (para.4), well control equipment to prevent blowouts (para.5), protection against hazardous atmospheres and explosion risks (para.6), emergency routes and exits (para.7), ventilation of enclosed workplaces (para.8), room temperature (para.9), the floors, walls, ceilings and roofs of rooms (para.10), natural and artificial lighting (para.11), windows and skylights (para.12), doors and gates (para.13), traffic routes (para.14), dangerous areas (para.15), room dimensions and air space in rooms – freedom of movement at the workstation (para.16), rest-rooms (para.17), outdoor workplaces (para.18), pregnant women and nursing mothers (para.19) and handicapped workers (para.20).

Under Part C further obligations are then imposed in relation to fire detection and fire-fighting (para.2), remote control of safety equipment necessary in emergencies (para. 3), communications systems, both general and emergency (para. 4), safe assembly points and muster lists (para.5), means of evacuation and escape (para.6), the holding of safety drills (para.7), sanitary equipment (para.8), first-aid rooms and equipment (para.9), accommodation (para.10), helicopter operations (para.11) and safety and stability in the positioning of installations at sea (para.12).

The question which must be asked is to what extent is it possible to reconcile the immense detail of the obligations imposed by the draft Directive with the stated aim of the post-Cullen regime to avoid the prescription of 'detailed measures to be taken'? The Health and Safety Commission's Consultative Document (No 34) on regulations to implement the Framework Directive admitted that (para.4)

the provisions of EC directives tend to be more prescriptive and detailed than objective setting regulations made under the HSWA in the UK.

The Health and Safety Commission appears to consider that the requirements of the Extractive Industries Directive can be met without altering the planned post-Cullen regime, but this appears rather optimistic. It may well be that the new regime is forced to become detailed and prescriptive in order to fulfil the UK's European obligations, so that the benefits Cullen sought to gain are lost.

4.0 SUMMARY

This Chapter has examined a most complex question, which has thrown up a number of issues. Accordingly, it may be helpful to offer a summary of the main points which have been made.

1. Most British employment legislation, with certain notable exceptions now applies offshore. Thus, given that a number of legislative provisions purport to give effect to EC Directives, certain provisions of EC law can in one sense be said to apply offshore.

2. It is also the case that British legislation must be construed in light of relevant provisions of EC law as interpreted by the European Court of Justice, whether or not that legislation was designed to give effect to those provisions.

3. It is argued that EC law extends to any territory over which member states exercise jurisdiction and thus extends offshore. This would allow individuals to rely on provisions of EC law which are directly effective both horizontally as well as vertically; ie they can be relied upon by individual employees against their employers.

4. Certain Directives which do not have direct effect have arguably been improperly implemented in British legislation. Prominent here is the Acquired Rights Directive. Indeed, the implementing legislation does not extend offshore at all. It is argued that employees who have been disadvantaged by the imperfect implementation of this Directive, or by its non-implementation as regards offshore employment might have a remedy against the state on the basis of the *Francovich* case.

5. In terms of future developments in EC employment law the UK has traditionally opposed the augmentation of the rights of employees. Thus, given that unanimity continues to be required to introduce measures relating to 'the rights and interests of employed persons', further developments are unlikely, save in the area of health and safety at work where measures may be introduced by a qualified majority. It is further observed that the UK refused to sign the Social Protocol at Maastricht, whereby the other member states committed themselves to 'continue along the path laid down by the Social Charter of 1989'. Thus there is no realistic chance of the

employment measures of the Social Charter being adopted in the UK, apart from those with a health and safety dimension.

6. The main thrust of the recommendations of the Cullen Report is that 'the principal regulations in regard to offshore safety should take the form of requiring that stated objectives are to be met rather than prescribing that detailed measures are to be taken'. Thus the framework has been set up for the progressive replacement of existing regulations by new goal setting regulations. Moreover, the operator of any offshore installation will require to have a detailed safety case accepted by the Health and Safety Executive if the installation is to operate lawfully.

7.   At the same time the EC is progressing with its own considerable legislative programme in the field of health and safety at work. Central to this programme is Directive 89/391 – the so-called 'Framework' Directive, which contains general principles concerning the prevention of occupational risks, the protection of safety and health, the elimination of risk and accident factors, and consultation with workers. This has been relatively easily integrated into both the existing legislative framework and the proposed offshore regime, but these 'general principles' are to be supplemented by so-called 'Daughter' Directives, laying down detailed provisions on specific issues. In this regard particular attention is paid to the provisions of the draft Extractive Industries Directive, given its obvious relevance to offshore employment. The concern is expressed that were this to be implemented, the specification of obligations in such detail would run contrary to the emphasis of the new domestic regime.

Section 3

Environmental Law

Chapter 9

European Community Environmental Law

Colin T. Reid

1.0 INTRODUCTION

The aim of this Chapter is to provide a general overview of the development of the European Community's involvement in environmental issues and of its approach to them. Aspects of the impact on the member states, particularly the UK, will be discussed, followed by a very brief account of the substantive content of Community environmental law in several major areas. Finally, potential developments in Community law, taking account of both the changes to the Treaty once the Maastricht Agreement is fully implemented and the terms of the new Action Programme on the Environment, will be discussed.

2.0 HISTORY AND DEVELOPMENT

There is no reference to environmental matters in the original Treaties establishing the European Community; at the time it was created, such matters were not seen as being part of its sphere of interests. However, environmental issues slowly pushed their way on to the Community agenda. In part this was a feature of the general awakening to environmental concern during the 1970s. The UN Conference on the Environment in Stockholm in 1972 was both a reflection of, and a spur to, this growing awareness and it was after that meeting that a Community summit set in motion the Community's first environmental policies. In addition, the economic significance of environmental measures became apparent. Different environmental standards in different parts of the Community could result in considerable variations in the costs borne by manufacturers, and the free movement of goods throughout the Community was interrupted by differing national standards.

In giving effect to such concern there was a major problem in finding legal justification for Community action in this field, as the Community is only empowered to do what the Treaties allow it to do. For a long time the environmental initiatives survived on the basis of two articles of the Treaty of Rome:

1. **Article 100**, which deals with the approximation, or harmonisation, of laws affecting the establishment or functioning of the common market – in other words environmental measures were adopted as part of the general programme to ensure common standards throughout the Community on a whole range of issues so that goods made in one Member State can be freely sold in all the others and businesses in different states can compete on even terms; or
2. **Article 235**, which is a general back-up provision allowing the Community to take any action necessary to achieve its objectives in the absence of a specific power having been conferred.

Reliance on these two provisions was not very satisfactory and the legal basis for some action taken by the Community was somewhat questionable.

The issue was resolved, however, by amendments to the Treaty of Rome carried out by the Single European Act, taking effect in 1987. A whole new section was added to the Treaty, dealing with environmental matters (Articles 130R–130T). This now gives express authorisation for the Community to act in the environmental field, and sets down the general objectives and principles to be followed. The Articles will be amended on the coming into force of the Maastricht Agreement , but at the time of writing it is these provisions which govern the Community's environmental action.

The relevant legislative procedures for environmental measures are also laid down in the Treaty as amended, specifically in Article 130S. This matter will not be dealt with in detail, other than to note that there are procedural differences depending on whether Article 130S (environmental policy) is used to justify a measure or the more general provisions on the harmonisation of industry (particularly Article 100A), and that the position will become even more complex once the Maastricht Agreement is implemented. The differences concern the role of the European Parliament and whether unanimity or merely a qualified majority vote is required for a measure to be adopted by the Council of Ministers.

Article 130R(1) sets out the objectives for action by the Community relating to the environment:

(i)   to preserve, protect and improve the quality of the environment;
(ii) to contribute towards protecting human health; and
(iii) to ensure a prudent and rational utilisation of natural resources.

These are all very broad and laudable aims, and give the Community wide scope to act. In the particular context of this volume, it should be noted that the utilisation of natural resources is expressly included as a concern of the environmental policy.

Article 130R also sets out the principles on which the Community's actions should be based:

– preventive action should be taken;
– environmental damage should be rectified at source; and
– the polluter should pay.

These set a clear aim of avoiding environmental harm, not merely cleaning up afterwards, and therefore justify intervention at all stages of industrial and other processes to ensure that pollution or risks of contamination are eliminated in the design and operation of a process. It is not merely a matter of the Community being concerned with what is coming out of the end of a chimney or waste pipe. With respect to the adoption of the polluter pays principle, it should be noted that there are different views as to what this means in practice.

The Community thus has the power to embark on wide-ranging environmental measures, affecting all aspects of activity within the Community. The Treaty also states that environmental protection is to be a component of the Community's other policies (Article 130R(2)) – the relationship between environmental and other policies raises problems as shall be noted below.

3.0 IMPACT ON MEMBER STATES

In environmental matters the Community is very diverse. It is diverse physically in terms of geographical and climatic conditions, from the sub-arctic of the Scottish highlands to the near desert of southern Spain. It is diverse economically in the level and nature of industrialisation; this affects both the levels of serious pollution experienced throughout the Community (exacerbated by the inclusion of the eastern Länder of Germany), and the priority given to environmental protection as against projects promising economic development. It is diverse politically in terms of the level and nature of environmental concern felt by the public and politicians.

The impact of Community law has therefore varied – varied between states and for each state on different topics. On some points the standards agreed for the Community as a whole are much higher than those which had previously been adopted in a given state, on others the Community standards are lower. Where higher standards are agreed, member states struggle to comply; where lower, there is often a desire to maintain the previous higher standards.

In the United Kingdom, Community law has produced many changes. In most instances there was some basic framework of legal control already in existence, but the Community has had a major impact on the details and the standards to be observed. Overall in the UK perhaps three general changes can be identified in relation to environmental protection.

1. Community law has prompted action where there was no great political priority, *eg* in relation to water quality and sewage treatment. Community proposals have provided a focus for more general concerns about environmental matters and the UK has been forced to go along with higher standards (and the related expense) in areas where the government might have been happy to let things lie.
2. Particular Community measures on environmental assessment and access to information have led to much greater openness in the administration of environmental controls. Previously this was essentially a private matter between the regulatory authorities and the polluter.
3. Community law has led to the introduction of fixed standards in pollution control, both standards for emissions and quality standards, setting maximum

limits for pollutants in water, air etc. Previously UK law relied heavily on a more flexible approach, based on the concept of using the 'best practicable means' to reduce pollution, which allowed considerable variation depending on location, the nature of a process and the cost of reducing the pollution.

Two more general issues can be mentioned in relation to the impact on member states: the extent to which different national standards can be permitted, and the problem of compliance.

Some member states on particular issues want higher standards than it has been possible to agree at a Community level – is it permissible for them to maintain these? Here one runs into the problem of interfering with the common market; differing national standards are a barrier to the free movement of goods through the markets of the Community, therefore at first sight they should not be permitted. However, the European Court of Justice has ruled that measures imposed for environmental purposes can be acceptable even though they do operate as indirect barriers to trade.

This was decided in the *Danish Bottles* case,[1] arising from a Danish scheme for the sale of drinks in returnable bottles, which required producers to use only approved types of bottle. Foreign producers argued that this restricted their ability to trade in Denmark, and therefore contravened Community law. The Court held that environmental protection was a requirement of Community law and that therefore measures to this end could be permissible even though they conflicted with the Community's other objectives, most importantly the free movement of goods and services. However, such interference is acceptable only if the environmental measure is proportionate to the goal being achieved. In other words the measure must be reasonable in view of the benefit gained for the environment. In the particular case there were problems with the details of the Danish scheme, but the important point is the recognition by the Court that national environmental measures may be permitted even though they do interfere with the free movement of goods.

In the more recent *Wallonian Waste* case[2] the Court again allowed environmental measures to take priority over other Community policies. Waste was held to fall within the definition of 'goods' and a local ban on the importation of hazardous waste was declared unlawful as Community legislation on the matter was deemed to provide a complete system ensuring appropriate protection for the environment, so that there was no good reason for local measures interfering with the free movement of the waste. On the other hand, in the absence of any legislation at Community level providing appropriate safeguards, a ban on importing other waste was held to be acceptable in view of its environmental objective, although on the face of it the ban appeared both discriminatory and to deny the free movement of goods. Moreover, the Court did not subject the ban to any close scrutiny on the basis of proportionality, allowing its environmental purpose to overcome free movement without a detailed examination of the balance of interests.

It is thus clear that in some instances member states may be permitted to enforce their own environmental measures and that different rules and standards can apply

1. Case 302/86 *Commission v Denmark* [1988] ECR 4607, [1989] 1 CMLR 619.
2. Case C2/90 *Commission v Belgium* [1993] 1 CMLR 365.

in different states. The acceptance of stricter national standards is reaffirmed by the Treaty's express provision that individual states are allowed to impose more stringent environmental measures, subject to their general compatibility with the Treaty (Article 130T).

On the second issue of compliance, it is all very well for the Community to produce large quantities of environmental legislation, but these are worthless unless properly enforced. There are long-standing problems in ensuring that member states implement Community law and the environmental field has proved particularly difficult. This is partly because, unlike the position in other areas, there is rarely any individual who can claim direct harm or can claim to have been deprived of specific rights as the victim of non-implementation. For this reason several Community proposals contain measures endeavouring to make it easier for individuals and pressure groups to take action themselves, or at least to get the information with which they can apply political pressure.

If Community measures are not properly implemented, action can be taken by the Commission, and in many instances the Commission has instigated proceedings against member states before the Court of Justice for non-implementation of environmental provisions. Attempts are also made to keep the position under review by imposing reporting requirements on the member states to ensure that regular information is provided to the Community.

There is also a proposal for a European Environment Agency to collect environmental data and to some degree, as yet undecided, to monitor what is happening in the member states. Legislation is in place,[3] but the establishment of the Agency has been held up awaiting a decision on where it was to be based. This issue had become embroiled in bigger battles over the home of other Community institutions; the main logjam, over the home of the European Parliament, was broken at the Edinburgh summit in December 1992.

4.0 SPECIFIC POLICIES

The following is a very brief look at what the Community has done in several areas.

4.1 General

At the general level two important points can be highlighted:

(a) the requirement for a full environmental assessment before many major development projects, *eg* power stations, motorways, mines and large industrial works, can be approved – this ensures that the full impact on the environment is taken into account when the decision is taken whether a project is to proceed;[4]

(b) measures to ensure freedom of access to environmental information – a general provision has allowed the public (and, more significantly, pressure groups and the media) access to the records of industrial concerns and of the regulatory

---

3. Regulation (EEC) 1210/90 May 7 1990 (OJ 90/L120/1).
4. Directive 85/337/EEC June 27 1985 (OJ 85/L175/40).

bodies so that they can ensure that standards are being observed and that appropriate action is being taken when they are not.[5]

4.2 Air

Policy here has developed along three main lines:

(a) quality standards for products, *eg* prescribing maximum sulphur and lead content for petrols;
(b) air quality standards, setting maximum permissible levels of sulphur dioxide, nitrogen dioxide etc in the air;
(c) emission limits for specific items, *eg* motor vehicle engines and large combustion plants.

4.3 Water

There have been two main strands to the policy:

(a) the control of discharges into the aquatic environment, requiring specific authorisations and other regulatory controls;
(b) the setting of quality standards for water for particular uses, *eg* drinking, bathing, shellfish.

4.4 Waste

Here there has been a more varied approach, and policy is still developing. Initially there were specific measures on particular forms of hazardous and toxic waste, including their labelling and transport, but the emphasis is moving to more general measures attempting to encourage recycling, to reduce the production of waste and to impose liability on the producers, handlers and disposers of waste for any harm caused to the environment.

4.5 Noise

So far this issue has been approached by means of controls on noise produced by particular products, *eg* vehicles, lawn-mowers, household appliances.

4.6 Nature Conservation

There is a specific measure on the conservation of wild birds, and now a more far-reaching Directive on the conservation of natural habitats and many species of plant and animal.[6] The Community also participates in the operation of CITES, the international convention regulating trade in endangered species.

---

5. Directive 90/313/EEC June 7 1990 (OJ 90/L158/56).
6. Directives 79/409/EEC Apr. 2 1979 (OJ 79/L103/1) and 92/43/EEC May 21 1992 (OJ 92/L206/7).

5.0 THE FUTURE

How is Community environmental law likely to develop? There are two main places to look for an answer: the Maastricht Agreement and the Fifth Environmental Action Programme.

5.1 Maastricht Agreement (Treaty on European Union)

The Treaty amendments agreed at Maastricht in December 1991, will do several things as far as the environment is concerned.

1. The Community's commitment to environmental issues is strengthened. Environmental concern is built into the basic objectives of the Community in Article 2, where there will be reference to 'sustainable and non-inflationary growth *respecting the environment*' and to 'raising the standard of living and *the quality of life*'. Environmental policy will also become one of the expressly listed activities of the Community (Article 3). These changes make environmental issues a central concern of the Community.
2. It is emphasised that this environmental concern is to be integrated with the Community's other policies. This is apparent from the above quotations from Article 2, and even more from the amended version of Article 130R(2), which states that:

    Environmental protection requirements must be integrated into the definition and implementation of other Community policies.

    This is much stronger than the present statement that environmental policies 'shall be a component of' other policies.
3. A further principle is added to those on which Community action is to be based, namely the precautionary principle (Article 130R(2)). This means that one does not wait until it is proved beyond all doubt that something is causing environmental harm before acting, because by then it may be too late and irreversible damage may have been caused. Instead, one should act as soon as a realistic risk is identified. The best example of the operation of this principle is in relation to the greenhouse effect; at present nobody can be absolutely certain whether the greenhouse effect is in fact taking place, or what will happen in the future, but the precautionary principle states that in view of the risk, we should act now, not wait for another fifty years in order to be absolutely certain. The risks of getting it wrong and acting unnecessarily or acting too soon are less than those of getting it wrong and acting too late.
4. However, the amendments also create a risk of a greater fragmentation of environmental law. This arises first through the greater emphasis on the idea of subsidiarity, the principle of leaving as much as possible to member states and only taking Community action where action on that scale is necessary (Article 3B). This idea is already present in the environmental provisions of the Treaty (Article 130R(4)) but is now given much greater prominence for all aspects of the Community's activities. In practice, however, it may often be possible to

argue that environmental issues can only be dealt with properly on the larger scale as pollution does not stop at national frontiers.

Secondly, fragmentation may arise from the fact that the aim of Community environmental policy will be stated to be 'a high level of environmental protection taking into account the diversity of situations in the various regions of the Community'(Article 130R(2)). This opens the door to different standards in different places, *eg* in the eastern Länder of Germany or in poorer regions where economic development might be favoured over environmental protection.

5.2 Fifth Action Programme

The other main guide to future policy is the new Fifth Action Programme on the Environment, which was formally adopted in February 1993 and sets out the broad strategy for the Community in the next few years.[7] Energy policy is one of the areas identified in the Programme as requiring specific attention with the objective of ensuring that environmental considerations are fully taken into account in the development and operation of policy. Five more general aspects of the Programme:

1. There is reference to achieving 'sustainable development'. This key idea was identified by the World Commission on Environment and Development (Brundtland Commission) in its report Our Common Future in 1987 and calls on us to ensure that in meeting the needs of today we do not compromise the ability of future generations to meet their own needs. In practice it requires that we do not simply pursue short-term economic growth, but have regard to the broader picture.
2. As part of this, there is the emphasis already mentioned on ensuring that environmental concerns form part of the basis of all other policies. An integrated approach should be adopted; environmental policy should not be regarded as being in a compartment of its own.
3. Policy should be based on the precautionary principle, as already mentioned.
4. Environmental protection should be seen as a matter of shared responsibility. It is not just a matter for governments, but something for everyone: governments, industry, the public at large. It is not enough to rely on governmental action and controls. The Community must make sure that everyone is playing their part in changing practices and habits to ensure that a sustainable future is in fact achievable.
5. This leads on to an interest in using a broader range of instruments to achieve environmental policies. Not only the standard regulatory mechanisms of prohibitions, permits, quality standards, etc, should be employed, but also many other tools. The Community should endeavour to:

    – improve environmental data, so that we know the state of the environment and what we are doing to it;
    – carry out scientific research and technical development;

7. Council Resolution Feb. 1 1993 (OJ 93/C138/1).

- provide information and training for professionals and for the general public; and
- make greater use of planning, for industries and for land use in order to minimise environmental impacts.

The Community should also use the economic approach. This involves ensuring that industry makes clear its environmental policies and is aware of the environmental costs of what it is doing, *eg* by greater use of environmental audits. Various mechanisms should also be employed to 'internalise the externalities', to ensure that environmental costs are properly reflected in production costs and in the prices paid by those who use the final goods or services, *eg* by introducing charges for pollution permits etc and levies on goods which have high environmental costs. Taxes and subsidies could also be used to discourage undesirable and encourage desirable practices and to ameliorate the costs of changing to more environmentally acceptable ways of doing things.

The Commission is also hoping to encourage co-operation and common understanding within the Community by arranging meetings of the various national enforcement agencies and of the senior environmental civil servants from the member states to discuss strategic issues of common concern. Also in mind is a forum to allow environmental interest groups to meet together and with the Commission, strengthening their voice to balance that of the various industrial and trade groups which devote considerable energy to ensuring that their views are properly represented in Brussels.

Giving effect to these policies is likely to produce considerable environmental activity from the Community in the coming years. As well as the development of existing initiatives and those in the Fifth Action Programme, specific action can perhaps be expected on the following issues:

- the adoption of integrated pollution control, as opposed to dealing with single media, *eg* water and air, separately;
- measures on the prevention and management of waste, particularly concentrating on prevention of waste and increased responsibility for those who do produce it;
- attempts to reduce the consumption of energy from non-renewable sources.

Whatever happens, the Community will continue to play a leading role in shaping the environmental law and policy of Europe, and it seems certain that all areas of activity will have to take account of environmental factors in the shaping of their own policies. The environment is not a separate issue, to be dealt with by a separate set of policies and officials, but is an integral part of everything that we do. The challenge which the Community has taken up for the coming years is to ensure that the rhetoric of environmental concern is converted into reality in all facets of our business, work and daily life.

ADDENDUM. The Maastricht Agreement has been ratified by all twelve member states and came into effect on November 1 1993. It has also been decided that Copenhagen is to be the location for the European Environment Agency.

Further reading

European Community Environment Legislation (7 volumes.) (Commission of the European Community 1992).
Towards Sustainability (Fifth Action Programme) OJ 93/C 138/1.
N. Haigh, *Manual of Environmental Policy: the EC and Britain* (Longman, 1993).
S.P. Johnson and G. Corcelle, *The Environmental Policy of the European Communities* (Graham & Trotman, 1989).
L. Krämer, *EEC Treaty and Environmental Protection* (Sweet & Maxwell, 1990).
L. Krämer, *Focus on European Environmental Law* (Sweet & Maxwell, 1992).

Chapter 10

The Court of Justice and Environmental Protection

David Edward and William Robinson[1]

1.0 INTRODUCTION

The Treaties founding the European Communities contained no specific reference to protection of the environment or, indeed, to protection of the consumer. This reflected the relative unimportance, from a political point of view, of those issues at that time when the Treaties were drafted. The subsequent growth of political and public concern posed legal problems for the institutions of the European Communities, of which there are four: the European Parliament, the Council of Ministers and the Commission (the 'political' institutions), and the Court of Justice. The Single European Act, which was signed in 1986 and came into force in 1987, contained new provisions relating to the environment, but without resolving the pre-existing legal problems.

This Chapter examines the approach of the Court of Justice to two of the most compelling developments in the field of environmental protection: first, recognition of environmental protection as a counterweight to one of the fundamental principles of the European Economic Community, the free movement of goods; and second, the response of the Court to the lack of a definitive legal base in the original treaties for measures of environmental protection, and the new problems raised by the Single European Act.

Environmental protection has now become firmly established at the centre of Community objectives and is an example of the flexibility of Community law in responding to new political concerns. The Court's approach to consumer protection closely resembles its approach to environmental protection and shows many temporal and jurisprudential similarities.

1. The authors thank Jacqueline Minor, Legal Secretary at the Court of Justice, for a number of very helpful suggestions. The opinions expressed are entirely personal.

2.0 THE TREATY PROVISIONS

The closest reference to environmental protection included in the founding Treaties is to be found in Chapter III of the Treaty establishing the European Atomic Energy Community (Euratom). This provides for 'basic standards' and co-operation between member states, usually through the medium of the Commission, in the field of health and safety for workers and for the general public.[2] The Treaty refers, in particular, to the levels of radioactive contamination in the air, water and soil.[3] These provisions have given rise to one case concerning the disposal of radioactive waste from the French nuclear power station at Cattenom near the Luxembourg, German and Belgian frontiers: *Saarland v Ministry for Industry, Post and Tele-communications and Tourism.*[4]

Article 37 of the Euratom Treaty requires member states to furnish the Commission with data concerning the transfrontier effects of the disposal of radioactive waste, in order that the Commission can deliver an expert opinion. The French authorities authorised the disposal of radioactive waste from Cattenom without prior notification to the Commission. The Court ruled that the Commission's opinion, based on the findings of experts, was of 'very great importance ... [to the] ... protection of the population and the environment against the risks of nuclear contamination'.[5] It was therefore essential that member states provide the Commission with the relevant data prior to the authorisation of disposal plans, in order that the findings of the experts be fully effective.

However, even the Euratom Treaty deals with problems of environmental protection, which are now of acute public concern, only in outline. The European Economic Community Treaty (Treaty of Rome)[6] conferred no specific legislative powers and defined no specific Community objectives in the field of environmental protection. It was not thought necessary to derogate from the primary economic aims of the Communities with regard to such matters, and the derogations provided for in Article 36 of the EEC Treaty defining the permissible restrictions on free movement of goods,[7] were considered exhaustive.[8]

Political interest in environmental protection emerged, at Community level, at the Paris Summit in 1972,[9] partly due to the start of what has now become a string of environmental disasters.[10] But pursuit of environmental objectives in the wide fields

2. Art. 30–39 EAEC.
3. Arts 35, 37 and 38 EAEC.
4. Judgment Sept. 22 1988, Case 187/87, [1988] ECR 5013.
5. Ibid., points 13 and 11, respectively.
6. The Euratom treaty was in fact signed in Rome on the same day.
7. Art. 36 provides that, 'The provisions of Articles 30 to 34 shall not preclude prohibitions or restrictions on imports, exports or goods in transit justified on grounds of public morality, public policy or public security; the protection of health and life of humans, animals or plants; the protection of national treasures possessing artistic, historical or archaeological value; or the protection of industrial and commercial property ...'
8. See Judgment June 17 1981, Case 113/80 *Commission v Ireland (Re Restrictions on Importation of Souvenirs)* [1981] ECR 1625.
9. Meeting of the Heads of State or Government of the member states, Oct. 19–20 1972. See also the Conference of the Ministers responsible for environmental questions held in Bonn, Oct. 31 1972, and the United Nations Convention on the Human Environment, Stockholm 1972.
10. *Eg Amoco Cadiz*, Seveso, Three Mile Island, acid rain, the pollution of the Rhine, Bhopal, Chernobyl, *Exxon Valdez*, global warming etc.

of water, air, waste, chemicals, noise and flora and fauna was limited by the lack of legal basis in the Treaties. The first of the Community's Environmental Action and Research Programmes in 1973[11] was therefore based on the slender references to 'the constant improvement of the living and working conditions of [their] peoples' in the Preamble, and to 'harmonious' and 'balanced' economic development and expansion in Article 2 of the EEC Treaty. The adoption of legislation by the Council, for example the 1975 Directive on Waste,[12] was based upon Articles 100 (approximation of legal provisions which directly affect the functioning of the Common Market)[13] and 235 (measures necessary to achieve one of the objectives of the Community for which powers have not otherwise been provided).

Although criticisms were made of the Council's legislative approach[14] Articles 100 and 235 in conjunction, or Article 235 alone,[15] were used extensively as the legal basis for further legislation. Perhaps more significantly, these developments at Community level were paralleled by initiatives at national level in the fields of environmental and consumer protection which brought the member states into conflict with the treaty provisions on free movement of goods. Purposive interpretation of the objectives of the treaty was necessary in order to accommodate these new political concerns.

3.0 THE RULE OF REASON

In 1979, in its *Cassis de Dijon* judgment,[16] the Court of Justice recognised that the derogations provided for in Article 36 were not sufficient to cope with overriding considerations of national policy such as effective fiscal supervision, protection of public health, prevention of unfair trading practices and consumer protection. The Court enunciated a 'rule of reason' which would allow member states to give effect to such overriding considerations, inelegantly referred to as 'mandatory requirements',[17] in regulating the marketing of goods. Until recently, it was assumed that the doctrine of 'mandatory requirements' could be invoked only where the national rules in question were 'indistinctly' applicable – that is, applicable without distinction to goods of domestic origin and goods imported from other member states. As will be seen later, this is not necessarily so.

Although environmental protection was not one of the 'mandatory requirements' specifically mentioned in *Cassis de Dijon*, the Commission, the Netherlands and Denmark soon afterwards invoked it as such in the *FNMBP* case.[18]   That case

---

11. OJ C112, Dec. 20 1973, p.1.

12. Council Directive 75/442/EEC July 15 1975 on waste, OJ L194, July 25 1975, p.39.

13. The need to ensure that competition was not distorted was cited as the element in the functioning of the common market which required the approximation of national legal provisions by Art. 100.

14. See, *eg*, the 22nd Report of the House of Lords Select Committee, Session 1977–78.

15. See, *eg*, Council Dec. 82/72/EEC Dec. 3 1981, concerning the conclusion of the Convention of the conservation of European wildlife and natural habitats (OJ L38, Feb. 10 1982 p.1).

16. Judgment Feb. 20 1979, Case 120/78 *Rewe-Zentral AG v Bundesmonopolverwaltung für Branntwein* [1979] ECR 649.

17. 'Mandatory requirements' was the phrase used to translate the French *exigences impératives*. A better translation would be 'overriding needs'.

18. Judgment Dec. 17 1981, Case 272/80, *Criminal proceedings against Frans-Nederlandse Maatschappij voor Biologische Producten BV* [1981] ECR 3277. See in particular point 8 and pp.3282, 3284, 3285.

concerned the question whether Netherlands legislation requiring prior approval of plant protection products could be invoked to prevent the marketing of 'Fumicot Fumispore' lawfully marketed in France. The Court noted the point but found that the requirement of prior approval for such products already fell within Article 36.

In *Procureur de la République v Association de défense des bruleurs d' huiles usagées (ADBHU)*[19] the Court was asked whether certain elements of Council Directive 75/439/EEC on the disposal of waste oils,[20] including the administrative zoning of the collection and disposal of waste, were compatible with the fundamental treaty principles of freedom of trade, free movement of goods and freedom of competition. (The Directive had been enacted on the dual legal basis of Articles 100 and 235.) The Court held that 'the principle of freedom of trade is not to be viewed in absolute terms but is subject to certain limits justified by the objectives of general interest pursued by the Community',[21] and that environmental protection is 'one of the Community's essential objectives'.[22] Environmental protection cannot, however, justify discriminatory or disproportionate measures, and Advocate General Lenz emphasised that it was 'especially important' that absolute territorial protection was not contemplated.[23]

Environmental protection as an exception to the Treaty rules on free movement came up next in the *Danish bottles* case.[24] The question was whether the Danish compulsory deposit-and-return system for beer and soft drinks bottles fell within the rule in *Cassis de Dijon*. Advocate General Slynn believed that it did not do so, both because it was, in effect, discriminatory as between Danish and non-Danish producers and because it was disproportionate.[25] However, the Court repeated its ruling in the waste oils case that environmental protection is an essential Community objective, referred to the environmental provisions brought into force in the Single European Act and, on that basis, ruled that the Danish system was, at least in part, justified since ' ... the protection of the environment is a mandatory requirement which may limit the application of Article 30 of the Treaty'.[26]

The difference of approach between the Court and the Advocate General in the *Danish bottles* case illustrates the difficulty of finding objective criteria to judge whether national rules purportedly aimed at environmental protection are in reality disguised non-tariff barriers. Are they in truth 'indistinctly applicable' as between domestic and imported products and dictated by overriding policy considerations, or are they only dressed up to appear so?

This question became even more acute in *Commission v Belgium*, which concerned the importation of waste products into the region of Wallonia.[27] The Walloon Regional Executive had imposed a ban on the importation of all waste products into their region, including importation from other regions of Belgium. On

19. Judgment Mar. 23 1983, Case 240/83, [1985] ECR 531.
20. OJ L194 1975, p.23.
21. Supra note 19, point 12.
22. Supra note 19, point 13.
23. Supra note 19, pp.534 and 535.
24. Judgment Sept. 20 1988, Case 302/86, *Commission v Denmark*, [1988] ECR 4607.
25. Ibid., p.4625.
26. Supra note 24, point 9.
27. Judgment July 9 1992, Case C2/90, [1993] 1 CMLR 365.

the face of it, the ban offended, not only against the principle of the free movement of goods, but also against the provisions of two Directives on the transfrontier shipment of hazardous waste.[28]

A preliminary point arose as to whether waste of no monetary value is 'goods' to which the Treaty rules on free movement apply. The Advocate General and the Court agreed that objects carried across a frontier with a view to commercial transactions (in this case the transaction by which the waste would be disposed of for payment) are 'goods' within Article 30.[29] They disagreed however about the application of the rule of reason.

Advocate General Jacobs held that, although environmental protection falls within the scope of the 'mandatory requirements' exceptions to Article 30, those exceptions could not be relied upon in this case as the national rules in question were 'plainly not indistinctly applicable'[30] – that is, they were plainly discriminatory as between goods of domestic origin and goods from other member states. Although regional compartmentalisation of waste management accords with the principles of the Basle Convention[31] (self-sufficiency and proximity of disposal) and, potentially, with the amended Article 5 of Council Directive 75/442/EEC,[32] the measure in question clearly discriminated against waste originating in other member states and thus did not properly apply the international principles *at the Community level*.

The Court, however, drew a distinction between waste and other sorts of goods on the grounds of the peculiar characteristics of waste, and in particular the increased dangers caused by massive influxes into a certain region. It held that the measures in question, although not 'indistinctly applicable', could not be considered discriminatory (and therefore illegal under Article 30) since 'discrimination' was an unavoidable consequence of applying the principles of self-sufficiency and proximity (disposal as close as possible to the source of production), principles found both in Article 130R(2) of the EEC treaty as amended by the Single Act and in the Basle Convention.[33]

It is, at least in theory, open to question whether the discrimination in question was an unavoidable consequence of applying the principles of self-sufficiency and proximity. The nearest waste disposal plant *might*, in some cases, be in another member state and the principle of self-sufficiency is relevant only if the appropriate test is self-sufficiency *within national frontiers* – a test which might be thought no longer to be appropriate in a Community context. There were, however, genuine grounds for concern that Wallonia might become 'the dustbin of Europe' and it

28. Council Directive 74/442/EEC on waste, supra note 12, and Council Directive 84/631/EEC on the supervision and control within the European Community of the transfrontier shipment of hazardous waste (OJ 1984 L326, p.31).

29. The Court, supra note 27, point 28. Advocate General Jacobs at point 22 of his Opinion Sept. 19 1991.

30. At point 20 his Opinion Jan. 10 1991.

31. The Basle Convention on the Control of Transboundary Movements of Hazardous Waste and Their Disposal, Mar. 22 1989, *International Environmental Law*, (Deventer and Boston: Kluwer 1991), p.546. The underlying principles being self-sufficiency in waste, and the reduction of transportation by proximity to the source of production.

32. As amended by Council Directive 91/156/EEC Mar. 18 1991 (OJ L78, 1991 p.32), Art. 1.

33. See supra note 27, points 30–36.

would be unwise to draw conclusions of general application from a rather special case.

In particular, *Commission v Belgium* should not be seen as authority for the proposition that member states have *carte blanche* to partition markets on national or regional lines in real or purported pursuit of environmental goals. On the other hand, the case does illustrate the strength of the commitment to environmental protection as a Community objective.

It is important also to explain an aspect of the case which has given rise to some misunderstanding. Although the Court held that the Walloon Regional Executive was entitled to legislate against the import of waste for disposal, it held that the Executive was not entitled to do so in respect of hazardous waste. The reason for this, at first sight extraordinary, conclusion was that the measure in question was in direct contravention of the hazardous waste directive. It was therefore a measure which the Executive could not lawfully take, and which the Court could not lawfully authorise.

4.0 ENVIRONMENTAL LEGISLATION

Recognition of the political priority now afforded to environmental protection at a substantive level has been accompanied by a significant refinement in the legal basis of environmental legislation. The Single Act added three articles to the EEC Treaty as Title VII on the Environment,[34] and the inclusion of this Title was, as has been seen, invoked by the Court as a reason for recognising environmental protection as a 'mandatory requirement'. Article 130R sets out wide-ranging Community objectives, including the quality of the environment, human health and the prudent and rational use of natural resources. Article 130S goes on to empower the Council, after *consulting* with the European Parliament and the Economic and Social Committee, to legislate by *unanimous* vote to achieve these objectives.[35]

The Council's power to legislate under Article 130S has not, however, established a universal legal basis for environmental measures. The Single Act's adoption of the principles of Lord Cockfield's White Paper[36] also introduced Article 100A on the approximation of laws with the aim of completing the single market as set out in Article 8A. Unlike Articles 100, 235 and 130S, legislation under Article 100A involves the *co-operation* procedure with the European Parliament and only a *qualified majority* in the Council. Article 100A(3) requires the Commission, in any proposals concerning health, safety, environmental protection and consumer protection, to 'take as a base a high level of protection'. The significance of this provision lies in the fact that, under Article 149(1), the Council can amend a Commission proposal only by unanimous vote. A member state wishing to maintain a high level of protection can therefore block any watering down of a Commission proposal provided that that proposal starts from a high level.

34. Art. 25 of the Single European Act inserted Arts 130R, 130S and 130T as Title VII of the Treaty of Rome.
35. Art. 130S(1).
36. *Completing the Internal Market* COM(85) 310 Final.

The result is that the Treaty contains potentially conflicting procedures for adopting environmental protection legislation which did not exist during the period of reliance upon Articles 100 and 235 (both requiring unanimity) before the passing of the Single European Act.

The correct procedure for the adoption of environmental protection legislation came before the Court in the *Titanium dioxide* case[37] which concerned the legal basis on which the Council had adopted the second titanium dioxide directive.[38] The Commission, supported by the Parliament, challenged the fact that the Council had adopted the directive under Article 130S, thus excluding the procedure of co-operation with the Parliament. The Commission had proposed the directive, prior to the Single European Act, under Articles 100 and 235, and had subsequently changed the basis to Article 100A. The Council's preferred use of Article 130S minimised the legislative input of the 'greener' Parliament.

The Court held that although the legislation had the dual aims of environmental protection and the elimination of disparities in the conditions of competition, it was necessary to establish its 'centre of gravity' in order to determine the most appropriate of the two incompatible procedures. Drawing upon the wording of Article 130R(2), which provides that environmental protection '. . . shall be an integral component of the Community's other policies', the high base level of protection required by Article 100A(3) and the democratic prerogatives of the Parliament, the Court asserted the predominant role of Article 100A in measures with dual objectives. Where measures are adopted to harmonise national rules with a view to completing the Internal Market, Article 100A is the correct legal base. The Court referred to the 'burden upon the undertakings'[39] created by the environmental measures prescribed as a justification for according precedence to Article 100A.

The 'centre of gravity' approach does not, however, exclude Article 130S as the correct legal base in every case. Case C155/91 *Commission v Council*[40] concerned the correct legal base for Council Directive 91/156/EEC, which amended Council Directive 74/422/EEC on waste. The Commission challenged the Council's adoption of the Directive on the legal base of Article 130S, since there was also a Single Market objective. The Council, however, sought to limit the *Titanium dioxide* case to 'exceptional' cases where it is necessary to choose between legal bases when dual, or mixed, objectives are equal. The Court held that, although the directive had an effect on the operation of the Single Market, its primary aim was to protect the environment through management of industrial and domestic waste. Indeed, the directive could not be regarded as promoting free movement of waste within the Community, first, because of the proximity principle and, second, because protection of the environment, as a mandatory requirement, justifies exceptions to Article 30. The directive's ancillary purpose of harmonising the conditions of competition and trade was not sufficient to require the adoption of legislation on the basis of Article 100A. The case therefore establishes that Article 130S, as a legal base, is

37. Judgment June 11 1991, Case C300/89 *Commission v Council*, [1991] ECR I-2867.

38. Council Directive 89/428/EEC June 21 1989 laying down procedures for harmonising programmes for the reduction and eventual elimination of pollution from the titanium dioxide industry (OJ L201, July 14 1989 p.56).

39. Supra note 37, point 23.

40. [1993] ECR I-939.

not confined to matters such as establishment of the European Environmental Agency.[41]

The tensions between the principles of democratic legislative input and the need to choose between two conflicting legal bases for measures of environmental protection may, to some extent, be released by the partial harmonisation of procedures in the Maastricht Treaty on European Union. This provides that Article 100A is to be governed by Article 189B (co-operation and conciliation) and Article 130S by Article 189C (co-operation). Although both procedures allow the Council to legislate by qualified majority, there are differences in the Parliament's powers. But the legal basis question will not be wholly resolved by the Treaty, especially as difficulties may arise from the application of Article 139S(2), requiring unanimity for defined environmental areas. Nor is certainty for the future assured by the fact that, in the minds of some at least, environmental legislation is seen as a candidate for the axe of subsidiarity.

5.0 CONCLUSIONS

The EEC Treaty did not include environmental protection as a distinct objective of the Community, but development of political and public concern required the Court to balance protection of the environment with the explicit economic principles of the Treaty. The case law of the Court suggests that, at least as far as the Court is concerned, this initially unmentioned Community objective can now be taken to rank amongst the Community's central objectives and, potentially, as a fundamental priority. The legislative process, even as developed by the Single European Act and by the Maastricht Treaty, perpetuates the initial difficulties of the lack of a definitive legal base and is likely to remain a source of tension between the member states, the Commission and the European Parliament.

41. See Council Regulation 1210/90/EEC May 7 1990 on the establishment of the European Environment Agency and the European environment information and observation network (OJ L120, May 11 1990, p.1), adopted upon the sole base of Art. 130S.

Chapter 11

The Environment: Recent Trends in Law and Policy: The United Kingdom Example

Denzil Millichap

1.0 INTRODUCTION

The major force behind developments in environmental law in the United Kingdom is the European Community. This has both a 'substantive' and a 'procedural' impact. Particular initiatives taken at the EC level thus find their way into UK legislation – usually by way of legislation implementing EC directives. This also means that the civil law approach of Continental countries has an increasing influence on the legal concepts employed in UK legislation and case law. The existence of the two traditions (Civil Law and Common Law) does create certain problems – especially for the courts who now have to take account of EC law in an increasing number of cases.

Further problems are created by the historical evolution of environmental law in the UK.[1] Piecemeal legal developments in the UK over the centuries have created anomalies and uncertainty: harmonisation of the UK environmental law corpus is thus important in terms of creating a workable legal framework within which the environmentalist, the regulator and industry can operate. This may also require the establishment of a specialised environmental law court able to handle these different strands in an efficient manner. Such an institution may also be able to handle the marriage of civil law and common law approaches more effectively.

However, the target will not stand still. Environmental legislation continues to flood out of Brussels and Whitehall. The courts will be faced with more and more

---

1. *Cambridge Water Company v Eastern Counties Leatherwork plc*, [1994] 2 WLR 53(HL), illustrates the importance of the various heads of liability under tort to present-day pollution problems. Even regulatory authorities (*eg* the National Rivers Authority) may prefer to use those case law rules and principles that have been developed incrementally to protect private property rather than use regulatory powers to (for example) sue a polluter or landowner to obtain the necessary fund to clean up a problem.

cases involving public law, private law and criminal law issues. There will be
further tension both *within* the UK environmental law 'code' and also *between* UK
law/legal culture and the law/legal culture of the EC.[2] Such tensions are already
apparent – for example in the scrutiny by EC institutions of UK implementing-
legislation.[3] The activism of the EC in environmental law not only drives forward
much of UK environmental legislation, it also may influence some of the fundamental legal concepts that are central to the Common Law tradition.

One hallmark of that tradition is the emphasis of English law on a property-based
conception of legal rights and duties: this does not always sit happily with the civil
law approach which is more willing to place limits on the exercise of rights – even
to the extent of recognising positive duties to others. Another difference between the
two traditions perhaps lies in the greater emphasis (in interpreting legislation)
placed by the courts on purposive reasoning: an approach which focuses invariably
on the underlying (social, political and economic) purpose of the legislation under
examination.

The first section looks at one potential conflict for the future between the civil law
and the common law approach. The example comes from the Netherlands – a
country whose geographical and geological situation makes it particularly sensitive
to environmental issues. This is the problem posed by liability for damage to the
'non-owned environment'. This example also has particular relevance to the
petroleum industry as it involves tanker pollution.

2.0 THE NON-OWNED ENVIRONMENT

The traditional concern of the English courts to protect identifiable property rights
is often held out as the key thread in legal developments in the UK. That concern
may, however, in the light of environmental law and policy not be appropriate as the
touchstone of legal developments in the EC context. Environmental pollution can
damage not only 'ordinary' property – buildings etc which are owned by someone –
it can also damage and destroy those elements in the environment which are not
owned. The Common Law tradition may find it very difficult to develop concepts (in
the absence of legislation directed to this problem) that go behind private property
rights and their protection. In the absence of legislation the issue of compensation
for damage to the flora and fauna that live freely on land and in the sea will not be
addressed in the way which the Netherlands courts have (as is shown below).

The legislative approach can fill the gap. Pollution (the most obvious example
being oil pollution problems) of the marine environment has in fact led to, in many
cases, specific legislation (linked to international conventions). Such legislation
seeks to regulate a potentially polluting activity. It may also form the basis of a
compensation system if pollution does occur.[4]

In the United States, the Oil Pollution Act 1990 (a response at federal level to the
Exxon Valdez accident) established liability for damage caused to natural resources

2. Woolf LJ, 'Are the Judiciary Environmentally Myopic?', *Journal of Environmental Law* (1992),
Vol. 4, No.1, p.1. L. Kramer, 'The Open Society, Its Lawyers and Its Environment', *Journal of
Environmental Law* (1989), Vol.1 No.1, p.1.
3. The conflict regarding the implementation of the EC Directive on environmental assessment in the
UK is one recent example: this is discussed below.

resulting from oil spills. Liability covers the cost of restoring, replacing, rehabilitat-
ing or acquiring an equivalent for the damaged resource as well as the diminution
in value pending restoration and reasonable assessment costs. Nearer home there is
the example (of particular relevance perhaps for the UK offshore industry) of the
Norwegian Pollution Control Act of 1989. This established strict liability for
damage caused by pollution from an installation. If such pollution affects the non-
commercial exercise of rights commonly enjoyed over the use of open spaces then
the government or private associations with a specific legal interest in the assertion
of such rights can claim restoration costs of a reasonable level from the owner of the
facility.[5]

In addition to these specific statutory codes there is a more interesting development from the Netherlands. This involves a judgment of the District Court of
Rotterdam of March 15 1991. In this case[6] an oil spill from a tanker had polluted the
sea water of the North Sea and the coasts of Zeeland and Zuid-Holland. Thousands
of seabirds were affected and the Netherlands Association for the Protection of
Birds planned and executed a rescue operation to remove the birds, clean them up
and ultimately release them.

This involved co-ordinated activity with various local bodies which ran bird
centres and bird shelters. The Association then sought to recover the costs incurred
in this rescue programme against the owners of the ship. The claim was made on the
basis of general principles of tort law as set out in the Netherlands Civil Code. An
initial problem was that the Association did not have any property interests which
were directly damaged by the oil spill – they did not own the seabirds which had
been affected. The problem of giving the non-owned environment a legal foothold
was thus faced by the Court – without having any specific statute law to rely on. The
District Court however approached the issue in the following way. It held that
although the birds were 'non-owned property' their 'maintenance and protection
have to be seen as a general interest which deserves to be protected in the
Netherlands according to common opinion nowadays'. The general interest in
protecting and conserving such elements of the environment was therefore held to
be an interest which could be protected by the law. The next stage in the argument

4. In this respect the following are relevant at the supra-national level:
– The 1969 Civil Liability Convention (and 1984 Protocol).
– The 1971 Fund Convention for Oil Pollution Damage.
– The 1954 International Convention on the Prevention of Pollution of the Sea by Oil (and 1962, 1969
    and 1976 Protocols).
– The 1976 Protocol to the 1969 International Convention on Civil Liability for Oil Pollution
    Damage.
– The London Convention on the Prevention of Marine Pollution by Dumping of Wastes and Other
    Matter 1972, as amended.
– The London Convention for the Prevention of Pollution from Ships 1973 (and 1978 Protocol).
– The Oslo Convention for the Prevention of Marine Pollution by Dumping of Wastes and Other Matter
    1972 (and 1983 Protocol).
– The Paris Convention for the prevention of Marine Pollution from Land Based Sources 1974.
5. Contrast the position in the UK, where the Merchant Shipping (Oil Pollution) Act 1971 imposes
strict liability on the owner of a ship carrying persistent oil in bulk for the escape or discharge of such
oil. The owner is liable for any damage caused, for the cost of measures reasonably taken to prevent or
reduce such damage, and for damage caused by such measures taken. The 'damage' which can be
claimed for under the Act is limited to property damage and *does not* cover ecological harm.
6. District Court of Rotterdam, Mar. 15 1991, NJ 1992, 92 – 'The *Borcea*'.

was then to find that the Association's interests could be identified with that general interest; the Court, in that respect, said:

In view of the objects of the plaintiff and the activity which it has been carrying out for the realisation thereof during 90 years . . . that general interest must also be seen as the plaintiff's own interest.

The Court further said:

. . . it is only logical that the plaintiff who is entitled to prevent or stop its interests from being harmed, could also claim the damage which is sustained as a consequence thereof or be compensated for the costs which it incurred in order to limit or prevent the consequences thereof by the party who affected its interests.

The Court also had to conclude that the owners of the ship acted unlawfully towards the Association. The Court stated that the owner:

. . . could and should have known that the interest to maintain and protect seabirds is considered an interest to be defended by law and that measures are taken to stop the results of oil pollution as much as possible.

The contrast with the well-publicised *Rose Theatre* case in the UK is striking.[7] The High Court refused to give standing to an association specifically formed to promote the 'historic built environment' represented by the Rose Theatre. The association had no property rights at stake (the common law tradition and its emphasis on protection of private property rights clearly had a great influence) and so had no identifiable interest which the court would recognise. The court made reference to the fact that an individual of acknowledged distinction in the field of archaeology would not have such standing and this was apparently an appropriate analogy. The criticism of this case may have influenced the same judge to adopt a slightly more forgiving approach when he dealt with a case involving proposals to develop heathland on which some rare amphibians were living.[8]

He held that a non-incorporated association could have sufficient standing due to its long association with the site, its financial input into the site and that it was given power under a condition of the planning permission to catch and relocate rare species prior to development.

Where important environmental interests have to rely on a human agent to protect their 'rights' the UK law will have to make significant developments in its jurisprudence to cover such situations. The range of interests which the law will recognise will have to be expanded beyond those that are proprietorial in nature. The problems of a narrow view of standing will also have to be faced. Common interest groups will then be able to promote those interests affected by ecological damage. Interest groups and pressure groups are already active (for example bringing private prosecutions against those in breach of environmental law standards) in promoting environmental interests. However, the UK Government's implementation quite recently of a Directive on access to environmental information has been criticised for not dealing with the problem that faced the Rose Theatre Trust in establishing standing. The implementation of the access to information Directive relies for its enforcement provisions on the mechanism of judicial review. If a body fails to

7. *R v Secretary of State for the Environment ex parte Rose Theatre Trust* [1990] 1 All ER 754.
8. *R v Poole Borough Council ex parte Beebee, Journal of Environmental Law* (1991), Vol.3, p.293.

comply with the legal norms, the sanction of judicial review will not be available to those who do not have a direct interest of a proprietorial nature. Landowning interest groups such as the National Trust may be able to avoid such difficulties – relying on their proprietorial interests. However, pressure and interest groups without that proprietorial interest are likely to fail to meet the tests for standing. Those interests they represent may therefore suffer as a result of the UK's implementation of a Directive which fails to take account of certain weaknesses in the approach of the courts to environmental issues.

How might the UK courts deal with the issue of giving standing to an environmental interest represented by a pressure group? One relevant authority from a common law jurisdiction does provide a full discussion of the importance of accommodating such an approach. The arguments for the extension of standing were set out in a dissenting judgment in a well-known case in US law. Thus in *Sierra Club v Morton* the dissenting opinion by Justice Douglas focused on the 'jurisprudential' arguments for admitting a claim by a pressure group seeking to protect an environmental interest in the absence of any injury to their property interests.[9] The pressure group failed on the standing issue.[10] However, the approach taken by the dissenting judge may well find favour with some of the more adventurous judiciary in the UK who have indicated a wider concern for accommodating environmental issues within a reformed legal framework. Such a view may therefore parallel the Netherlands approach which looks further than mere 'property-based' harm to the plaintiff.[11] The Netherlands precedent could also be important as regards the formulation of EC legislation in this field. (This is not to say that less adventurous decisions in other EC member states will not have a restraining influence.) The recognition of giving standing to environmental interests in this way may therefore find expression in future Directives and Regulations. The UK courts and Parliament may therefore have to face head-on the need to expand the environmental law jurisprudence to match such developments. The proposal for a Directive on civil liability for environmental damage (although held in limbo for the moment) clearly raises this issue. Other problems (proof, causation, joint tortfeasors, etc) will no doubt arise but the clear signal given by the Netherlands case is something that cannot be ignored as indicating a trend for not only Netherlands law but perhaps EC law in general.[12]

9. *Sierra Club v Morton* 405 US 727.

10. By coincidence the link with the Netherlands sea-birds case involving the *Borcea* is underlined by the dissenting judge's reference (in his discussion of the problem of legal personality) to maritime law and the fiction that a ship has a legal personality. Thus at p. 741, Justice Douglas made reference to the fact that ships have legal personalities in litigation involving maritime disputes. He went on to say that this and other examples of legal fiction should also indicate the appropriateness of giving standing to items of the natural environment such as valleys, rivers, lakes, estuaries etc. He further went on to say that those '. . . people who have a meaningful relation to that body of water – whether it be a fisherman, a canoeist, a zoologist, or logger – must be able to speak for the values which the river represents and which are threatened with destruction'. This link between the general interest in recognising that inanimate objects in the environment have legal status and then allowing those individuals or groups with a special interest in protecting such elements of the environment is thus apparent from this dissenting judgment.

11. This emphasis on protecting property is an approach which would most probably defeat claims in the UK.

12. On Jan. 1 1991 the new Environmental Liability Act 1991 (*Umwelthaftungsgesetz*) came into force in Germany. This introduced strict liability for damage to property caused by industrial facilities. It did not introduce liability for environmental damage caused to the non-owned environment.

3.0 LEGISLATIVE ACTION BY THE EC

If we turn to specific EC action in the environmental sphere it is possible to discern important legal and policy initiatives that show the trend towards a body of legal norms designed to conserve and enhance the environment in a way which UK law and policy has not yet fully comprehended. The first two examples taken here relate to EC directives whose implementation has indicated that the EC (through its various organs) is promoting a view of environmental interests which puts them above economic interests. The first example involves infringements of the Directive relating to wild birds. The EC Directive 79/409/EEC on the conservation of wild birds required member states to give special protection to specified habitats of protected birds through designating 'special protection areas'. The German Government had built a dyke which, according to the Commission, had disturbed birds which enjoyed special protection under the Directive and had damaged a special protection area. The German Government argued that the sole purpose of these operations were to secure the safety of the dyke and that in planning and executing the works the competent authorities had taken account of the conservation objective of the Directive and had balanced these against the aims of coastal protection. The European Court found in the *Leybucht* case[13] that once an area had been designated as a special protection area pursuant to Article 4(1) of the Directive then a later Article (Article 4(4) – which allowed the modification or reduction of the areas) could only be used on exceptional grounds. The Court interpreted these 'exceptional grounds' by reference to the 'general interest' which was represented by the ecological objective of the Directive – the protection of wild birds. Accordingly other interests recognised by the Directive in Article 2 (economic and recreational aspects) were not interests which had an equal or greater importance than the ecological objectives of the Directive. Although the decision of the Court was that the German authorities had not infringed the Directive, it is clear that the subordination of economic interests to environmental ones is not something at which the court will baulk.

In assessing the case the Court was clearly taking the purposive approach. As EC legislation (in common with civil law legislation in general) invariably contains a large number of prefatory remarks relating to the purpose of the legislation the examination of such purposive clauses by the courts directly influences their analysis and so has a direct bearing on the final decision. Other directives in the environmental field contain such initial purposive clauses and so the approach of the European Court in interpreting environmental legislation must clearly, in the long term, influence the way in which English courts approach such law. This will often involve subordinating economic interests to environmental interests when it comes to interpreting environmental law.[14] However, the UK Government (the Department of the Environment) has not necessarily taken on board the real import of the *Leybucht* case in framing its revised policy as to how local planning authorities

---

13. *Commission of the European Communities v Federal Republic of Germany*, Case C57/89, *The Times Law Reports*, Mar. 20 1991.

14. Other more general aspects of the impact of interpreting and applying EC law in member states (the direct effect doctrine etc) are of course relevant but will not to be discussed here for reasons of brevity.

should approach their consideration of development proposals affecting special protection areas. The UK planning regime has used existing statutory designations to give protection under existing law instead of creating a special legal mechanism for the purpose of protecting such areas. In advising local planning authorities on the appropriate way to assess development proposals, the Department of the Environment has not applied the more stringent approach of the ECJ (where economic interests cannot be a basis for prejudicing special protection areas) in relation to such designated sites. The potential for infringement proceedings for improper implementation of the Directive is therefore very real should a development proposal be given permission which affects such an area but does not meet the more stringent criteria which the ECJ found to be necessary. This implementation problem also arises in the second example noted below.

The second example deals with an EC directive relating to environmental assessment – 85/337/EEC. The most recent stage of this particular conflict between the European Commission and the UK Government is set out in a European Commission press release of July 31 1992. Seven specific instances involving 'infrastructure' projects had been the subject of attention by the European Commission. These involved motorway extensions/works, a rail link between London and the Channel Tunnel, a road project in East London affecting Oxleas Wood and a British Petroleum development at Kinneil in Scotland. The latter two projects, according to the European Commission, had not been subject to proper assessment as required by the environmental assessment Directive. In the first situation it was felt by the Commission that the Department of Transport (the body responsible for the project) had failed both to identify and assess the main environmental effects that the project would have in relation to soil and fauna (namely mammalian, reptilian and amphibian populations). The Directive specifically sets out a list of environmental 'receptors' which need to be addressed where it is found that significant effects are likely to occur by virtue of the project. As regards the British Petroleum development the view of the Commission was that the Directive's requirements as regards consultation with the public and consideration by the competent authority of the environmental information were not followed in the assessment procedure. On one view these instances may be seen as merely 'teething problems' in getting to grips with a complex system and procedure. However, since the Commission is considering the extension of environmental assessment to policies, plans and programmes it is clear that such complexity will multiply.

A more rigorous analysis of the appropriate balance between development interests and those of the environment is also apparent at the policy level. In this respect, the policy initiatives in the Fifth Environmental Action Programme break new ground. Its very title (Towards Sustainability) indicates the dramatic shift away from one of the basic tenets underlying the Treaty of Rome. Balanced economic growth (seen as crucial in preventing economic and military conflict in Europe) of EC member states was the central aim of the Treaty. Economic growth was accepted *per se* – it merely had to be balanced in order to avoid political and economic conflict and the risk of (military) catastrophe. The Fifth EAP questions that basic assumption that growth is good *per se*.[15] Growth must be sustainable. The

---

15. Commission of the European Communities 'Towards Sustainability' Mar. 27 1992 COM(92) 23 Vol. II.

underlying rationale being that unsustainable growth will bring with it environmental catastrophe. This new policy approach thus emphasises a view of environmental protection that clearly puts the 'social' use of resources at a premium. It remains to be seen whether such a fundamental change in the aims of the European Economic Community will in fact be accepted and find expression in legislation and concrete policy initiatives. If it does then perhaps the European Economic Community will give way to the 'European Environmental Community'. For industry this basic shift from balancing growth to controlling growth such that it is sustainable will have major consequences. Already the current initiatives on, for example, reduction of sulphur content in petroleum products are going to involve a very significant investment in the EC petroleum industry.

4.0 IMPLEMENTATION AND ENFORCEMENT

A particular feature of the UK presidency of the EC in 1992 was an emphasis on the enforcement and implementation aspects of environmental legislation and policy. Initiatives have therefore been taken to set up a network of enforcement agencies so that information, strategies and techniques can be shared. This will enable a more realistic picture to emerge of the effectiveness of regulation and to show how particular member states are dealing with the implementation of EC directives, etc. The UK Government has suspected that the proclaimed environmentalism of certain countries, when it comes to setting up legislative mechanisms and procedures, does not actually seep through into positive enforcement and implementation at the ground level. One problem with this approach is that the countries which do implement the directives in an efficient manner will thereby impose extra costs on industry which other EC countries (less thorough with implementation) are avoiding. This particular focus of the UK Government is therefore tied in with the issue of the interaction between environmental regulation and industrial competitiveness of member states.

If we turn to enforcement of specific environmental standards, it is clear that recent developments in UK practice are important for industry. Environmental issues are now important and have a very high profile among the public. This increased visibility of environmental issues is mirrored in (so it seems) increased concern for implementation/enforcement issues. The National Rivers Authority (NRA) is a good example of a regulator seeking to improve its image as a protector of the environment and a determined opponent of the polluter.

It is clear that the courts are also viewing environmental infractions as contraventions requiring swift and punitive action. The activities of both regulator and judiciary in the punishment of offenders is borne out by the recent record of the NRA in pursuing a vigorous and activist approach to enforcing provisions of the Water Resources Act 1991. The legislation itself mirrors the increased concern for making the polluter pay. Offences, including the 'making or continuation of a discharge' are prosecuted by NRA inspectors on a strict liability basis with a maximum penalty, in the Magistrates' Court, of £20,000. This represents a recent tenfold increase in the maximum imposable fine, reinforcing the enforcement armoury of the inspectors.

How has this legislation been used in practice? In the period from January 1992 to end-July 1992 the NRA brought 269 cases to court, an increase of about 25 per cent on the same period in the previous year.[16] In September 1991 the NRA published a report[17] indicating a 'dramatic fall' in the number of serious pollution incidents, down from 658 in 1990 to 386 in 1991. The NRA stated that this was due to its tough and rigorous pollution prevention and control measures and the strong signals being sent by the courts (via increased fines). Such action by the NRA in the last two years has indicated a greater willingness to use the courts to penalise polluters who overstep the bounds set by the regulations.

Fines are not now the only credible and accepted weapon of the regulator. The law allows other penalties. Recently one such weapon was used for the first time and, in effect, sets a precedent for its use in other situations where the circumstances merit vigorous enforcement action against those who are actually in control of a company's activities. That weapon is the disqualification of a director from holding office. Thus a director, as a result of his quarry company being fined for a health and safety offence, was disqualified under the Company Directors Disqualification Act 1986, section 2.[18] The firm had failed to observe a prohibition notice issued by the Health and Safety Executive and so failed to protect employees from falling rocks. The Lewes Crown Court considered that a fine (levied against the company and the director) was not sufficient punishment and so imposed a two year ban under section 2 of the 1986 Act. The liability of directors etc for offences under environmental law committed by their companies is based on a provision whose terms are frequently repeated in the various principal statutes dealing with environmental regulation. In the health and safety area this provision is section 37 of the Health and Safety at Work etc Act 1974. Provisions with similar or identical wording appear in the Town and Country Planning Act 1990 (section 331), the Environmental Protection Act 1990 (section 157) and the Water Resources Act 1991 (section 217). The combined effects of such provisions, the disqualification power and this particular case from the health and safety field mean that regulatory authorities are given the green light to make applications to the courts for the disqualification of directors: naturally the criminal courts would tend to make such orders only where a good case can be made out for driving home the point that environmental protection is an important goal which may need to be supported in some cases by disqualification. A clear and calculating breach of control that involves prejudice to an important 'environmental interest' (safety of workers in the working environment being a clear example) would thus be needed before the courts would consider imposing such a penalty. In terms of the special provision making directors etc liable a wilful breach of the relevant controls would probably have to be shown before the courts decided to exercise their powers to disqualify. Since pressure groups are sometimes now to be found taking action in the criminal courts against polluters there is clearly a possibility that such orders will be sought during private criminal prosecutions.

16. 'NRA Pollution Prosecutions January–July 1992' *Environment Business* Suppl. Oct. 21 1992.
17. 'Water Pollution Incidents in England and Wales 1991: Second Annual Report Water Quality Series No. 9', NRA Sept. 1991.
18. *Health and Safety Executive v Chapman, The Independent*, July 1 1992.

5.0 SUBSIDIARITY

Political events in the wake of Maastricht have had their effect on the future course of environmental legislation and policy in the EC. A central issue is the operation of the principle of subsidiarity as regards EC environmental policy and its implementation via a legislative programme. It has been suggested that subsidiarity (whatever the precise definition of it may turn out to be) would point to EC member states being the primary decision-making bodies as regards environmental regulation, etc. However, it is more likely that the majority of EC member states will take the view that the interrelated and regional nature of environmental problems – which is more evident on the Continent than in the UK – means that Brussels is the more appropriate place for setting the basic standards and mechanisms. This will also help to ensure that there is a 'level playing field' throughout the EC as regards environmental regulation. The principle of subsidiarity may mean that, in particular instances, the more detailed aspects of environmental regulation will be left to member states but it is more likely that the special concerns posed by pollution (which is no respecter of national boundaries) would in general point to the need for action from the top rather than the bottom. An increasing emphasis on the subsidiarity principle (once it is defined to the satisfaction of all) will therefore lead to discussions about local regulation in particular and limited circumstances, rather than relying on local regulation as the normal basis for dealing with environmental issues. (Whether the UK Government is, in effect, looking for the subsidiarity principle to provide an opt-out on environmental regulation akin to that enjoyed in respect of the Social Charter is a matter which might be a subject for debate – but not here!)

6.0 CONCLUSION

Recent developments (in both law and policy) in the EC and the UK indicate that the impact of environmental law liability upon industry will be increasingly important. Risk management (avoiding or reducing to an acceptable degree the risk of civil liability, criminal liability and administrative action) is going to become a key feature of business practice in the 1990s: such will be the reaction as policy initiatives are translated first into EC legislation and then into domestic law in member states. In many things the US experience indicates how events might turn out, the problems that will be encountered, the costs that will have to be borne and the defensive mechanisms that will have to be instituted. Legislation can be influenced at Brussels and Whitehall. Influencing public opinion is something that is much more difficult. The realistic approach is thus one of attempting to influence the detail rather than prevent at all the increased regulation of activity which affects the environment. This ties in with the increased importance for business of knowing the specific issues (as regards environmental liability) arising from past and present activity affecting the environment. In this respect, an environmental audit of such activity is perhaps an essential prerequisite of the effective management of risk as the decade progresses. With such information the business concerned can at least then plan its defences, cost its solutions and implement its strategies at a pace which is least damaging to its general corporate goals. Such a proactive approach is necessary since the trends apparent in the last few years may presage a further tightening of environmental regulation.

Section 4

Oil and Gas

Chapter 12

Planning Considerations for the Oil and Gas Industry

David Brock

1.0 INTRODUCTION

There have been several important changes in planning law in the United Kingdom in the last few years. These include the implementation of EEC Directive 85/337 requiring an assessment of environmental effects of certain projects, the consolidation of the Town and Country Planning Acts in 1990, and the subsequent amendments to those Acts by the Planning and Compensation Act 1991, the implementation of controls over hazardous substances, and a plethora of new Government policy guidance notes, a number of which are still at the draft stage, including those on pollution control and nature conservation issues.

The whole tenor of the changes has been a tightening of controls and a gradual shift away from the presumption in favour of development, which has been a hallmark of the planning system since 1947, to a more restrictive regime where forward planning and environmental considerations are given greater weight.

The planning law system is the place where the public can most easily make its voice heard. The extensive public consultation system provides a forum. Public concern about changes and the environment is easily expressed in the planning system. Partly as a consequence of this, many new provisions have an environmental flavour.

This Chapter considers the most significant changes for the oil and gas industry. A key document which deals explicitly with overlap and the relationships between planning law and pollution control law is the draft Planning Policy Guidance (PPG) Note on planning and pollution control.

2.0 THE DRAFT PPG ON PLANNING AND POLLUTION CONTROL

In 1990, in its White Paper on the Environment *This Common Inheritance*, the

Government undertook to 'consider the need for . . . guidance on the relationship between planning and pollution control in the light of new measures in the Environmental Protection Bill'.

In December 1991, the Department of the Environment commissioned a study by Environmental Resources Ltd in association with Oxford Polytechnic into the relationship between planning control on the one hand and pollution and waste management control on the other. The aim of the study was to provide information to assist the Department in the preparation of the new guidance necessary following the implementation of the Environmental Protection Act 1990.

The resulting draft PPG was published for consultation in June 1992, and the consultation period ended on August 10. The contents of the draft PPG will be of interest to the oil and gas industry in relation to its land-based operations, as a number of the processes which the industry undertakes require pollution control consent under the Environmental Protection Act 1990 in relation to integrated pollution control (IPC) or local authority air pollution control (LAAPC) and for any discharges to controlled waters. The prescribed processes for which IPC consent is required include:

(a) Reforming or refining natural gas.
(b) Odorising natural gas or liquefied petroleum.
(c) Producing gas from coal, lignite, oil or other carbonaceous material.
(d) Purifying or refining any product of any of the processes described above or converting it into a different product.
(e) The loading or unloading or handling or storage of, or the physical, chemical or thermal treatment of crude oil, stabilised crude petroleum, crude shale oil or any associated gas.

The industry also, of course, needs discharge consents from the National Rivers Authority (NRA) for discharges to controlled waters – which include coastal waters.

The construction of new facilities where a prescribed process is going to be carried on, or in which a process needing a discharge licence is going to be undertaken, needs planning permission. So do extensions to existing facilities. The requirement for planning permission and pollution control consents therefore create the possibility of duplication of controls.

The draft PPG starts from the premise that planning control should not duplicate pollution control (paras 1.1, 1.25). This is a matter of key importance to any developers intending to carry out potentially polluting developments because it means they will be able to make their application for planning control safe in the knowledge that the local planning authority will be able to make its decision on the planning merits taking into account all material considerations. These considerations may well include the need for authorisation under the Environmental Protection Act, IPC or LAAPC for the carrying out of a prescribed process, or the need to obtain a licence from the NRA for discharge of water into controlled waters. These are just some of the matters which the local planning authority will take into account in making its planning judgement. They should not of themselves predetermine how the decision on the planning application will be made.

The advice given suggests that there should in future be a considerable flow of advice between planning authorities and the pollution control agencies. The classic problem for a planning authority, asked to give permission for a specialised development, is the need for specialist advice. To some extent this has been exacerbated by the requirements for environmental assessment. The authority will be presented with an environmental statement prepared by the applicant and its advisers. How is the planning authority to judge the statement without advice from its own experts? As environmental assessments often deal with air and water quality, the pollution control authorities have a natural role to play. Furthermore, where a pollution control authorisation is to be obtained, they will later be dealing with the applications for these authorisations.

In turn, this leads to another dilemma, this time for the developer/industrialist. With the advent of integrated pollution control which can control layout and design of buildings, how is the developer/industrialist to ensure that it is not caught between conflicting requirements of the planning authority on the one hand and the pollution control authority on the other?

Finally, there is the question of pollution policies in the development plan.

How does the draft PPG address these issues?

2.1 Consultation and Advice

The draft PPG begins its advice on this with the uncontroversial statement that:

... applicants should be able to provide sufficient information on the pollution aspects of the proposed development, with the advice of the pollution control authorities, to enable a sound planning decision to be made (para.3.3).

It then goes on to advise planning authorities to obtain advice from the pollution authorities in the case of a development which seems likely to raise significant pollution issues. The pollution control authorities are to be asked whether the development is likely to meet pollution control objectives (para.3.6).

In para. 3.9, the planning authority is advised that where consultation reveals that there is likely to be an insuperable obstacle to the granting of a pollution control authorisation, then one of three courses may be chosen:

(i)   consideration of the application may be delayed until the pollution control authority is reasonably likely to be satisfied;

(ii) conditions may be attached, limiting the use to processes which are not subject to pollution control;

(iii) the permission may be refused if the only use for the development is one for which there is no reasonable prospect of a pollution control authorisation.

It will be obvious that pollution control authorities will have a great deal of power if the PPG is adopted in its current state. As consultees, they will almost be in a position to direct refusal of all applications for planning permission. This is a power which was taken away from highway authorities in 1988. Thus, applications for a development which necessitates a pollution control authorisation will need to be supported by material which adequately describes the pollution control measures. A convincing case that the relevant criteria can be met will be desirable. Without it, the pollution control authority, no doubt pressed for time, might conclude that the authorisation would not be given when applied for.

This new requirement, which will effectively apply to any planning application of importance, will mean that development proposals will have to be formulated in much greater detail at an earlier stage. This might be considered unfortunate. An application for planning permission is often made to establish the principle of development at that site. It may be made before the land is purchased, or as part of a contract which is conditional on planning approval. The draft PPG will lead to far greater expenditure at the outset. One way round this may be to make applications in generic terms, for example for a general industrial (B2) building. This, however, for the oil and gas industry, necessitates careful consideration of use class B2, to ensure that the proposed use does not fall within use classes B3, B4, B5 and B6, which are excluded from B2.[1]

It also seems that para. 3.9 will in fact achieve the very duplication of control which the draft PPG sets out to avoid. It is difficult to see what harm there can be in granting permission for a development which is then not given its pollution control authorisation.

2.2 The Conflicting Requirements of Planning and IPC

The most likely ground for conflict between these two regimes is in the design and layout of buildings. These matters have always been controlled by the planning system. Under IPC, they are also controlled by Her Majesty's Inspectorate of Pollution (HMIP). This is because under the Environmental Protection Act 1990 Section 7 conditions are to be imposed on authorisations to ensure that in carrying on a prescribed process the best available techniques not entailing excessive cost, (BATNEEC) will be used. Section 7(10) provides that BATNEEC can include design, construction and layout of buildings.

A couple of obvious examples show how conflict could arise:

(i) The planning authority requires chemical storage to be located near to the site entrance to minimise on-site vehicle movements. HMIP requires storage away from the road because of the risk of polluting the storm water drainage systems in case of spillage.

(ii) The planning authority requires the stack to be below a certain height to avoid piercing the horizon. HMIP requires it to be higher to minimise air pollution.

The draft PPG urges close consultation between the pollution control and planning authority in such circumstances to try to resolve the matter (para.3.10). This has the merit of pragmatism and it is difficult to see what else the draft PPG could say in the absence of 'harmonising' legislation.

One solution would be for the applications for planning permission and IPC authorisation to be made at the same time, thus ensuring that all the relevant information is available, but leaving it to the planning authority to reach its own decision on the planning merits in the light of all the relevant considerations including the likelihood of IPC consent being granted. It would be even better if both the permission and the authorisation could be granted simultaneously. This would avoid the possibility of one authority revising its requirements. This approach, however, includes all the expense of front-end loading. At least it has the

---

1. In Feb. 1994 the Department of the Environment proposed abolishing use classes B3–B6 and widening B2 to encompass them. If this goes ahead a generic B2 application will be more attractive.

benefit that both applications will be considered in the light of the fullest information. It might also avoid double expense in preparing two environmental assessments.

In its March 1993 report on Environmental Assessment and Integrated Pollution Control, the working party (chaired by the author of this chapter) of the United Kingdom Environmental Law Association, and the Institute of Environmental Assessment recommended that consideration be given:

(i)   To establishing an optional tandem procedure which would utilise one assessment and ensure that conflicts between the requirements of the planning authority and HMIP, specifically, in regard to overlaps inherent in BATNEEC do not occur or are resolved in both consent procedures.
(ii) To ways of allowing developers to submit one assessment document which would serve the planning purposes and IPC application.
(iii) To methods of reducing conflict between the requirements of the planning system and IPC.

This report has generated considerable interest and has been sent to the Department of the Environment and HMIP.[2]

2.3 Pollution Control Policies in the Development Plan

The Government has proposed wider environmental policies in Development Plans. The advice given in the draft PPG is reasonably encouraging to industry:

[Development Plans] should make realistic provision for the types of industry or facility which may be detrimental to amenity or a potential source of pollution (para.2.5).

It also suggests that authorities drawing up local plans should identify land suitable for potentially polluting development. Authorities are then encouraged to provide 'State of the Environment Reports', as a method of establishing a baseline of data and of measuring progress.

3.0 THE PLANNING (HAZARDOUS SUBSTANCES) ACT 1990

This Act came into force on June 1 1992, and it introduces for the first time a separate system of control over the presence of hazardous substances on, over or under land. Control is to be exercised by the relevant Hazardous Substances Authority (HSA) which will usually be the same body as the local planning authority.

The Act applies only to England and Wales. Similar provisions amending the Town and Country Planning (Scotland) Act 1972 are now in force.

2. The draft PPG was considered by the High Court in *Gateshead MBC v Secretary of State for the Environment and Northumbria Water Group PLC* [1994] JPL 255. The Deputy Judge, Jeremy Sullivan QC, held that the existence of the IPC System was a material consideration which the planning authority should take into account. He also stated that in cases where the pollution effects could not be dealt with at all under IPC, the planning authority could refuse planning permission. However, he said there was no hard and fast line. The case is going to the Court of Appeal.

The Planning (Hazardous Substances) Regulations 1992, which also came into force on June 1 1992, specify the hazardous substances and the controlled quantities for the purposes of the new consent requirement and also provide certain exceptions. It also sets out the procedures for obtaining consent and for enforcement.

The substances which, if present at or above the controlled quantities, will be subject to the new hazardous substances consents requirements, include liquefied petroleum gas, any gas flammable in air and various liquefied gases.

The substances listed are drawn from the Control of Major Accident Hazards Regulations 1984 (CIMAH) and Notification of Installations Handling Hazardous Substances Regulations (NIHHS). They do not include all the substances to which those two Regulations apply. As a first stage check, if a site is affected by those regulations, managers should look at the Planning (Hazardous Substances) Regulations 1992 to see if materials held are also listed in those regulations. Storing a hazardous substance without consent is a criminal offence with a maximum penalty of £20,000 on summary conviction or an unlimited fine on conviction on indictment.

3.1 Deemed Hazardous Substances Consent – Section 11

Deemed consent could be claimed where a hazardous substance has been present on, over or under a site during a 12-month period immediately preceding the coming into force of the Act on June 30 1992. In such cases a valid claim had to be made to the Hazardous Substances Authority within six months, *ie* by no later than November 30 1992. The application had to be made in the prescribed form. Provided a valid claim was correctly and accurately made, hazardous substances consent was automatically deemed to be granted subject to the standard conditions. The authority in that case is limited to determining whether the claim had been validly made. If it considered the claim was invalid, it had to give this opinion within two weeks of receipt of the claim.

The standard conditions include prescribing the maximum aggregate quantity of the substance that may be present on, over or under the land. They are designed to ensure that there is no significant change in the manner in which a substance is kept without the HSA having the opportunity to exercise detailed control.

If no valid claim for deemed consent was made by November 30 1992, the right to deemed consent will have been lost.

3.2 Obtaining Hazardous Substances Consent When it is First Proposed to Store Hazardous Substances

Because, from June 1 1992, it has been necessary to obtain hazardous substances consent for any new storage of a hazardous substance, if a new facility is to be built or if a hazardous substance is going to be stored for the first time, a consent must be obtained before storage.

A consent will also be necessary for any substances which have not been held for long enough to qualify for a deemed consent. A transitional exemption to deal with this situation was introduced in the commencement order for the Act. It provides that no offence is committed and no contravention notice can be issued in respect of the presence of a substance without consent for a period of 28 days from the commencement date. Furthermore, if an application for consent is made within this time period, the exemption is continued for eight weeks or until determination, whichever is the earlier.

Before an application for hazardous substances consent is made, publicity must be given to the application by way of a notice in a local newspaper, a site notice and notice to any other person with an interest in the land. The form of this notice is prescribed in Schedule 2 to the 1992 Regulations. The application form is also prescribed in Schedule 2 of the Regulations.

The hazardous substances authority must then consult the Health and Safety Executive and other public bodies including the National Rivers Authority.

Although the Health and Safety Executive has no power to direct the authority to refuse an application where the authority are minded to grant consent against its advice, it must give 21 days' notice in order that the Health and Safety Executive can decide whether to request the Secretary of State to call-in the application.

The Hazardous Substances Authority considers the application in much the same way that it would for a planning application. That is to say, it must have regard to any material consideration including the provisions of the development plan. Because the Planning (Hazardous Substances) Act 1990 is also a 'planning act', Section 54A of the Town and Country Planning Act 1990 also applies. This means that a decision must be in accordance with the development plan unless material considerations indicate otherwise. It is somewhat odd that such a technical matter as a hazardous substances consent should be subject to the very political provisions of a development plan. This makes it all the more important to be alive to the implications of Section 54A which is dealt with in Section 4 of this Chapter.

Appeals are to the Secretary of State and the spirit of the procedure for an inquiry or written representation Appeal under the Town and Country Planning Act will be applied as appropriate.

3.3 Inter-relationship with Planning Permissions

The Government issued Circular 11/92 with the Regulations to give guidance on the new system. It advises that in cases where both planning permission and hazardous substances consent will be required, it will now be sensible from both the developer's and the authority's point of view for the related applications for hazardous substances consent and planning permission to be dealt with together. The circular goes on to advise that this does not necessarily mean that similar decisions should be given on both applications. For example, although a local authority may decide, having considered the potential risk to the local community arising from the proposed presence of a hazardous substance, that there is no good reason for withholding hazardous substances consent, it may nevertheless determine as the local planning authority, that planning permission should not be granted for the associated development because of the wider planning considerations, such as the adverse effect of the proposed building on the local scene or inadequate access arrangements/traffic problems.

3.4 General Development Order 1988 and Use Classes Order 1987

With the introduction of the specific planning controls over the presence of hazardous substances, the former restrictions in the General Development Order and the Use Classes Order in relation to 'permitted development rights' for the construction or use of facilities likely to involve the presence of hazardous substances and the use of certain land have now been removed. Thus, express planning permission may not be required but instead hazardous substances consent will have to be obtained.

3.5 Calculating the Quantities; and Exemptions

3.5.1 Calculating the Quantities

In calculating the quantity of the substance, account is to be taken of the amount of the substance on, over or under other land (or in or on any part of the structure) which is within 500 metres of the land in question and is in the control of the same person. This provision is intended to ensure that where sites are close to each other and are controlled by the same person, consent will be required where the aggregate quantity equals or exceeds the controlled quantity on all the premises. It should be noted that the person in control of the land may not necessarily be the same as the legal owner, for example two adjoining sites may be under the ownership of two different companies but both may be controlled by the same parent company which is in effective control of the operations on both sites. Alternatively, a site may effectively be under the control of a tenant rather than a freeholder. It should be noted that under Section 39(3) of the Act, any two bodies corporate are to be treated as being one person if one is a subsidiary of the other or both are subsidiaries of the same body corporate. The purpose of this provision is to ensure that the Act is not circumvented in the case of adjoining sites which are essentially under the same control.

3.5.2 Exemptions

(a) Pipelines – the provisions relating to hazardous substances consent do not apply to the presence of substances in cross-country pipelines. Instead, existing controls relating to such pipelines as set out in the Pipelines Act 1962 will continue to be relied upon. However, any substances contained in that part of the pipeline which is on, over or under the site to or from which it leads will have to be aggregated with other substances on the site for control purposes. Similarly if the pipeline is wholly within the site it will be included in the calculation.

In relation to public gas suppliers undertakings an exemption is being provided for gas in a service pipe.

(b) Temporary presence during transportation – the temporary presence of a hazardous substance while it is being transported is exempt unless the substance is unloaded. There is no statutory definition of temporary presence. It will therefore be a matter of fact and degree. Similarly, unloaded is not defined.

3.6 Hazardous Substances Consents – Conclusion

The new regime for hazardous substances is an important crossover between health and safety law, environmental law and planning law. The planning law system has a number of assets to bring to the subject, not least its well-established appeal system. Bringing hazardous substances into the planning system in this way was, however, done before Section 54A was passed and there must be some concern about how local authorities will use Section 54A in relation to hazardous substances.

4.0 SECTION 54A OF THE TOWN AND COUNTRY PLANNING ACT 1990 – SECTION 18A OF THE TOWN AND COUNTRY PLANNING (SCOTLAND) ACT 1972

4.1 Why is Section 54A so Important?

Section 54A of the Town and Country Planning Act 1990 is a new provision, which makes serious changes to the assumptions underlying the planning system. It provides that:

Where, in making any determination under the Planning Acts, regard is to be had to the development plan, the determination shall be made in accordance with the plan unless material considerations indicate otherwise.

The section was added as a Government amendment to the Planning and Compensation Bill in its final stages in the House of Commons on June 19 1991 in response to sustained criticism from Tory backbenchers and Clive Soley MP, then Opposition spokesman on housing and planning, that developments were being approved which were contrary to the development plan. It redefines the function of the development plan in making planning decisions.

Section 54A has to be read in relation to planning applications in conjunction with Section 70 of the Act, which states that in determining an application for planning permission:

. . . the [planning] authority must have regard to the provisions of the development plan so far as material to the application and to any other material considerations.

Since the introduction of the modern planning system in 1947 there has been a presumption in favour of development. This presumption was stated by Lewis Silkin MP during the debates in the House of Commons on the Town and Country Planning Act 1947 and has been consistently restated, most recently in Circulars 22/80, 14/85 and PPG 1.

The classic statement of the presumption is:

There is always a presumption in favour of allowing applications for development having regard to all material considerations unless it can be shown that the development will cause demonstrable harm to interests of acknowledged importance.

The new PPG1 published in March 1992 to reflect Section 54A, states:

It [the planning system] should operate on the basis that applications for development should be allowed, having regard to the development plan and all material considerations unless the proposed development would cause demonstrable harm to interests of acknowledged importance.

At para. 25 it states that decision makers should have regard to the development plan and, if it is material to the development, it must be taken into account, and the decision made in accordance with the plan unless material considerations indicate otherwise. The effect is probably to introduce a presumption in favour of the development plan.[3] An applicant who proposes development which is clearly in conflict with the development plan will need to produce convincing reasons to demonstrate why the plan should not prevail.

This means it is of the utmost importance that industry participates and takes an interest in the plan-making process. It will be difficult later to obtain permission for a proposal which does not accord with the policies in the plan. Because Section 54A also applies to hazardous substances consents it is essential that plans are scrutinised to ensure that they do not prohibit (deliberately or inadvertently) the storage of hazardous substances. They should also make appropriate provision for new industry seeking to locate in the area and which will need to store hazardous substances. Similarly, appropriate provision should be made for the needs of industries already in the area to expand, which may take their quantities of hazardous substance storage through the thresholds in the new Regulations.

The draft PPG on planning and pollution control advises that development plans should contain policies on polluting developments. Thus scope exists for planning authorities to write policies excluding polluting industries. For this reason, it is important to plan forward and monitor the proposals in development plans.

In addition, applicants will risk an award of costs against them if they pursue appeals but are unable to produce substantial evidence to support the contention that there are material considerations justifying an exception to the policies of the plan.

4.2 How Can the Content of the Development Plan be Influenced?

All parts of the development plan are subject to public consultation. They are scrutinised by various quasi-appellate bodies before approval.

The plan consists of the Structure Plan and the Local Plan. Often there will be minerals plans and waste plans. In unitary authorities, the Structure Plan and Local Plan coalesce in a Unitary Development Plan. Their procedures are as for a local plan.

The Structure Plan is prepared by the county and contains strategic policies. It is no longer allowed to contain much detail. There is a formal public consultation period. Then, taking representations into account, the plan is put on deposit. Formal objections

---

3. Cases such as *St Albans District Council v Secretary of State for the Environment and Allied Breweries Ltd* [1993] JPL 374, *Sainsbury plc v Secretary of State for the Environment and Bexley LBC* [1993] JPL 651 and *South Lakeland District Council v Secretary of State for the Environment and Halpin* [1993] JPL 644, indicate that the change may be more one of emphasis rather than radical change. At a political level however, the plan is undoubtedly a key determining factor.

can be made. The plan is then subjected to an Examination-in-Public, before a panel appointed by the Secretary of State. The panel reports to the county which can make amendments as it sees fit. The resulting document is the Structure Plan.

It will be seen that there are two opportunities to make representations and participate in the formulation of the plan.

There is a similar provision for the local plan (prepared by the district council), with important differences. The local plan is a much more detailed document. It will have policies for specific sites, as well as policies for protection of the countryside, town centres and conservation areas.

The power of the county or district council to disregard the recommendations of the panel or inspector is rarely used in respect of key policies. Indeed, on some of the few occasions when the power had been used for a key policy in a local plan, the plan has been called-in by the Secretary of State.

Examinations-in-public are conducted on an inquisitorial basis; local plan inquiries on an adversarial basis. The procedure is relatively informal, although the subject matter is specialised. Members of the public frequently represent themselves. There is no requirement to be advised by lawyers or planning surveyors, although for projects where there is much at stake it is obviously important to devote such resources as are commensurate with the scheme to achieve the right result.

4.3 Section 54A – Conclusion

This section has brought about a significant change to the UK planning system. It has created a new presumption in favour of the development plan. The inclusion within its scope of policies on hazardous substances consent is somewhat curious. It has important ramifications for industry, however. It is important to monitor the policies in development plans and to participate in the plan-making process to ensure that future opportunities and requirements are adequately provided for.

5.0 NATURE CONSERVATION

5.1 Draft PPG on Nature Conservation

A draft planning policy guidance note on nature conservation was published for consultation in February 1992. It sets out the principles and policies which apply in relation to nature conservation priorities in land use planning with the aim of ensuring that existing nature conservation obligations are fully met.

It advocates a very restrictive approach to any development on Sites of Special Scientific Interest (SSSI) which will normally include Ramsar sites (designated under the Ramsar Convention as Wetlands of International Importance especially as waterfowl habitats), Special Protection Areas (SPAs) designated under the EC Birds Directive and Special Areas of Conservation (SACs) designated under the EC Habitats Directive. SPAs and SACs will form a nature conservation network to be called Natura 2000.

The Government is obliged to implement the Habitats Directive by June 1994. It intends to publish the Town and Country Planning (Habitats) Regulations which will provide that Articles 6 and 7 of the Habitats Directive be given direct statutory force for SPAs and SACs through the planning system. This will mean that any development in or near a SPA or a SAC will be subject to environmental assessment. If the assessment shows that the development could have a negative effect on the integrity of the site the development will only be allowed if there is no alternative solution and there are imperative reasons of overriding public interest to outweigh its international importance. In future, applications for planning permission in SSSIs, SPAs and SACs will almost invariably be called in for Ministers to decide. The Town and Country Planning (Habitats) Regulations will also amend the Wildlife and Countryside Act 1981. Under that Act it is a criminal offence to carry out operations in an SSSI which have been prescribed by English Nature or its counterpart conservation agencies in Scotland and Wales. However, if the operation is permitted by planning permission, that affords a complete defence to any criminal charge. The Regulations will remove that defence. This will damage the value of existing planning permissions for development in SSSIs, SPAs and SACs.

Many of those sites are in coastal areas and will thus be of importance in selecting sites for expansion and new development.

The new planning policy guidance is necessary to take account of the decision of the European Court in *EC Commission v The Federal Republic of Germany*, Case 57/89. In this case the Commission brought an action under Article 169 of the EEC Treaty alleging that by undertaking construction work which damaged the habitat of protected birds in a Special Protection Area designated under Article 4 of the Birds Directive 79/409 the Federal Republic of Germany had failed to fulfil its obligations under the Treaty. The work in question was extension and reinforcement of existing sea defences. The defence works in the case would result in a reduction of the SPA. The Court held that member states had no general power to modify or reduce a SPA once declared, otherwise they would escape from their primary obligation to protect such areas. A reduction could only be justified on exceptional grounds corresponding to a general interest such as the prevention of flooding or the need for coastal protection superior to the ecological interest envisaged by the Directive. General economic and recreational interests would not of themselves justify a reduction of or disturbance to special protection areas.

Pipeline works which could affect a site designated as an SPA or SAC may not therefore be justified under the terms of the Birds or Habitats Directive. Indeed, a major gas pipeline (Europipe) running from the North Sea through the Wadden Sea to Emden in Germany had to be put in a 2.5km tunnel running under the protected wetlands to avoid potential impact on an SPA.

There are some 230 candidate sites for SPA designation around the United Kingdom of which 73 have already been designated. In addition the government is under an obligation to designate SACs under the Habitats Directive by June 1995. If all of these sites were designated it could make it very difficult for pipelines to be routed to avoid an SPA or SAC. Furthermore in view of the above decision the works would probably not be justifiable under the terms of the Directive if they interfere with an SPA or SAC.

5.2 Marine Consultation Areas

The UK Government is consulting interested bodies on the introduction of a system of Marine Consultation Areas. These will be areas which are both of great importance to nature conservation but where there is a significant potential for further activities to conflict with this conservation interest. The essence of the system is that those who take decisions affecting those areas should seek and take into account the advice of conservation bodies on the likely impact of their proposals. Marine Consultation Areas would vary in size but would generally cover an area extending from high water mark to a limit of six miles out to sea and extending over several miles of coastline. In cases where a Site of Special Scientific Interest already extends from landward to low water mark, the Marine Consultation Area begins at the low water mark.

The impact of a proposed development on a Marine Consultation Area would be a material consideration under the Planning Acts.

6.0 PPG 20 ON COASTAL PLANNING

This review would not be complete without reference to the guidance note on the need for a co-ordinated approach to coastal planning issued by the Government in September 1992. It is the first time that the Government has produced comprehensive guidance on this issue.

The note defines the coastal zone for planning purposes noting that in many places it will only be a narrow strip because the local planning authority's jurisdiction under the Town and Country Planning Act 1990 ends at the mean low water mark.

It summarises the various statutory, non-statutory and international designations which may affect coastal areas and notes that in coastal areas, particularly estuaries, the effect of development on other interests such as wildlife and beauty of the landscape can be acute and widespread and advises that potentially damaging impacts should be avoided.

Local authorities are urged to make realistic provisions in their development plans for development in areas away from the coast. Specific advice is given for development which requires a coastal location as follows:

(i) In relation to major development such as refineries, ports and oil and gas terminals, it notes that proposed developments of national and regional importance which require a coastal location will normally be included in the development plan. Such proposals will usually require an environmental assessment.

(ii) In the case of mineral development, including oil and gas, the advice in mineral planning guidance notes is emphasised. Given the sensitivity of many coastal areas, exploration for and exploitation of such minerals needs to be undertaken with care. Where mineral working is permitted in areas designated for landscape conservation, careful control over a development by means of conditions minimising environmental effects is required.

(iii) In respect of energy generation, the national interest in new power stations must be balanced against any potential impact on the environment, both in landscape and ecological terms. These issues are to be assessed in the context of the environmental assessment which is normally required for such developments.

The guidance note urges local authorities to incorporate and co-ordinate their efforts in the coastal zone particularly around estuaries. It emphasises the need for local authorities to involve other relevant agencies fully. In preparing development plans, planning authorities are urged to undertake a detailed analysis in order to define the coastal zone for planning purposes. Within the zone they are required to define those parts of the coast which will be subject to policies safeguarding the environment, the parts of the coast where ideal opportunities for development exists, and those parts where physical constraints and hazards such as the risk of flooding or erosion either make development inappropriate or require the imposition of special conditions on planning consents.

Local authorities are encouraged to gather information on the physical processes which affect the coastal area, the quality of the coastal environment and landscape designations affecting it and development impact, working closely with English Nature and the National Rivers Authority. This information should then be used to provide a firm basis for development plan policies which carefully assess the potential risks of development, limit the damage to the environment and guard against piecemeal loss of significant coastal habitats and landscapes.

The Department of the Environment has commissioned research to define the earth science information which is needed to assist the formulation of planning policies and the determination of planning applications in coastal areas.

7.0 CONCLUSION

There have been a number of important recent developments in planning law which are of significance to the oil and gas industry. The draft PPG on planning and pollution control is amongst the most important. If adopted as drafted, it will give considerable power to the pollution control authorities. Applications for planning permission for development which also needs IPC authorisation, a discharge consent or other pollution control permit, will in future need to be accompanied by details of how the requirements of those permits will be met.

The new legislation on hazardous substances draws planning and health and safety issues closer together. It gives much power to the Health and Safety Executive. Coupled with Section 54A of the Town and Country Planning Act 1990, the possibility exists for a very restrictive regime.

Since the coming into force of Section 54A, the presumption in favour of the development plan which it creates has led to much greater participation by industry in the development plan process.

Concerns about nature conservation and coastal planning have surfaced in further draft and issued planning policy guidance notes.

All these matters reflect an increasing public concern with (and political response to) environmental matters, which is finding its means of expression through the planning system – probably the most developed environmental code the UK has. The oil and gas industry should watch developments, respond to consultation papers where necessary, monitor local plans, participate in the plan-making process where necessary, and take these matters into account in preparing planning applications for new installations.

ADDENDUM. The law is stated as at 31 March 1994.

Chapter 13

Acreage Portfolio Management[1]

Georges Schneider[2]

1.0 INTRODUCTION

The United Kingdom sector of the North Sea has seen the emergence of acreage portfolio management in recent years. The resulting deals are made between companies that want to rationalise their acreage – *ie* to upgrade the value of their holdings through acquisitions and divestments while maintaining their overall position in the area. These companies often have well-established links within multiple joint venture partnerships. The deals include conventional farm-ins and farm-outs and straightforward cash sales and purchases. They also include an increasing number of acreage swaps that are a relatively new type of deal.

In the distribution of prospective acreage, most of the cards have been dealt and the many players now have to negotiate between themselves to improve their hands. These negotiations have to recognise the mutuality of interest between the parties in order to be successful. In this game, there can be many winners, with each player eventually finding his niche.

This Chapter presents the situation in the UK North Sea, how the deals are done and the role of the petroleum economist in the process. It has wider applications to other areas of the world as they reach maturity and may look to the North Sea as a model.

1. Copyright 1992 Society of Petroleum Engineers.
2. The author thanks Jane Raiser, Neville Brown, Fred Yong and Will Roach of Shell Expro for their contributions; Ellen Davies of Shell UK, Al Boulos of Conoco, Brian Turner of the Department of Energy, Dave Wilkin of Esso and Rob Jonkman of Shell Internationale for their advice and encouragement; and the managements of Shell UK Exploration & Production and Esso Exploration & Production UK for permission to publish and those of BP Exploration, Enterprise Oil plc, Lasmo plc, Amoco (UK) Exploration and Elf Exploration UK for their reviews.

2.0 BACKGROUND: SETTING THE SCENE

Acreage portfolio management has emerged from the distribution of licence blocks between companies.

2.1 Overview: UK North Sea Acreage

In the UK Continental Shelf, licences are awarded by the Government, mainly on a discretionary basis, in licence rounds which are held at regular intervals. The size of the licence blocks is small relative to the Netherlands or Norwegian blocks. Originally the area of a block was about 260 sq kms in the far south and 200 sq kms in the far north. However, after subdivision through partial relinquishments and subsequent reissues, the average block size is now around 120 sq kms. This decrease in size has increased the chance that discoveries extend across block boundaries. At the end of 1990, a total of 668 offshore blocks (or sub-blocks resulting from relinquishments) were under licence in the North Sea part of the UK Continental Shelf. Another 70 blocks were awarded in the Twelfth Round of licensing in May 1991.

As of March 1991, there were around 170 companies (of which 35 were operators) owned by 115 parent companies, which held equities in UK North Sea licences. The 15 largest licencees held about two-thirds of the acreage and the next 15 largest another one-sixth.

Most blocks are held by joint ventures of three to five partners, and discoveries which straddle two or more blocks are owned by even more partners. This situation has resulted in fragmentation of holdings and complex field partnerships.

2.2 Emerging Issues

Most of the larger fields in the UK North Sea were discovered early on. The play is now in a mature stage and exploration yields smaller, technically more difficult hydrocarbon accumulations which require application of new appraisal and development technologies. A comparison of 1995 forecasts[3] with 1985 actual production shows a dramatic increase in the number of small fields and the concurrent decline in production from large fields. Fields producing above 100,000 barrels of oil equivalent per day will contribute only about 40 per cent of UK oil and gas production in 1995, down from 70 per cent in 1985. As a consequence, the unit operating costs for new oil and gas fields under development and for probable future projects are expected to be higher than for their predecessors (see Figure 1). This trend can be mitigated by combining small field developments into clusters sharing a common infrastructure.

With production from existing fields on the decline, unit operating costs for these fields are also bound to increase, a trend which is often exacerbated by the necessity to treat increasing volumes of produced water. Therefore ways must be found to hold or reduce these costs, either by demanning or decommissioning facilities, or by

3. CountyNatWest–WoodMac, 'North Sea Service': KEY 16–39, (Nov. 1991).

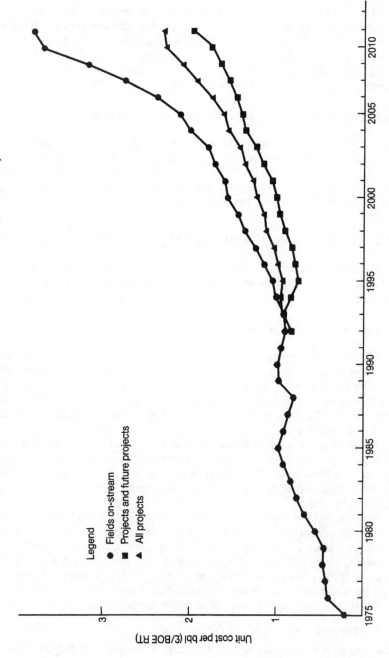

Figure 1. Operating Costs for UK North Sea Projects
(source: CNWM Nov. 1991 Business Publications)

Legend
● Fields on-stream
■ Projects and future projects
▲ All projects

Unit cost per bbl (£/BOE RT)

utilising ullage in existing infrastructure as it develops and bringing the new, smaller fields into production as satellites at a lower cost.

The current status with respect to acreage holdings further complicates field developments. For example the Britannia Field, which straddles five blocks, has 12 partners, although some rationalisation has already occurred. Complex partnerships tend to delay decisions and to incur high management costs. The level of ownership complexity tends to increase considerably when several small fields have to be developed jointly in a cluster and to share common facilities.

2.3 The Need to Manage the Acreage Portfolio

As a consequence of these increasing complexities, there is a growing need to manage the acreage portfolio and to rationalise ownerships in individual fields or in clusters of fields. The geology of the UK North Sea is reasonably well known and the more prospective acreage has been licensed. Companies wanting to improve their position have now to negotiate between themselves.

3.0 CONCEPTS: DEFINING THE GOALS

In the drive to maximise value by redistributing petroleum assets, many companies approach portfolio management by building up heartlands and balancing cash flows over time.

3.1 Building Up Heartlands

A heartland is a geographical area within which a particular company wishes to retain most of its licence blocks, and attempts to reinforce an already dominant acreage position through acquisitions. This assumes the definition of areas needed for a company to survive as a business. Illustrating a largely subjective concept, the term of 'heartland' is probably more descriptive than the phrase 'core areas' or 'poles of development'.

A significant acreage position allows economies of scale and facilitates cluster developments. Operatorship can also sometimes be a strong motive. Some companies have been successful in building up from their ownership in major fields and concentrating their efforts on clusters of discoveries located near the infrastructure under their control.

The heartland concept may call for the acquisition of exploration blocks in the vicinity of existing licence holdings. Also, companies often attempt to gain higher per cent equities in blocks they already own. Lasmo, for example, after two deals involving licence block 16/12a, announced in a press release of July 19 1990: 'Lasmo already has interests in several blocks in this significant oil producing area and these transactions further consolidate that position'.

Heartlands have one or more of the following features:

3.1.1 Regional Knowledge

The company holding the acreage builds up a regional knowledge which puts it in a better position to recognise the real value of such acreage, to win competitive bids and to devise a successful exploration programme.

3.1.2 Access to Infrastructure

Reinforcing the heartland is justified by utilising spare capacity available in the company's infrastructure and taking advantage of a favourable competitive position to gain a share of the profit from adjacent field developments. It also contributes to reducing operating costs through sharing logistic bases and transportation systems and to extending the life of the existing infrastructure.

3.1.3 Long-Term Potential

True heartlands should ensure long-term continuation of the business. Ideally they will contain a high proportion of undeveloped reserves and provide entry points to new plays and proximity to prime open acreage. Declining fields with nearly depleted reserves and located in areas of little remaining exploration potential would not, in the author's opinion, form the basis of a heartland for the future.

3.1.4 Technological Expertise

In technically difficult developments, the licence holder can gain a competitive edge from application of novel technology and build a 'niche' heartland. Then he also needs to possess adequate human and financial resources to support these developments.

3.2 Balancing Cash Flows

Reasons for rephasing future cash flows can be:

3.2.1 Tax Efficiency

The party acquiring a producing field usually gains a tax shelter for its future exploration expenditures. In some cases this enables it subsequently to nurture a dynamic farm-in strategy.

3.2.2 Production Profile

In September 1989, Shell and Esso agreed to swap a 9 per cent equity in the Fulmar Field with Amoco for 25.77 per cent in two potential future projects. From the point of view of Shell and Esso the main benefit of the deal was a net positive balance in hydrocarbon resources and a production increase in the long term. Conversely, with the swap of equities in the Franklin and Markham fields with Elf Exploration UK plc, Ultramar plc was 'increasing earnings per share by bringing reserves into production as quickly as possible'.[4]

3.2.3 Investment Phasing

However 'nice' it can be to have a large number of field development projects in hand, this situation can create an unbearable burden on cash requirements. The company may then want to trade out of one project in order to alleviate the financing of the other projects.

4. Press release Aug. 21 1991.

3.2.4 Manpower Stability

Manpower may be a constraint just as much as cash availability, particularly if the company is an operator. Rather than hire and fire, it may find it preferable to phase the development of projects in its portfolio. Manpower considerations also add an incentive to maintaining the production profile and the level of activity in the long term.

3.3 Restructuring

Having said all this, concentrating on heartlands or rephasing future cash flows remain conservative strategies aimed at improving company performance within the existing business. Companies with more expansionist ambitions would want to create new heartlands through taking over competitors. This type of acquisition, which I would call a restructuring deal, is beyond the scope of this Chapter although it may contain an element of portfolio management. An illustration of a restructuring deal with an element of balancing the cash flow, is the May 15 1991 letter from the chairman of Enterprise Oil to shareholders which explained: 'The reduction in the Nelson interest will be balanced by the acquisition of a one-third interest in the assets of Occidental GB, thereby improving the overall balance of Enterprise's portfolio.'

Growth in this manner can result in rather dispersed portfolios, particularly in the case of repeated acquisitions. Thereafter, a period of consolidation becomes inevitable as demonstrated by several acreage package sales. This requirement has been further acknowledged by Lasmo plc in its offer for Ultramar of October 21 1991,[5] which states: 'The merger will create opportunities for asset rationalisation.'

4.0 FACTS: FEATURING THE RATIONALISATION DEALS

The year 1990 saw a moderate level of trading activity in terms of volume of discovered reserves after the years of the mega-deals in 1988 and 1989 (see Figure 2). The activity increased again in 1991 and was, for the main part of the year, focused on acreage rationalisation although there was also a resurgence of restructuring deals with the takeovers of Occidental Petroleum (Great Britain) Inc and Ultramar.

4.1 Inventory of Deals

4.1.1 Number of Holdings Assigned

Excluding the share deals which are outside the scope of this Chapter, a total of 134 equity interests in licence blocks or in field ring fences changed hands in 75 deals

---

5. Lasmo plc, 'Offer by J. Henry Schroder Wagg & Co Limited on behalf of Lasmo plc for Ultramar plc': p.16, (Offer Document, Oct. 21 1991).

Figure 2. UKCS Deals 1980–91
(excluding corporate deals other than complete takeovers) (Source: CNWM)

during 1991. This represents an increase of activity over 1990, when 110 transfers were completed.

4.1.2 Level of Activity in Volume

In 1991, complete takeovers accounted for two-thirds and acreage rationalisation for one-third of the volume of discovered reserves traded. Within the latter category, if an attempt is made to include undiscovered potential, then cash deals have contributed more than half the volumes, swaps one-third and farm-ins the balance.

4.1.3 Farm-in/out Activity in 1990–91

Hailed as the 'year of the farm-ins', 1990 saw a resurgence in this activity from the levels of 1988 and 1989 as companies strove to increase their exploration effort. In part this was also in response to the Department of Energy's encouragement to deal with fallow acreage (blocks without a well for 10 years). There were 20 farm-ins reported in 1990 and this activity grew still further in 1991, with 31 reported.

4.1.4 Acreage Swaps

Since Elf pioneered swaps of acreage in 1986, there was a steady level of activity in 1987–90 with an average of more than five swaps per year. This number more than doubled in 1991 with 12 swaps reported, all of which were done between partners on either one or both sides.

4.2 Analysis

Further analysis reveals the emergence of a new type of deal with the following features:

4.2.1 Deals Between Partners

The need for portfolio management has generated an increasing number of friendly, win-win deals of which a majority are between partners in the blocks in question. This not only applies to the new swap deals but also to the more traditional deals with two-thirds of the farm-ins and three-quarters of the cash deals, reported during 1991, between partners. After a particular deal is concluded the parties will often continue to work together, in different partnerships, and so clearly they need to maintain a good business relationship.

4.2.2 Emergence of Swaps

The willingness of companies to trade acreage for their mutual benefit is best demonstrated by the emergence of swap deals.

Although acreage rationalisation is not necessarily done by swapping, negotiations will often start from that premise. In practice it is often difficult to find properties which match exactly and the deal may end up as a straightforward cash sale or a mixed asset swap and cash payment. However, the intent of reciprocity which prevailed at the start, will continue to colour the negotiation until the end.

4.2.3 Value Gap Motivation

Traditionally, the rationalisation deals have been dictated more by differences in perception of value than by financial distress. Many deals are done between parties who intend to remain active in the North Sea. They share the same goal of creating wealth by the exploration and production of hydrocarbons and they also share the will to stay and continue to pursue that goal. This commonality of interests remains paramount in the negotiation of this type of deal even if some sales are also prompted by the need to raise cash.

5.0 PERCEPTIONS: FINDING THE VALUE GAP

The required feature emerging from a quick review of rationalisation deals is the recognition of value gaps by both parties so that they can reach a deal that is mutually beneficial. These differences in perception of values are often influenced by corporate cultures. They are easier to identify when companies know each other well, which may be another reason why deals are often done between partners.

5.1 Reserve Reporting

A potential buyer may have a perception of higher volumes than those recognised by the vendor. Knowledge of oil and gas fields is never perfect even though it improves as the field produces and original assumptions are tested through actual performance to the end of field life. This uncertainty is seldom recognised to its full extent which leads to wide differences in perceptions between the various petroleum engineers performing independent evaluations. Variation in reserves estimates remains the most important reason for a value gap between buyer and seller.

The analysis of historical reserves reporting of some North Sea oil fields provides illustrations of such differences in perception. Towards the end of field life, it often appears that the field will produce more than expected and there follows an anomalous period when the remaining reserves seem to stay constant in spite of continuing production. At that stage in its life, the value of a producing field, which is based on remaining reserves, becomes very sensitive to small changes in estimates of ultimate recovery.

5.2 Case Study: Forties Field

The history of reported reserves in the Forties Field (see Figure 3), comparing oil-in-place and ultimate recovery, shows an initial optimism in oil-in-place, followed by a downward adjustment and a period of more or less constant estimates. The estimated recovery factor was initially quite low and small upward revisions were regularly made until 1985 as 'the reservoir continued to out-perform expectations'.[6] At the final equity determination in 1987, the operator increased the oil-in-place by nearly 20 per cent back to the original level, with a lesser relative increase in Ultimate Recovery.

6. J.M. Wills and D.K. Peattie, 'The Forties Field and the Evolution of a Reservoir Management Strategy': p.22; *North Sea Oil and Gas Reservoirs-11*, The Norwegian Institute of Technology (Graham & Trotman, 1990).

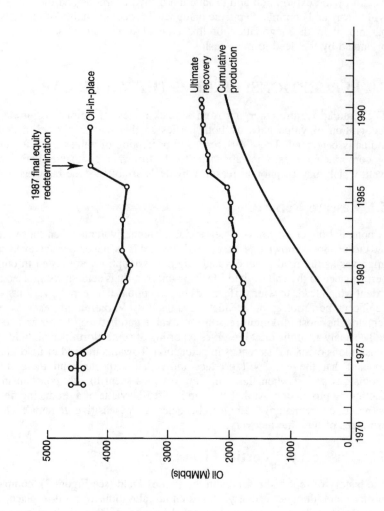

Figure 3. Forties Volumetrics Historical Trends

Reservoir simulation work has shown significant variations in recovery efficiency, a critical factor in estimation being the residual oil saturation. A review of core sample analyses in the Forties Field shows that results of some techniques lead to significantly higher residual oil saturations than results by other methods (see Figure 4). Depending on which analysis technique is preferred, various degrees of conservatism could be reflected in estimates of recovery factors and this would create a value gap between parties.

5.3 Cost Estimation

The gap in perception of value may also come from expectation of lower costs of future development or operation through the application of more cost-effective technology by the buyer. Changes in technology may result in non-commercial reserves becoming valuable at some time in the future. Early recognition of this possibility, combined with an acceptance of higher risk, will give the advantage to the buyer over a more cautious seller.

5.4 Fiscal Aspects

Quite often, the value gap is enhanced by differences in fiscal positions. Through its purchase of an equity in the Hutton Field from Amoco in 1990, Ultramar was reported by CountyNatWest–WoodMac to have 'gained some useful Corporation Tax shelter'.[7] An even clearer case, is the string of eight Forties Field Units sales and purchases by companies short of Petroleum Revenue Tax shelters since BP sold 11.65 per cent of the Forties Field in 1984.

Tax position may also be a strong consideration behind farm-in and farm-out deals dependent on the prevailing fiscal regime in respect of exploration expenditures.

5.5 Strategic Advantage

The most difficult gap to evaluate is that arising from the desire to secure a strategic advantage. An international company may wish to rebalance its portfolio geographically. Within the North Sea some companies may try to achieve a balance between oil and gas.

5.6 Utility

Assessment of the geological risks is also a very subjective component of a value gap. This is illustrated again by most farm-ins, whereby the original equity holder may be more risk averse than the exploration company which takes the risk of farming-in.

7. CountyNatWest–WoodMac, 'North Sea Report, Number 214': p.18, (Feb. 28 1991).

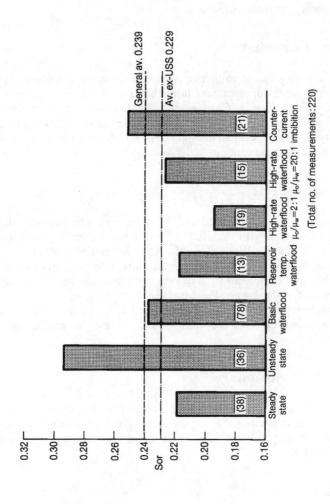

Figure 4. Forties Field – Residual Oil Saturation

6.0 THE BUSINESS PROCESS

Since rationalisation deals are essentially motivated by differences in perceptions of values, the petroleum economist will play a central role within the portfolio management team throughout the business process which leads to a deal.

6.1 Target Identification

It is clear that a company which intends to remain active in the North Sea will not spontaneously put good quality assets on the market. Chances are small that acreage which fits one's strategy can be found only by reacting to public offers. Portfolio management requires a proactive attitude, assuming that an offer can be made to the potential vendor which in return would satisfy his own aspirations.

On the basis of scouting information obtained through press releases or data exchanges, the company involved in portfolio management draws up a shopping list of strategic assets and identifies the asset owners. Exploratory contacts are made to express interest in a target asset and to determine whether a party is willing to trade.

Analysis of recent deals made by companies can shed some light on their motives. From this information, the buyer should attempt to outline possible deal structures which might satisfy both parties (sale, farm-out or swap) before contact is made with a potential trader.

The main concern during the identification phase is to avoid the risk of missing opportunities. However, the business process following identification is quite manpower intensive and a balance must be found between evaluating all opportunities and missing some.

6.2 Screening Economics

Early identification of a value gap will help targeting the acreage and ranking opportunities in order of preference. At that stage only scouting information is available and a full economic analysis is not required. The economist will use unit values derived by analogy with better known acreage or similar prospects. This approach requires professional experience and a familiarity with the technical parameters which are critical to the value of the acreage under consideration.

It is equally important that the economist has a thorough understanding of the value of his own company's acreage. This is necessary in order to identify trading blocks which may have more value to another party and can be offered as part of the consideration in a deal. The drive for portfolio management has created a market for petroleum assets in the UK North Sea and the economist needs to have a feel for the value of his company's assets on that market as well as the internal value carried by the company which may be quite different.

Established views and also a different level of knowledge can hamper a balanced judgement about one's own properties as compared to those of a competitor. The position of the economist allows him to be more detached and to adopt a more objective view of the property.

6.3 Due Diligence

The screening process is performed with limited information and most of the data not directly accessible. Often, it will be followed by viewing additional data. The parties then share available factual information in an open manner and in good faith. The data room typically contains well logs, seismic surveys, production tests, plus such other information as is necessary to perform a full evaluation or to validate an existing interpretation. It also contains financial data and agreements. It must be complete so as not to mislead the potential buyer. The party showing the data has a duty of 'true representation' which will generally be confirmed in the sale and purchase agreement when the deal is completed.

There must be a genuine intention to do business on the part of the buyer, so that the seller will be confident that the information he provides will not be used for any other purpose. This undertaking is generally covered by a confidentiality agreement.

6.4 Full Evaluation

Data viewing is usually followed by a quick review to confirm the attractiveness of the assets on offer. In the affirmative, the buyer will then proceed with a full technical and economic evaluation. Once the data room has been visited, both buyer and seller have access to the same set of data. However the information unavoidably remains incomplete and there is scope for considerable variation in the interpretation of these data.

The buyer will be given some time for his evaluation and he will normally put together a multidisciplinary team of geologists, engineers and economists for that purpose. For a complex deal a large company may involve 20 to 30 professional staff, fortunately not all on a full-time basis.

Although the economic evaluation happens only at the end of a sometimes long technical evaluation, the author believes it is important that the economist should be involved at the outset, to advise on which technical parameters are most important for assessing the value and thus require further scrutiny. Time is of the essence and it is desirable not to have to redirect work at a late stage of the evaluation.

Very often the process will include evaluating the acreage from the point of view of both buyer and seller and the economist must be familiar with the tax and financial positions of all parties concerned.

6.5 Negotiation

The negotiation can proceed as soon as the evaluation is completed. The negotiating team is normally much smaller, (eg, three or four staff) and would include a professional business negotiator. The key members of the evaluation team will stay on call to support the negotiators. The economist in particular will be calculating the consequences of the demands from the other party on the value of the deal and trying to understand their economic motivation. He will also assist the negotiator in establishing his negotiating range and in recognising both the upside value and the downside risks in the deal.

The process of negotiation will often result in changing the deal structure and the economist will have to perform repeated evaluations throughout the process until the deal is agreed . . . or aborted.

6.6 Legal Framework

Agreement on the value and structure of the deal is not the end of the process. There are still the legal terms to negotiate and a large amount of paperwork to go through, the most notable of which include:

(i) Partner Consents; depending on the terms of any Joint Operating Agreements, there may still be the risk of pre-emption which can scupper the deal.
(ii) Ministerial Consents and Approvals; the Department of Energy will give particular attention to the competence and plans of the incomer and to the number of participants and any change of operator in the licence.
(iii) Agreement for Sale of the Interest; warranties and indemnities, providing proper protection for the buyer, form a critical part of the sale and purchase agreement. They may thus require lengthy negotiations.
(iv) Documentation; the agreements will include, in the case of non-producing acreage, licence assignment, interest assignment and novation of joint operating agreement and, where appropriate in the case of producing acreage, also assignments of all other agreements.

There is no deal until legal completion and it is best to keep the same negotiating team, with the additional support of a lawyer, rather than to leave it to newcomers to draft the legal terms. Seemingly trivial clauses can sometimes have significant effects on the value of a deal. The economist will thus have to remain involved until legal completion and to be alert to the repercussions of the legal drafting of the Agreements.

7.0 CONCLUSIONS

This Chapter demonstrates the need for acreage portfolio management at the stage of maturity which has been reached in the UK sector of the North Sea. It has outlined the goals, the main features of the deals, and the business process. Portfolio management is a manpower intensive activity but the reward is a more cost-effective company which has a better understanding of the strengths and weaknesses of its portfolio and a clearer vision of its future. It is also an exciting task to which economists, engineers and geologists can bring different viewpoints allowing a balanced assessment of both their own and the other party's acreage.

The traditional role of the petroleum economist involves the provision of economic analysis of data compiled by geologists and engineers, which in itself is important. However, this alone, is, in the author's opinion, insufficient in the context of portfolio management.

In order to respond in a timely manner, the economist needs to be an active member of the evaluation team from the outset, challenging preconceived ideas, looking for upside potential and assessing downside risks. He also has to be involved at an early stage of negotiations, establishing negotiating ranges and developing mutually beneficial deals. He will thus make an essential contribution to promoting the development of the business within agreed corporate strategies.

The business process involves sharing information in an open manner and negotiating in good faith. Companies which often will remain partners, need to adhere to high ethical standards in their dealings.

Negotiation of rationalisation deals involves a level of reciprocity which is not always fully accepted. The negotiators should therefore avoid confrontation and follow the Doctrine of Mutuality of Interests.

Further references

Alfred J. Boulos, 'Mutuality of Interests Between Companies and Governments – Myth or Fact?' *Energy Law '90* (International Bar Association/Graham & Trotman, 1990) p.3.

Chapter 14

Basic Structure and Recent Developments of Joint Operating Agreements

Adrian Hill

1.0 NATURE OF THE JOINT OPERATING AGREEMENT (JOA)

Worldwide, exploring for and producing oil and gas is normally done on the basis of joint ventures. The participating companies generally prefer to share the risks involved, with each having several rather than joint obligations; it also enables them to hold wider portfolios of assets than they would be able to support if these assets were wholly owned. In some parts of the world these joint ventures are organised as corporations; examples are the old Kuwait Oil Co involving BP and Gulf Oil or NAM, the joint venture between Shell and Esso in the Netherlands.

An alternative in the United Kingdom would be a formal partnership under the Partnership Act 1890, but this would involve joint and several liability on the part of the partners. This particular problem could be avoided by a limited partnership under the Limited Partnership Act 1908, but in this case the partners other than the managing partner would be precluded from taking any part in the management of the partnership.

Generally, and almost invariably in the United Kingdom Continental Shelf (UKCS), companies prefer to organise their joint ventures or consortia, as unincorporated associations, with their joint venture arrangements governed by a joint operating agreement (JOA). It is the arrangements of this type that will be considered in this Chapter. The main reasons for the preference for the unincorporated association are to do with the tax transparency that this arrangement allows, with each venturer being able to claim directly tax allowances on the expenditures it makes. It also provides a simpler form of organisation, with no separate corporate structure having to be formed and maintained. In this Chapter only operating agreements relating to exploration and production operations will be considered, though the term operating agreement is used also for the contract governing joint ventures in other operational areas in the oil industry, for example transportation by pipeline. The form of operating agreement to be considered here will be mainly that which was developed in the UK in the mid 1970s by the British National Oil Corporation (BNOC). Prior to that time a wide variety of operating agreements were in use in the UK, most of them based on models imported from the United States which were often far from suitable because of the different ownership regime and economic and operating conditions found in the UKCS. Following the formation of BNOC in 1976, it was a condition for the award of a production licence in the fifth and sixth licensing rounds that the licensees enter into an operating agreement with BNOC in a form satisfactory to the Secretary of State. As a result BNOC developed, in negotiations with the oil companies, a pro forma JOA for the fifth round. This has become something of a norm, or at least a starting point, for nearly all subsequent JOAs negotiated in the UK, even though it was not a required text at any time after the sixth round held in 1979. It has also been adapted for use in operating agreements in other parts of the world and has strongly influenced the International Model Form Operating Agreement put together by a committee of the American Corporate Counsel Association (ACCA) and the (US) Association of International Petroleum Negotiators (AIPN) in 1990.

The operating agreement is normally negotiated between the licensees of a petroleum production licence or other similar mining title after its award. In most parts of the world outside North America petroleum in its natural condition in strata is vested in the state and the production licence will accordingly be granted by the state. In countries where direct state participation in oil operations is required, the operating agreement is normally used as one of the means of implementing this, by making the state oil company a party to the JOA. This is no longer the position in the UK, though it still remains necessary for the terms of the JOA to receive the prior approval of the Secretary of State, under the terms of the licence.

2.0 CONTENTS OF THE JOINT OPERATING AGREEMENTS

2.1 Participating Interests

The operating agreement will declare the respective participating interests of the parties, expressed in percentage terms. This function is of particular importance in the UK as the production licence does not set out percentage interests but provides that where there is more than one licensee the obligations are to be joint and several. In line with the risk-sharing intention of the parties, the agreement will also state that the participants' interests will be several and not joint or collective and declare that there is no intention to establish a partnership. It is by no means certain that such declaration will be binding on third parties, so the JOA will normally contain mutual indemnities under which each party will be indemnified by the others against any liabilities incurred by it in excess of its percentage interest.

The percentage interest of each party will normally govern the sharing of the costs and the fruits of the joint operations, although there is likely to be provision for disproportionate sharing of costs in some events, for example in the event of sole risk or default, which will be considered later. Disproportionate sharing also occurs when there is a carried interest, for example of a state oil company during the exploration phase of operations, as in Norway and several other countries.

2.2 Appointment of the Operator

For reasons of efficiency it is normal for one of the parties to an operating agreement to be appointed as the operator for carrying out the 'function of organising or supervising all or any of the operations of searching or boring for or getting petroleum'. The quoted words are taken from Model Clause 24 (in the numbering of the Petroleum (Production) (Seaward Areas) Regulations 1988) which requires the approval of the Secretary of State of the entity which is to carry out this function. Failure to obtain this approval is grounds for revocation of the licence. The operator is normally the participant with the largest percentage interest. Model Clause 24 does not require the operator to hold a participating interest and so it can be an affiliate of a participant.

The operating agreement will enumerate in broad terms the duties of the operator, which include the preparation of an annual programme of works to be carried out and a budget in respect of this; the carrying out of this programme when it has been approved; the provision of reports and information to the non-operators; and generally the carrying out of all technical and advisory services required for the efficient performance of the joint operations. The agreement will also contain provisions governing the terms on which the operator can resign or be removed.

It is the practice of the industry for the operator to carry out its functions on a cost-of-service basis, without making any loss or gain as a result of the operatorship. In view of this it is almost always provided that the operator, in its capacity as such, will not incur any liabilities to the non-operators for any losses or liabilities arising from the joint operations except in the case of wilful misconduct on the part of the operator. Wilful misconduct will normally be defined as 'an intentional and conscious, or reckless, disregard by any of the operator's or its affiliates' officers, directors or employees of any provision of the operating agreement or of any agreed programme'. It is further normally provided that wilful misconduct will not include any error of judgment or mistake made by any officer, director or employee of the operator or its affiliates or by any agent or contractor of the operator in the exercise in good faith of any function, authority or discretion conferred upon the operator. Frequently it is also provided that liability for wilful misconduct will only be engaged in respect of the acts of employees having a managerial or supervisory position. Furthermore, because of the very large sums of money that are potentially involved, it is also normal for the JOA to provide that, even in the case of wilful misconduct, the operator will not be liable for any inability to produce petroleum, loss of production, loss of profits or any other similar consequential loss or damage.

2.3 Control of the Operator

In the exercise of its functions the operator will be subject to the control and supervision of an operating, or management, committee established by the JOA and on which each of the participants will be represented. In particular, this committee will be charged with approving the annual programme of works and the budget and for making decisions relating to the joint operations to be carried out which the operator will then be authorised and required to conduct. The operating committee will reach its decisions according to an agreed voting procedure set out in the agreement. This will normally specify a percentage vote – the so-called passmark – which must be obtained before a decision becomes binding on the participants. The passmark is normally a sensitive issue and will usually be aimed to ensure that the operator cannot unilaterally make decisions but at the same time will not be a figure so high as to make it difficult for decisions to be reached or which will give parties with small interests a disproportionate power to prevent decisions being reached. A figure in the order of 70 per cent is common. If the operator's percentage interest is or is likely to exceed the passmark, it may be provided that any vote to be valid must be supported by at least one participant in addition to the operator.

2.4 Sole Risk and Non-Consent

The normal rule that no decision can be made unless the passmark is reached, and the converse that any vote which reaches the passmark is binding on the minority who voted against, gives rise to serious potential problems which the operating agreement will normally seek to mitigate. To prevent potentially fruitful operations being thwarted because the passmark cannot be reached, the JOA will normally contain a so-called sole risk clause which enables some of the parties to carry out a particular operation at their sole risk and cost, notwithstanding that it has not been approved as a joint operation. This will enable, for example, an exploration well to be drilled at the sole cost of one or more, but not all, of the parties. If it results in a discovery the other parties are normally given the right to participate in the development of that discovery on condition that they pay to the sole risk party a substantial premium to compensate it for the sole risk it assumed in making the discovery. Such premium may be up to ten times the cost of the sole risk operation. For tax reasons it is normally found in UKCS JOAs that the premium will be discharged in the form of the non-sole risk parties carrying the sole risk party for the costs of appraising or developing the discovery, up to the amount of the premium.

To address the problem of the minority parties voted into a decision they opposed, the operating agreement is likely to contain certain so-called non-consent provisions. These enable any party which voted against the proposal to refuse to participate in the operation in question, at the cost normally of being excluded from any future rights in respect of that operation. In high cost areas such as the UKCS it is common to allow non-consenting only in respect of decisions to develop a field. The BNOC pro forma, for example, denied any party voting against a proposal to drill an exploration or appraisal well the right to non-consent because of the likely detrimental effect this would have on the willingness of the other parties to proceed with the operation in question, on account of the additional burden of having to assume the share of the costs of the non-consenting parties. This approach is still commonly followed in more recent JOAs. (For a fuller discussion of sole risk and non-consent clauses see Chapter 15.)

2.5 Financial Control

An important aspect of control of the operator is control by the operating committee of the expenditures to be made by the operator. In addition to the approval of an annual budget, individual items of significant expenditure will be subject normally to control by an authority for expenditure (AFE), a document which itemises the expenditure in question, usually of a capital nature, and requires the approval by participants who together hold the voting passmark. Outvoted participants are bound by the approved AFE which authorises and requires the operator to incur the expenditure or enter into the commitment described in the AFE.

An attachment to the JOA, known as the accounting procedure, will specify the expenditures that the operator is permitted to charge to the joint account and which are to be borne by the participants according to their percentage interests, or as otherwise specified. The accounting procedure will also give the non-operators audit rights in connection with the joint account and the items debited to it. It will also normally authorise the operator to make cash calls against the non-operators to meet each participant's share of the expenditures on the joint operations to be met during the following month. The accounting procedure also usually spells out certain general principles such as the intent that the operator will make no profit or suffer any loss as a result of being operator; that there shall be no duplication of charges debited to the joint account and that appropriate accounting principles will be followed.

2.6 The Operator's Contracting Function

It is normal in the oil industry for the carrying out of many of the activities of the joint venture to be contracted out by the operator to third party contractors. The extent of contracting out will normally be left to the discretion of the operator, though the costs incurred will be subject to the financial controls already mentioned. The JOA will normally provide that, notwithstanding any such contracting out, the operator will remain responsible to the non-operators for proper performance. Under the influence of the BNOC pro forma, which greatly extended the concept of non-operator control over the operator's activities, the operator's contracting function tends to be closely supervised in UKCS JOAs. These normally require the operator to carry out competitive tendering and subject the operator to varying degrees of control with regard to the preparation of lists of contractors to be invited to bid and the terms of the contracts to be entered into. In the current climate of soaring costs for offshore operations, some of these controls are probably not in the best interests of the venture as they can add to costs and cause delays which may result in loss of opportunities for securing optimum contracts. UKCS JOAs nowadays normally provide that the operator is to contract as agent for the joint venture as otherwise non-operators will be technically strangers to the contract and therefore, because of the lack of third party beneficiary rights under English contract law, may encounter difficulties in recovering their share of any damages for breach of the contract. As a matter of convenience (and the JOA may require it), contracts placed by the operator will often contain a 'channelling provision', requiring the contractor to look only to the operator for performance of the contract, with a view to avoiding involvement of the non-operators as principals to the contract in any legal action brought by the contractor.

2.7 Default

The question of default in relation to operating agreements has given rise to more legal discussion in the UK than any other aspect of JOAs. Because of space constraints, it is possible here only to touch on some of the issues that arise.

To avoid the need to register default provisions in operating agreements as charges (that is to say security interests) under the Companies Acts, JOAs which are subject to English or Scottish law have, since the early days of UKCS operations, avoided the creation of liens or other forms of charge, fixed or floating, over the joint venture assets of a participant who has defaulted in meeting its cash calls or share of expenditures incurred. Instead the practice evolved that a defaulter's interest under the production licence and the JOA was made subject to forfeiture (conditional upon the Secretary of State's consent) if the default continues for a specified period, commonly 60 days. If the right to forfeiture is exercised, the normal provision is that the defaulter's interest will be assigned to the non-defaulters in the ratio of their respective interests or in the proportions in which they have contributed to meet the default, if different. The rationale for this is that forfeiture of interest is not considered to be a security interest and therefore does not require registration at the Companies Registry as a charge. The all-or-nothing nature of forfeiture, however, itself gives rise to legal problems, namely the question of whether a forfeiture provision is an unenforceable penalty under well-known principles in both English and Scottish law or additionally whether, under another equitable principle, relief against forfeiture can be obtained from the courts. Because of the greater risk of forfeiture being considered penal during the production phase, that is after very considerable expenditure on development has been incurred by the defaulter (with the result that there could be an enormous discrepancy between the value of the interest forfeited and the loss caused to the non-defaulters by the default) it was for a time widely considered that the default clause should be rewritten, after a decision had been made to develop a field, in order to reduce the potential penal element.

Despite a number of recent cases in the English courts (none of which involved default under a JOA but which did relate to analogous situations) indicating that equitable relief against forfeiture is available from the courts on a discretionary basis, the general view as to the legal problems surrounding the forfeiture clause is now certainly more relaxed than it was a decade ago. In a recent case, *Jobson v Johnson* [1989] 1 All E.R. 621 (CA), it was held that, even if a penalty is identified by the court, the provision will not simply be struck out *in toto* but will be given effect, though in such manner as to prevent any windfall gain being made by the non-defaulting parties by ensuring that they will only recover the amount of their loss plus interest. This the court can do by ordering the sale of the asset in question; the proceeds will be used first in meeting the amount of the default and interest, with the balance being taken by the defaulter. Furthermore, with relief against forfeiture and penalties being equitable and discretionary remedies, the defaulter will have to 'come to court with clean hands' and will therefore have had to remedy the default prior to seeking any relief and it could be that relief in the form of reinstatement will not be granted if there is a likelihood of repeated default.

2.8 Disposal of Petroleum

A JOA will normally entitle each party to lift separately its entitlement at a delivery point, which is to be agreed, at or near the place of production. This obligation to take separately in kind is considered to be the essential element that distinguishes an unincorporated joint venture from a partnership under the Partnership Act 1890, as there is no element of carrying on a business in common with a view to profit. Each party to the JOA realises its own profit by separately selling its liftings or appropriating them to its own refining operations. It also avoids joint marketing which could give rise to tax and antitrust problems for US companies involved in the venture. In addition to the right to take separately in kind, the parties will be obliged to make arrangements to lift their share of production from the agreed delivery point; this they will do by entering into appropriate arrangements to transport the production from the field. This provision normally determines the scope of the exploration and production JOA; operations beyond the agreed delivery point will generally be outside the scope of this JOA. If these operations are also carried out by the participants on a joint venture basis, either dedicated solely to the field in question or in relation to a pipeline system serving a number of separate fields, these arrangements are likely to be the subject of other joint operating agreements, dealing with the transportation and the shore processing and terminalling operations, and which will contain many of the features of the exploration and production JOA, such as those dealing with ownership interests, operatorship and decision making. Alternatively, the offtake may be through a pipeline system owned by third parties, in which case it will be the subject of a transportation agreement involving the payment of a tariff.

Because of the many variables that govern the physical offtake from an oil field (dedicated pipeline for a single field, pipeline system serving several fields or offshore loading into tankers at a loading facility near the field, without any pipeline to shore) it is not normal for the operating agreement initially entered into at the time of the grant of the production licence to contain detailed offtake provisions governing the physical offtake, as it is not feasible to stipulate these until the physical arrangements have been decided upon. Instead the parties commit themselves to enter into appropriate detailed offtake arrangements at a later stage.

The disposal of petroleum clause will however usually set out some broad principles to govern the offtake. These are often aimed at requiring the parties to lift their entitlements when produced and not allow them to 'play the market' by not lifting when market conditions are unfavourable, with a view to 'making up' their underlift at a later stage when conditions may be better. Exercise of such make up rights can prejudice the interests of other parties when the offtake facilities are operating at capacity, as the other parties would have to reduce their offtake entitlements to accommodate the make up oil. To prevent this, UKCS JOAs have traditionally provided that petroleum not lifted at the time it is produced will be deemed to remain in the ground for the benefit of all of the parties when it is eventually produced, resulting in serious loss of entitlement on the part of the underlifter.

2.9 Assignment and Withdrawal

The right to assign interests under a JOA are normally made subject to the approval of the assignee by the other parties in respect, at least, of its financial standing, or to pre-emption rights in favour of the other parties. As the assignment of interests under the production licence without the consent of the Secretary of State is grounds for revocation of the licence, it is normal to provide that no assignment will be effective until the Secretary's approval has been obtained. An assignor will also be required to ensure that the assignee enters into an agreement, usually a novation, with the other parties, by which the assignee assumes its share of the obligations under the agreement and establishes privity of contract with the other parties.

Withdrawal from a JOA implies assumption by the other parties of the withdrawing parties' obligations. It is therefore normal to prohibit withdrawal prior to completion of the required work programme under the production licence or, after a decision to develop the field has been made, until the development is complete. Other than in these circumstances it is frequently provided that a party wishing to withdraw can require the other parties, or any of them, to acquire its interest at no cost and that if they fail to do so this shall be deemed to be a decision by all the parties to abandon the joint venture and to bring the licence and the JOA to an end.

2.10 Miscellaneous

The operating agreement will normally contain a number of other provisions of the sort normally found in commercial agreements, such as a *force majeure* clause, confidentiality obligations and dispute resolution provisions. It is not necessary to consider these here as operating agreements present no unique problems in these areas.

3.0 RECENT DEVELOPMENTS IN OPERATING AGREEMENTS

Although the basic form of contemporary UKCS operating agreement remains largely similar to that pioneered by the BNOC pro forma of 1977, there have been a number of changes in recent years.

3.1 Abolition of State Participation

A major change in the UK in recent years has been the elimination, as the result of changes in government policy, of direct State participation in exploration and production activities through a State oil company which is a party to production licences and JOAs. Initially, following the election of the Thatcher Government in 1979, the British National Oil Corporation was stripped of many of its privileges and its role, under most of the licences subsequently awarded, was restricted to the right to become a party to the licence and the existing JOA at the time a decision was made to develop a field, with a right, under a required amendment to the JOA, to opt to acquire up to 51 per cent of the production of each of its co-licensees at market price and to participate at operating committee meetings to the extent required to monitor this right. Over the years these rights were progressively reduced. First, BNOC's exercise of all its options to acquire oil (most of which existed under participation agreements in relation to licences awarded in the first four licensing rounds) were cancelled and BNOC was then abolished, though the State for a time retained the right, through a new organisation known as the Oil and Pipeline Agency (OPA), to reactivate the options under the JOAs and OPA continued to trade in royalty oil taken in kind. These last vestiges of UK State participation however disappeared after the decision of the Government in June 1988 that OPA should cease its trading activities and that all state participation provisions, including the options and the rights to receive information about operations, should be deleted from all existing JOAs. This process of amending JOAs was conducted on an agreement-by-agreement basis over a two year period.

With the disappearance from the scene of BNOC (which acted as a non-operator in most of the joint ventures in which it participated) there has been a trend to loosening the control of the non-operators over the operator and to allow more discretion to the operator. With the current need to contain costs to maintain the profitability – and possibly even the survival – of UKCS operations, this trend is likely to increase. It is likely to be most marked in the controls over the exercise by the operator of its contracting function. This is likely to be reinforced by the need to comply with the EC Utilities Directive, with its aim to eliminate national preference in contracting and to promote non-discriminatory and open procurement practices. This will, for example, make it difficult for the operating committee to exercise control over bidding lists. (For an in-depth discussion of the EC Utilities Directive's impact on the upstream oil and gas industry see Chapter 4.)

3.2 Abandonment

Decommissioning operations after field abandonment is within the scope of most existing operating agreements. What is usually lacking is adequate obligations as to the provision of security to meet each participant's share of the abandonment costs, which may prove a serious problem with some participants, particularly those whose only revenue producing asset was the field which is being abandoned. A great deal of effort has been devoted in recent years to developing appropriate provisions. A basic consensus has developed within the industry as to how these provisions should be structured and a number of JOAs have been supplemented to incorporate such provisions. However, only a minority of JOAs have been supplemented in this way and serious difficulties have frequently been encountered in getting all the parties to a JOA to accept the security provisions, particularly in the case of existing producing fields. (For a fuller discussion of abandonment security issues see Chapter 17.)

3.3 Pre-Emption Clauses

The advisability of including pre-emption rights in assignment clauses is being widely re-examined. At present about half of the JOAs for the UKCS are thought to contain pre-emption rights (or its alternative, the first right to negotiate). Their basic purpose is to enable existing participants in a joint venture to increase their stake in any successes won, rather than allow an outsider to come in, where at least one of the existing participants is prepared to match the offer made by the outsider. In a time when there is a strong trend towards companies rationalising their portfolios by concentrating on areas of strategic interest to them and disposing of other interests, pre-emption rights are being seen as a disadvantage. They certainly delay disposals of interests and they may well deter some potential assignees from devoting the considerable time necessary to evaluate and negotiate a deal in the knowledge that it may well be pre-empted. Furthermore it is recognised that pre-emption rights can often be circumvented by structuring disposals in packages, involving interests under more than one licence, which cannot be matched by any of the participants.

3.4 Default Clauses

There have been some recent attempts to provide for the better working of these clauses. For example, to discourage repeated defaults in meeting cash calls on time some JOAs now provide that, following each successive default, the period allowed to remedy the default before the defaulter's interest becomes subject to forfeiture should be progressively reduced down to a minimum of, say, seven days.

To facilitate the mechanics of effecting the forfeiture, a number of agreements now include powers of attorney by each participant in favour of the others, empowering these others to execute the necessary assignment documents to give effect to the forfeiture in case the party in default fails to do so. This obviates the need to make application to the court if the defaulter proves uncooperative, which is likely to be the case.

Where abandonment security provisions are agreed, the scope of the default clause in the JOA will normally be extended to cover breaches of the obligation to provide, or to renew, security in accordance with the agreement.

Following the reduced concern over legal problems related to enforcing forfeiture provisions as discussed above, there appears now to be little drive to amend default clauses, when a decision is made to develop a field, to reduce the chances of their being attacked on the grounds that they are a penalty or are subject to equitable relief against forfeiture.

3.5 Unitisation

Although this chapter has not addressed the subject of unit operating agreements, that is operating agreements for fields which have been unitised as they cross licence boundaries, two recent developments in relation to unit operating agreements deserve a mention. First, there is a trend towards adopting fixed unit interests which are not subject to one or more later redeterminations as more is learnt about the unitised reservoir through development drilling. Even though the fixing of equities before the reservoir's characteristics are fully known carries considerable risks in getting matters wrong, it has become widely recognised that the cost, time and effort, and the disrupting of relationships between the competing licence groups,

caused by lengthy redetermination exercises may considerably outweigh the benefits to the parties of any greater precision in the matter of unit equities. Second, to
avoid the lengthy delays that have frequently been experienced in getting developments under way through failure of the unit interest owners to agree a single unit
operator for the unitised field, it was agreed in 1991 between the two contenders for
the operatorship of the Britannia Field, that the operatorship should be shared
between the two companies. The Department of Trade and Industry has no objection
in principle to the concept of a shared operatorship – and in fact welcomes it if it can
result in the speeding up of the development of unitised fields. (For a fuller
discussion of the concept of unitisation and unit agreements see Chapter 16.)

3.6 Generally

Mention has been made earlier of the International Model Form Operating Agreement prepared by the ACCA and the AIPN. It is considered that this is likely to have
little impact in countries such as the UK or France where the form of operating
agreements is well established. It may prove useful however in areas of the world
where the form of JOAs is not so well entrenched. A feature of the model is that for
many of its provisions it includes a number of fully drafted alternative ways of
dealing with the matter in hand, which may prove helpful to negotiators and their
legal advisers.

Another development, in countries such as the UK where it is open to parties to
enter into bidding agreements to apply jointly for petroleum licences, is that it has
become the practice of some oil companies to require the operating agreement to be
fully negotiated at the bidding agreement stage. This can reduce considerably the
period required to negotiate the agreement and it ensures that a fully termed
agreement will be in effect very shortly after the licence is awarded, so avoiding a
legal hiatus with regard to the terms that are to govern the joint operations.

A theme underlying a number of the developments mentioned in the final section
of this chapter relates to ways of reducing the costs of carrying out operations under
the JOA. As previously mentioned, this could be a matter of major importance in
ensuring the longevity of UKCS operations. Cost-saving arrangements such as the
sharing of warehouses and supply vessel chartering and the like, as well as
integrated computerised management systems, are very much to the fore in many
companies' thinking and some of the more standard provisions in operating
agreements may well need some amendment to reflect these changes in operating
practice.

Chapter 15

Sole Risk and Non-Consent

Tom Winsor

1.0 INTRODUCTION

This Chapter deals with sole risk and the related subject of non-consent in United Kingdom joint operating agreements (JOAs). (See Chapter 14 for an overall discussion of JOAs.) The treatment of this controversial subject in JOAs in other parts of the world varies considerably in several important respects, and it is important to remember that this chapter is concerned with commercial practice in the UK jurisdiction.

Sole risk is undeniably the most exciting part of the JOA. It is where the parties have disagreed. It is based in discord and disharmony when the amounts of money involved can be enormous. Non-consent is perhaps not quite as glamorous or inflammatory.

Both are rooted in disagreement within the group. Both are the antithesis of a joint venture, because, in a nutshell, they allow a member of the group who dissents from the decision of the Operating Committee on a particular matter – usually a well – to disregard that decision and follow its own preference. They are destructive of cohesion.

2.0 THE PASSMARK

Whether or not sole risk or non-consent provisions may be likely to be invoked will depend to a very large extent on the passmark. Decisions are made in oil and gas joint ventures by the Operating Committee. Each of the licensees will usually have a seat on the Operating Committee and a vote corresponding to the size of his equity interest. The size of the passmark in the JOA is purely a matter of commercial negotiation.

Very often parties will disagree on proposals put to the Operating Committee. They will vote and the proposal will be agreed or rejected. The issues of whether to invoke sole risk or non-consent rights and what their consequences will be will arise when a member of the group disagrees with the decision the Operating Committee has taken.

3.0 THE DIFFERENCE BETWEEN SOLE RISK AND NON-CONSENT

The main difference between sole risk and non-consent is the support given to the matter in question when it was considered and voted on in the Operating Committee.

It is a fundamental principle of these provisions that the matter in question has been put before the Operating Committee first. The difference between the two is, essentially, that whereas with 'non-consent' the non-consenter elects not to take part in a project which has been agreed the Operating Committee, with 'sole risk' the sole risker is determined to proceed with something which the Operating Committee has decided *not* to do.

There are usually, though not for any logical reason, differences in the consequences of being a non-sole risk party and a non-consenting party.

4.0 NON-CONSENT

Once a non-consent election has been made, in many cases the parties that do go forward with the project without the non-consenter, do so in very much the same way as they would if the project was being carried out on a sole risk basis. In those circumstances, much of what follows about sole risk will be equally applicable to non-consent. It is important to note, however, that 'stand-alone' non-consent clauses may not be drafted so as to harmonise with sole risk provisions, and in such cases the divergencies in procedures and consequences can be considerable.

A right of non-consent gives a member of the group who has been outvoted on the Operating Committee a chance nevertheless to opt out of the project which the majority members of the consortium have approved. It is the most blatant exception to the principle that all members of the group will abide by the passmark decisions of the Operating Committee. Non-consent provisions are not by any means the rule in JOAs. North Sea exploration JOAs almost invariably include sole risk provisions, but relatively few also contain non-consent rights.

Non-consent clauses are usually encountered in groups where there are parties which are financially significantly weaker than the others, where there are also one or two dominant parties, and where the equity interests of the minority parties are not large enough to have any real chance of influencing the decisions that are made.

In such cases, the large and strong parties are sometimes prepared to concede that if a minority party is profoundly opposed to a proposal which has been passed by the Operating Committee, mainly through the use of their usually decisive voting power, that party will be permitted to opt out. It should always be remembered that it is by no means invariable practice that the co-venturers will agree to depart from the principle of majority rule being binding on all group members even in these cases of significant imbalance in voting power. After all, the minority co-venturers will almost always have known the make-up of the group and the balance of power within it when they agreed to join it. The large co-venturers can justifiably say that if non-consent rights were not agreed at the licence application stage there is no reason why they should concede them later, when the JOA is being negotiated.

Whilst the sole risk provisions in modern UK JOAs are in fairly standard form, non-consent rights vary sometimes quite considerably. The variations usually relate to:

(a) when the non-consent decision has to be made – at the budget approval stage, or at the later authority for expenditure (AFE) stage?
(b) the types of project which can be the subject of a non-consent decision – for example the whole annual work programme, individual wells, seismic, projects over a certain financial threshold? and
(c) the consequences of a non-consent decision, mainly whether or not the non-consenter has the right to participate in the project at a later stage (similar to the right of a non-sole risk party to 'back-in' later), and what premium they should pay to do so.

There is no uniformity in these provisions, and they are very much a matter for individual commercial negotiation at the time.

The foregoing is the case in relation to non-consent to exploration and appraisal work. However, it is almost invariable practice in North Sea and onshore UK JOAs that every party will have a right of non-consent when it comes to a development. It is not hard to see why that should be. Developments are usually enormously expensive. If a member of the group is so opposed to the development that he would rather have no part of it than be compelled to provide a share of the expenditure against his will, it is probably better to let him opt out at the beginning. To have an unwilling party as a participant in a development could be seriously disruptive, partly because he may be inclined to frustrate the development plan by always trying to persuade other members of the group to amend it or not to approve AFEs, and partly because if he is unable to find his share of the expenditure there seems little point in waiting for him to default and having to go through the difficult and sometimes complex process associated with the default of a co-venturer and the ultimate forfeiture of his interest in the venture when the group wants to press on with the development itself, not to be distracted by the consequences of one member's financial problems.

An important feature of non-consent at the development stage is that it can arise twice. The first time is after the development programme and budget has been approved. The second time is if the Secretary of State has required a material amendment to the proposed development plan. In that second case, all members of the group usually have the right to reassess their participation in the project, and those who opted out in the first place can reconsider their decisions and elect to participate after all (perhaps because the Secretary of State has required amendments which removed the original dissenters' objections). Conversely those co-venturers who initially elected to participate can also think again.

However, once the members of the group who do elect to participate are committed there will usually be no further opportunities for non-participants to join at a later stage.

5.0 SOLE RISK

5.1 Introduction

Sole risk provisions are clauses which enable parties to a joint venture to proceed with a project which has been rejected by the Operating Committee.

The sole risk clause is usually the longest clause in the operating agreement and until the last few years it was hardly ever used. That is not to say parties did not use the *threat* of invoking the sole risk provisions as a way of coaxing or cajoling their co-venturers into agreeing to projects they were lukewarm about doing – that kind of thing takes place all the time – but relatively rarely has a sole risk well actually been drilled, and never to the author's knowledge has there been a sole risk development in the UK sector of the North Sea.

5.2 Objections

Before the sole risk regime will be invoked there will have been objections to a proposal made to the Operating Committee. Taking the example of an exploration well proposal, the objections might be:

(a) technical objections – the dissenters do not agree on some aspect of the proposed well – perhaps its location or objective;
(b) financial objections – the well proposal is too expensive or too elaborate, or the detractors may not be able to afford to drill the well at the time proposed;
(c) strategic objections – the detractor may have interests in nearby or neighbouring blocks and might prefer that the well be drilled in a place or to a depth which will produce data which will be more useful to it in its assessments of its outside interests, at the same time ensuring its co-venturers share the costs of obtaining that data;
(d) timing or priority objections – the objecting party may simply think that the group should defer spending money in that year because the objector wishes to devote its financial resources to other blocks that are higher in its individual corporate priorities;
(e) political objections – the party in question may want to frustrate the carrying out of certain work for all sorts of reasons – perhaps to convince his co-venturers that the work should be done by another operator, or some other kind of dealing in the interests should take place.

For these or any of a number of other reasons, the proposal will have failed to get the necessary Operating Committee passmark vote of approval.

If the parties in favour of it feel strongly enough about it, they can initiate the sole risk procedure.

5.3 Motives for Proposing Sole Risk Work

It is apposite first to consider what may be the motives of a party which initiates the sole risk procedure. He may not be entirely the principled white knight of oil and gas exploration – the brave angel of enterprise and exploration, boldly going where his co-venturers are too lazy, too complacent, too timid or too tightfisted to tread. He may have his dark side too. His reasons may be strategic – wanting to force the pace much faster than older and wiser heads think prudent, or perhaps compel already financially hard-pressed smaller co-venturers to stay out of the project to enable him to take a larger share of something which perhaps everyone agrees is a good prospect. He may have a drilling rig on long-term charter with nothing else to do – he may need to find work for it, and at daily charge-out rates which are higher than the prevailing market price. The list goes on.

The standard sole risk clause does not discriminate between the Machiavellian sole risker and the brave spirit. Either of them can forge ahead alone. Usually it does not matter how small a percentage interest in the group the sole risker has. Very few JOAs contain a lower limit on the equity interest of a party proposing a sole risk project. Theoretically, a party holding a one per cent – or even smaller – interest could force the pace, much to the discomfort and inconvenience of the other co-venturers.

Having decided to propose a sole risk project, the sole risker must study the sole risk provisions of the JOA very carefully. The financial and other consequences of making a procedural mistake can be very considerable.

5.4 Constraints on Proposing Sole Risk Projects

There is very often a provision early in the sole risk clause which acts as a block on sole risk work being proposed at all until the work obligations under the licence have been completed. The purpose of this restraint is simply to maintain some degree of cohesion in the early stages when the minimum work obligations, which were agreed by all the co-venturers at the outset, are carried out.

It is also a fundamental principle that the sole risk work must not conflict or interfere with work which has already been approved as a joint operation.

5.5 Types of Sole Risk Project

It is not every kind of activity that can be proposed on a sole risk basis. Only operations of significance usually qualify and this means usually wells or an entire development.

Occasionally a provision is encountered in a JOA which allows a party to shoot seismic on a sole risk basis, but these clauses are not usually very well developed and it is often not clear what the consequences are if the other parties do or do not want to make a late participation election, or if that seismic identifies a structure which is eventually developed.

More usually, sole risk projects fall into one of the following categories:

(a) an exploration well – a wildcat well which is intended to penetrate a geological formation which has not been drilled before;
(b) an appraisal well;
(c) drilling or deepening an existing discovery well down into a different geological horizon which has not yet been tested; usually this kind of work requires

Operating Committee approval even though it is being proposed on a sole risk basis because of the risk that the joint discovery will be damaged by the sole risk work;

(d) deepening, sidetracking or testing a well which is being drilled as a joint operation; usually an Operating Committee decision to abandon the well will be needed before this further work can go ahead on a sole risk basis; and

(e) the development of a discovery.

5.6 Proposal of Sole Risk Project

Having determined that the work in question qualifies as sole risk work and that the necessary preconditions have been satisfied, the sole risker then has to propose the project formally as one which he is prepared to carry out on a sole risk basis. This involves a sole risk notice to the other co-venturers. The essential part of this process is that the other members of the group must be given a full and fair opportunity to assess the merits of the proposal in order to decide whether or not to participate with the sole risker.

Having been rejected by the Operating Committee, the proposal will of course come as no surprise to the other members of the group. However it is important that the sole risker lays the proposal before his co-venturers in the way set down in the JOA. This will involve him stating exactly what he proposes to do, what the costings are (these may be quite different from what the Operating Committee rejected), and when he proposes to start the work. The notice will also usually have to include a statement whether or not any joint property will be needed for the well. The overriding requirement of the JOA is that 'all relevant information' must be included in the notice. This is where the sole risker can trip himself up. Where does he stop? What does he withhold from his co-venturers? The short answer is that he should hold nothing back. It is safer for the sole risker to provide everything that is relevant and perhaps some things that are not than to fail to include relevant information which might later form the basis of a challenge to the validity of the sole risk procedure.

When they have received the sole risk notice, the other co-venturers then have the right to elect whether or not to participate in the project with the sole risker.

This is perhaps the stage of highest tension in the process. It is when each co-venturer must re-examine his earlier decision on participation and satisfy himself that the decision which he is now asked to take is the correct one. The consequences of being wrong can be quite Draconian. It is at this stage also that the bravery of the sole risker usually pays a dividend. Other members of the group may well find that they accept that there is a case for the work and they would rather pay their shares now than face the significantly adverse consequences later. It is important to remember that work is not rejected by the Operating Committee only on technical grounds. It may have been rejected on cost grounds or timing considerations – all the co-venturers may agree the prospect is worth drilling; their objections are to when it is to be carried out. A sole risk proposal can therefore be a very effective way of accelerating the parties' work objectives and forcing the co-venturers to put the proposal to the top of the agenda. If the well is truly worth drilling, it is very unlikely any co-venturer will elect to be a non-sole risk party on any other basis.

The other members of the group will usually have 30 days to elect whether or not to take part. The procedure for initiating sole risk work when there is already a rig on location and the proposed work is, for example, sole risk testing or deepening, needs to work faster. Usually the other group members are given as little as 48 hours to respond to the sole risk notice.

If the parties who wish to participate together hold the Operating Committee passmark vote, the proposal will usually be treated as having been approved by the Operating Committee and it will proceed as a joint operation.

However, if the proposal is supported by parties whose total voting power is insufficient to make up the passmark, the sole riskers are entitled to proceed alone. They have to start carrying out the sole risk project within a certain time – usually six months – as it would be unfair for the sole riskers to be able effectively to sterilize the prospect for years ahead.

5.7 Carrying out the Sole Risk Project

Once the sole risk group has been formed, its members are in charge of the sole risk operation. The non-sole riskers make no financial contribution and generally speaking they are entitled to none of the fruits. The sole riskers, as the name implies, take all the risks. They pay all the costs, and, since the licence obligations are joint and several, they are normally also required to indemnify the non-sole riskers against any costs or liabilities associated with the sole risk project.

The sole riskers make up their own Operating Committee, they decide amongst themselves what their individual equity stakes will be in the project, and they own the data that results. The non-sole risk parties do not receive daily drilling reports or any of the operational reporting or involvement that they would expect to have if the project was carried out as a joint operation. The sole riskers form a group within a group, and the insiders are the ones who are in control.

It is not, however, true to say that the non-sole riskers are never allowed to see the well data. They do have rights of access to the information but their rights are more restricted in terms of timing. They have to be shown the data from the sole risk project after it has been completed so that they can make their assessments of the project's success and decide whether or not to make a late participation election.

The operatorship of the sole risk project is a matter for the sole riskers. If the operator approved under the licence is a member of the sole risk group then it is natural for him to be the operator for the sole risk project. If that is not so, however, it is up to the sole riskers to find an operator. That may be the licence operator carrying out the work as a contractor, or it may be one of the sole riskers, or they may get a non-group member to operate for them. The JOA usually provides that the licence operator may refuse to carry out a sole risk project.

The JOA also usually contains provisions which deal with the right of the sole riskers to use joint property. This includes jointly owned data and any well which the parties have drilled jointly. This is usually only relevant in the case of a sole risk deepening, sidetracking or testing.

If the sole risk project turns out to be as disappointing as the detractors originally asserted, that will usually be an end of the matter.

However, it may also be that the sole riskers were right in their assessment of the prospectivity of the target. They may make a discovery, or the appraisal well they drilled on a sole risk basis may have led to the find being declared commercially exploitable. It is at that point that it becomes necessary to examine sole risk payments and late participation elections – what are usually known as 'back-in rights'.

5.8 Sole Risk Payments and Back-in Rights

If the sole risk project is a success, for example an exploration well flows well and the structure appears strongly to merit full appraisal, the non-sole risk parties may face a difficult choice – whether to elect to participate in further work on the prospect and pay the price, or remain a non-participant, forgoing a share in any fruits of the venture.

The JOA normally provides that if a non-sole risker wishes to take part in the appraisal, further appraisal or development of a discovery, he has the right to do so. The terms in which he may do so can be fairly ferocious.

First, he has to pay to the sole riskers whatever he would have paid towards the costs of the project if it had been a joint operation. By doing so, he acquires an equity stake in the project corresponding to that payment. Second, if the project proceeds to development, the JOA usually provides that, in addition to his normal cash calls under the development or operating programme and budget, he must pay the sole riskers ten times the amount he paid upon electing to participate late.

Some JOAs require a non-sole risker making a late participation election to provide the ten times payment in cash at the beginning of the development, out of taxed profits. So structured, this is often regarded as impossibly expensive. Others provide for him to 'carry' the sole riskers through the development and if necessary beyond, meeting their cash calls as well as his own until he has made the full late participation payment. Still other forms of JOA provide for the sole riskers to receive the late participation payments out of the non-sole riskers' share of production, perhaps leaving the non-sole riskers with a small share of production but taking the lion's share until the payment has been made in full.

The implication of this regime is that unless the non-sole risker accepts that he must make these enormous payments, he has no rights in the geological structure which is being developed. He cannot participate in decisions and he has no right to any production from it. So he is faced with a choice – to participate in the project having opted out in the early stages he must pay ten times what he would have paid had the project been a joint operation; if he elects not to do so, he is excluded from the field altogether. It can be a very difficult choice to make. That is why when a party formally proposes work on a sole risk basis, it is often found that the other members of the group discover the proposed work's technical merits which had eluded them when they voted against it in the Operating Committee, or that it is not so difficult to find the necessary money to fund the project in this year's corporate budget after all!

Most JOAs do not set down explicit time limits for the late participation election to be made. What they do say is that if a non-sole risker wishes to participate in further work on the sole risk structure he may only do so if he accepts an obligation to make these payments. JOAs also usually make provision for the fact that the development may take place years after the sole risk project was first carried out by including an inflation indexation of the base value of the late participation payment.

5.9 Sole Risk Development

Sole risk development is a simpler matter as far as the JOA is concerned. It has been explained above that it is almost invariable practice in modern UK Continental Shelf JOAs that no co-venturer can be compelled to take part in a development against his will, and will always have a right of non-consent.

There are three main features which distinguish sole risk development from other kinds of sole risk project. These are:

(a) because everyone has the right of non-consent when it comes to development, there is no material difference between sole risk and non-consent in this case – the question whether the project received passmark support at the Operating Committee does not make much difference;

(b) the time limits within which parties have to make their elections whether or not to participate in the sole risk development vary according to whether the development plan proposed is the one which the Operating Committee rejected (in which case a relatively short time is allowed for elections to be made) and whether the plan is substantially different from the one which was rejected by the Operating Committee, when a longer time is given for parties to consider their positions; and

(c) once the sole risk development is under way, the dissenters who have opted out are permanently excluded. There are no rights to participate in the development at a later stage.

Before sole risk development can be proposed the JOA normally insists that any joint appraisal programme has been completed.

When a sole risk development proceeds, the JOA usually provides for part of the licensed area to be 'carved out' and set aside for the sole riskers going forward with the project. It provides for the creation of a sub-area in which the sole riskers have exclusive rights. Delimiting the sub-area can be problematic. The JOA usually provides that it is the geological structure which is being developed together with the surface area above it.

The purpose of including the surface area in the sub-area is to ensure that the sole risk development has unimpeded access to the necessary area in priority to later joint operations. It is also usually provided in the JOA that the surface area of the sub-area must be retained by the licensees when they are surrendering any part of the licensed area, which they can do at any time. Were it not for these protections it might be possible for dissenters to engage in 'spoiling tactics' against the sole riskers.

The JOA will usually also provide that as far as the sole risk development is concerned, the JOA will apply in the manner of a separate contract to the rights and obligations of the sole riskers. This means that everything that is said about joint operations applies privately amongst the sole risk parties. The non-sole riskers have the benefit of an indemnity from the sole riskers, they have no late participation rights, so they have no further interest in the project.

The JOA will also usually provide that if one of the parties participating in the development wishes to exercise rights of assignment or withdrawal, he must do so for his interest in the development – the sub-area – and the remainder of the licensed area; in other words that there should be no separate right of assignment or withdrawal in relation to the sub-area.

5.10 Onshore

This Chapter has dealt with the sole risk regime as it normally applies in UKCS JOAs. The onshore UK licensing regime is currently significantly different from the offshore. Whereas offshore there is a single licence – a petroleum production licence (albeit since 1988 split into three terms instead of two) – onshore a different licence is needed for exploration, appraisal and development. If the onshore JOA is correctly structured and contains adequate mechanisms for the transition from one licence to another, the sole risk provisions can mercifully be much shorter.

For a fuller explanation of the commercial practices of holders of UK petroleum licences, both offshore and onshore, in relation to sole risk and non-consent, see Chapters 3 and 7 of *Taylor and Winsor on Joint Operating Agreements* (Longman, 1992).

Chapter 16

Unitisation

Michael P.G. Taylor

This Chapter provides something of an overview of unitisation, it is taken primarily from a UK standpoint and is broadly divided into four parts. The first part defines unitisation and sets out ways in which units interest are determined. The second part discusses the UK Government's powers as regards unitisation, and the third section describes the structure and contents of unit agreements. The remainder of the Chapter takes a brief look at cross-border unitisation, commenting on a situation where an oil and/or gas field crosses an international boundary.

1.0 INTRODUCTION

In the Minister for Energy's Report to Parliament in April 1992, details are given of 46 offshore oil and condensate fields in production on the UK sector of the Continental Shelf (UKCS) as at the end of 1991 of which 18 are shown as falling within areas covered by more than one licence. The equivalent figures published for gas fields indicate a total of 34 UKCS gas fields in production of which 20 fall within areas covered by more than one licence.

Whenever a field fails to fit neatly within the area covered by a single licence, the question arises as to whether the holders of each licence should be able to develop, and subsequently produce petroleum from, that part of the field falling within their licence, or whether the field should be unitised, *ie* developed and subsequently operated jointly by the holders of all the relevant licences with the resulting production from the field divided between them in agreed proportions irrespective of actual production from the portions of the field underlying each of the relevant licensed areas.

In the example shown in Figure 1, the field in Block 1/1 (covered by Licence P.1) extends into Block 2/2 (covered by Licence P.2). In order to develop and operate the field as a unit, the licensees of Licences P.1 and P.2 would need to enter into a unit agreement.

Figure 1.

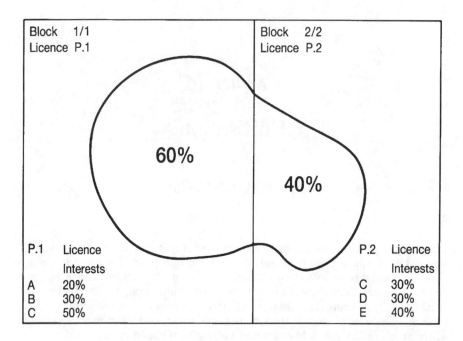

One of the most important functions of the document will be to establish the respective interests of each of the licence groups in the unitised field. These interests are normally referred to as 'tract participations'. In the example, the P.1 licence group has a tract participation of 60 per cent and the P.2 licence group has a tract participation of 40 per cent.

The unit agreement will also establish the interest of each individual licensee in the unitised field. This is normally referred to as a 'unit participation' or 'unit interest'. The unit participation of each licensee in the field is equal to: percentage interest of licensee in own licence x tract participation of its licence group.

In the example, A has a percentage interest of 20 per cent in Licence P.1 but has no interest in Licence P.2. Therefore its unit participation will be 20 per cent x 60 per cent, *ie* 12 per cent. C's unit participation will be (50 per cent x 60 per cent) + (30 per cent x 40 per cent), *ie* 42 per cent.

As a general rule, a company will be obliged to pay its unit participation proportion of costs and will receive its unit participation proportion of the petroleum produced from the unitised field.

2.0 TRACT PARTICIPATIONS

The initial tract participation of each licence group will be negotiated and agreed and set out in the unit agreement. Negotiation of tract participation is likely to be a lengthy and difficult process, particularly where, as is usually the case, the basis upon which the initial tract participations are calculated is to be used in any subsequent redetermination of tract participations.

The usual method of determining tract participations is by reference to stock tank oil originally or initially in place (STOOIP or STOIIP). This means the total quantity of petroleum in the reservoir prior to commencement of production. This method has the advantage of being relatively easy to estimate and agree, and the final STOOIP figure can usually be determined a few years after development drilling has been completed. However it suffers from the disadvantage that no distinction is made between those reserves which will in fact be produced, and those which will have to be left in the ground.

If the holders of one licence perceive that their tract is likely to make a greater contribution to production from the field than the tract participation that would be allocated to it on the basis of STOOIP, it may well be argued that tract participation should instead be based upon recoverable reserves of the field underlying each tract. However there are difficulties with this:

(a) There are the practical objections that estimates of future recoverable reserves are notoriously imprecise while a final calculation will not be possible until the field has been depleted and upon depletion there will, of course, be no remaining reserves for making a final adjustment of production.

(b) There are objections of principle. The most serious of these is that the relative recoverable reserves of each tract will be affected by the development plan itself with the result that a decision to base tract participation upon recoverable reserves may result in each licence group being more concerned to maximise the recoverable reserves of its tract rather than concentrating on developing the field in the manner which is most beneficial to all parties.

(c) A further problem is that basing tract participation upon recoverable reserves ignores the fact that reserves which are not recovered may, nevertheless, play an important part in the production process through displacing reserves which are produced.

One compromise is to base tract participations upon moveable oil, *ie* oil which is capable of movement within the reservoir even if not actually produced. Another form of compromise is to adopt STOOIP as the basis for determining tract participations, but to make some adjustment where one tract is likely to make a disproportionate contribution to the recoverable reserves.

3.0 TIMING OF UNITISATION

UKCS fields are usually unitised prior to development, for two main reasons:

(a)   It will generally be in the commercial interests of the holders of the relevant licences to develop the whole field from the outset as an integrated operation to avoid wasteful technical duplication.

(b)   With only rare exceptions, the Department of Trade and Industry (DTI) will wish to see a fully signed unit agreement submitted with the development plan for the field in question. This is because:

   (i)   it has an interest in ensuring the maximum economic recovery of petroleum and the field will almost invariably have to be developed as a single entity to achieve this;

  (ii)   in the DTI's view, the unitisation arrangements are more likely to be fair and equitable if the unit agreement is negotiated before huge development investments have been made by the licensees, by which stage they might feel under pressure to try and squeeze out for themselves the most favourable (and probably unrealistic) deal; and

 (iii)   in the past any delay in production which might be caused by delay in negotiating unitisation arrangements between the two licence groups would in turn delay receipt by the Government of petroleum revenue tax, and this would be against the national interest. However, the Finance Act 1993 has abolished petroleum revenue tax for fields where the Secretary of State's consent for development was granted after March 16 1993.

The practice to date of the UKCS whereby fields are generally unitised prior to development is in strong contrast within that onshore in North America where unitisation, either voluntary or compulsory, usually takes place only after the commencement of production, frequently in response to the need for secondary recovery operations.

4.0 GOVERNMENT CONTROL

The UK Government has two important powers under a petroleum production licence which, in practice, enable the Government to compel licensees to unitise a field which straddles the licence boundaries.

   (i)   The Secretary of State's approval to the development of a field is required under the terms of the licence (model clauses 17–18). A representative of the then Department of Energy stated (at a 1991 conference on unitisation) that they 'will act to ensure that no actions which may result in the capture of hydrocarbons from adjoining acreage can take place unless the agreement of the licensees of that adjoining acreage has been obtained'. The same Department of Energy representative said, some years ago, that the Department depends upon 'persuasion rather than any direct sanctions' to get operators to settle their differences although 'at the crunch point permission to develop a field will not be given unless a field is unitised'. Although refusal to consent to a development of part of the reservoir is not the same thing as actively compelling unitisation, the effect may be the same. The Department's strong preference is for unitisation arrangements to be agreed before the licensees embark upon development of the field because, in the view of the Department, the unit agreement is more likely to be fair and equitable if negotiated at this stage.

       An alternative to agreeing unitisation at the outset may be for one licence group to go ahead with the development with the other licence group giving a 'waiver' but this is only likely to be a solution where nearly all the field is within one licence area; the holders of that licence are able to develop the field satisfactorily by means of operations conducted upon their licence area; and the holders of the adjoining licence are willing to give a waiver so as to allow the development to proceed.

Where the agreement of the licensees of adjoining acreage has been obtained by way of waiver the DTI will probably allow the holders of a licence comprising a majority of the field's reserves to proceed to develop that portion of the field. In cases of waiver, it is likely that the neighbouring licensees will require an undertaking that unitisation discussions will be commenced if they so require, (if, for example, the portion of the field underlying their licence area turns out to be larger than they had first thought).

(ii)   Under model clause 28, the Secretary of State has power to give notice to each of the licence groups involved, requiring them to develop the field as a single unit if he considers that this would be 'in the national interest in order to secure maximum ultimate recovery of petroleum and in order to avoid unnecessary competitive drilling'. The wording of this model clause seems to contemplate the possibility of each of the licence groups competing to be the first to extract the petroleum from the common reservoir. This in effect would amount to a right of 'capture' if petroleum from that part of the reservoir under, for example, Block 2/2 flowed into the area of the reservoir beneath Block 1/1 and was extracted from development wells on that block. Apparently consistent with this idea, the licence granted by the Crown confers on the licensees an 'exclusive licence and liberty ... to search and bore for, and get, petroleum in the seabed and subsoil under [the licensed area]'. There is nothing to say that the licensee does not have the right to extract such petroleum as may lie under the licensed area at any given time. If petroleum in a common reservoir strayed into the licensed area from the adjoining block, the licensee would on this basis have the right to extract it. However, the DTI has made it known in no uncertain terms that it does not believe that such a right of capture applies to petroleum on the UK Continental Shelf. How it will manage to square this view with the fact that it can only require and compel unitisation in order to secure the maximum ultimate recovery of petroleum *and to avoid unnecessary competitive drilling* remains to be seen if competitive drilling is not an accepted concept in the first place! So far, this power under model clause 28 has not been used but it would be interesting to see how the DTI could justify its use where a field extended into another block where the licensees refused to give a waiver but at the same time had no intention of commencing any competitive drilling themselves.

Also under model clause 28, if the parties are unable to agree terms for the unitised development and operation of the field, the Secretary of State may prepare and impose a scheme 'which shall be fair and equitable' to the holders of each licence. This power has never been exercised, and the DTI may well be reluctant to become technically involved to the extent of preparing a scheme itself, but the existence of the power encourages licensees to reach agreement between themselves rather than risk having terms imposed upon them by the DTI.

5.0 UNIT AGREEMENTS

The development of a field as a single unit by the holders of more than one licence will require a new agreement which will largely, although not entirely, replace the Joint Operating Agreements (JOAs) which are in place for the respective licences. This new agreement has two principal functions.

First, it provides for the unitisation of the field, and second, it provides for the development, operation and ultimate abandonment of the unitised field. Since it provides for the development and operation of the field, it will contain many provisions which are common to ordinary licence JOAs, but will also contain a number of additional provisions which are only required in the case of unitisation. All companies holding interests in the relevant licences will need to be party to the unit agreement.

In the United States, the practice is to have a unitisation agreement and a separate unit operating agreement but the practice in the UK is to have one document combining both functions. The full title of this document is usually 'unitisation and unit operating agreement'.

A unit agreement will generally include clauses dealing with the following matters:

- Definitions including, in particular:
  - Unit area
  - Unitised zone or unitised reservoir
- Duration
- Creation and effect of unit
- Tract participations and unit interests
- Redetermination
- Consequential adjustments following redetermination
- Unitised substances
- Enlargement of unit area
- Unit operator
- Unit operating committee
- Programmes and budgets
- Non-unit operations
- Sole risk
- Costs and accounting
- Default
- Abandonment
- Confidentiality
- Assignment and withdrawal

Many of these clauses are similar to the equivalent clauses found in ordinary JOAs governed by the laws of England and Wales. The clauses which are not found in a typical JOA of this type, or which differ significantly from the equivalent provisions of a typical JOA governed by the laws of England and Wales, are described below.

5.1 Definitions

The unit agreement will include a number of defined terms not needed in an ordinary JOA. The 'unit area' will be defined by reference to specified coordinates and will broadly correspond to the aerial extent of the field as known at the time the unit agreement is entered into. The 'unitised zone' or 'unitised reservoir' will be the stratigraphic sequence within the unit area containing the field.

5.2 Creation and Effect of Unit

Provision will be included in the unit agreement to the effect that the interests of each of the participants in the unitised zone, and in all petroleum produced from that zone, are unitised in accordance with the terms and conditions of the unit agreement and that unit operations are to be conducted as a single integrated operation in accordance with the unit agreement. It will also be provided that any previous agreements entered into between any of the parties which contain provisions conflicting with the unit agreement are amended to eliminate the conflict, but that nothing in the unit agreement is to be construed as resulting in any assignment of licence interests.

5.3 Tract Participations and Unit Interests

See sections 1.0 and 2.0 above.

5.4 Redetermination

There will normally be provision for periodic redetermination of tract participations. Where this is the case it should be noted that the tract participations of the relevant licence groups are those established at the final redetermination while the tract participations originally set out in the unit agreement or established in any interim redetermination are merely provisional. This important principle of unitisation is reflected in the retrospective adjustments which are made following a redetermination, and is the reason why a redetermination is not thought to constitute a disposal for capital gains tax purposes. The unit agreement will need to set out:

(a)   the number and timing of the redeterminations,
(b)   the basis upon which the revised tract participations are to be determined; and
(c)   the procedure to be followed for redetermination.

To take each of these in turn:

(a)   *Number and timing of redeterminations*
      Each redetermination is likely to be an expensive and time-consuming process and this factor must be taken into account in deciding upon the number and frequency of the redeterminations. It has been estimated that an average redetermination exercise can keep 12 people fully employed for two years at a cost of some £2m. For redetermination to be cost-effective it therefore needs to result in a material alteration to the ownership equities at stake. If initial estimates are fair (and it is likely that they will be) alterations will be marginal. There is clearly an argument for the proposition that there should be no redeterminations at all, and one respected

unitisation expert has argued that there should be no more than two, even on a large field. Companies may also bear in mind that 'fixed equities' are increasingly possible due to advances in the accuracy of seismic surveys. However, most companies seem unwilling to forgo the possibility of increasing their unit participation just to avoid the cost of redetermination (and the risk that their unit participation may be reduced!). Also, the more redeterminations there are, the less likely it is that one of them will result in a dramatic and potentially damaging change in the tract participation of either licence group and the companies may therefore perceive a need, in the interests of economic certainty, for several interim redeterminations followed by final redetermination once all the development wells have been drilled and a reasonable amount of production experience obtained.

It is undoubtedly best to call for a redetermination when a balance of data is available across the whole structure, but this is unfortunately a rare occurrence because development wells will generally be drilled only into parts of the reservoir which are known to be fruitful. If however the availability of balanced data is delayed, it could have a huge impact at the time of the final redetermination.

Timing of redetermination may be determined on various different bases:

(i)   it may be agreed in the unit agreement that redetermination is to take place at a predetermined time, (which is, when it comes to it, almost sure to be an unsuitable time!); or

(ii) it may be fixed to take place at certain 'milestones' in operations (*eg* commencement of production, or drilling of the fifteenth development well); and/or

(iii) it may be specified that it will occur at the election of a participant or licence group.

It is generally preferable to specify for some element of conscious decision making at the time, rather than merely fixing a number of dates years in advance.

(b) *The basis upon which the revised tract participations are to be determined*

The basis upon which revised tract participations are to be determined will generally be the same as that used in determining the original tract participations, although this is not necessarily the case. For example, STOOIP may have been used to calculate the original participations while the unit agreement could provide for a redetermination later in accordance with recoverable reserves. This would, however, seem to be rare in practice.

(c) *Redetermination procedures*

The redetermination procedure will normally be very detailed. Its purpose is:

(i)   to identify and narrow down areas of disagreement between the licence holders as to the various complex geological, geophysical and reservoir engineering issues involved in the redetermination, and

(ii) to provide a method for resolving any remaining disagreement, usually by referral to an independent expert.

To take each of these aspects in turn:

(i)   When a redetermination is called, raw data will be supplied from the unit area and made available to all the participants. This will be known as the 'common database' and constitutes the material which will be used in order to try and reach agreement on the revised tract participations. (Some interpreted data may be allowed into the common database if the parties agree.) There will be a cut-off point after which no further data of any description is admitted. The parties will then try to thrash out between them an agreement on the revised tract participations and this may take some considerable time. Formal objections may be referred to an expert, but if this does not occur after a certain time, the existing equities will continue in force.

(ii) If formal objections are submitted to an independent expert, the extent of his power and discretion will depend upon the extent to which it has been circumscribed under the terms of the unit agreement. In *Arco British Limited and others v Sun Oil Britain Limited and others* (unreported, December 1988), the Court of Appeal decided that, in the absence of clear contractual provision to the contrary, the powers of an expert appointed for the purpose of conducting a redetermination extend to a discretion to revise figures when necessary in order to correlate data from different sources and achieve overall accuracy. If the parties are concerned by this, then the scope of the expert's appointment under the terms of the unit agreement should be clear and specific from the outset. It may be possible to set out his terms of reference in detail in an Appendix to the unit agreement.

When considering the terms of a dispute resolution procedure in a unit agreement, the negotiators should also consider the following additional points:

(i)   From a legal point of view to appoint an expert to decide a dispute blurs the traditional distinction between an arbitrator (who commonly fulfils a judicial role deciding a dispute) and an expert (who traditionally provides a professional opinion which both parties agree to accept to prevent a dispute from arising). The appointment of an expert in order to determine a dispute does not, in the view of the courts, automatically confer upon an expert the status of an arbitrator. This may be welcome from the point of view of parties who are wishing to avoid the application of the Arbitration Acts (which, amongst other things, provide for appeal to the courts in certain circumstances) but there is a correlated disadvantage in that there is no ready-made body of law (such as the Arbitration Acts) to fall back upon if the expert procedure does not work or there is a dispute between the parties as to how it should be interpreted.

(ii) From a practical point of view, there are disadvantages in having a lengthy negotiating process between the various participants, followed by a separate, equally (if not more) lengthy expert determination process. Delay and expense are obvious. Less obvious perhaps is the tendency for the adversarial nature of the procedure to cause each participant to take the most extreme position in its own favour when presenting its own technical submissions to the expert. This is because the expert is probably less of an expert than the owners themselves in relation to the matters at issue and, being under severe time constraints, it is more than likely that he will adopt a 'middle ground' solution. It is natural therefore for each party to adopt the most extreme position possible, a tendency which is viewed, not least by the DTI, as being extremely unprofessional. It may get to the point where the quality of the submissions to be made to the expert becomes more important in the minds of the parties to the dispute than trying to reach agreement between themselves. In order to encourage parties to be more reasonable, the DTI has indicated that it would perhaps prefer to see a 'pendulum determination' solution, *ie* whereby the expert is required to plump for either one side's case or the other, rather than take the middle ground. This would encourage all submissions to be more reasonable.

(iii) Some modern unit agreements contain something called the 'Guided Owner Process' as a dispute resolution procedure. Under this, the two separate 'participants-negotiation followed-by-expert' procedures are replaced by a single negotiation between the participants, with the expert present throughout. Delays in getting the process under way due to disagreements over data and procedural issues are avoided by addressing these in advance within a set and enforceable timeframe. The guided owner process provisions ensure that (a) the 'expert' is a multidisciplinary team which is appointed at the outset of the redetermination and works in parallel with the participants, witnessing (unless everyone agrees otherwise) every equity redetermination technical meeting and thus discouraging the adoption of extreme positions, and (b) the equity redetermination process is divided into 'key steps', each of which is a collection of detailed procedures which must be completed and agreed before moving on to the next key step. The fundamental requirement is that, at each key step, the participants must agree all matters outstanding at that point. If they cannot, the expert will determine the outstanding deadlocked matters and the process will then move on to the next key step on schedule.

5.5 Consequential Adjustments Following Redetermination

Costs and production must be adjusted following each redetermination. The principle is generally that, following each redetermination, the parties should, so far as possible, be put in the position they would have been in had the new tract participations prevailed from the outset. Parties whose unit participations have increased (and who therefore have invested too little to date) will therefore make payments to those whose unit participations have reduced (and who therefore have paid too much), so that, after the adjustment payments have been made, each party has paid its unit participation proportion of all unit expenses to date.

There will also need to be an adjustment of past production but, assuming this is to be in kind rather than in cash, the adjustment will be made out of future production. It is usually agreed that a proportion of future production should be set aside and allocated amongst the parties whose unit participations have increased (in addition to new unit participation proportions of the remaining production) until the cumulative production which they have received equals their new unit participation proportions of total cumulative production from the field. Slightly surprisingly perhaps, it should be noted that the adjustment of production is generally by reference simply to the difference between the volume of past production allocated to each party in accordance with the old unit participations and the volume which would have been allocated in accordance with the new unit participation. A case could be made for taking into account after-tax values at the time of original production as compared to after-tax values at the time of adjustment.

The adjustment provisions give rise to a number of issues, *eg*:

(1) Should interest be paid to an over-investor upon the adjustment of capital? On the face of it, the answer would seem to be that it should (and an interest element is often incorporated to provide some return on the over-investment (*eg* 1 per cent over LIBOR)), since the intention is to put the parties in the position in which they would have been had the new participations prevailed from the outset. However, if the participants whose interests have reduced are to receive interest on the adjustment payments they receive, should the parties whose unit participations have increased receive some form of uplift on the adjustment of production in their favour? If so, how should this be calculated?

(It should be noted that, where it is provided that payment should be made representing an adjustment of capital plus interest, the paying parties will generally be obliged to deduct tax (at the standard rate of income tax) from the interest element. This was decided in a case involving the Ninian field (*Chevron Petroleum (UK) Limited v BP Petroleum Development Limited* [1981] STC 689). The recipients should generally be able to recover the amount deducted by way of an offset against their corporation tax liabilities (or a payment from the Inland Revenue if they have no corporation tax liability) but such a recovery may take some time.)

(2) What is the best basis for fixing the proportion of future production to be set aside by the parties whose unit participations have decreased to enable the parties whose unit participations have increased to recover their shortfall in past production? If this proportion is not sufficient to enable the shortfall to be made good within a specified period, should there be provision for the proportion to be increased and should there be provision for payment in cash if there are insufficient remaining reserves to enable the shortfall to be recovered from future production?

(3) Particular difficulties, meriting a paper of their own, can arise where the participants holding interests in a unitised gas field have agreed to sell gas to different buyers. An adjustment of production in these circumstances could result in those participants whose interests have reduced having insufficient gas to satisfy their contractual obligations while other participants, whose interests have increased, have surplus gas. It would be open to the participants to overcome this particular difficulty by ensuring that their respective contracts provided sufficient flexibility to allow for adjustments

of production but this would tend to reduce the attractiveness of the contract from a buyer's point of view and thus reduce the price which the seller was able to obtain. These problems are likely to become more common in future as the UK gas market opens up. Effective solutions seem possible but are still being developed. It will be important to ensure that the timing of redetermination adjustments under the unit agreement is consistent with any relevant notice periods required under the gas sales contract.

(4)   If the adjustment of production is to be spread over a lengthy period, should the adjustment of costs also be spread over a lengthy period?

These matters are not easy to resolve even if all parties are willing to assume fairly small changes in tract participations at an early stage in the field's production against a background of profitable operations and stable or rising oil prices. They become extremely difficult where it is felt that the circumstances may be not so favourable.

5.6 Enlargement of Unit Area

Another provision which is exclusive to unitisation agreements is that dealing with the enlargement of the unit area. There will probably be provision for enlarging the unit area in the event that the field is found to extend beyond the boundaries of the original unit area. Such an enlargement may require the approval of all parties (in which case it may be provided that such approval is not to be unreasonably withheld) or the approval of the unit operating committee, or it may be treated as a matter to be determined upon its technical merits with reference to an independent expert should the parties be unable to agree. The principle which is generally accepted is that the unit area should encompass the entire unitised field in so far as it falls within the area covered by the relevant licences. However, the parties must decide what they mean by a field; for example, is it sufficient for the petroleum within a proposed extension of the field to be in pressure communication with the petroleum which is already subject to the unit agreement, or must it be in continuous hydrocarbon phase?

Where the unit area is enlarged to include an extension of the field, there will probably need to be a redetermination of tract participations.

Some unit agreements also include provision for reduction of the unit area.

5.7 Unit Operator

The usual operator/non-operator conflicts will be present and are likely to be heightened in the case of the unit agreement. 'Usual operator/non-operator conflicts', meaning in this context the conflicts which arise as a result of the divergent interests of the operator and the non-operators, the former of whom will wish to have maximum freedom to conduct joint operations, including hiring contractors, spending what it considers necessary (in the light of its experience) and keeping administration to a minimum, without the interference of the non-operators, and the latter of whom will, conversely, wish to protect their investments by requiring financial control, involvement and consultation at all stages of operations. In addition to these conflicts, there may well be disagreement as to which party should be operator, with the holders of each licence probably wanting their licence operator to be the operator of the unit.

5.8 Unit Operating Committee

In the same way, when deciding upon the percentage vote required for decisions of the unit operating committee, the holders of each licence will probably wish to ensure that resolutions cannot be passed by vote of the holders of the other licence alone. This will be particularly relevant where a large portion of the unitised field is in one licensed area and only a small part in the other. The holders of the licence with the majority share of the unitised zone will not want to be frustrated by the holders of small equity interests while conversely the minority parties will want some means of protecting their interests.

One solution is to provide that any decision requires votes in favour of it from at least one party from each licence group. If this solution is adopted, it will also usually be necessary to ensure that if a company, either itself or through its affiliate, has an interest in both licence groups, that company's vote may not be considered in satisfying the requirement.

Another solution is to set a passmark higher than the tract participation of any single licence group, but since tract participations can alter, some further protection may therefore be required by members of the minority group, such as that described above.

5.9 Non-Unit Operations

Provision will be included regarding the conduct of non-unit operations by the parties within the unit area. The overriding principle, however, is that the unit operations have priority and so there is unlikely to be an unfettered right to carry on non-unit operations or use unit facilities for this purpose. Normally there will be a provision whereby any party wishing to carry out non-unit operations within the unit area, even if this does not involve the use of unit facilities, must satisfy the other parties that the conduct of the non-unit operations will not interfere with unit operations. The party conducting the non-unit operations will usually be required to indemnify the other parties against any losses which may be incurred as a result.

In some unit agreements the only type of non-unit operation which is permitted within the unit area is drilling from a mobile drilling rig to a target depth either deeper or shallower than the unitised zone. In other cases, however, the unit agreement permits the unit facilities to be used for drilling non-unit wells after the development drilling has taken place and perhaps even for other types of non-unit operation, *eg* the parties may be allowed to use unit facilities for processing petroleum from satellite fields within the area covered by one of the licences provided they are outside the unit area.

Although the use of unit facilities will in any event be subject to the principle of not interfering with unit operations, there may well be spare capacity. This raises the question of what payments should be made to the joint account for such use. A number of positions can be taken. It can be argued that the use by a party of the unit facilities for non-unit operations should be regarded as a use by a third party to be charged at a full market rate. At the other extreme it can be argued that the capital costs of the unit facilities have been paid for already by the parties to the unit agreement and, if there is any spare capacity, unit participants should be entitled to use it without having to pay anything more than the incremental costs involved. There are of course a number of possible compromises. For example a party may be allowed to use its unit participation share of any spare capacity upon favourable terms while more onerous terms would apply if it were to use any spare capacity in excess of this.

Frequently, the solution adopted is simply to defer the issue by providing that the terms upon which the unit facilities may be used by the parties for non-unit operations are to be determined by the unit operating committee at the relevant time. This is a difficult issue, especially where the parties are well aware that one licence group is more likely than the other to use unit facilities for non-unit operations.

5.10 Sole Risk

The purpose of a sole risk clause in a unit agreement is usually to allow one or more members of a licence group to drill an appraisal well in that portion of the unitised zone falling within their tract participation at their own sole risk and cost, *eg* if they believe the result will be of assistance to them during a redetermination of tract participations. Data from the sole risk well may be made available to all the unit participants and the well may be adopted as unit property if it is thought best by the unit operating committee to complete or suspend it. (For a further discussion on sole risk clauses see Chapter 15.)

5.11 Default

There are several other issues which are addressed in an ordinary JOA but which may need to be dealt with differently in a unit agreement.

The most important of these is default although assignment and withdrawal may also prove difficult. A UK Continental Shelf JOA will normally provide for a defaulter to transfer its interest to the non-defaulters if the default is not remedied within a specified period of time (forfeiture provision) although there may be a provision for reassignment of a reduced interest at a later date (withering provision). If a forfeiture or withering provision was included in the unit agreement, the result would be that an interest might be assigned from the holder of one licence to all the remaining parties to the unit agreement, which would include the holders of the other licence. This would involve a licence assignment and is generally considered undesirable for a number of reasons including potential legal difficulties, the conflicts of interest which may arise and the fragmentation of interests which could result.

For these reasons, most unit agreements either adopt a default procedure which does not involve any transfer of the defaulter's interest but merely deprives the defaulter of any rights under the unit agreement until the default is remedied, or provides for the other holders of the defaulter's licence to make good the default. In the latter case, forfeiture provisions in the unit agreement or the licence JOA may apply as between the holders of the relevant licence, and may result in a transfer of the defaulter's interest but only to the other holders of that licence. The problem of group default *ie* default by all the holders of a particular licence is sometimes addressed but is obviously unlikely to occur in practice. If it is addressed, the agreement will probably provide for the non-defaulting group to make up the shortfall whilst consulting with the government to determine what to do next!

5.12 The Licence JOAs

It should not however be assumed that a unit agreement would entirely replace the licence JOAs. Although the unit agreement will govern the development and operation of the unitised field and will impose restrictions on any other operations carried on within the unit area, operations carried out in the remainder of the area covered by each licence will continue to be governed by the licence JOA. In addition, each licence JOA will generally continue to apply, as between the parties to it, to matters pertaining to the unit area except in so far as overridden by the unit agreement. The unit agreement will generally include a provision to the effect that, in the event of any conflict between a licence JOA and the unit agreement, the unit agreement will prevail. However, subject to this, the provisions of each licence JOA will apply, as between the parties to it, in parallel with the provisions of the unit agreement. For example, a party may be free to assign its unit participation under the unit agreement but may nevertheless have to offer it first to the other parties to its licence JOA if this confers a right of pre-emption. (For a further discussion on JOAs see Chapter 14.)

5.13 Cross-Border Unitisation

An oil and/or gas field can of course also cross an international boundary, and by way of example three fields in the North Sea, Frigg, Statfjord and Murchison, straddle the median line between the UK and Norway. In such a situation the DTI, for example, is powerless to require the licensees of the other government involved to develop the field as a unit.

However, as in this case of the UK and Norway, the two governments may enter into a treaty in respect of the exploitation of the field in question. The purpose of such a treaty will be to ensure concerted action by the two governments and eliminate potential conflicts which might arise by incorporating a procedure to agree on almost all important matters. For example, paras 2 and 3 of Article 2 of the Frigg Treaty provided that:

2 The two Governments shall consult with a view to agreeing a determination of the limits and estimated total reserves of the Frigg Field Reservoir and an apportionment of the reserves therein as between the Continental Shelf appertaining to the United Kingdom and the Continental Shelf appertaining to the Kingdom of Norway. For this purpose the licensees shall be required to submit to the Governments a proposal for such determinations.

3 The two Governments shall endeavour to agree the apportionment of the reserves of the Frigg Field Reservoir before production of the reserves commences. If they are not able to do so, then pending such agreement, the production shall proceed on the provisional

basis of a proposal for the apportionment submitted by the licensees, or if there is none, on the provisional basis of equal shares. Such provisional apportionment shall be without prejudice to the position of either Government . . .

As a matter of UK law, such treaties do not bind the respective licensees directly and consequently the licensees in the Frigg, Statfjord and Murchison cases have undertaken to have regard to the terms of the relevant treaty when exploiting their field and determining and apportioning its reserves. Governmental bodies may have additional powers, the DTI for example has the power, under model clause 29, to direct the UK licensees 'as to the manner in which the rights conferred by the licence shall be exercised' in cases of cross-border unitisation.

Chapter 17

Abandonment of Offshore Petroleum Production Installations

Gareth Jones and Mark Saunders

1.0 INTRODUCTION

As the end approaches of the useful economic life of an offshore petroleum production facility the owners and/or operators must face vexed and costly questions. What duties does the owner have on the disuse of the facility? Must it be removed? What are the options? What has to be done about pipelines? Must all the costs be borne by the owners? Is there tax relief? A number of oil producing areas have already had to contend with these issues in practice, in particular the Gulf of Mexico and East Coast USA and, increasingly, the North Sea. This Chapter approaches such issues primarily from the perspective of the UK experience while making some observations based on the experience of other states.

The structure of the Chapter is to examine the international guidelines, then to look at the legal and fiscal background, policy, practice and some reported cases of abandonment and finally to consider what response to these issues is made by companies engaged in petroleum production to share the burden and risks of paying for abandonment. This structure is contained in the following sections:

2. *International Obligations*
    This section examines the principal conventions from the UK's point of view. The comments made in relation to the UK's international position, however, would be the same for other states party to those conventions.

3. *The Petroleum Act 1987*
    This now forms the principal legislation in the UK.

4. *Abandonment – Costs and Taxation*
    Statistics on costs for certain North Sea coastal states are examined and, in relation to the UK, are considered in the context of its fiscal regime.

5. *Policy and Practice*
    This considers the principal source of current international practice and

239

      describes cases of reported abandonment, principally in the North Sea,
      showing how that practice has affected plans and methods of abandonment.
      This is followed by a section on special aspects of UK policy.

6.   *Abandonment Agreements*
      This section examines the types of provisions that members of UK
      Petroleum Licence Groups are entering into in order to respond to the
      financial challenges of abandonment costs.

The term 'abandonment' can be confusing. There is no surrender of ownership
rights consequent on ceasing to use a petroleum production facility or pipeline.
'Decommissioning' might be a more appropriate term but abandonment continues
to be used to connote the ceasing of production from an offshore field or the
decommissioning of the related platforms and pipelines or both of these. Abandonment of the wells themselves however will occur during the stage of exploration and
appraisal as well as at the end of a field's productive life. Under the Model Clauses
incorporated into UK production licences the Secretary of State's consent is needed
for the abandonment of any well and for the final cessation of production.
Conditions may be imposed by the Secretary in relation to his granting consent to
these activities.

2.0 INTERNATIONAL OBLIGATIONS

The Geneva Convention[1] on the Continental Shelf of 1958 deals with the exploitation of petroleum and other natural resources on the Continental Shelf. With respect
to the abandonment of offshore structures the key questions are whether installations have to be removed, and if not, whether they may be left wholly or partly in
place. Article 5(5) of the Convention states that − 'Due notice must be given of the
construction of any such installations and permanent means for giving warning of
their presence must be maintained. Any installations which are abandoned or
disused must be entirely removed.'

    However, for some time past, there has been evident a tendency among directly
affected states to avoid entire removal as a mandatory policy and instead to try to
establish standards and criteria for partial removal which could meet with general
acceptance. It is not surprising therefore either that the Government's stated view is
that in complying with its international obligations the 1958 Convention must be
interpreted in a manner consistent with customary international law or that the
Government supports a generally held view that Article 5(5) does not now reflect
customary international law.

    There is some support for this view. The fifty four states who are party to the
Convention represent 'a minority of states, even of maritime states (although it does
include the major maritime powers) and . . . it is clear that the figures will not now
increase'.[2] It is commonly accepted there is not enough evidence of a clear practice
on the part of non-ratifying states for entire removal of offshore structures so as to

---

    1. See *United Kingdom Oil and Gas Law* by Daintith and Willoughby para. 2, 002 ff.
    2. Blanche Sas, 'An Update on the Legal Aspects of Offshore Abandonment' IBC Conference on
Decommissioning and Removal of Oil Structures Apr 19–20 1989, p.2.

support the view that the Convention as a whole has come to be accepted as representing customary international law.

However, the arguments by which the UK, a ratifying party to the Convention, might now claim that the total removal obligation is no longer binding on it can appear unconvincing. These arguments include (1) the provision has ceased to have legal effect since it has fallen into desuetude (2) the provision was established to overcome problems of navigational safety which through improved technology and experience have shown themselves not to require the total removal of structures and (3) the circumstances which gave rise to the total removal rule have changed fundamentally.

Despite the inconclusive nature of supporting arguments, there is a widely held view that customary international law on abandonment of offshore structures is reflected in the principles set out in the United Nations Convention on the Law of the Sea of 1982 (UNCLOS) and not in the 1958 Geneva Convention. Article 60.3 of UNCLOS states 'Any installation or structure which is abandoned or disused shall be removed to ensure safety of navigation, taking into account any generally accepted international standards established in this regard by the competent international organisation. Such removal shall also have due regard to fishing, the protection of the marine environment and the rights and duties of other states. Appropriate publicity should be given to the depth, position and dimensions of any installations or structures not entirely removed.'

Article 60.3 seems to hold to a basic rule of removal which is capable of being modified if international standards permit.

UNCLOS is not yet in force and the UK and US and other key states have not ratified it. If this delay is resolved then the possibility of partial abandonment will apply to the UK. However, even after ratification and coming into force it has been argued[3] that as between the UK and a state which is bound only by the 1958 Convention it is the Convention which will apply unless in due course of time new developments in abandonment practice become sufficiently widespread and accepted so as to amount to new customary international law which might release Convention states from the total removal rule of Article 5(5).

If international practice is engaged in by the vast majority of states in the belief that it is obligatory, it forms new international law. Article 60(3) provides a starting point for a new practice on abandonment.

Article 60.3 of UNCLOS permits partial removal of installations. This measure of discretion as to the method of abandoning offshore structures means that decommissioning may involve:

1. leaving the facilities in place;
2. partial removing and toppling of the facilities;
3. wholly or partially removing the facilities and then dumping them in deep water; and,
4. wholly or partially removing the facilities and taking them onshore.

Article 60.3 refers to standards set by the competent international organisation. Although no competent international organisation is referred to in the text of UNCLOS, the International Maritime Organisation (IMO) has become recognised

3. Rosalyn Higgins QC, 'Abandonment of Energy Sites and Structures: Relevant International Law' *Journal of Energy and Natural Resources Law* Vol. 11, No.1 (1993) pp.9–10.

as, *de facto*, the competent organisation in question. The IMO has now adopted standards relating to removal of offshore structures which are examined later in this Chapter. These standards have proved of considerable importance to formulation of the UK Government's policy on abandonment. In other words these standards are already treated in the UK as reflecting customary international law.

In October 1989 the IMO adopted its 'Guidelines and Standards for the Removal of Offshore Installations and Structures on the Continental Shelf and in the Exclusive Economic Zone' (IMO Guidelines). The new standards, while very involved, restate a general rule of removal which is subject to an exception permitting non-removal or partial removal if consistent with the new standards. The coastal state, having jurisdiction over the structure, may decide whether it can remain in whole or in part, by reference to safety, the effect on other uses of the sea, environmental effects, risk of shift, excessive costs, technical feasibility, risks of injury to personnel engaged in removal and determination of new use or other reasonable justification for allowing the installation or structure or parts of it to remain. What is more, the coastal state can apply these criteria on a case-by-case basis. The IMO Guidelines set out circumstances where total removal is required and these are looked at later.

Mention needs to be made also of the Oslo Convention for the Prevention of Marine Pollution by Dumping from Ships and Aircraft of 1972 which applies to the North Sea and North Atlantic ('the Oslo Convention') and the Convention on the Prevention of Marine Pollution by Dumping of Wastes and Other Matter – otherwise called the London Dumping Convention[4] signed in 1972 and in force since 1977.

The London Dumping Convention (LDC) has yet to finalise its views on the IMO's Guidelines which were distributed in the IMO's consultative process to all interested international organisations. There is agreement that abandonment on site and toppling of offshore platforms should be considered as dumping within the LDC provisions. Apart from a strong minority view to the contrary from Germany, there is also general agreement that where a toppled platform is converted to another use such as an artificial reef this falls within the description of activity under LDC rules which does not constitute dumping. In the first case the disposing party would require a permit which could only be granted in accordance with LDC rules and would be subject to controls pursuant to the LDC provisions, while in the latter case it would be sufficient to obtain a licence from the relevant Coastal State. The Oslo Convention has drawn up further specific guidelines regarding abandonment in its waters. While IMO Guidelines deal with all cases of abandonment, the Oslo Guidelines apply to disposal at sea of fixed structures (although the text deals also with disposal *in situ*). The technical criteria for disposal at sea are not necessarily mandatory and a contracting party could issue a permit in appropriate cases even if all criteria are not met.

The Oslo Convention currently applies stringent criteria as to depth of waters (2,000 metres) and distance from landfall (150 nautical miles) for deep water dumping. These could prohibit partial disposal methods for structures. It may be expected that North Sea coastal states will be likely to interpret the criteria under the Oslo Convention as subject to the IMO Guidelines.

4. The London Convention on the 'Prevention of Marine Pollution by Dumping of Wastes and other Matter' – Dec. 12 1972.

The general view seems to be that the above international conventions do not apply to pipelines and their important position in relation to abandonment will therefore depend largely on the relevant national law. In the UK steps have already been taken to address the issues of how and when to remove pipelines.

One example of how the Dumping Conventions can impact on proposals for abandonment is where Elf was recently refused permission[5] to dump its Northeast Frigg platform in a Norwegian fjord. The governor of Rogaland County withdrew a permit to dump the structure in Nedstrandfjord. Elf was asked to file a new application to the state pollution inspectorate providing proof that other methods of disposal would be unreasonably costly and it expects abandonment of the platform to take place in summer 1994.

3.0 THE PETROLEUM ACT 1987

As far as UK law on abandonment is concerned some limited statutory powers did exist for example under the Coast Protection Act 1949 in relation to structures such as platforms and under the Petroleum and Submarine Pipe-Lines Act 1975 ('the 1975 Act') in relation to pipelines. The 1975 Act deems a pipeline to be abandoned once it has been unused for three years. The Model Clauses governing petroleum licences provide that the Secretary of State's consent is required before any facilities may be abandoned. The Secretary may stipulate conditions or standards to be adhered to in respect of abandonment under these provisions and, in the event of default, may commission any relevant works and recoup the costs. However, it was accepted that these provisions did not provide a comprehensive framework. Abandonment or decommissioning of platform installations and pipelines is now regulated by the Petroleum Act 1987 which remedied a number of deficiencies in the earlier legislation.

There is no legal requirement in the UK to remove offshore installations or pipelines on cessation of production but the Secretary of State now has powers to require removal of installations or pipelines after they have been abandoned for production purposes. These powers are set out in Part 1 of the Act which is the most important piece of UK domestic legislation on abandonment.

The Act provides that the Secretary of State may by serving notice under Section 1 of the Act call for an 'abandonment programme' from (principally) the owners of interests in the platform or pipeline (who will typically be the licensees under the relevant production licence).[6] Those parties who are served with a Section 1 notice may be required to consult with specified interest groups. If the parties served with a Section 1 notice fail to prepare an abandonment programme, or if the Secretary of State rejects a programme that they have prepared then he has power to impose an abandonment programme of his own design.[7]

In practice the Department will be notified at an early date of any proposed cessation of petroleum production from an offshore field. The licence obligations require a cessation of production plan three years or so prior to the expected date.

---

5. *FT North Sea Letter* Sep. 30 1992.
6. Petroleum Act 1987 ss.1(1) and 2.
7. Petroleum Act 1987 s.5.

This is then likely to be followed by a notice under Section 1 of the Petroleum Act for an abandonment programme to be submitted. The owners on whom the Section 1 notice is served will be expected to consult fishing organisations for their views on the programme and to obtain an independent report on the programme.

An abandonment programme must estimate the costs of specified abandonment measures and provide for the timing of these operations and in the case of partial removal, the programme must indicate what further maintenance may be necessary.[8]

The abandonment programme may be rejected or approved by the Secretary who also has power to make modifications to it and to specify conditions which might apply to the programme.[9] He may also withdraw approval at the request of any one or more of the parties who prepared it.[10] The persons who prepare an abandonment programme share joint and several liability to carry out the abandonment programme which the Secretary has approved or imposed.[11] Failure in carrying out the work or complying with any condition could lead to a remedial notice from the Secretary and if not complied with the Secretary may execute the works himself and seek reimbursement.[12] Failure to comply with any remedial notice given by the Secretary is a criminal offence. Any breach of the Act by a company can also involve liability for its directors, secretary or managers if the breach is committed with their 'consent', 'connivance' or 'neglect'.[13]

In addition to the owners of the installation the Secretary may extend liability for preparing an abandonment programme – and therefore for carrying out an abandonment programme – to the holding or subsidiary or sister subsidiary companies of the owners of the installation including companies in which only a 50 per cent interest is held.[14] A bank will, however, not be liable for compliance with a Section 1 notice by reason only of holding an interest in an installation or pipeline by way of security for a loan.[15]

The Act should be a catalyst to the formulation of abandonment agreements. These are agreements between the owners of interests in offshore platforms or pipelines who share joint and several liability for the costs of abandonment. The key areas which need to be dealt with in abandonment agreements are how to provide for the preparation of an abandonment programme and how to fund and provide security for each owner's share of these costs.

There is no legal obligation for co-owners of installations to conclude abandonment agreements but since the original parties are jointly and severally liable for the abandonment programme and because this liability may extend within groups of companies there is a strong incentive for the parties to enter into abandonment agreements to ensure that all the co-owners make valid and binding security arrangements for abandonment costs so as to protect each other against one of them defaulting or going into liquidation.

8. Petroleum Act 1987 s.1(4).
9. Petroleum Act 1987 s.4.
10. Petroleum Act 1987 s.7.
11. Petroleum Act 1987 s.8.
12. Petroleum Act 1987 s.9.
13. Petroleum Act 1987 s.13.
14. Petroleum Act 1987 ss.2(1)(e), 2(2)(c) and 2(5).
15. Petroleum Act 1987 ss.2(1)(d) and 2(2)(b).

Another incentive to encourage abandonment agreements is contained in the Act. Where the Secretary has been and continues to be satisfied that adequate arrangements (including financial arrangements) have been made to ensure a satisfactory abandonment programme will be carried out then he will require a programme to be submitted only by the owners of the relevant facility (this will usually be the licensees themselves) and not their associated companies.[16] Consequently, if the abandonment agreement referred to above is contained in a Joint Operating Agreement the Department's approval should be sought to the effect that it amounts to adequate arrangements under the Act for abandonment purposes.

The Secretary of State may make regulations relating to abandonment but none has yet been issued nor are any envisaged as a result of Government statements of policy. Such regulations could prescribe standards and safety requirements in respect of dismantling, removal, disposal and the prevention of pollution.[17]

Provision is also made to ensure that the owners of the installation will be able to fund their obligations. If the Secretary is not satisfied of this he may by notice require the relevant person to take such action as he may specify.[18] This power is wide enough for the Secretary to require the owners of the installation to enter into security agreements for abandonment. It is thought not to be present policy to use the power in this way.

Part III of the Act establishes a security zone of 500 metres around each installation. The Act makes it an offence for any vessel to enter this safety zone and provides that, in such event, both owner and master shall be guilty of an offence.[19] The purpose of the exclusion zone is, of course, to minimise risk of collision. The Government is keen to place reliance on the security zone's existence as an effective deterrent to third party claims after abandonment has occurred.

In exercising his powers under the Act Section 1 Notices have been served on the owners of UK installations giving preliminary notice that they should submit an abandonment programme by such date as may later be directed by the Secretary. No such date has yet been specified and no further action has yet been taken in relation to such Notices.

4.0 ABANDONMENT – COSTS AND TAXATION

4.1 Costs

It is important to obtain an idea of the scale of costs likely to be involved in decommissioning offshore installations and pipelines. In autumn 1990 there were 110 steel platforms weighing up to 5,000 tonnes in the southern North Sea and 37 steel platforms weighing up to 50,000 tonnes or more and 10 large concrete gravity platforms weighing up to 200,000 tonnes or more in the deeper waters of the central and northern North Sea.[20]

16. Petroleum Act 1987 s.3(2) and (3).
17. Petroleum Act 1987 s.11.
18. Petroleum Act 1987 s.10.
19. Petroleum Act 1987 s.21.
20. *UK Oil and Gas Law* supra. note 1, para. 1-759.

Decommissioning operations will be far more costly if they involve the total removal of structures. In 1988 the UK Offshore Operators' Association (UKOOA) estimated that the cost of removing all offshore UKCS facilities would range from £4.4bn for total removal to £2.9bn for partial removal in accordance with IMO Guidelines.[21]

In 1990 the Government declared that removal of abandoned facilities should comply with IMO Guidelines. The requirements for total removal in low water conditions set out above would require (as at March 1990) the entire removal of 111 of the 155 fixed installations currently on the UKCS.

It has been estimated that if all the existing installations on Norway's shelf are removed and broken up the total cost would be $7.3bn and higher than the estimate made in early 1992 by the Norwegian authorities at the equivalent of US$6.2bn. Like the UK Government, Norway's authorities have refused to permit petroleum licence participants to set aside tax-deductible funds for abandonment costs.

In addition to the platforms over 3,500 miles of pipelines have been laid of which about 60 per cent are of 30in diameter or greater.

Cost estimates for removal of pipelines can vary widely since the lifting of large bore pipelines off the seabed is a difficult and costly task. The cheapest option is for the pipeline to be flushed and sealed, the next cheapest is to bury the pipeline *in situ*, but lifting and removing the pipeline is vastly more expensive. Cost estimates for one pipeline removal apparently ranged from £2m for a 'flush and seal' method to £100m for complete removal.

There is an obvious desire to contain decommissioning costs given the sums involved and the widely differing estimates for different removal methods. The Government also has an interest in this issue. Prior to the petroleum taxation changes contained in the Finance Bill 1993, it was estimated that as much as 80 per cent of abandonment costs would have been borne by the taxpayer in some cases through fiscal incentives for abandonment costs given to oil companies. The rate of petroleum revenue tax on existing fields is now to be reduced from 75 per cent to 50 per cent and is to be zero for new fields which will likely increase the percentage of abandonment costs borne by the oil companies. While it is beyond the scope of this Chapter to examine the impact of these changes in taxation, even after their implementation it is likely the majority of abandonment costs could be paid for through 'lost' taxation revenue. Management of total costs is therefore a key determining factor in Government policy. For example the 1987 Government policy statement in its 'Brown Book' confirmed that 'The Government's main objective will be to institute an effective abandonment regime which, whilst taking account of the requirements of international law, the safety of navigation, fishing and environmental interests, will aim to minimise the costs of abandonment in each case.'

4.2 Taxation

The following is a very discursive outline of the tax effects of abandonment costs and recourse should be made to specialist texts on the subject.

21. See House of Commons Energy Committee Fourth Report – Decommissioning of Oil and Gas Fields – Mar. 20 1991 ('Energy Committee Report') – para.12.

As a general rule, abandonment costs can be relieved in calculating both corporation tax (CT) and petroleum revenue tax (PRT).

The main changes introduced by the Finance Acts of 1990 and 1991 were:

(i) Costs of bank and financial guarantees taken out to provide security against an oil field participator's default in paying its share of abandonment costs can be relieved against CT and PRT.[22] This will further encourage the provision of security under abandonment agreements where such security is required. However, payments into trust funds to provide for future abandonment costs are not allowable expenses for tax purposes. This is a major disincentive to the use of trust funds in abandonment agreements.

(ii) If licensees are forced to pay a defaulting licensee's share of costs under their joint and several liability these costs can be relieved for the purposes of CT and PRT.[23] However, the participants 'must have taken all reasonable steps by way of legal remedy to secure that the defaulter meets the whole of its liability'.

(iii) There is relief from CT for abandonment costs incurred within three years after cessation of the company's ring fence trade.[24] However, this period may be insufficient to ensure tax relief for all costs if operations are prolonged during the run-down period for the field. Also, there is doubt as to whether there is any relief for costs of meeting residual liabilities such as maintenance costs after abandonment.

(iv) A new capital allowance of 100 per cent of expenditure on closing down all or part of a producing field under an abandonment programme is available for CT[25] and any losses resulting from this capital allowance can be carried back three years.[26]

(v) The scope of abandonment expenditure allowable against PRT has also been significantly extended so that all expenditure in closing down, decommissioning, abandoning or wholly or partly removing any qualifying asset can be relieved against PRT.[27]

The tax reliefs available to oil companies will produce widely varying net of tax costs for abandonment expenditure as between participants in the same field. The three year time limits on carry back of losses will be insufficient if a company has not paid equivalent corporation tax during that period. The three year limit on relief for expenditure after production has ceased will be inadequate if expenditure is incurred later and that company does not have other producing field interests within its ring fence trade. These factors are bound to influence the parties' attitudes on issues as to the type of abandonment programme to adopt and its date for implementation.

22. Finance Act 1991 ss.62, 103 and 104.
23. Finance Act 1991 ss.64 and 108.
24. Finance Act 1990 s.60.
25. Finance Act 1990 s.60.
26. Finance Act 1990 s.61.
27. Finance Act 1991 ss.103 and 104.

5.0 POLICY AND PRACTICE

5.1 IMO Guidelines

As mentioned above the UK Government has stated it will comply with the IMO Guidelines and its policy is to adopt a case-by-case approach taking into account the IMO Guidelines in making a decision on each abandonment programme. A key principle is that 'abandoned or disused installations or structures on any Continental Shelf or in any exclusive economic zone are required to be removed, except where non-removal or partial removal is consistent with the following guidelines and standards'.[28] The IMO Guidelines therefore state those cases where partial removal of the structure is permitted; they also provide for certain cases where total removal is required.

The IMO Guidelines provide for:

(i)   a requirement to evaluate on a case-by-case basis the effect on safety of navigation, rate of deterioration of the relevant structure, its effect on the marine environment, the risk that the structure will shift position in the future and the possibility of alternative uses of a disused structure.[29] These factors are likely to influence UKCS abandonment programmes;

(ii) consideration of 'the costs, technical feasibility, and risk of injury to personnel associated with removal of the installation or structure'.[30] A State may therefore decide not to require removal on grounds of technical difficulties, excessive cost or undue risk to personnel.[31] It has been noted that there are 10 large concrete gravity platforms in place and it may well be that, owing to their colossal mass, it would be exorbitantly expensive to remove these structures.

The emphasis on cost as a relevant factor is noteworthy. This mirrors the Government's policy to seek to contain abandonment costs in view of the fact that most of such costs will be met by the taxpayer. It may also be noted that safety of personnel engaged in the removal is considered important. This was a factor in allowing the remains of the Piper Alpha to be left on site and it has been stated that the decision to permit on-site toppling of the Piper Alpha remains is not a precedent;

(iii) complete removal of all existing structures in less than 75 metres' water depth and weighing less than 4,000 tonnes in air (exclusive of any deck or superstructure since these will require removal in any event);[32]

(iv) complete removal of new structures put in place after January 1 1998 in less than 100 metres' water depth, and weighing less than 4,000 tonnes in air (exclusive of deck and superstructure);[33]

28. IMO Guidelines Annex Art. 1.1.
29. Ibid. Art.2. 1(1)–2.1 (6), excluding 2.1(5).
30. Ibid. Art. 2.1(5).
31. Ibid. Art. 3(5).
32. Ibid. Art. 3.1.
33. Ibid. Art. 3.2

(v)   the possibility of leaving a structure entirely in place where it does not interfere with other uses of the sea;[34]

(vi)   in cases of toppling or partial removal there must be an unobstructed water column of 55 metres over any remains[35]. The UK Government has increased this to 75 metres for the northern part of the North Sea on grounds of safer navigation for naval submarines;[36]

(vii)   complete removal will be required in waters used for internal navigation[37] or where residues would be displaced from location by waves and tides.[38]

Application of the IMO Guidelines would mean as at March 1990 the total removal of 111 out of 155 UKCS structures. This is due largely to the fact that most structures are located in the shallower waters of the southern North Sea and indicates the constraints of applying partial removal methods in the North Sea to reduce costs.

5.2 Examples of Reported Abandonment

While such practice to date as exists in relation to North Sea abandonment has tended to indicate total removal, closer examination of the circumstances usually shows that such abandonment complies fully with IMO Guidelines. It is anticipated many installations on Norway's shelf might be left in place as it would be costly and difficult to remove them. Norway's Petroleum Act Committee has advocated oil companies making greater use of floating production units. Three structures on the Netherlands Continental Shelf have been removed since the water depth in the relevant location was less than the IMO Guidelines minimum. There is a similar UK example with the abandonment of the Argyll/Duncan/Innes complex and the Forbes field referred to below.

In the US there has been established quite an extensive programme of converting abandoned rigs to artificial reefs to boost fish stocks. In the Gulf Coast the 'Rigs to Reef' programme was active throughout the 1980s and was carried out at state level under Congressional guidance. The toppled structures were relocated to locations suitable for attracting fish or crustaceans. There have been environmental counter-arguments based on the damage caused by the initial toppling or the towage to the new site but in appropriate cases the new use would seem to provide a positive approach to the problem of abandonment.

Until recently the only significant facility to be abandoned on the UKCS was Piper Alpha. After considering various matters (primarily safety) the Piper Alpha platform was abandoned by means of pull vessels and explosives which effectively toppled the platform. There was then follow-up survey work to ensure that there was a 75 metre water clearance above the toppled platform. The Government has been keen to point out that this should not be seen as a precedent for abandonment.

34. Ibid. Art. 3.4(2).
35. Ibid. Art. 3.6.
36. Letter from Department of Energy to BRINDEX Feb. 12 1991.
37. IMO Guidelines Art. 3.7.
38. Ibid. Art. 3.9.

In June 1991, the Secretary of State for Energy approved the abandonment programme for the Crawford field installations. The programme provided for total removal of all field facilities, leaving a completely clear seabed and for post-abandonment seabed monitoring and the abandonment was completed, substantially, later that year. At the end of 1991 four draft abandonment programmes were under discussion with the UK's then Department of Energy.

In August 1992 it was reported[39] that an agreed abandonment programme had been finalised for Hamilton Oil's abandonment of the Argyll/Duncan/Innes complex and the Forbes field located in the southern basin of the North Sea. The first two phases of the Argyll abandonment which includes removal of all flexible pipes and flowlines has now been largely completed. Platforms are to be totally removed since they stand in less than 55 metres of water. However, it is significant that the larger 10in Esmond pipeline which is already buried is to be left in place after seawater flooding and sealing. The recovered sub-sea facilities are to be scrapped. The major cost item is the heavy-lift barge for removal of the topsides, jacket and conductors. All that will remain once the Argyll facility has been decommissioned will be one large concrete manifold base.

Another interesting feature of this abandonment programme is that it involved the recovery of wellheads and a general debris clearance.[40] From this it can be seen there can be a coincidence of the operator wishing to maximise the recovered value of equipment on decommissioning with the general scheme of best international practice to leave the seabed in something close to its original state. Argyll was the UK's first North Sea oil field to come on stream (on June 11 1975) and its successful abandonment has attracted favourable publicity.

One of the most important factors for an oil company in developing any abandonment programme has been to exploit any proven means of deriving the maximum value, having regard to disposal and treatment costs, from recovered structures or materials. New uses for offshore infrastructure and equipment or the materials they contain are being developed all the time thus reducing to some extent the problems of ultimate disposal. If no alternative use can be found materials often have to be consigned to landfill sites after removal and disposal of toxic substances.

Improvements to methods and engineering techniques to assist removal of heavy structures are continuing. There are also improvements in methods for disposal of ancillary equipment such as flowlines. For example, the methods used for flowline disposal in the Argyll field apparently resulted in a four to fivefold cost saving over conventional methods.[41]

Ninteeen ninety-two saw the abandonment of the Linnhe field as well as Argyll, Duncan and Innes. Northwest Hutton may be abandoned in about one year's time according to the rate of progress of Amoco's proposals for the cessation of production following discussions with the DTI.

There continue to be regular press reports now of activity by companies engaged in the North Sea costing proposals for removal of production installations of different types. This is not surprising given that adherence to IMO Guidelines in this

39. *FT North Sea Letter* Aug. 7 1992.
40. *FT North Sea Letter* Jan. 27 1993.
41. *FT North Sea Letter* Dec. 16 1992.

region is likely to provide in most cases a primary indication in favour of the removal option.

Problems associated with pipeline decommissioning are no less interesting. The report[42] of BP Exploration's decommissioning of the redundant 32in Forties offshore pipeline provides some interesting insight into this issue. Since it was originally laid in a trench most of the length of the pipeline is now buried. British Petroleum sought approval to leave the pipeline *in situ* and 'as is' (after being depressurised, cleaned and filled with seawater). However, in view of its close proximity to the new Forties 36in line there will be ongoing inspection of the abandoned line over a 30 year review period and provision of status reports on its condition. Finally, there will need to be a co-ordinated approach to abandonment of both the old 32in line and the new 36in line at the end of the latter's operating life.

5.3 Safety Provisions

Following the *Piper Alpha* disaster the recommendations of the Cullen Report have mostly been given statutory effect by the Offshore Safety Act 1992. The Health and Safety Executive now has the statutory power to carry out a wide-ranging programme of revising and updating the existing offshore safety regime including the functions of securing safety, health and welfare of persons on onshore installations or engaged on associated pipeline work and the safety of the installations and pipelines and of their construction and dismantling.[43] Existing legislation on those matters may now be enforced by the Health and Safety Executive which has set up a special Offshore Unit for this purpose. The HSE has power to enlarge or modify the statutory provisions by regulations made under the Health and Safety at Work etc. Act 1974.[44] The new provisions may have an impact on the operating plans for producing fields. BP recently stated as a reason for accelerating the abandonment of the Thistle field that Cullen Report safety expenditure could not be quantified.

Operators will now be required to submit a Safety Case for each installation which will have to be accepted by the Health and Safety Executive. This Safety Case will have to be formally updated for each major modification during the life of an installation and this will include the abandonment stage. Consequently, in developing an abandonment programme a Safety Case will be required to be submitted to the Health and Safety Executive.

5.4 Energy Committee Report and Government Response

Significant statements on abandonment policy were made in the House of Commons Energy Committee Report Fourth – Decommissioning Oil and Gas Fields – of March 1991 ('the Report') and in the Government's Response of July 1991.[45]

42. *FT North Sea Letter* Aug. 7 1991.
43. Offshore Safety Act 1992 s.1.
44. Offshore Safety Act 1992 s.1 and Part 1 Health and Safety at Work etc Act 1974.
45. House of Commons Energy Committee Sixth Special Report 'Government Observations on the Fourth Report from the Committee (Session 1990–1991) on Decommissioning of Oil and Gas Fields' July 10 1991 ('Government Response').

Fifteen recommendations were made in the Report which are summarised below.

1. The Committee approved the Government's use of a case-by-case approach to decommissioning while recommending that the Government should publish general requirements and limit its discretion to technical matters. The oil industry had voiced concern that a wholly flexible system would lead to more rigorous criteria being imposed.[46] In response the Government pointed to the general requirements which it had notified to UKOOA and BRINDEX (British Independent Oil Exploration Companies) that UK policy would be consistent with the IMO Guidelines but stated it was not appropriate to make a more definite statement of requirements for decommissioning. The Government had no intention of exercising its powers to make regulations under Section 11 of the Petroleum Act at present.[47]

2. The Committee recommended examination of the oil industry's claim that total removal of structures is more dangerous than partial removal.[48] In its response the Government noted that assessment of risks of this type should form part of the safety case required at the abandonment stage of the platform.[49]

3. The Committee was concerned at the environmental impact of the disposal of the oil polluted drill cuttings piles at the base of installations and recommended the introduction of guidelines to avert their dispersal in connection with the total removal of installations.[50] Since this issue is currently being pursued by the Paris Commission the Government view is that introduction of guidelines would be premature.[51]

4. The Committee were keen to urge consideration of the marking of exclusion zones around partially removed installations at sea surface level. This was prompted by concern that marking of partially removed structures on nautical charts would not be adequate to protect fishermen who accidentally strayed into the exclusion zone around the platform.[52] The Government would require new powers to implement this and appears to have reservations about taking such action.[53]

5. It was recommended that compensation for loss of fishing catch proved to result from loss of access should be provided.[54] In the Government's view the compensation case has not been made out.[55]

6. It was recommended the possibility of using abandoned platforms as artificial reefs should be considered.[56]

46. Energy Committee Report, supra, note 21, para. 11.
47. Government Response para.8–12.
48. Energy Committee Report para.15.
49. Government Response para.13.
50. Energy Committee Report para.18.
51. Government Response para.15.
52. Energy Committee Report para.24.
53. Government Response para.17.
54. Energy Committee Report para. 27.
55. Government Response para.20
56. Energy Committee Report para.29

7. The Committee recommended that pipelines on or under parts of the sea-bed which were unstable should be removed to reduce danger of debris or obstruction to sea traffic.[57] The Government currently recognises this problem which is still being investigated.[58]

8. The Committee urged the Government to preserve the options of toppling and deep water dumping where permitted by the IMO Guidelines.[59] The Government concurs with this.

9. The Committee proposed the setting up of an independent body to determine what cost, safety and environmental considerations in respect of offshore installations and pipelines were in the best public interest.[60] The Government is not of the view that there is a need for a new independent body in view of its constant monitoring of these issues, the fact that it takes a case-by-case evaluation to each abandonment programme, and that this approach would also be used by the Health and Safety Executive in relation to safety cases.[61]

10-12. These recommendations related to suggested measures to discourage the spread of debris, to provide for penalties and for clean-up operations.[62]

13. Significantly the Committee endorsed the UKOOA proposal to transfer legal liability in decommissioned structures to the Government in return for a single payment of an amount sufficient to fund ongoing costs. This was one of the most radical of the Committee's recommendations.[63] The Government is most reluctant to assume the residual liabilities of decommissioned structures. It does not wish to become a potential defendant in perpetuity for third party claims. In its response it stated that the risk of third party claims arising after completion of abandonment was slight as a result of the exclusion zone.[64]

14. The Committee recommended a longer period than the three years currently permitted for carrying back losses for corporation tax purposes so as to offset decommissioning costs fully.[65] The Government repeated its view that it was not reasonable to extend the period of three years permitted for the carry back of such losses.[66]

15. The Committee also urged re-examination of the issue of tax relief for payments into abandonment trust funds to give security against premature abandonment or the default of participants.[67] The Government's view is that it is unclear that the take up of funds in such circumstances would be sufficient to merit the extra complexity of amendments to the tax system.[68]

57. Energy Committee Report para.32
58. Government Response para.23.
59. Energy Committee Report para.33.
60. Energy Committee Report para.33
61. Government Response paras 27 and 28
62. Energy Committee Report para.38
63. Energy Committee Report para.42
64. Government Response para.37.
65. Energy Committee Report para.50.
66. Government Response para.41.
67. Energy Committee Report para.51.
68. Government Response para.45.

5.5 Residual Liabilities

The key issue is who will be responsible for third party claims arising out of structures or equipment left in place following decommissioning and for claims arising from the carrying out of decommissioning works themselves. The IMO Guidelines urge that 'the coastal state should ensure that legal title to installations and structures which have not been entirely removed from the seabed is unambiguous and that the responsibility for maintenance and financial ability to assume liability for future damages are clearly established'.

As matters now stand, owners of offshore facilities retain all the liability of owners even after decommissioning. This is particularly pertinent to partially removed structures. In answer to concerns raised by the oil industry over the risk of residual liability, the Government's stated view is that if a vessel entered the 500 metre safety zone around the partially removed installation and was involved in an accident the owners of the installation would have a defence that the master had been negligent.[69] But the general view is that this presents no defence to a damages claim, for example, for lost fishing nets. In addition, there remains the possibility of further pollution arising or debris breaking free if the decommissioning operations are not entirely successful.

6.0 ABANDONMENT AGREEMENTS

Abandonment agreements received a fresh impetus following the passing of the Petroleum Act 1987. Indeed, since the passing of that Act one operator, BP, has been seeking the introduction of a security agreement in respect of each of the UKCS fields in which it has an interest.

An abandonment agreement is an agreement between the co-owners of an installation which may deal with the preparation of an abandonment programme and budget and/or how to find and provide security for each owner's share of abandonment costs. The co-owners will have entered into a Joint Operating Agreement at the commencement of their association as licencees under the relevant licence and this document is the focal point of discussion of provisions dealing with abandonment. (For an in-depth discussion of Joint Operating Agreements see Chapter 14.) The format of abandonment agreements is that they are usually annexes to or a part of modern Joint Operating Agreements (JOAs). Most 'older' JOAs dealt with abandonment only in general terms. A typical 'abandonment' clause in an older style JOA used to state merely that if the parties decide to abandon any joint property, the operator shall try to recover and dispose of whatever may be economically and reasonably recovered (or which the law requires to be recovered) and the net costs or proceeds shall be debited or credited to the joint venture parties as appropriate.

The following is a typical clause of this type.

---

69. Government Response para.37.

Disposal and Abandonment

1. If the Operator shall consider that any item of the Joint Property is no longer needed or suitable for the Joint Operations the Operator shall, subject to the provisions of the Accounting Procedure, dispose of the same.

2. If the Participants shall decide to abandon the Joint Operations, or any part thereof, the Operator shall recover and endeavour to dispose of as much of the Joint Property as may be determined can economically and reasonably be recovered or as may be required to be recovered under the Acts, the Licence or any other applicable law, and the net cost or net proceeds therefrom shall be charged or credited to the Joint Account.

Some JOAs extended this general statement and would state that by the time for submitting an Annex 'B' development programme the parties would agree an abandonment agreement to deal, among other things, with 'an equitable sharing of liabilities between the Participants' and the 'provision of security therefor'. This is essentially an agreement to agree and probably of little contractual effect. However, there would typically be a sanction against a minority opinion preventing execution of the abandonment agreement if consented to by parties holding the required voting percentage. The relevant clause would commonly state as follows:

3. Without prejudice to Clause 2 above it is agreed that following any proposal made to the Joint Operating Committee for the Operator to prepare a development programme and budget for a particular discovery the Participants will before submission of an Annex 'B' to the Department of Energy agree the terms of an Abandonment Agreement which should, *inter alia*, include an equitable sharing of liabilities between the Participants and the provision of security therefor provided that in the event of failure to obtain unanimous agreement of the Participants to the terms of such Abandonment Agreement the provisions of this Clause 3 shall be deemed to have been satisfied for the purpose of enabling the submission of an Annex 'B' if the Participants who have agreed the terms of such Abandonment Agreement hold in aggregate a Percentage Interest not less than that specified in Clause (Pass Mark Clause) and provided further that in such event the Participants shall use all reasonable endeavours to obtain unanimous agreement to the terms of the Abandonment Agreement as soon as practicable after such submission.

6.1 Common Features in Abandonment Agreements

The JOA has to be approved by the Department of Trade and Industry and the abandonment clauses or the annex contained within it are certainly capable of forming an approved abandonment arrangement under Section 3(2)(3) of the Petroleum Act thus preventing associates of the JOA parties from being required to submit an abandonment programme. Abandonment agreements will vary according to the circumstances but they should seek to deal with (1) how to agree the terms and costs of an abandonment programme and (2) how to provide security for abandonment costs.

(1) *The Abandonment Programme and Budget*

A formal procedure is needed to determine what actual abandonment operations are to be carried out, and when, and to provide for the related costs to be budgeted.

Some JOAs adopt provisions for abandonment as part of the annual budget procedures. On this basis the operator would be authorised prior to the commencement of the financial year in which he considered that first abandonment is likely to occur, to submit to the operating committee a proposed abandonment programme budget for review, revision and approval. The operator would then be required in each succeeding year to submit an update of that programme and budget with details of any new costs to be committed in the relevant year. The annual programme and budget would be required to be approved by the operating committee by the start of each year. Once approved, the operator should be authorised to submit the abandonment programme and budget to the Secretary of State for approval under the Petroleum Act.

Since there may well be serious problems in all JOA parties reaching agreement on a particular abandonment programme and budget some JOA parties might prefer to provide for abandonment programmes and budgets to be prepared prior to first commercial production of petroleum from the field even if any attempt at budgeting the costs is bound to be indicative only of the scale of costs.

Whatever the timing arrangements in the JOA for agreeing abandonment programmes these may be upset by a Section 1 notice under the Petroleum Act. If the Secretary of State requires an abandonment programme to be submitted prior to the operating committee reaching agreement on the abandonment programme and budget the operator might for example be given further powers in the JOA in order to ensure that the JOA parties are not in default of any statutory obligation to submit an abandonment programme. In that event the operator might be given authority to prepare an abandonment programme and budget and submit it to the Secretary of State without prior operating committee approval – although clearly the operator should be required to follow as closely as possible such guidelines for the abandonment programme as had been determined by the operating committee. Revisions could then be proposed by the JOA parties after submission of the abandonment programme. There could, however, be no guarantee that any proposed revisions would be acceptable to the Secretary. The JOA will have to provide that all parties must pay their share of costs of the abandonment programme whether it is an approved programme or one imposed by the Secretary of State.

(2)   *Security for Abandonment Costs*

Security is clearly perceived by the oil industry as of vital importance. The costs of abandonment will be considerable. Since JOA parties share joint and several liability under the Petroleum Act they must be sure that if any of their number defaults there will be adequate security to fund the defaulter's liabilities. Thus, abandonment agreements should oblige the parties to provide security for their share of abandonment obligations and describe the type of security and when it will be required. Provision should also be made for failure to provide security.

The usual JOA remedy of forfeiture in the event of payment defaults, *ie* the defaulter loses its share of revenues, will not generally be adequate to provide for funding of these liabilities. By the time abandonment is an issue the field will probably be in decline and the defaulter's future revenues could well be less than its share of abandonment costs.

6.2 Types of Security

The types of security for abandonment costs which are commonly seen in practice are:

1. Parent company guarantee.
2. Bank guarantee or letter of credit.
3. Trust fund.

Since a parent company guarantee (even a bank guarantee) has the attendant risk that the parent (or the bank) may become insolvent, most agreements provide that any guarantor must have a defined credit rating. Examples include 'a credit rating of AA- or better by Standard & Poors Corporation' or an 'Aa rating (whether graded 1, 2 or 3 or otherwise qualified) or better by Moody's Investors Service Inc'. If, as is increasingly the case, renewable letters of credit are used to provide security, then it is important that the stipulated credit rating should be made to apply on each renewal.

Deciding on the type of security can prove to be a major source of disagreement among JOA parties. For the most substantial of oil companies a parent company guarantee may well suffice if the parent has a high credit rating. For a smaller company the ratio of abandonment liabilities to its net worth may be such as to justify the JOA partners in demanding other security. Providing security for abandonment obligations will be more costly for smaller companies. A standby letter of credit can cost annually between 0.1 per cent and 0.5 per cent of its value.

The view of BRINDEX is that (i) the payment of cash into a trust fund or (ii) bank guarantees are the only 'totally secure' methods of providing security for abandonment.

6.3 Timing of Security

The UK Offshore Operators' Association's view is that the requirement for security should arise when the 'discounted cost of abandonment exceeds a predetermined proportion of the discounted value of the remaining reserves (typically 50 per cent – 75 per cent)'.

In most abandonment agreements the requirement to provide security is generally crystallised when the net remaining value of the field is equal to or below 150 per cent or 135 per cent of the projected costs of abandonment. The net remaining value is based on projected production less projected operating costs and taxes.

To determine when this trigger is reached requires constant monitoring. It also requires provision for expert determination if values cannot be agreed between the JOA parties.

Once the trigger has been reached the relevant field will have entered its 'run down period' and each year thereafter the parties will need to determine the value of security required to be provided by them in the light of the latest projection of abandonment costs yet to be incurred and the latest projections of production and of operating costs. This means that it is inevitable there will be fluctuations in the amount of security to be provided by participants.

The run-down period would normally end at conclusion of the abandonment works but consideration needs to be given to residual liabilities (as to which see below).

JOA parties will not wish to lock in their own cash flow to the security arrangements and will prefer to arrange for the issue of guarantees or letters of credit. In addition to this, while tax relief is available for the costs of maintaining guarantees and letters of credit such relief is not available for cash payments into an abandonment fund to provide for future costs.

The typical abandonment agreement will therefore commit the parties to maintain adequate security usually by way of guarantees or letters of credit and provide that if the security becomes inadequate or is not renewed cash payments will only then be made into an abandonment trust fund of such amount as together with any ongoing security is equal to that party's share of the estimated costs.

If, under such arrangements, a liability to make cash contributions arises then, in order to provide for a regular payment basis for the affected JOA parties, the operator will each year estimate both the remaining field production and the cost of abandonment so as to determine a unit cost for abandonment per barrel of production.

Having determined this, the operator will then cash call the parties (possibly monthly) according to the barrels of production or gas equivalent received by them and any funds raised would be paid into the abandonment trust fund. The abandonment agreement would typically provide that any surplus following the completion of the abandonment programme would be held on resulting trust and distributed pro rata according to contributions.

One significant problem which arises in determining the point in time at which the security agreement becomes effective is whether the calculation of the value of an interest in a field should be gross or net of the participants' taxation. The usual approach seems to be to calculate the value of each interest on an after-tax basis. Since the marginal tax rates of the JOA partners will differ from each other the safest course in doing so is to assume that the maximum rate of tax will be applied. However, for similar reasons abandonment costs will probably have to be calculated disregarding the benefit of any tax reliefs to the JOA partners.

Forfeiture of a participant's interest is not considered appropriate as a sanction for not maintaining the required security in view of the risk that the value of the defaulter's interest is approaching its share of abandonment costs. However, forfeiture would still be likely to be resisted by JOA parties with a smaller interest since they could be overruled on decisions as to acceptability of their security. It is for these reasons that the trust fund with a requirement to make cash payments is seen as the most effective way of dealing with security defaults. Of course, failure to make a cash call to the trust fund would have to be treated as any other cash default under the JOA.

If a trust fund is to be established, the trust document is often contained in an annex to the abandonment agreement. Normal trust law considerations will apply. The purpose of the trust will need to be defined for example 'to pay for the costs of abandonment of Field X'. There will need to be a trustee (which can be a trust corporation). There should be provisions concerning the permitted types of investments for funds paid into the trust fund.

Some abandonment agreements do not go into the complexities of a trust fund. They merely stipulate that the security for abandonment costs will be a guarantee or an irrevocable standby letter of credit of the appropriate credit rating. Any default in providing such security would then be dealt with under the standard JOA default provisions.

6.4 Other Issues

Abandonment agreements should also seek to address the problem of residual liabilities. These are particularly relevant where a platform or pipeline is partially left in place. The JOA parties will have to decide what are the residual liabilities (typically maintenance and inspection of decommissioned structures) and what the ongoing costs of these will be. Based on this they will need to decide whether or not to retain insurance and security arrangements to cover such residual liabilities, at what level and for how long.

7.0 CONCLUSION

In conclusion, a number of general policy considerations which are likely to be applied by the UK Government in approving abandonment programmes are now reasonably settled. How these will be applied in each case is less clear in view of the Government's policy of approaching each abandonment proposal on a case-by-case basis. As far as owners of installations are concerned, they have real incentives to seek to agree abandonment programmes and to provide adequate financial arrangements by way of security for abandonment programmes. In practice there are often significant differences in the financial and fiscal positions of individual participants making agreement on these issues difficult to achieve in addition to the complexity created by technical and environmental issues.

As more fields begin to enter their decline phase the costs of abandonment obligations and the securing of such costs will become increasingly pressing concerns to oil companies. There remains the risk of an abandonment programme being imposed by the Secretary of State if one is not agreed in time by the participants. It will be interesting to see how the industry responds over the next few years to these pressures.

Chapter 18

Gas Contracts in the European Context

Michael Stanger, David Aron, Charles Robson

1.0 INTRODUCTION

Gas is becoming one of the most important fuels used in Europe. It is considered to be an environmentally acceptable fuel as it produces substantially lower emissions than its main competitors, coal and fuel oil. This fact, in particular, is leading to the growing use of gas for the generation of electricity.

Changes and developments in Europe are discussed below in a general context. More specific information is given of one market, the United Kingdom, to enable the subject to be covered in more detail.

2.0 STRUCTURE OF THE EUROPEAN GAS INDUSTRY

2.1 Organisation

The European gas industry is dominated by a number of very large companies mostly associated with the international oil industry. The state plays a significant role in a number of countries such as the Netherlands and Italy although there are plans to reduce state involvement in some European countries. The gas industry in the UK is dominated by one company, British Gas plc, which until recently was state owned.

Competition only exists to any significant extent in the UK and Germany. Competition in the UK involves the use of a single integrated transportation system. Competition in Germany is carried out using competing transportation systems serving different areas.

2.2 Consumption

Gas consumption in Europe in 1991 was 275.4bn cu m.[1] Gas production in Europe in that year was 198.8bn cu m with the balance being made up almost entirely by imports from Russia and Algeria. Indigenous production therefore represented 72 per cent of total demand in that year. Gas consumption is dominated by only five countries (France, Germany, Italy, the Netherlands and the UK) which represent 87 per cent of total demand. The largest user of gas in Europe is Germany, followed by the UK.

Users of gas in most countries are usually described by sector. Generally the residential and commercial sectors use about half of the gas, with the remainder being used by industry. For the Netherlands and the UK (both large producers and consumers) the residential and commercial sectors represent more than half of the total demand.

The growth of the use of gas for power generation is quite marked. By 1995 it is expected that the total gas market in the UK will have grown by 25 per cent with almost all of this increase being attributed to the use of gas for power generation. Demand in Italy is also expected to grow dramatically. Overall, the expected use of gas for power generation in the European Community is expected to more than double in the period 1990–2000.[2]

All the European markets have to deal with the problem of peak requirements in the winter period caused by the winter heating load. It is generally not economic to provide transportation facilities to cover the full peak requirements but they can be handled in a number of different ways. In France, Germany and Italy there are large underground storage facilities which as well as providing peak supplies also act as a strategic reserve. The Netherlands does not have storage but relies on its substantial offshore reserves. Other countries such as Belgium and the UK rely on interrupting industrial customers to meet their peak winter loads.

2.3 Supply

The largest supplier of gas in Europe is Russia, which is not surprising as Russia is estimated to have over 40 per cent of the world's gas reserves. Nearly half of German consumption is provided by imports from Russia, and about 30 per cent of Italian consumption.

The next largest supplier in Europe is the Netherlands, followed by the UK. Norway currently produces about 14 per cent of European production and is the fourth largest supplier. It is likely that Norway will become the dominant indigenous producer in the next 10–20 years, based on its very large undeveloped gas reserves.

Nearly all the imports of gas to Europe are transported by pipeline. Small quantities are, however, imported as liquefied natural gas (LNG). The main supplier of this is Algeria which exports LNG to Belgium, France, Italy and Spain. Libya exports a small quantity of LNG to Spain.

1. *BP Review of World Gas,* Aug. 1992.
2. *Energy in Europe – A View to the Future*, Commission of the European Communities, Sep. 1992.

3.0 CURRENT DEVELOPMENTS

The European gas market is going through a period of intense change. A number of major pipelines are in the process of construction, and these will further accelerate the development of the market. Norwegian gas fields are currently connected by one pipeline to Germany and two parallel lines to the UK. A further line (Zeepipe) is currently being finished which will connect Norwegian reserves directly to Belgium. Another line, planned to be completed in 1995, (Europipe) will land in Germany.

Algerian exports by pipeline are expected to increase dramatically within the next few years. Algeria is already connected to Italy, and a parallel line is being built. A new line will connect Algeria with Spain, and a connection from Spain to France is under consideration. An additional Russian line is planned that will go to Germany via Poland.

At the margins of Europe integration of the gas system is also under way. Ireland was linked with the UK in 1993. Greece has plans both to develop an import terminal for LNG and to construct a pipeline to Bulgaria allowing the purchase of gas from Russia. The question of third party access to the pipelines in Europe is a matter of intense debate. (See for further discussion Chapters 6 and 7.) The European Commission has published a Draft Directive[3] which would allow companies which buy more than 25m cu m of gas per year to buy from suppliers anywhere in the Community. This Directive has not obtained sufficient support and it is unclear how this issue will be resolved.

4.0 UNITED KINGDOM PERSPECTIVE

4.1 Introduction

The last few years have seen a marked increase in the level of trading in gas from the UK Continental Shelf (UKCS). This has been due largely to two factors: the increased use of natural gas as a fuel for power generation, and governmental stimulation of competition in the gas supply industry.

Until 1991, EC Directive 75/404 had prohibited the use of natural gas for power generation on the grounds that such use was a waste of a finite natural resource. Not least because of the emergence of public environmental concerns, the EC has now lifted this restriction. At the same time regional electricity companies, gas producers and others were being encouraged to compete in the power generation and supply markets of the newly privatised electricity industry.

Following the investigation of the Monopolies and Mergers Commission (MMC) into the gas supply market in 1988 the then Director General of Gas Supply, Sir James McKinnon, became increasingly involved in the negotiation of restrictions and undertakings from British Gas plc as a form of surrogate competition to curb some of the practices of the monopolist gas supplier in the UK. This surrogate competition has proved to be a poor substitute for the real thing, and by the time of

---

3. 'Completion of the Internal Market in Electricity and Gas', Jan. 1992.

the second MMC reference in July 1992 it had become clear that direct steps were needed to foster real competition in gas supply. The MMC concluded that the development of competition would best be achieved through the divestment by British Gas of its gas trading arm and the gradual removal of its domestic gas supply monopoly, resulting in the abolition of the monopoly by 2000–2002. Michael Heseltine, the President of the Board of Trade, decided that the abolition of the monopoly need not be delayed as the MMC envisaged. He proposed that from April 1996 the whole of the non-domestic market should be open to competition together with a proportion of the domestic market determined by the Director General of Gas Supply. The government's proposals for reform are discussed further at 4.4 below.

There follows an outline description of the physical structure of the UK gas supply industry and a brief summary of the transactions involved in supplying gas to consumers in the UK.

4.2 Infrastructure

4.2.1 Pipelines

UK gas fields are almost entirely offshore, whereas points of consumption are almost exclusively onshore. The relative proximity of fields to points of consumption means that pipelines are the only economic method for transporting gas in the UK market, and well-developed pipeline systems exist, both offshore and onshore. All but the largest new developments must make use of the existing pipeline system, and a network of related contracts has been developed which will apply to the sale of gas from any new development.

The regimes for offshore and onshore pipeline systems are quite different and will be considered separately.

4.2.2 Offshore Transportation

The pipeline systems of the UKCS are facilities built in order to develop particular fields and have generally been funded and are owned by oil and gas production companies with interests in the relevant fields.

The network, therefore, is not integrated. Individual pipelines are independently owned and, to a greater or lesser extent, the cost of their construction has been a field development expense. Tariff revenue generated from transporting a third party's gas from a new development is additional revenue for the pipeline owners.

The construction and operation of offshore pipelines is governed by the Petroleum and Submarine Pipelines Act 1975 which makes provision for non-proliferation, minimising disruption and enabling third party access.

Offshore pipelines are, by their nature, point-to-point pipelines which serve to transport the gas physically from the point of production to a point on shore –usually the closest point of access to the onshore transportation network.

4.2.3 Onshore Transportation

The onshore pipeline network is almost exclusively owned and operated by one company, British Gas plc, which 'inherited' the network from the Gas Council and the 12 area boards in 1986.

It consists of a national transmission system, a regional transmission system and a distribution system, each one being at successively lower pressure. It is fully inter-connected and operates, in essence, as a 'big bottle' – gas can enter the system at various landing points and be taken from the system at virtually any point. The system has to be kept in balance but gas delivered at a landing point is only notionally transported to the point of consumption – in all probability the gas delivered into the system will not be the gas taken from the system at the point of consumption.

The construction and operation of most pipelines in the British Gas onshore pipeline network is governed by the Gas Act 1986 pursuant to which British Gas, as a 'public gas supplier', has a statutory right to construct pipelines to enable it to supply gas. The construction and operation of onshore pipelines by any other person or for any other purpose is governed by the Pipelines Act 1962 which contains similar provisions in relation to onshore pipelines as apply to offshore pipelines pursuant to the Petroleum and Submarine Pipelines Act. Both onshore statutory regimes contain provision for third party access.

4.2.4 Processing

A degree of processing is necessary offshore, at or near the point of production, in order to make produced gas fit for transportation through offshore pipelines – in particular, to prevent clogging or damage to the pipelines. For this reason there is an entry specification to all offshore pipelines. Such processing is carried out by facilities constructed for the purpose or, increasingly commonly, by existing facilities belonging to third parties in return for a processing tariff.

There is a strict entry specification for the British Gas onshore pipeline network, to safeguard the network and to standardise the quality of the gas within it. The majority of gas processing is carried out onshore, just before entry into the British Gas network, by the owners of the relevant offshore pipeline system, as part of the offshore transportation service.

4.3 Contracts

The physical stages involved in the supply of gas in the UK are:

1. Production.
2. Offshore processing.
3. Offshore transportation.
4. Onshore processing.
5. Onshore transportation.
6. Consumption.

Depending upon the identity of the buyer and the point of sale, however, four different basic contractual structures can exist:

1. Producer sells to British Gas at entry to the British Gas system. British Gas sells to consumer at point of consumption.
2. Producer sells to consumer at entry to the British Gas system. Consumer negotiates onshore transportation with British Gas.

3. Producer sells to gas marketer at entry to the British Gas system. Gas marketer negotiates onshore transportation with British Gas. Gas marketer sells to consumer at point of consumption.
4. Producer sells to consumer at point of consumption. Producer negotiates onshore transportation with British Gas.

The following contracts will typically be involved in all of these arrangements.

4.3.1 Offshore Processing and Transportation Contracts

Gas from offshore fields is generally bought on long-term contracts, very often for all of the economically recoverable reserves of the field. Offshore transportation contracts must provide flexibility to allow for daily variation in rates of production and decline in field performance. A daily nomination procedure is normally used to let the operator of the pipeline system know what quantities of gas a field group would like delivered into the onshore transportation system on each day and what quantity each field group will deliver into the offshore transportation system on that day. The producer is invariably responsible for ensuring that gas delivered into the offshore transportation system complies with the entry specification, and the offshore pipeline system operator is invariably responsible for ensuring that the gas delivered into the onshore transportation system meets the required specification.

Transportation charge structures vary considerably but normally contain a capacity charge element (rather like a booking fee) and a commodity charge element (which reflects the quantity of gas actually transported in the system).

Onshore, but before delivery into the onshore transportation system, the gas will undergo more rigorous processing to remove valuable natural gas liquids (NGLs) for separate sale, and to bring the gas up to the specification of the onshore transportation system.

4.3.2 Commingling and Allocation Agreements

Where more than one field group uses the same pipeline system to transport gas, the production from each field is commingled with the production from other fields, and all parties involved must agree on a basis for allocating the commingled gas stream on exit from the offshore transportation system. Commingling and Allocation Agreements operate on a daily basis by reference to the daily nominations and deliveries made by each field group using the system on that day.

4.3.3 Balancing Agreements

Each participant in a field will have a right, independent from the rights of all other participants, to dispose of its entitlement to gas from that field. Where more than one purchaser buys the gas from a field, each will consume gas independently of the others which may result in the participants lifting their respective entitlements to gas disproportionately on a day-to-day basis. A balancing agreement is required in these cases to ensure that at the end of the field's life each participant will have had the benefit of all of, and no more than, its gas entitlement.

4.3.4 Onshore Transportation Agreements

British Gas has, since the MMC report of 1988, produced a series of standard form transportation contracts pursuant to which it will transport gas for a number of different circumstances. The terms of the contracts vary greatly as to duration and quantities but generally all provide for a nomination procedure, an obligation to try to keep deliveries and offtakes in balance and a tariffing structure. The operation of the onshore gas transportation and storage network is at the centre of the reforms being undertaken following the second MMC investigation. The reforms include establishing an onshore transportation network which is equally accessible to all and a system of transportation charges which is transparent and flexible so that transporters are left free, as far as practicable, to make their own decisions regarding their storage and back-up requirements. The proposals for reform are discussed further at 4.4 below.

4.3.5 Gas Sales Agreements

Generally the scale of the investment, both for production facilities and for pipelines, is such that long-term gas contracts have been required. Performance of the parties' obligations is usually measured on a daily basis however, and the agreements are structured accordingly. Overall, they are designed to guarantee for the buyer a reliable and flexible supply of gas, and to guarantee for the seller a predictable and adequate cash flow.

Gas contracts are of two main types: supply contracts and depletion contracts. In a supply contract an agreement is made to supply a fixed volume of gas over a number of years, possibly up to 25 years, but is not necessarily tied to gas produced from a particular field. A depletion contract generally involves the purchase of the entire output from one gas field. The production from most gas fields usually involves a period of build-up followed by a number of years at a constant rate known as a plateau. Following the end of the plateau there is a decline period which ends at an economic cut-off. A depletion contract will need to address the issues that arise out of this, and the economic termination may often need to be agreed by an expert. Both types of contract will typically include the following features.

The buyer will be required to nominate to the seller how much gas it requires to have delivered to it on each day. Its nomination rights will be subject to certain agreed limits defined by reference to a daily benchmark quantity – the 'Daily Contract Quantity' or 'DCQ'.

The maximum daily rate is important for both parties. The higher the maximum rate is in relationship to the average daily quantity the more valuable the gas is because it can provide peak capacity. A high maximum rate that is only likely to be used for a short period is generally unattractive to a gas producer as it means that expensive capacity is not fully used.

There will be financial incentives on the seller to deliver on each day the quantity of gas nominated by the buyer, usually in the form of discounts in the price payable if the seller fails to deliver the nominated quantities.

Similarly, there will be financial incentives on the buyer to nominate and take delivery of at least an agreed benchmark quantity of gas each year – the Take or Pay Quantity.

If the buyer takes less than this quantity it will usually have to pay the seller a sum in addition to the sums payable for gas actually delivered and taken. The buyer will generally be credited with 'Make Up Gas' equivalent to the additional sum paid, and in the following year, after an agreed quantity of gas has been taken at full price, the buyer may take such Make Up Gas at a reduced price or free of charge.

If the buyer takes more than the Take or Pay Quantity in a year it may be credited with 'Carry Forward Gas' which it may use to reduce the size of the Take or Pay Quantity in subsequent years.

In addition to these basic mechanisms a typical gas sales agreement will also deal with start up and commissioning of the seller's and buyer's facilities, price indexation during the life of the contract, and what relief (if any) each party is to be entitled to if it is unable to perform its obligations by reason of events beyond its control – *Force Majeure*.

The types of index used for price adjustments are a matter for negotiation and will usually reflect the gas producer's interests and the market that its customer operates in. Typical factors could include the price of oil and oil products, inflation, price of coal, etc.

4.4 Future Developments

The second MMC investigation into gas supply in the UK is likely to result in the most far-reaching changes to the market since the privatisation of British Gas in 1986. Michael Heseltine has decided that the emphasis of reform is to be the rapid opening of the market to competition rather than the dismemberment of British Gas. His proposals include opening the domestic market to competition in April 1996 but subject initially to a volume limit on the aggregate share of the market which new suppliers will be permitted to supply. That volume limit is to be increased a year later and, provided that the necessary administrative systems are seen to be operating satisfactorily, will be removed altogether in April 1998 so that the market will be fully open to competition from that date.

A new statutory framework for domestic gas supply will be required and the government has indicated that, subject to Parliamentary time, it intends to introduce the necessary legislation by April 1996. This will include a new regime of 'domestic gas supplier' and a Network Code governing the operation of the onshore pipeline network.

The objective of the reforms is to achieve effective, sustainable competition. That competition, it is hoped, will result in lower gas prices for consumers or, at least, a reduction in the rate of increase of gas prices. It will almost certainly result in an increase in the number of companies involved in the chain of gas supply from the point of production to the point of consumption. The basic framework of contracts between these various companies, and the principal contract terms are, however, likely to remain broadly as described in the previous sections.

Section 5

Energy Financing

Chapter 19

Financing Petroleum Agreements

C.J.V. Robson

1.0 INTRODUCTION

The focus of this Chapter is to describe the typical type of financing agreements which are currently used to finance North Sea petroleum projects whether they are in the course of development or have been developed and are producing.

The chapter will not deal with agreements entered into by oil companies which are straight corporate liabilities even though they may be related to petroleum projects since these are indistinguishable from general corporate obligations. In the past, the major oil companies were able to obtain straight corporate debt for whatever purpose on the basis of simple financing documents and highly advantageous terms to the extent that they were very often able to dictate the legal arrangements. In the light of the fragility of the banking system and the recent results produced by BP it remains to be seen whether this remains the case.

However, the chapter will deal with the agreements which are entered into to finance borrowings for petroleum projects on a non-recourse or limited recourse basis (*ie* borrowings where the lender is not relying upon a corporate covenant but on the success of the project and the income generated by the asset owned by the borrower). To put it another way if the project fails the loans will not be repaid and the lenders will have no remedy against any other member of the group. The banks having evaluated all factors are taking the project risk. Not surprisingly the banks obtain a high margin for this risk and the documentation needs to include a suitable negative pledge covenant.

2.0 HISTORICAL BACKGROUND

In the early days of the development of the North Sea in the United Kingdom in the 1970s legal and financial advisers were extremely confused as to how these financings should be structured. The amounts involved in developing prospective fields in the North Sea were very great in conventional terms and the borrowing companies were anxious to have the borrowings insulated from the main group to avoid any impact upon the main group in the event of the project going wrong and repayment of loans being required. For example, in the case of Tricentrol plc which is now part of Arco, the borrowing required to finance its share of the Thistle field was nearly two and one half times the then market capitalisation of the parent company and clearly any recourse to the parent group in the event of default would have meant the collapse of the whole group. To avoid this, petroleum interests were often held in a special purpose subsidiary which itself was the actual borrower.

The majors have been known to borrow through special purpose subsidiaries in difficult parts of the world with no parent company guarantee, the bankers relying, to some degree, on the belief that a major oil company would never at the end of the day allow its subsidiary to become insolvent and perhaps upon some vague type of comfort letter. However, there has been a considerable amount of litigation in recent years on the status of comfort letters and whether they, in effect, are designed to be genuine letters of comfort and no more or whether they should have some legally binding effect. There is however no need within the scope of this chapter to discuss this in any greater detail.

So far as the lenders were concerned it will come as no surprise to hear that traditional banking practice required the giving of some form of security which, in the event of default or insolvency, would enable the lenders to realise the assets, the subject of the security, to recover the monies advanced. One should bear in mind that we were talking at this stage about an oil province which had not been developed and of which there was very little experience and a great deal of nervousness about whether the projects could be successfully completed and what would happen if they were not.

Take the Piper and Claymore fields for example, of which Occidental was the operator and where the interests were held by all parties in special purpose subsidiaries. Because the loans were being organised through the London Market, the various finance agreements were governed by English law and it was thought appropriate that the borrowing companies should give debentures creating fixed and floating charges in favour of the banks under English law over the whole of their interests in the project, their interests in the licence, their participating interests under the operating agreement and their interests in all the relevant infrastructure and hardware.

On the other hand legal advisers noted that the oil fields were, in fact, in Scottish waters with the pipelines and terminals being situated in Scotland and in order to complete the circle it was thought appropriate to have back-to-back Scottish security and English lawyers were faced with becoming acquainted with Scottish assignations in security – whose role was not entirely clear – and also Scottish floating charges (even more arcane) under the Companies (Floating Charges and Receivers) (Scotland) Act 1972.

In retrospect all of these arrangements were largely illusory although they did at the time give comfort to the lenders that they had some form of asset over which they could exercise a right of sale in the event of default. However, this would probably have been difficult and was form rather than substance, although it would be true to say that these arrangements did establish a level of priority and prevented anyone else asserting prior claims except for the fact that the rights of the other members of the consortium in the event, for example, of a failure to pay cash calls would always have priority. Thankfully, the efficacy of these highly complicated security arrangements has never been tested.

A similar search for security took place in loans to Norwegian companies where the initial solution was to deem the drilling platform to be a ship and record the mortgage in the Norwegian Ships Registry. There are now in place specific statutory provisions.

As the North Sea became a more mature developed petroleum province in the United Kingdom, Norway and the Netherlands, the nervousness of lending on such projects became less and most lending is now carried out on an unsecured basis, again in a special purpose subsidiary to ensure that the assets remain intact and free of any prior third party claims. None the less, whether it is of any use or not, the security structure has continued to be used where the borrowing is made by a subsidiary of a very small group. It continues to give the lenders something of a warm feeling.

Leaving these rare cases aside, in broad principle it would probably be true to say that there has been established a fairly uniform pattern for financing agreements for petroleum projects although their length and complexity will differ depending upon whether the project is in the course of development or whether the project has in fact already been developed and is producing. It may also differ as a result of the identity of the parties so that the terms of a loan to an Elf Aquitaine company by Crédit Lyonnais (both of which are organisations in which the French state has a shareholding) might be on significantly different terms from those available from American banks.

3.0 CURRENT PRACTICE

The earlier rather bland statement as to unsecured loans disguises the fact that the detail of any financing arrangements and the terms of the documentation can vary substantially so that, taken in the round, when the detail is analysed one document may produce a very different result from another.

Irrespective of the status of the project the borrower will be looking for the highest degree of flexibility and the maximum protection available against the whims of intransigent bankers. It will want to ensure that development cost variances, currency fluctuations and movements in the oil price do not produce surprises or events of default. It will want to be satisfied that having budgeted on the basis of certain funds being available at a particular time to fund expenditure nothing can occur which would enable the lenders to withhold a drawing of funds or prevent an outstanding advance from being rolled forward to the next period.

Equally, the lenders will want to ensure that they have a degree of control over the movement of funds, that the project is being developed or operated in a proper manner, that the borrower is acting in an appropriate way and that monies are not being advanced to disappear, not down a black hole but into a dry hole. At the end of the day it is the duty of the lawyers involved in the transaction to achieve a balance between the respective interests of the borrowers and lenders. It is dismaying sometimes to see the sterile arguments which can go on almost indefinitely on the minutiae of the language of financing agreements. It remains important to distinguish the wood from the trees.

3.1 Due Diligence – Legal and Economic

It is important first to examine the steps which are undertaken as a prelude to the financing documentation.

In the first place, it should be established that a borrower has the necessary title to the asset to be financed and this requires checking that a valid licence or permit exists and that it has been properly issued or transferred to the borrower. In the case of the United Kingdom it would be a licence on a joint and several basis issued under petroleum legislation dating back to 1934 which in itself would not indicate what the beneficial interests of the parties would be in the respective project. There is no indication in the licence of the percentage interest which any party holds. This will be established by the interests indicated in the relevant operating agreement or unitisation agreement as the case may be.

There will also be a geological and technical study of the project and whether the field is in development or developed makes little difference particularly as although geology is fundamentally a precise science, knowledge of it will frequently change as more information becomes available. In the case of a project in development there will also be some form of engineering study so that the lenders can be reasonably confident that on the basis of the geology and the proposed engineering the expected quantity of petroleum can be extracted. Someone will also have to calculate the basic economics of the project with assumptions as to exchange rates, inflation rates, future interest costs and discount rates, hydrocarbon prices and currency. These days there will also be an estimate of future abandonment costs at the end of the project and the anticipated tax treatment.

In the case of a limited recourse or non-recourse borrowing there will also have to be some evaluation as to where other risks are to lie. For example are the lenders to take the political risk. In 1974 with the advent of a Labour government there was considerable concern about nationalisation or expropriation, whatever you call it, in the event it was called participation by the British National Oil Corporation. No-one has been greatly concerned about this aspect through the Thatcher/Major years with the Government's emphasis on privatisation. It would, however, be relevant in other jurisdictions and the lenders might seek specific cover for this one event from another group company.

3.2 Financing Agreement

A typical non-recourse or limited recourse financing agreement will contain all the usual clauses which you would expect to see in a financing which was not linked to any special project.

It might be a revolving facility under which amounts can be drawn and repaid and then redrawn at the end of any relevant interest period. It may have a foreign currency option which is beloved of all corporate treasurers and which is regarded as giving a considerable degree of flexibility. That is the right to draw the loan in a currency other than the original currency, which would probably be dollars, *eg*, sterling, Yen, Deutschmarks or even ECU although, at the end of the day, most treasurers appear to come to the conclusion even with the ability to hedge that they are not in the business of foreign currency speculation and although these clauses are argued about at length they are not frequently used, except where the revenue includes oil (dollar priced) and gas (sterling priced) to match loans and revenues.

There will be the usual clauses dealing with increased costs resulting from changes in circumstances, either upheavals in the foreign currency markets or changes in law which affect the cost to the lenders of providing the funds and, again, despite the fact that they give great anguish in the negotiations, with the borrowers resenting the insistence of the lenders in having virtual autonomy in deciding what this cost is, there is little experience of them being actually invoked. There was some discussion after the 1987 crash and after the invasion of Kuwait that they might need to be considered. There will also be the usual boilerplate clauses dealing with confidentiality, illegality, notices and governing law. One of the great advantages of English law (but not necessarily Scottish law) is that it is perceived as being relatively neutral and there have been petroleum project loans between a syndicate of non-UK banks and a non-UK borrower where neither side trusted the law of the jurisdiction of the other and opted for English law as the middle course.

More particularly, however, in petroleum financings there will be detailed provisions for preparing estimates on how the project is likely to develop both at the inception of the financing and throughout its course and detailed provisions designed to calculate the cash flow which it is expected the project will generate and the residual value of the project to a particular date at any one time. The representations and warranties, covenants and events of default which will be referred to later have a material bearing on policing these crucial areas.

There will be a projection at the inception of the loan of, *inter alia*, the oil in place and its quality, anticipated reservoir performance and recoverable reserves, timing, future oil prices and interest and in the case of a project under development, the future development costs and the likelihood of over-runs. As noted above any projection will also have to take into account the touchy area of abandonment costs. Based upon these projections there will then be an estimate of the net cash flow which the field is expected to generate. It is on the basis of these projections that the lenders decide, bearing in mind the non-recourse nature of the loan, how much can safely be advanced.

The structures of the repayment obligations under financing agreements of this kind are extremely varied. It is possible simply to apply a percentage of the net cash flow towards the repayment of the loan, it is also possible to have a target for repayment, sometimes called a reduction schedule, so that excess net cash flow can be used by the borrower as it sees fit or if there is a deficiency carrying it forward to the next period or the back end of the loan, the latter a concept not beloved of lenders. It is possible to provide for repayments of fixed amounts but this would be unusual these days because of the inherent uncertainties of projects of this kind and the fact that it is not possible to forecast precisely how much money will be available in any period.

Bearing in mind that the total amount available under any financial arrangements is unlikely to be drawn in one amount, arguments will arise as to whether once a projection has been made it holds good for the whole period of the loan or for a particular period even though in practice it is discovered subsequently that the projection will not turn out as expected so that even though a later projection downgrades the previous estimates the borrower can continue to roll over an advance which has already been made but, perhaps, not draw any fresh amounts. This is essentially a matter for negotiation.

Formalising in the documentation how and when projections are to be made and the assumptions upon which they are to be based is an exceedingly complicated process involving computer models, specialist banks, independent experts in the event of disputes and perhaps ultimately some form of arbitration. It is not necessary to attempt to go into greater detail in this chapter.

In order to make this system work there are representations and warranties given at the beginning of the loan, there will be covenants (both negative and positive) to operate throughout the course of the loan and then there will be events of default which will trigger acceleration of repayment. Because of the inherent uncertainties of petroleum projects, which have been alluded to, the practice has developed of not calling the relevant events *events of default* but *designated events*, in order that the cross-default provisions which may exist in the parent group's own financing arrangements are not triggered. Whatever you call them they have the same effect of acceleration and whether on a true legal construction merely calling something a *designated event* as opposed to an *event of default* cures the cross-default problem is far from clear. In exceptional cases, there may be a half-way house with a series of so-called suspensive events which are not *designated events* or *events of default* but which hold everything in limbo until the position clarifies.

3.3 Specific Provisions

So far as representations and warranties are concerned these should be relatively straightforward in that they should be matters within the knowledge and control of the borrower. It should be able to confirm that it has been validly incorporated, that there is a valid licence, that the appropriate consents and approvals for development have been obtained and that its interests are free of any charges, mortgages or encumbrances. It should also be able to confirm that the information which it has supplied to the lenders for the purposes of making the loan, usually in the form of an information memorandum with all the relevant field and economic data is, so far as it is aware, reasonably accurate and not misleading.

The initial warranties are largely mechanical in nature but the question arises whether they should be deemed to be repeated when the loan or any part is rolled over or when a future drawing is required. Circumstances may have changed outside the control of the borrower which prevent it from giving representations and warranties in precisely the same terms if called upon to do so at that time. Most lenders would probably accept that it is not reasonable to impose the same absolute representations and warranties upon the borrower with reference to an indeterminate time in the future but would expect that they should remain materially correct. This seems to be a fair middle course. If events have occurred which render the information supplied wholly inaccurate or misleading, whether or not due to the actions of the borrower, it would seem reasonable that the lenders should have an opportunity of reviewing their position.

So far as the covenants are concerned, as mentioned earlier these can either be positive or negative. Positive covenants will compel the borrower to take certain actions with a view to having the project developed or operated to its maximum potential. These covenants could involve obtaining appropriate consents and approvals, performing relevant obligations under the field agreements, co-operating in the field development, taking all reasonable steps to ensure that the project is developed, operated and maintained in a good and workmanlike manner in accordance with good oil field practice and relevant legislation, and that the best price is obtained for any petroleum extracted. In particular, there will be a covenant to prepare projections from time to time in a proper way in accordance with the financing agreement which will enable the lenders to monitor how the project is going.

The critical thing to bear in mind here is that most fields are developed by consortia so that, unless the borrower has a controlling voting interest in the project, in certain instances it cannot give absolute covenants since it is not within its power to do so but can only give covenants within the framework of the consortium arrangements to the extent of its own percentage interest.

The negative covenants are the reverse side of the mirror and will be designed to ensure that the interest in the project is not diminished by any unilateral act of the borrower. It should be noted, of course, that the lenders will have the ability, in certain circumstances, either through an agent bank or a majority of banks to waive compliance with the various covenants.

Bearing in mind that this discussion is focusing on unsecured loans it should not be difficult for the borrower to covenant that it will not dispose of any of its interests in the project or incur any other third party borrowings and matters of this sort.

The critical area in a project loan is the clause dealing with events of default or designated events whatever they may be called and this is where the greatest degree of difficulty can be experienced.

There are some matters which are genuine defaults such as failure to pay interest or capital when due, failure to carry out obligations, failure to take out appropriate insurance and failure to meet appropriate cash calls but you will also find categorised as events of default matters over which the borrower has no control. For example, the economics of the project may have been predicated on the basis of certain ratios. A frequent test is that the net present value of the field calculated to the date of final maturity of the loan will always be a particular multiple of the amount outstanding under the loan. As oil prices, currency values and interest changes the net present value may increase or decrease and on this basis it would be deemed to be an event of default if the relevant ratio is not met. It could also be an event of default if the estimate of the future cashflows would not be adequate to amortise the loan by the expected date. It is rather hard to use such a pejorative term in relation to matters which result from such extraneous factors but it is likely that the financing agreement will be drafted in this way.

Many hours are spent in negotiating the precise language of the events of default to cater for the respective interests of borrower or lender so that it must be appreciated that legally there is a world of difference in emphasis between language which says for example that there will be an event of default if 'there has been in the opinion of the bank any material adverse change in the business, assets, financial condition or prospects of the borrower or any subsidiary since a particular date' (a wide-ranging definition vesting considerable discretion in the bank) compared with language which reads 'there has been any material adverse change in the financial condition of the borrower and its subsidiaries taken as a whole since a particular date' (a wholly objective standard).

Equally one can appreciate the difference between the language which categorises something as an event of default if 'any other event or series of events whether related or not occurs which in the opinion of the bank would *or might result* in a material adverse effect' as compared with 'any other event or series of events whether related or not occurs which would result in a material adverse effect'. A similar polarisation.

In a highly volatile and potentially rapidly changing world lenders will prefer the wider test whereas borrowers will much prefer more objective assessments.

4.0 CONCLUSION

Though a cursory sketch of the types of agreements involved in petroleum financings this Chapter attempts to highlight those legal issues of particular relevance to borrowers and lenders in the petroleum sector and how such issues may be potentially dealt with.

Chapter 20

Derivative Instruments for Energy Industries

James L. Gunderson

1.0 INTRODUCTION

'Derivative' is a term used to group together different contractual instruments that were originally developed in different markets for different purposes. Although the term came into common use relatively recently, some of the instruments referred to as derivatives have been in existence for centuries. Most of the others were anticipated in the academic literature of the 1960s and 1970s. Today they are grouped together because major banks, securities houses and other market makers view them as useful tools for managing price risk.

A derivative instrument is a contingent claim (or a bundle of contingent claims). Its value (and each of the future payment obligations it consists of) depends on the values of more basic underlying variables. One can imagine derivative instruments contingent on almost anything, but most are contingent on the prices of key commodities or securities. To be a suitable basis for a derivative, an asset should be relatively standard, there should be substantial future supply, substantial and diversified demand and significant price variation over time. Today there are major markets in several cities around the world for a whole range of derivatives based on agricultural commodities, metals and other raw materials, financial assets, securities and various energy products.

Derivatives have a number of different functions, but in the energy industries their most important use is as a means of transferring or 'hedging' price risk. This chapter will describe the four principle types of derivatives and their main functions. There are endless variations, but most others are derived from or are combinations of these.

2.0 FORWARD CONTRACTS

One of the simplest forms of derivative is the forward contract. It is an agreement to purchase or sell a specific quantity of something at a price specified now, but to be delivered (and usually to be paid for) at a specified future date. As the contract approaches maturity its value increases or decreases as the market's view of the future value of the asset rises or falls.[1]

Much of the legal basis for development of a forward market was achieved in Western mercantile law by the early thirteenth century. The most important of these developments included the bill of lading and other transportation documents, the notion of transfer of ownership by transfer of transportation documents rather than actual delivery of goods, and an objective measure of damages for non-delivery of goods based upon the difference between the contract price and the market price.[2]

The earliest forward contracts in northern Europe were probably those developed by Dutch whalers in the sixteenth century. Selling whale products forward before sailing not only helped them finance their voyages, but also made it possible to fix a better price for their product.

Europe's wildest early forward market was also in the Netherlands: the tulip bulb market of the 1630s. Buying tulip bulbs in the winter for future delivery when they were lifted in June became a normal practice around 1634. As prices rose with demand, negotiable tulip bulb contracts began trading vigorously in organised groups (colleges) that convened at specific taverns at specific times.[3] Speculators who saw new opportunities in the tulip bulb 'paper' fuelled the market, so that by lifting time in 1636 prices were three times what they were two years earlier. The rise in prices continued to accelerate until they peaked the following winter, amid anxiety among the growers that a crash might leave them with worthless stocks. In early February panic did set in, prices dropped hourly and the contracts for future delivery eventually became worthless.

Asia's first forward contracts were developed in Japan about 60 years after the collapse of the Netherlands tulip market. The Tokugawa Shogunate required the feudal lords (*daimyo*) to spend four months of each year in attendance at the Shogun's court in Edo (Tokyo), and to leave their families there when they returned home to oversee their estates, requiring the *daimyos* to spend considerable amounts of their finances on maintaining two establishments in the luxurious style required by their rank (thus diverting their funds away from military purposes).[4]

---

1. For the other factors affecting forward prices see the text accompanying notes 31–35 below.

2. H.J. Berman, *Law and Revolution: The Formation of the Western Legal Tradition* (1983), pp. 348–51. 'In addition to the extension of credit by sellers to buyers through negotiable instruments and other devices, buyers also extended credit to sellers through various types of contracts for the purchase of goods to be delivered in the future, to be purchased by the seller and resold, and the like. Once again, such contracts presupposed the existence not only of a developed market but also of a belief in the future of the community that made up the market and a concept of time as a factor to be valued in commercial transactions.' Ibid. at p.351.

3. Transactions were usually carried out 'through the plates', where wooden disks were distributed to prospective buyers and price negotiations were reflected in chalk marks on the disks, or 'through the nought' where the seller would provide a bonus for the highest bidder at auction (the amount of the bonus being placed in a design on a slate). Bidding was also carried out through Dutch auction, where the seller begins at a high price, reducing it until a bid is offered. For a general description of the 'tulip mania', see S. Schama, *The Embarrassment of Riches* (1987), pp.349–63.

4. W.S. Morton, *Japan: Its History and Culture* (1975), pp.123–4.

To raise the cash needed to meet these expenses, their rice (collected as rent on their estates) was hauled to market in Edo or Osaka. They inevitably spent more than they had, so they began buying goods on credit and were forced to pledge their rice before it was available for delivery. Merchants became rice brokers and the *daimyos* started selling warehouse receipts against supplies they had stored in the country or in rented warehouses in the city.[5] These warehouse receipts became forward contracts.

From the sellers' viewpoint this market in warehouse receipts developed as a means of accelerating receipt of revenue. However, for the merchants it was not only a means of earning interest but a way of locking in the price of rice to be received in the future.[6]

To the extent a forward is used as a means of purchasing a physical asset (albeit in the future), it is not really a derivative in the sense of this Chapter.[7] The early forward contracts discussed so far are of interest to the extent that they were developed into tools for hedging the risk of price changes. Japanese rice contracts did so by becoming a combination of forward contract (the obligation to deliver – and take delivery – in the future) with an advance of the purchase price.

To use our rice merchant and *daimyo* as an example, imagine that the merchant had less rice inventory than he expected to sell in the future. If he actually had obligations to sell more in the future than he had in inventory, he would be 'short' of rice. Being short rice, if there is some problem of supply in the near future, such as a major series of warehouse fires, he could be exposed to higher rice costs at the time he would need to buy. He could hedge that risk by establishing an opposite position in the rice forward market. If he buys rice forward, he will be 'long' in forward rice (compensating for his short physical position) and reduce his future price risk.

The *daimyo*, to the extent he had more rice on route to the market (or yet to be harvested) than he had committed to sell, would be 'long' in rice. Even if he did not need to sell rice forward to get an advance from the merchant to satisfy his immediate cash needs, he might want to protect the value of his rice until it was sold. To hedge his 'long' position, he would sell rice forward (take a 'short' forward rice position) to reduce or eliminate that risk. By reducing that worry he would be freer to concentrate on his main activities (*eg* court intrigue).

The forward price of the rice would naturally depend on supply and demand. The amount of rice forward contracts offered for sale by the *daimyos* would depend both on their desperation for immediate cash and their desire to hedge prices. The demand for those contracts would depend on the merchant's desire to hedge or speculate. But the merchant could hedge or speculate not only by buying forward, but also by buying immediately ('spot') and holding the rice to cover his short position or until prices rise as anticipated. The principle difference to the merchant would be the storage and other costs of holding the rice (the 'cost of carry'). He will

5. See G.B. Sansom, *Japan: A Short Cultural History* (1978), p.471 and P. Kaufman, *The Concise Handbook of Futures Markets: Money Management, Forecasting and the Markets* (1986), pp.15–16.

6. In fact the merchants not only hedged prices but speculated, so that between 1710 (when a full-fledged futures market developed) and 1718 rice prices tripled and then crashed to half of what they had started at. Sansom, op cit., ibid., pp.471–472.

7. If a forward contract is not being used as a means of purchasing a physical asset, it may be treated as a futures contract under certain finance or securities laws. See text accompanying notes 17 and 18.

buy forward if the forward price is less than the spot price plus the cost of carry. Unlike the case of the seasonal tulips in the Netherlands where only forward contracts were available, where the commodity can be stored the price of forward contracts will depend on this arbitrage between forward prices and spot prices together with carrying costs (including interest).[8]

Forward contracts can be standardised or specially tailored. Our *daimyo* might want the contract to fit his specific grade of rice, and the quantity and delivery date to fit his particular plans. The merchant, on the other hand, might want it to be as generic as possible, since he is probably writing several of them and would like to minimise his administrative costs. Generally speaking standardisation allows more trading of a particular type of contract, and the resulting increase in volume tends to reduce the transactions costs. Since the contract is directly negotiated between the buyer and seller (what we call an 'over-the-counter' agreement), it can be as standard or specially tailored as the parties wish.[9]

Because the transaction is over-the-counter, the merchant has to worry about the creditworthiness of the *daimyo*. For example, if the *daimyo* has too many debts, his rice might be seized by other creditors before the delivery date. In that case the merchant may not only lose the rice (and the money advanced for it), but default on a contract for sale to another buyer.

The risk that one party may pay or deliver while the other becomes bankrupt before he pays or delivers (*ie* where simultaneous payment and delivery is impracticable) is known as 'settlement risk'. It is dealt with in modern derivative contracts through agreement to net in advance of the settlement date any reciprocal obligations for the same class of asset for the same settlement date.[10] A second type of netting, default netting, is intended to address the risk that one party may become insolvent before the settlement. Where the forward contract is an executory contract for one party to deliver a commodity and the other money, default netting requires that it be possible to rescind the contract upon insolvency and set off resulting losses and gains. Otherwise the insolvency administrator may be able to select profitable contracts for performance and unprofitable ones for repudiation.[11]

Specially tailored over-the-counter contracts also normally present transferability problems. Most jurisdictions require the consent of one party before another party can transfer its obligations and responsibilities to a third party. Thus if the *daimyo* wanted to close out his short forward position by transferring his responsibility to another *daimyo*, he would have to find the merchant and get his permission. The

8. H. Working, 'The Theory of Price of Storage', 39 *American Economic Review* pp.1254–62, (1949).

9. Standardisation is another element regulatory bodies consider in applying regulations on futures trading. See text accompanying notes 14 and 15.

10. For settlement netting to work a receiver in bankruptcy should not be able to reopen the netting by claiming recovery of the commodity delivered or amounts purportedly discharged by netting. This should not present a problem under English law but may be a problem in certain other European jurisdictions. See P.R. Wood, 'Netting in Commodities and Financial Markets', *Financial Derivatives: The Legal Issues*, Euromoney Training, July 1992.

11. Rescission is apparently easier (and in some cases mandatory) under Austrian (mandatory), Belgian, English, Italian (mandatory), Netherlands (mandatory) and German (mandatory) law than it is under French law. Set-off is permitted in Austria, Denmark, England, Finland, Germany, the Netherlands, Italy, Norway and Scotland while it is apparently forbidden in Belgium, France, Greece, Luxembourg, and Spain. Ibid.

merchant might be reluctant to give advance permission for assignment since that would not give him the opportunity to evaluate the new counterparty's credit-worthiness.

To gain the advantages of transferability, the Japanese rice forward contracts became negotiable instruments. Today parties concerned with transferability in over-the-counter contracts often address the problem by including early termination provisions into the contract, but that often requires complex valuation and price setting provisions.

2.1 Crude Oil Forward Contracts

As stated above, most derivatives are based upon key commodities which are relatively standard, in substantial future supply, for which there is substantial and diversified demand and significant price variation over time. Crude oil has been a key commodity for quite some time and future production of oil has played a role in energy finance for more than a century (beginning with Crédit Lyonnais' loans to the 'Nobel brothers' Baku ventures in the late nineteenth century).[12] But, until the early 1980s there was not enough price volatility to warrant a major derivatives market. Before then almost 90 per cent of the world's oil was sold under long-term contracts based on prices set by the majors, and the rest was bought and sold by the majors. From then on 90 per cent of the world's oil was available on the spot market and price volatility became substantial.

Standardised crude oil forward contracts are one of the ways producers, refiners, traders and end-users can hedge the risks arising as a result of the increased price volatility. For example, North Sea Brent blend forward contracts[13] are agreements for the sale or purchase of a 500,000 barrel cargo of Brent blend to be delivered in a specified month FOB Sullom Voe, Scotland. Brent forward contracts are entered into by telephone and confirming telex specifying the names and addresses of the buyer and seller, the cargo reference number, the month forward, and the price in dollars per barrel, all other terms and conditions being standardised.

The high degree of standardisation of Brent forward contracts permits the same cargo to be purchased many times in a series of back-to-back transactions, called 'chains'.[14] These chains can create a good deal of tension as the deadline approaches for the original seller of the cargo to give notice of the three-day loading range (the 'lay days') when the cargo will be ready for delivery. Under each of the contracts in the chain, this 'nomination' obligation must be fulfilled by 5:00pm fifteen days prior to the first lay day, so if the original seller waits until 4:55pm to notify the first buyer in a chain, there would probably be defaults down the chain when the 5:00pm deadline passes.[15]

12. D. Yergin, *The Prize* (1991), p.60.
13. For descriptions of various other crude oil and oil product forward contracts see B. Sas, 'Legal Aspects of Risk Management and Forward Oil Trading: The Forward Oil Markets and their Contracts', 7 *Journal of Energy and Natural Resources Law* 1, (1989).
14. Due to these long chains letters of credit are common where the credit rating of the buyer so warrants, as well as letters of indemnity where shipping documents are not yet available.
15. For what its worth, the Shell form of Brent contract includes a provision obliging the parties in a chain to communicate information they are obliged to pass on to third parties (such as nominations) as expeditiously as possible.

Where a party occurs twice in a chain, the length of the chain can be reduced by 'book out' of the series of transactions (the 'circle') between that party's two positions. The book out of the forward contracts replaces them with financial settlements.[16] Upon maturity of the contracts title passes sequentially among the remaining parties in the chain.

Because so many participants in the Brent forward market do not actually take delivery, there is significant risk that Brent forward contracts will be treated as futures contracts under the UK Financial Services Act 1986 (FSA).[17] The FSA applies to any person trading or arranging contracts in the UK for the sale of a commodity under which delivery is to be made in the future at a pre-agreed price unless the person is engaged solely in contracts 'made for commercial purposes'.[18] Persons covered by the FSA must either fit under a specific exclusion, be specifically authorised by the Securities and Investment Board as 'permitted persons'[19] or be authorised through membership in FSA-recognised self-regulating bodies.

The Securities and Futures Authority Ltd[20] is the body responsible for oil and product traders, defined as 'Oil Market Participants' (OMPs), and registration as a member with that body automatically makes an OMP an 'authorised person'. In addition to the FSA and the Securities and Futures Authority Rules (which include Conduct of Business Rules), OMPs are subject to the Securities and Investment Board's Oil Market Code of Conduct[21] and Principles of Investment Business.[22]

2.2 Electricity Forward Contracts

There are several reasons one might be surprised to find electricity underlying a derivative instrument. It is not durable (it cannot be stored in bulk). It is as much a service as it is a product. Since most electricity is transmitted over a national or regional grid, once it has been generated it loses its identity (one cannot identify a particular 'cargo' as coming from a particular generator or as having been delivered to a specific customer).

---

16. See *Voest-Alpine Inter Trading GmbH v Chevron International Oil Company Ltd.* [1987] 2 Lloyd's Rep. 547.

17. '[A]lthough delivery intention is only one of a number of indications, the fact that only a minority of transactions in the Brent market result in delivery means that most market participants regard it as unsafe to rely on a commercial purposes exclusion from the definition of futures.' Securities and Investment Board, *SIB Consultative Document on the Future Regulation of the Oil Markets* 2, (1988).

18. FSA, Schedule 1, § 8.

19. FSA, Schedule 1, § 23a.

20. The Securities and Futures Authority Ltd (SFA) is the successor to The Securities Association and the Association of Futures Brokers and Dealers (which was formerly the body responsible for oil traders) which merged in Apr. 1991. The Association of Futures Brokers and Dealers' rules have been superseded by the SFA Rulebook issued on Apr. 1 1992.

21. SIB 'Oil Market. Code of Conduct', Guidance Release 4/88, dated Mar. 1988.

22. For a general discusssion of these rules see N. Turck, 'Regulation of Oil Trading: A US and UK Legal Update (or) Death of *Transnor*', in *Energy Law '92*, (Graham & Trotman, 1992), pp.99–104. See also B. Sas, 'Legal Aspects of Risk Management and Forward Oil Trading: The US and UK Regulatory Regimes' 7 *Journal of Energy and Natural Resources Law* pp.142–6, 1989.

In England and Wales[23] where electricity forward contracts were developed, electricity prices charged by generators and paid by retail suppliers (the regional electricity companies) and large industrial customers are determined through a pool.[24] Each morning at 10:00am the generators declare to the National Grid the amount of generating capacity available for each half-hour until 12:00 noon on the following day. At the same time large industrial consumers notify the National Grid of their forecast of demand for each half-hour from 9:00pm through all of the following day to 12:00 noon on the next day, as well as the maximum price per half-hour that they are willing to pay. After combining those forecasts with an overall consumer demand forecast (taking into account historical demand, weather conditions and other relevant factors), the National Grid Company then calculates the lowest price (called the 'system marginal price') at which enough offers can be accepted to supply demand for each half-hour time slot.

All generators sell at the same 'pool purchase price' based on the system marginal price,[25] and the regional electricity companies and large industrial users purchasing directly from the National Grid purchase at the related 'pool selling price'.[26]

Variations in demand in different half-hour slots and changes in generating capacity can result in a great deal of price volatility. In response, the generators and regional electricity companies developed two types of hedging contracts. In the so-called 'one-way contract', the generator agrees to pay the customer the difference between the pool selling price paid by the customer and a price agreed in advance. When the payment received is subtracted from the market price for electricity to be

23. While the following discussion of electricity forward contracts is limited to England and Wales, Norway also has a spot market pricing system for electricity, and could develop a forward contract system as well. Under the Norwegian Energy Act, which came into effect at the beginning of 1991, consumers as well as utilities can freely participate in the spot market. The principle difference between the Norwegian system and the English system described below is the fact that Norway's is almost entirely a hydro-electric system. Shortages of capacity are normally a function of the amount of annual snow and rainfall rather than the complex issues facing fossil fuel generation plants. Consequently the spot price of electricity in the Norwegian system is more directly a function of immediate supply and demand, without the 'capacity payment' element referred to in note 25 infra.

24. Under a structure for electricity supply introduced on Mar. 31, 1990 by the Electricity Act 1989, the output of generating plants are pooled to meet the combined requirements of customers under a Pooling and Settlement Agreement signed on Mar. 30, 1990. Production of electricity is divided principally among two fossil fuel based generating companies, National Power and PowerGen, and one nuclear based company, Nuclear Electric. Transmission of electricity from generating plants (as well as from interconnectors with France and Scotland) across the National Grid is now the responsibility of the National Grid Company PLC, which is owned indirectly by the 12 regional electricity companies responsible for distribution of electricity over their respective local networks. See S. Beharrell, 'The Electricity Pool in England and Wales: The Generator's Perspective' 9 *Journal of Energy and Natural Resources Law* 45, (1991).

25. The pool purchase price due to generators (also called the 'pool input price') is calculated for each half hour, and includes not only the system marginal price, but also (i) a payment for ancillary services, such as keeping generating station on standby or operating in such a way as to maintain voltage stability, and (ii) a 'capacity payment' based upon an estimate of the probability that capacity will be inadequate to supply demand during the particular half hour in question, multiplied by the difference between the system marginal price and a rate per kWH set by the Department of Energy as the cost of such a lost load. Ibid.

26. The pool selling price (also called the 'pool output price') is equivalent to the pool purchase price plus an amount to compensate the National Grid Company for the costs of reserves, availability of plant, forecasting errors, transmission constraints, ancillary services and marginal plant adjustments.

paid, the net effect is a 'cap' or ceiling on the amount that the customer will have to pay for the electricity. In the 'two-way contracts' the customer is also required to pay the generator the difference between the pool purchase price (or in some cases the pool selling price) and the price agreed in advance.[27] Not only is there a cap on the amount the customer has to pay, but the difference payment the customer must make in case of lower than expected market prices results in a 'floor' or minimum amount the generator will receive for electricity.

Under the UK Financial Services Act 1986 these contracts are 'contracts for differences'[28] (since there is cash settlement based upon the difference from the market price rather than actual physical delivery), so as with certain oil forward contracts persons arranging or trading them must either fit under a specific exclusion,[29] be specifically authorised by SIB as permitted persons or be authorized through membership in FSA-recognised self-regulating bodies. The UK members of the pool have applied for and received from SIB authorisation as permitted persons on the basis that their main business is not investment business and the contracts are related to their main business.

In October 1991 the major regional electricity companies and the generators (including Electricité de France and the Scottish generators) launched a more formalised over-the-counter market for two-way contracts, now called electricity forward agreements, with standard terms and conditions, for trading during fixed hours during the day through a broker, GNI Ltd. The broker matches potential buyers and sellers placing bids or offers to GNI Ltd over the telephone, and negotiates on behalf of each party on an anonymous basis. Once all details of the trade are agreed, the broker discloses the names of the parties, and if each party accepts the name of the other the agreement becomes binding and a confirmation is sent to the parties by the broker.

The 48 half-hour pricing periods in each day are grouped into six four-hour periods. The same four-hour period during each week is then grouped in either both days of the weekend or the five weekdays of that week. For example the four hours between 7:00am and 11:00am on Saturday and Sunday form one unit for trading purposes and those same hours on Monday through Friday form another unit. An electricity forward contract can be for a single week or a strip of weeks, generally up to one year.

Electricity forward agreement prices are quoted over the S&P Comstock price screen system and trading takes place by phone or fax during late morning and early afternoon. Settlement is through payment by one party of the difference between the actual average price during the agreed period and the agreed price. The settlement day follows the prevailing arrangements for the electricity pool (eg 28 days after the end of the week in question).

---

27. Variations in contract terms are also made to take a generator's specific characteristics into account. For example in a 'non-firm contract' the payments for differences would only be made when the particular power station concerned was declared available.

28. FSA, Schedule 1, § 9.

29. For example, Electricité de France would be excluded as an overseas person under FSA, Schedule 1, Part IV. To qualify as an overseas person, one must have no permanent place of business in the UK and not carry on a business there.

2.3 Financial Forwards

Forward rate agreements are forward contracts for interest rate payments over specified periods in the future. They enable companies planning to borrow in the future or deposit funds in the future to fix the rate of interest in advance, before the funds are actually deposited or borrowed. For example one could imagine an agreement for three months LIBOR on an assumed £5m 'notional' amount for six months beginning in three months. Interest periods of three, six or 12 months are common and can be fixed up to 18 months in advance. The forward rate agreement market began in 1983 and 'took off' after publication of standard terms by the British Bankers' Association in 1985.

A currency forward is an agreement to exchange a specific amount of one currency for another on a certain date in the future at a particular rate of exchange. The rate reflects the difference in the two currencies' interest rates and the prevailing exchange rate rather than a prediction of future spot rates.

3.0 FUTURES CONTRACTS

Futures are standardised, exchange-traded agreements to buy or sell a standard quantity and quality of an asset for future delivery at specific locations in predetermined months (usually on a quarterly basis). Think back to our Japanese *daimyo* and his selling of warehouse receipts to the rice merchants. Those forward rice contracts became negotiable and avidly traded among merchants, and one particular rice merchant named Yodoya came to dominate the rice market. In 1650 his house in Osaka became the the first commodities exchange in Japan and one of the first futures markets in the world.[30]

To be highly tradeable, the rice futures contracts had to be highly standardised. Their term was limited to any one of three four-month periods in a year, with no new contracts allowed in the last three days of each period. Settlement occurred on or before the last day of each period. Four basic grades of rice for each contract period were chosen by majority vote of the traders and the futures contracts had to be for those grades. All trades had to be cleared through a clearing house.

The trades by each party were actually trades with the clearing house so that any default by a trader affected only its side of a trade with the clearing house. The clearing house assumed that risk, so traders on the exchange would not have to worry about the creditworthiness of the other party to a trade. The clearing house took care of (and backed-up) the necessary lines of credit with each trader.

The intermediation of the clearing house in an exchange also eliminates problems related to 'closing out' a position. The trader who wants to get out of his futures position just needs to buy or sell the opposite contract.

The Chicago Board of Trade established the first modern futures exchange in 1865, and is still the biggest. The major exchanges for crude oil and petroleum product futures are the New York Mercantile Exchange (NYMEX) and the

---

30. P. Kaufman, op.cit., supra note 5, p.17. In 1697 the Dojima Rice Exchange was also set up in Osaka and became a futures exchange by 1710. W.S. Morton, supra note 4, p.130.

International Petroleum Exchange in London (IPE) and to a lesser extent the Singapore International Monetary Exchange (SIMEX).

After a trader representing a buyer and a trader representing a seller conclude a deal on the floor of an exchange, within a few hours the trade is registered with a clearing house. Almost all counterparty credit risk disappears as the clearing house puts itself between the buyer and the seller. All the principal UK derivatives exchanges (including the International Petroleum Exchange) use the London Clearing House, which is backed by an up to £200m guarantee, and margin procedures.

It is the margin procedures that distinguish modern futures exchange trading from the rice futures trading that took place at Yodoya's three centuries ago. In return for its clearing and settlement services, a clearing house for derivatives requires a security deposit, called the 'initial margin'. It also charges (or credits) the clearing member's account for changes in the value of the derivative beyond a certain limit. That charge or credit is called 'variation margin'. Each day until the maturity of the futures contract the increase or decrease in the futures price is determined and the trader's margin account is adjusted to reflect the gain or loss. The charge or credit to variation margin resulting from changes in futures prices each day is called 'marking-to-market'.

Futures contracts differ from forward contracts in that they involve less credit risk due to the intermediation of the exchange, most trading is done on margin, positions are normally closed out prior to maturity, and pricing differs because of the daily marking to market (which affects the timing of cash flows, which in turn affects the net present value of the futures position).

The first introduction of crude oil futures contracts on the NYMEX exchange in 1978 failed because of the absence of price volatility referred to earlier in connection with crude oil forward contracts. In 1983, by which time price volatility increased, the introduction of West Texas Intermediate crude oil on the NYMEX exchange was successful. Trading in crude oil futures began with contracts for delivery in up to six months, but have gradually extended to up to three years. The contracts are for delivery of West Texas Intermediate crude oil[31] in Cushing, Oklahoma. Pipeline space for delivery of physical crude oil must be reserved by the 25th day of the prior month, so WTI futures contracts terminate three days prior to the 25th day of the month before delivery.

3.1 Futures Prices

It was briefly mentioned earlier that the forward price should not be too far from the spot price plus the cost of carry. The fact that futures are marked to market (*ie* that variation margin is charged or credited each day to reflect daily futures price changes) affects the timing of cash flows, and has some effect on prices of futures (causing some difference from comparable forward prices).[32] The extent of the

31. Or alternatively one of six specified other grades, consisting of two Algerian grades, two Nigerian grades, a Norwegian grade and UK Brent Blend, all subject to a price adjustment against the WTI price.

32. J. Cox, J. Ingersoll and S. Ross, 'The Relation Between Forward Prices and Futures Prices', 9 *Journal of Financial Economics* pp.321–46 (1981).

effect of marking to market on futures prices v forward prices depends on the underlying asset, being less strong for commodities as opposed to financial assets.[33] The balance of this discussion will disregard the difference.

The most obvious difference between futures prices and spot prices is the delay in payments for futures, which allow the buyer to earn interest on the purchase price (less the margin) during the life of the contract while his counterpart in the spot market cannot. This factor, and the absence of storage or other carrying costs tends to increase futures prices relative to spot prices. On the other hand the inability to use the underlying asset (or collect dividends or interest on it) tends to decrease futures prices. In the case of futures on assets primarily held for investment, interest rates or dividend yields are crucial to pricing. But in the case of futures on commodities primarily held for consumption, other carrying costs and the demand for and supply of the underlying commodity are more important.

The relationship between spot and futures prices attracts an important source of liquidity to the market: the arbitrageurs. When they believe they perceive discrepancies between futures prices and cash prices they will take positions in one or both markets to profit when the discrepancies 'work themselves out'. In addition to providing liquidity to the market, arbitrage activity tends to drive down futures prices that are too high for short hedgers buying futures and drive up futures prices that are too low for hedgers selling futures.

What then is the role of market participants' expectations regarding the future course of spot prices? Futures prices provide forecasts that are no worse, and often better, than those available from sources using judgmental or econometric methods, such as the United States Energy Administration or the World Bank.[34] Another traditional view of forward and futures prices holds that businesses with inventory (long physical positions) do most of the hedging (taking short futures positions). As a result, there is more supply of futures contracts than demand, causing prices of futures to be generally lower than traders' expectations for the future spot price. According to the theory, this lower price provides the compensation (risk premium) necessary to induce speculators to buy futures (taking long futures positions) so that a market is available for the hedgers.[35] The risk premium is probably a function of expected price volatility.[36] Speculators may or may not require a risk premium to be induced to gamble on their 'view' of future price movements, but they are also essential providers of liquidity to derivatives markets.

3.2 Basis Risk

Despite the efficiency of the futures markets, hedging with futures does not provide perfect protection. The physical commodity being hedged is often of a particular

---

33. L. Meulbroek, 'A Comparison of Forward and Futures Prices of an Interest Rate-Sensitive Financial Asset' 47 *The Journal of Finance* p.381 (1992).

34. M.S. Kumar, 'The Forecasting Accuracy of Crude Oil Futures Prices', 39 *IMF Staff Papers* p.432 (1992).

35. This assumption is known as the Keynes-Hicks hypothesis, having been advanced by John Maynard Keynes and J.R. Hicks.

36. L.O. Scott, 'The Information Content of Prices in Derivative Securities Markets', 39 *IMF Staff Papers* p.596 (1992).

quality and in a specific location, while the future is based on a more standard commodity for delivery in another location which serves as a benchmark. Prices of physical commodities (called 'cash prices') and the futures used for hedging those commodities are normally correlated, but the spread between those prices usually varies. The difference between the price of the physical commodity and the derivative price is called 'basis'. Someone hedging a physical commodity with futures is exchanging the price risk of that commodity for the basis risk between the commodity and a comparable future. The advantage of using a more standard commodity for the future used in hedging is the transactions cost savings from the higher liquidity.

Historic trends do not provide a sufficient basis for judging basis risk. For example before the Gulf conflict, IPE gas oil futures prices historically moved in tandem with jet fuel prices, suggesting acceptable basis risk. However at the time an airline needed a jet fuel hedge most, at the inception of the Gulf conflict, jet fuel prices tripled while gas oil only doubled.

4.0 OPTIONS

Options are contracts granting the right (but not the obligation) to buy or sell an asset for a specified price (the 'strike price' or 'exercise price') within a specific time period (at expiration or until expiration). The purchaser pays the seller (or 'writer') of the option a premium for that right. The option buyer's risk is limited to the premium paid. Most exchange-traded options for crude oil or petroleum products are actually options for futures.

Call options grant the holder the right to buy the asset at the agreed price (establishing a price ceiling) while put options give the holder the right to sell the asset at the agreed price (establishing a price floor). American-style options allow exercise at any time during the life of the contract while European-style are exercisable at expiration. Modified American options provide for exercise on specific dates (eg monthly or quarterly) while so-called 'Asian'-style options are exercisable on one date but valued by reference to a 'strike-index' which averages several price 'samples' over a specified period.

Forwards and futures include an upside for the buyer if prices for physicals go up balanced by a downside risk if prices go down. Options are much more versatile than forwards or futures because they enable the user to separate the upside price potential (represented by a purchased call option) and downside price risks (represented by a sold put option) of the underlying asset. Combinations of options, called spreads, come in almost unlimited varieties and can be used to build almost any type of derivative instrument.

4.1 Pricing Options

The five most important factors in pricing an option are the strike price, the amount of time until expiration, the current price of the underlying asset, real interest rates (net of any yield on the underlying asset), and volatility of the spot price of the underlying asset. Pricing of European-style options has been facilitated in recent years by the availability of various analytical models for deriving derivative prices.

The best known model, known as Black–Scholes,[37] is aimed at call options for corporate securities. It is based on the assumption that arbitrage will eliminate any risk-free profits available from combinations of options and the underlying securities. By constructing a riskless hedge using the call option and its underlying security the Black–Scholes model solves for either the option price or the hedge ratio. Unfortunately it requires assuming some important variables, such as that interest rates and price volatility will be constant, and does not take account of transactions costs (which would be significant under the assumption of constant rehedging every time the underlying stock price changes).

American-style options are more difficult to price using analytical models because they can be exercised at any time. Numeric techniques, such as averaging the results of randomly generated scenarios on a discounted basis provide an alternative approach.

The principle model for petroleum derivatives is the two-factor model published by Rajna Gibson and Eduardo S. Schwartz in 1990.[38] Unlike Black–Scholes, which focuses on volatility of the underlying asset, the Gibson–Schwartz model also takes account of changes in the convenience yield (the value of actually owning the physical consumable commodity).

4.2 Option Price Movements

The extent that an option price changes when the price of the relevant underlying asset changes is called the option's delta. If the option's price moves to the same extent as the physical asset, the delta equals one. If it moves only half as much as the underlying asset, the delta is 0.5. The delta of an option is used to calculate the amount of the underlying asset that must be held or sold short to offset any risk from the option.

According to Black and Scholes, if a stock option's delta is 0.5, then at any given moment in time you can completely hedge the risk of selling that option (ie a short option position) by holding 0.5 shares of the underlying stock. But the riskless position doesn't last long since the option's delta changes with time. Gamma is the rate of change in an option's delta. A small gamma means the delta changes slowly and a hedge based on the delta at a given time will last longer. Theta is the effect on the option price as it approaches expiration. Theta is usually negative, meaning the option becomes less valuable as it approaches expiration.

4.3 Warrants

Warrants are options issued in primary markets through public and private placements. Their return is linked to the performance of an underlying equity, commodity

37. F. Black and M. Scholes, 'The Pricing of Options and Corporate Liabilities', *Journal of Political Economy*, pp.637–59 (May–June 1973). Modifications of the Black–Scholes models have been published since to take into account various aspects of particular options, such as transactions costs and different intervals between adjustment of hedging positions (Hayne E. Leland, 1984) and the specifics of foreign exchange options (Mark B. Garman and Steven W. Kohlhagen, 1983).

38. R. Gibson and E. Schwartz, 'Stochastic Convenience Yield and the Pricing of Oil Contingent Claims' 45 *The Journal of Finance* p.959 (1990).

or index of equities or commodities. Many warrants issued in connection with Eurobonds do not require any additional payment of a strike price at the time of exercise. Call (or 'bull') warrants give the holder the contractual right to obtain the excess (if any) of the value of the referenced asset on the exercise date over the strike price, while put (or 'bear') warrants give the holder the excess of strike price over the exercise value.

The London Stock Exchange permits warrants of up to five years linked to equities of companies other than the warrant issuer, currencies, metals, oil or indexes of any of those types of assets. In contrast to the other derivatives mentioned above, the main rationale for issuers of commodity warrants is to reduce their cost of funds. This might be by providing an alternative to linking a bond issue to equity (*eg* where the issuer cannot issue any more equity), or by accessing investors they might not reach otherwise (*eg* investors with a hedging requirement but no access to the OTC market – such as individuals or managers of portfolios limited to listed securities).[39]

Shortages of medium and long-term capital for project financing has encouraged project sponsors to consider combinations of commodity warrants and notes or bonds, called 'commodity linked' notes or bonds. A 'petro bond', for example, might carry a fixed interest rate coupon with a part of the face value of the bonds denominated in barrels of oil (giving it a bull warrant effect by rewarding the investor with higher principal if oil prices go up).

The short-term over-the-counter equivalent of a commodity warrant/bond combination is the commodity loan, popular in the gold mining industry but of potential interest to energy concerns. A common form of commodity loan is a revolving credit facility secured by the commodity producer's reserves. When the commodity producer decides to draw funds, it specifies the loan amount in commodity units (*eg* barrels of oil) and the duration of the loan. The revolving credit agreement will provide the formula for computing the total amount of commodity units due at maturity (including interest and principle). Although short-term, the loan hedges the reserves of the borrower in that the value of the loan declines if the commodity value declines.[40]

5.0 SWAPS

Swaps are over-the-counter transactions whereby two parties exchange streams of payments (cash flows) at certain times in the future according to some pre-arranged formula. The formula could be based on an interest rate calculation, the spot price of an asset or any other suitable variable. They work like a series or 'strip' of forward contracts, and are often analysed that way.

Whereas futures were developed in the commodities markets centuries ago and options were developed in the commodities and equities markets in the nineteenth

---

39. For a general discussion of some of the more noteworthy oil-linked primary market offerings (including BP's New York Stock Exchange listed 'Prudhoe Bay Royalty Trust'), see X Trabia, *Derivatives: From Options to Oil Warrants and Synthetic Oilfields* (1993).

40. See K. Leong, 'Structured Derivative Products: Commodity Price Hedging for Producers and Consumers', *The Columbia Journal of World Business* pp.74–5 (Summer 1992).

century, swaps were developed in the financial markets less than 15 years ago. Swaps evolved from parallel loans in different currencies arranged in the 1970s to avoid UK tax on foreign exchange transactions for foreign investment. A UK company would loan sterling to a foreign company in the UK, while a foreign affiliate of the UK company would borrow foreign currency from the foreign company or its affiliate.

5.1 Currency and Foreign Exchange Swaps

In the late 1970s parties began directly swapping different currency payment streams (now called 'currency swaps') to avoid the cross-default problems inherent in parallel loans among affiliates. At the same time currency swaps were coming into use, borrowers in the Euromarkets found they could issue notes or bonds in one currency and arrange forward exchange contracts to convert the proceeds and coupon and principal obligations into another currency. For example in 1979, Orion Royal Bank issued Deutschmark notes and hedged them into US and Canadian dollars, with lower overall borrowing costs than if it had borrowed directly in US or Canadian dollars. This structure became known as a 'foreign exchange swap'.

At the beginning of the 1980s, the World Bank found it could only satisfy its large borrowing needs in the large dollar denominated Eurobond market and US domestic market. This posed a problem for the bank because at that time the dollar was a higher interest currency than the German mark or Swiss franc and the bank had a policy of borrowing and lending in low-interest currencies. In August 1981 the World Bank found a solution when it issued $290m in Eurobonds and then swapped the fixed dollar denominated interest and principal on those bonds with IBM for German mark or Swiss franc denominated obligations, bringing currency swapping wide attention in the international financial markets.

Cross-currency swaps today normally consist of a commitment by one party to make periodic payments based on either fixed or floating rates to a counterparty, who commits in return to make periodic payments to the other in a different currency. There is usually an exchange of principal at the beginning and end of the swap. Currency swaps no longer require a party interested in a swap to find a counterparty with the 'mirror image' of its problem. The currency swap market for combinations of US dollars and Japanese yen, Swiss francs, Australian dollars, Deutschmarks and Canadian dollars are liquid in maturities of up to 10 years. Banks can arrange a swap with one party, partially offset it with a transaction with another party and then hedge its 'residual' position in the spot foreign exchange and interest rate futures market. While currency swaps are primarily used to convert funding advantages in one market into a favourable position in another, they can still be used to work around exchange controls in some countries.

5.2 Interest Rate Swaps

In 1979 a London banker arranging currency swaps realised that fixed rate interest obligations could be swapped against floating rate obligations in the same currency without the exchange of principal at the beginning and end of the swap. A 'fixed-for-floating' swap in 1982 by the Student Loan Marketing Association in the US gave interest rate swaps wide attention.

Just as different companies and institutions have different funding advantages in different currencies, they may also have different funding advantages in the fixed interest rate and floating rate market. A company or institution with a higher credit rating has a comparatively easier time borrowing in the fixed interest rate market while a company or institution with a lower credit rating has a comparatively easier time borrowing in the floating interest rate market. Consequently, when a higher rated institution wants to borrow at floating rates or a lower rated company wants to borrow at fixed rates, they each may be best off borrowing in their stronger market and swapping into the desired market.

The classic 'plain vanilla' swap involves one party who commits to make periodic payments based on floating interest rates (often six months LIBOR) on an imaginary ('notional') principal amount and a counterparty who commits in return to make periodic payments based on fixed interest rates on the same notional amount. But unlike the currency swap, there is no exchange of principal at either the beginning or the end, so the ultimate credit exposure each party is taking on is less than in a currency swap with comparable 'interest' payments. Most interest rate swaps are in dollars and compute the floating interest rate obligation on the basis of LIBOR.

The other main type of interest rate swap is the 'basis-rate' or 'floating/floating' swap, in which one floating rate based on one reference (*eg* three months LIBOR) is exchanged for another floating rate based on a different reference (eg three month US T Bills).

Just as options permit the separation of the upside potential or risk of a forward or future from the downside risk or potential, caps and floors permit a similar separation of the up and down sides of swaps. In 1985 a group of 20 US banks arranged a $2.75bn issue of floating rate notes (FRNs) which limited how high the interest rate payable under the note could 'float'. That limit or maximum interest rate payable meant that if market interest rates exceeded the limit, the issuer was relieved of the obligation to pay the difference between the market rate and the maximum under the FRN. The bank then sold the right to be paid the difference between maximum rate payable under the FRN and the market rate separately for an up-front fee (mostly to savings and loan institutions interested in limiting or 'capping' their short-term borrowing costs against their returns on longer-term loans).

The protection against interest rates over a certain level enjoyed by the issuers of the FRNs and purchased by the savings and loan institutions became known as 'caps'. Purchasers of caps are often willing to pay for them in whole or in part by accepting 'floors', which set a minimum on the floating rate they will pay even if market rates drop lower. Today caps and floors on interest rates denominated in US dollars, sterling, Deutschmarks, yen, Swiss franc and lira are large and liquid and are actively traded in an over-the-counter market for one to five years maturities.

5.3 Commodity Swaps

Swaps transactions involving an exchange of 'floating' and 'fixed' commodities appeared in 1987, after large securities firms involved in financial markets as well as forward and physical oil markets began offering hedging services to their customers,[41] and US regulators allowed banks to deal in direct transactions in commodities, commodity futures and forward contracts.[42] As with 'plain vanilla' interest rate swaps, one party commits to make periodic payments based on a floating reference, but instead of using interest rates at the time of each payment, the floating payor in a commodity swap pays the spot market price of the commodity on the payment date. Instead of multiplying the interest rate by the notional principal of the loan, the spot commodity price is multiplied by the notional quantity of the commodity. Again as with the interest rate swap, the fixed payor pays a fixed amount on each of the same payment dates as the floating payor, but instead of being based upon long-term interest rates it represents an estimate of the time-weighted average of the commodity's forward price for each of the payment dates contemplated in the swap.

One of the advantages of swaps over other energy industry derivatives is the long duration available. Crude oil swaps of up to five years are quoted regularly in the *Petroleum Economist*. Another advantage is the operational simplicity of their cash settlement as compared with the forward markets. With respect to many grades of crude oil and petroleum products swaps have overtaken the role of forward contracts for risk management.[43]

Swaps on the differential in price between two underlying commodities (called 'spread' swaps or 'margin' swaps) have also become popular, particularly 'crack spread' swaps used by refiners to fix the spread between crude prices and their refined products. Commodity linked price caps (essentially the commodity swap's answer to European-style call options) that put an upper limit on particular commodity prices, and price floors (European-style put options) that put a lower limit on prices, have been finding their way into energy industry financings.

5.4 Documentation and Negotiability

In the same way that the British Bankers' Association stimulated the forward rate agreement market with their standard terms, a US-based organisation, the International Swap Dealers' Association, Inc, accomplished the same thing in the currency and interest rate swap markets with their 'Code of Standard Working, Assumptions and Provisions for Swaps' in the mid-1980s. Today the ISDA Master Agreement provides the standard for the industry.

Since 1991 the ISDA has been developing amendments to the ISDA Master Agreement and 'Commodity Derivative Definitions for Cash-Settled Transactions' so that ISDA forms may be conveniently used for commodities transactions. However there seems to be some reluctance to use such extensive documentation in commodity swaps, with different institutions proposing their own forms of master agreements.[44] Since swaps are over-the-counter instruments, they cannot be sold without a cumbersome process of credit evaluation of the buyer and the

---

41. See M. Annesley, 'Strategies for Risk Management Using the Paper Markets', in *Energy Law '92*, (Graham & Trotman, 1992), p.66.

42. K. Leong, supra note 40, p.75.

43. M. Annesley, supra note 41, p.70.

44. For a recent overview of documentation issues see E. O'Shea, 'Making Sense of Commodity Derivatives' 12 *International Financial Law Review* 36 (1993) and Chapter 21, this Volume.

counterparty that is not selling. In most cases swaps are only sold when the buyer and the non-selling counterparty already have a master agreement with each other in place. Parties to a swap also have the option of early termination under the complex valuation provisions included in ISDA-based agreements. The third option is to 'unwind' or 'reverse' the swap with another swap.

Currency unwind swaps are very complex transactions requiring consideration of interest rate changes as well as foreign exchange rate movements and co-ordination of several parties. Interest rate swap reversals are like a currency unwind swap without the foreign exchange aspect. The party reversing its swap simply enters into a new swap with the same or a different counterparty that is the reverse of the original swap. In a swap 'closeout' one party simply receives or pays the counterparty an upfront payment which brings the internal rate of return of the fixed-rate cash flow to a market level. The fixed-rate matches the floating rate as a consequence, bringing the swaps value to zero.

6.0 CONCLUSION

The petroleum industry has been built on risk sharing to a greater extent than almost any other. Financial and commodity derivatives have broadened the range of parties to whom different components of energy-related risks can be transferred and increased the number of alternative ways those risks can be spread. In many cases derivatives can be used in financings to reduce several risks at the same time.

For example in 1989, Sonatrach borrowed US dollars under a scheme linking interest rates payable to the extent average oil prices in a given year were above or below $18 per barrel. During the first year one dollar above $18 per barrel would increase the relevant interest rate by 0.5 per cent. An additional dollar above that would add another 0.25 per cent. During the second year one dollar above $18 per barrel would increase the relevant interest rate by 0.5 per cent, the second dollar by an additional 0.5 per cent and the third dollar by 0.25 per cent. In essence the lenders received a cap on oil prices, receiving significant amounts for limited increases in the market price. Sonatrach paid higher financing as its revenues increased. Other aspects of the scheme also increased the interest rate if credit exposure increased due to falling oil prices.

In project financings, where debt is to be serviced and repaid out of the revenues of the project, currency risk (where the sales revenue of the project is different than the currency of the financing) and price risk (sales prices too low or supply costs too high) are among the challenges facing lenders and sponsors. (For a fuller discussion on project financing see Chapter 19.) Currency derivatives have become a common tool in project financing to deal with the first risk. For price risks, the traditional approach in project financings has been take-or-pay contracts, where the buyer agrees to pay a minimum price for goods or services whether or not they end up actually taking them. However in a world of increasing volatility in energy prices, fixed price take-or-pay contracts are becoming rarer. One would expect commodity derivatives to be increasingly considered to deal with price volatility.

Chapter 21

English Law Documentary Practice in the Off-Exchange Commodity Derivatives Market

Eoin O'Shea

1.0 INTRODUCTION

Although currently enjoying a broader audience of participants than at any previous time in their history, off-exchange (or 'over-the-counter') commodity derivatives are not a new product. Recently, however, steadily increasing volumes of transactions and the involvement of greater numbers of participants in the off-exchange commodity derivatives markets have focused attention on the legal and documentary issues which distinguish commodity derivatives.

This Chapter examines the legal principles underlying current documentary practices in the off-exchange, cash-settled commodity derivatives markets, contrasts and compares them with those in the physical market (*ie* physical settlement) and briefly distinguishes the varied types of documentation which have evolved.

2.0 ASSUMPTIONS

In order to focus on a discussion of commodity derivatives in the context of English legal practice, it has been necessary to make certain assumptions.

These assumptions are the use of English governing law and the submission to English jurisdiction in relevant documentation and that, in compliance with all relevant laws and regulations applicable to it, an entity would be capable of participating as principal in fixed income off-exchange derivative products which do not involve a commodity element (such as interest rate and currency exchange derivative transactions).

Non-English law matters are not discussed – readers are urged to consult with local lawyers expert in commodity derivatives in respect of all foreign law and

297

regulatory aspects applicable to this business. In particular, your attention is drawn to US legal and regulatory considerations under the Commodity Exchange Act (as recently amended by the Futures Trading Practices Act of 1992).

3.0 CERTAIN TERMS

The description 'derivative' will be generally used throughout rather than the more ubiquitous 'swap', which seems increasingly to be misused in a generic fashion to encompass many diverse types of derivative transactions which may not, like a swap, involve the exchange of liabilities (eg options).

The terms 'derivative' and 'derivative transaction' are used to describe the broad range of off-exchange financial transactions, products and instruments, which derive from (or are predominately attributable to) primary financial transactions, products or instruments which exist independently (whether on-exchange or otherwise) of the relevant derivative or derivative transactions.

The terms 'commodity' and 'commodities' are used in the sense of primary products of raw material principally being 'energy commodities' (ie oil and gas) but also including 'precious metal commodities' (ie gold, silver and platinum) and 'non-precious metal commodities' (ie aluminium, lead, zinc and copper). They are not used to describe 'paper' commodities such as equity or debt securities or 'soft' commodities such as sugar or cocoa.

4.0 STRUCTURE OF A COMMODITY DERIVATIVE TRANSACTION

The basic structure of a commodity derivative transaction is shown in the following diagram. In this example of a 'swap' transaction, the concept is very straightforward – an agreement between two parties to enter into the periodic exchange of fixed for floating US$ payments. The floating payments are calculated by reference to an agreed 'index'. As a consequence, the party receiving fixed payments (ie the floating payer) has its exposure to price decreases in the underlying commodity reflected in that index 'hedged' at the agreed 'fixed' price. In return for the payment of floating amounts, the floating payer transfers its floating exposure to the movement in price of the underlying commodity to a fixed exposure to its derivative counterparty. The fixed payer similarly 'hedges' its exposure to price increases by paying predetermined fixed amounts.

For the purposes of calculating floating payments and fixed payments, both parties assume a 'notional quantity' of units (in this case 'barrels') under the transaction. Since the transaction is cash-settled, the notional quantity does not represent any actual delivery of barrels but is simply an arithmetic convenience corresponding to the exposure of the oil producer to the underlying commodity it chooses to 'hedge'.

Most other derivative transactions are simply variations on this theme. For example an option may reflect the value of the right to buy or sell the commodity at a future point (or points) in time at a predetermined 'strike-price'. Essentially, in

Example Fixed/Floating US$ Commodity Swap Transaction referenced to price of Brent blend crude oil:

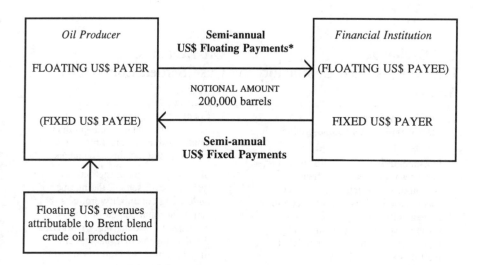

based on movement in price per barrel of Brent blend Crude oil, as quoted under the heading 'Spot Crude Price Assessments: International: Brent' in the issue of Platt's Oilgram that reports prices on the relevant date for price determination

return for a single fixed payment (known as the 'premium'), the buyer of the option obtains protection (or can take a view) on the future floating price of the underlying commodity. If structured correctly, such an option would provide the fixed price payer (or 'buyer') with the right to receive from its derivative counterparty (the 'seller') a future floating cash amount which corresponds to its future exposure to the movement in the underlying commodity.

5.0 PHYSICAL MARKETS V CASH-SETTLED MARKETS

Although any commodity derivative transaction may be structured to incorporate physical settlement, commodity derivative transactions are typically cash-settled. Commodity derivative transactions are ultimately applied as risk management (or 'hedging') tools which supplement or which are secondary to exposures originating in the relevant primary market (or under other commodity derivative transactions).

This distinction between the cash-settled and physically-settled markets is reflected in the different types of documentation which each market has generated, each having developed over many years forms of documentation to accommodate the particular legal and credit perception of their respective markets.

The following table should help illustrate some of the primary documentation issues which distinguish these two markets:

Off-Exchange Physically-Settled Commodity Market

1. Form of Agreement

Master agreements (single-product/ 'single-shot' agreements).

Documentation may be 'focused' on one or a very limited number of commodity products with distinct specifications. This tends to keep the agreement relatively concise and 'product-specific'. In addition the types of transactions contemplated may be extremely limited, perhaps including only delivery and payment obligations and 'book-outs' (*ie* the ability to cancel mutually off-setting positions).

It is not uncommon to incorporate by reference 'Standard Terms and Conditions' of third party major market participants. Master agreements are reasonably common. Short-form 'single-shot' telexes are widely used which may rely on the weight and perspective of a 'trading relationship' to make up for any dearth of legal detail.

2. Delivery

Physical settlement including extensive terms relating to delivery (*ie* insurance, delivery location, method of delivery, transfer of title and grading specifications) and the parties' duties in connection therewith.

Off-Exchange Cash-Settled Commodity Market

1. Form of Agreement

Master agreements (multi-product usually although sometimes single-product)/'single-shot' agreements.

Since derivative transactions are typically cash-settled, the number of underlying commodity products that can be accommodated in a single agreement is extensive. A marketing disadvantage is that one agreement may become 'cluttered' trying to cover too many commodity indices. In addition, many different types of transactions (with associated provisions) may be contemplated *ie* swaps and options.

Credit sensitivity and capital adequacy concerns drive enthusiasm to obtain master agreements wherever possible. Short-form 'single-shot' documentation generally unacceptable due to the level of legal detail which is expected.

2. Payment

Cash settlement with brief and extremely straightforward correspondent bank payment instructions.

3. **Market Disruption/*Force Majeure***

'Market Disruption' of price reference usually not considered in depth (if at all).

'*Force Majeure*' provisions are prevalent (although actual content can vary considerably), reflecting the hazards which may beset physical delivery.

3. **Market Disruption/*Force Majeure***

'Market Disruption' provisions are common to cover the possible disruption or breakdown in the availability of the relevant floating price, the formula or method by which it is calculated, the source from which it is obtained, the suspension or discontinuance of any related futures contract (*ie* used for hedging) or a change in the specification (*ie* the content, composition or constitution) of the underlying commodity.

In a market whose principal function is to provide effective risk management based on hedging strategies, 'Force Majeure' provisions are predominately considered inappropriate since the events they seek to cover usually represent an inalienable part of the risk which is being managed (*eg* Gulf crisis in 1991).

More specific 'Illegality' and 'Tax' provisions and a general reliance on common law doctrines of frustration are preferred.

4. **Credit Provisions**

Outside of usual insolvency/ bankruptcy provisions and failure to pay/deliver, there are typically much shorter provisions relating to the continuing creditworthiness of a counterparty.

Delivery may be structured to be exclusively against payment (including the possibility of legal title passing but title documents being withheld) or credit support (*ie* a letter of credit) arranged/demanded. Creditworthiness sometimes assessed on 'relationship' or 'trading' basis.

4. **Credit Provisions**

Extensive provisions relating to continuing creditworthiness of counterparty (*eg* cross-default on general debt, merger protection, linkage to default under other derivative transactions and default events linked to creditworthiness of affiliates).

Dealers may have extensive resources devoted to credit assessment and monitoring since financial institutions frequently intermediate between lesser credits (*ie* taking credit exposure on both sides allowing the relevant counterparties to take its credit while it must assess each counterparty).

5. **Tax**

'On-balance sheet' activity. The imposition of tax is usually considered the responsibility of each party, i.e. it ought to manage its own tax affairs. Unique Petroleum Retention Tax issues arise with respect to petroleum products.

Unique Value Added Tax issues arise relating to the delivery of allocated precious metal bullion.

5. **Tax**

'Off-balance sheet' activity. 'Gross-up' protection for imposition of tax is demanded for greater degree of certainty. No Value Added Tax ought to apply by virtue of Schedule 6, Group 5, Item 1 of United Kingdom 1983 VAT Act.

6. **Payment Netting**

(*Ie* net payment during the life of a transaction for same – currency obligations arising on the same date.)

Usually consists of obligations which cannot be netted (*ie* currency versus commodity) so no netting is possible unless there is two-way business; however 'book-out' provisions are sometimes included.

6. **Payment Netting**

Netting of cash obligations (in same currency) for mutual/two-way cash obligations. Especially useful in a master agreement with payments under several transactions falling due on same date.

7. **Close-out Netting**

(*Ie* net payment following the default of a party.)

Where it exists, usually calculated on a 'two-way' basis (*ie* irrespective of which party defaults, the party which is owed is paid, usually less the damages and expenses of the non-defaulting party).

7. **Close-out Netting**

Historically calculated on a 'one-way' basis (*ie* non-defaulting party is not obliged to make a payment to a defaulting party) – however, fairness, enforceability and other regulatory concerns (*eg* recognition of netting for capital adequacy purposes) have recently brought about a sea-change to a 'two-way' approach.

8. **Settlement Period**

Settlement against commercial invoice – settlement period may be quite extensive (*ie* up to 30 days following delivery).

8. **Settlement Period**

Settlement automatically follows pre-agreed dates – no invoices required (although brief telexes confirming actual rates are usually exchanged) – settlement period is usually very brief, typically 2–3 days.

9. **Legal Resources**
Much greater willingness to do business on the basis of standard terms, usually based on (or expressly incorporating) standard terms and conditions of third party major market participants. In some instances, alteration of 'standard' commercial delivery terms/duties may not be perceived as expedient or time-efficient in a physical market where actual delivery of the commodity needs to take place within a finite period. Legal resources may be limited and parties may be reluctant to devote extensive time and resources to 'counterparty-by-counterparty' negotiation.

9. **Legal Resources**
Each institution tends to reserve its right either to produce its own form of agreement or extensively to negotiate what it determines to be the material terms of standard forms of master agreements (such as the Interest Rate and Currency Exchange Agreement published by the International Swaps and Derivatives Association, Inc). Financial institutions frequently employ comprehensive legal resources (whether internal or external) – and place a high emphasis on 'counterparty-by-counterparty' negotiation.

10. **Calculation of Damages (*ie*, Loss)**
Calculation of loss is relatively straightforward *ie* failure to pay or failure to deliver (and/or breach of duties associated with delivery and payment) – market liquidity assists assessment of loss since the quantum of damage is relatively easy to assess by reference to market prices.

10. **Calculation of Damages (*ie*, Loss)**
Calculation of loss is complicated by mutual executory nature of obligations under most derivative transactions – present value of unliquidated (or contingent, in the case of options) future obligations may be difficult to determine since, to some extent, any calculation involves taking a 'view' on the characteristics and volatility of a future market.

Due to the relatively illiquid nature of the commodity derivative markets (and the consequential difficulty in obtaining meaningful and competitive quotations), a straightforward indemnification for loss is the most popular method, followed in popularity by a loss calculation by reference to the average of a number of market makers' (or dealers) quotes. The quotation method follows the predominant practice in the more liquid fixed income (as opposed to commodity) derivatives markets.

11. Isolation of Agreement
Typically there is a limited relationship between the parties outside of the physical delivery/payment relationship. It is therefore possible to view their rights and obligations in isolation within one relatively narrow band of commercial activity.

11. Isolation of Agreement
A financial institution may frequently have other exposures to the counterparty (or its affiliates) through non-commodity related products (*ie* through lending or other banking activities). This potentially multi-faceted relationship will usually cause the financial institution to expect to see its protection under any legal document take account of that greater context.

12. Environmental Issues
Allocation (or avoidance) of responsibilities needs to be considered and compliance with relevant legislation addressed.

12. Environmental Issues
Not an issue in a cash-settled market.

13. Governing Law and Submission to Jurisdiction
Arbitration is frequently chosen as the most appropriate forum to reach a 'commercial' understanding in a cost-effective manner. It can make considerable sense where the movement of a physical commodity is 'frozen' in transit during a dispute, making timely resolution crucial to both sides.

13. Governing Law and Submission to Jurisdiction
Arbitration is usually avoided with heavy reliance placed upon comprehensive negotiated contractual protection and ultimate legal recourse to courts preferred for a greater degree of certainty. Since no physical commodity is 'frozen' in transit (*ie* all obligations are cash-settled) there is less urgency to reach a timely compromise.

6.0 FORMS OF DOCUMENTATION

There is currently no universally accepted form of agreement for documenting commodity derivative transactions; however, two broad trends can be identified, each bearing hallmarks attributable to the market from which it has originated.

Broadly speaking, commodity derivative documentation in the off-exchange markets has been produced by two principal categories of counterparties (and their respective legal advisers):

(a) financial institutions and financial intermediaries; and
(b) end-users, producers and refiners.

6.1 Financial Institutions and Financial Intermediaries

6.1.1 Credit Analysis – Counterparty Risk

Since it is generally not the objective of a financial entity to take a position in the derivatives market that it has not otherwise protected from a risk management perspective (or 'hedged'), it naturally follows that a financial entity will ultimately see its risk (provided it has done its risk management correctly) as counterparty credit risk. In other words, it will seek to eliminate the market risk associated with the volatility or variability in the price of the underlying commodity but will generally accept that, absent third party credit support, collateral credit enhancement or escrow-style arrangements, counterparty credit risk is an inalienable factor to be taken into account in doing business with a counterparty. The financial entity will accordingly attempt to control or manage that exposure by adjusting the amount and/or maturity of credit exposure that it will consider undertaking with its counterparty.

This type of credit assessment or analysis falls naturally into general 'banking' activity. Most financial entities tend to be either well structured and resourced themselves (or have banking affiliates which are appropriately structured and resourced) to analyse large volumes of this type of counterparty risk.

6.1.2 Origins of Off-Exchange Commodity Derivative Markets

Although exchange-traded commodity transactions (*ie* options and futures contracts) have been established for some considerable period of time, the off-exchange commodity derivatives markets have only relatively recently accumulated sufficient depth and liquidity to attract a substantial number of financial entities.

Financial entities have, however, entered the commodity derivative field bearing historic and well-established credit assessment techniques and expectations (together with associated requirements for legal certitude and protection) which have evolved from techniques developed and tested in the fixed income derivative markets.

6.1.3 Approach to Documentation – 1993 ISDA Commodity Definitions

This is reflected in the approach to documentation of financial entities. In early 1991, groups of the major participants in the fixed income derivatives markets in London and New York met under the auspices of the International Swap Dealer's Association, Inc (ISDA) to co-ordinate and establish, as formal documentation committees, amendments and definitions which would enable the 1987 ISDA Interest Rate and Currency Exchange Agreement (and its successor, the 1992 ISDA Master Agreement) to be used for commodity derivative transactions. The groups were predominately comprised of financial entities but also included representatives from the major producers, refiners and users in the oil, gas and metals industries.

The objective and concept was simple: to produce a booklet of 'Commodity Derivative Definitions' which would allow commodity derivative market participants to benefit from the use of predetermined defined terms and standardised terminology, following directly on the enormous international success in the fixed income markets of the ISDA 1987 Interest Rate and Currency Exchange Definitions and the 1991 ISDA Definitions. The booklet was published in July 1993.

One of the most striking features of the 1993 ISDA Commodity Definitions is the extensive number of underlying commodities that it seeks to cover. As mentioned earlier, since commodity derivatives are typically cash-settled – it is possible for a financial entity to enter into derivative transactions referenced to a very broad variety of commodity indices on a cash-settled basis, unencumbered by the unique idiosyncratic difficulties associated with entering into obligations involving physical delivery of the underlying commodity.

This eclectic collection provides a reference point for abbreviated definitions of the most 'popular' commodities, indices and price sources in the energy and metal markets. A great deal of thought and analysis/contribution from market participants has gone into this non-exhaustive list accurately to pin-point the most prevalent market practice and standards.

6.1.4 Comprehensiveness May Be a Drawback

A drawback however for physical market participants contemplating this form of documentation may be the very comprehensiveness of the 1993 ISDA Commodity Definitions. Although it has long been the legal approach of financial entities, where possible, to accommodate as many transactions (and products) under one 'master agreement' as is commercially sustainable in order to take advantage of any close-out, settlement netting and capital adequacy efficiencies which may be available, for the market participant that consistently deals in a low volume of transactions or in a limited number of products, the extra detail can be seen as superfluous or obfuscatory.

The mechanism of cash-settlement (as opposed to physical settlement) can also involve lengthy definitions concerning, for example, how floating rates/fixed rates are obtained, how settlement amounts are calculated, how the parties address the potential failure or breakdown of the relevant price source or index by reference to which they had hoped to calculate the variable price of the underlying commodity and the collapse/suspension of the exchange-traded market in that commodity or exchange-traded futures and options contracts relating to it.

6.2 End-users, Producers and Refiners

6.2.1 Credit Analysis – Counterparty Risk

Generally speaking, the objectives of end-users, producers or refiners, although consistent in some respects, fundamentally contrasts with those of financial entities since they will generally have an underlying exposure to the extraction, refinement or use of the underlying commodity. That exposure is further distinguished from the cash-settled markets in that it involves the physical delivery of the underlying commodity and is typically of a much shorter maturity. Whereas in the derivative market, maturities may extend out to five years, in the physical market (or cash-settled exchange-traded futures or options market), maturities will typically only go out, with any degree of substantial liquidity, to about 18 months.

This has very important repercussions on documentation. Accustomed to a market where the ultimate risk is relatively short in tenor, a physical market participant may take a short-term view of the future likelihood of legal uncertainty or potential credit exposure which may be much more pragmatic or 'commercial' than its more conservative commodity derivative market counterpart.

6.2.2 Origins of Physical Market

The trading market for some physical commodities clearly pre-dates the arrival of its distant derivative cousin by some considerable period (off-exchange physical forward markets date back to the sixteenth and seventeenth centuries). This has naturally allowed a considerable degree of market practice to evolve together with associated legal documentation requirements.

As was the case with their derivative counterparts, physical market participants have also brought to the derivatives market expectations and requirements based on their experience.

6.2.3 Approach to Documentation

There currently exists no universally accepted market standard form of documentation which physical market participants feel comfortable with in the derivative arena, although many of the leading participants (particularly those with substantial internal treasury trading personnel and/or with affiliates which are participants in the derivatives market) have produced their own standard form of agreement, usually relatively short and product specific.

For reasons discussed earlier, the reluctance to use 'fixed income' inspired ISDA-type documentation is marked. The experience of financial entities has been that they must be prepared to offer to their derivative clients in the physical market two sets of possible documentation; one ISDA-based and the other based on the more abbreviated forms available in the physical markets.

6.3 Typical Considerations Relating to the Content of a Commodity Derivative Master Agreement and Associated Transaction Confirmation

6.3.1 Agreement

  (i) *Preamble*

      Consider how many commodity products will be covered by the agreement? How will each transaction be confirmed – telex, facsimile and hardcopy confirmations? The precise legal name of your counterparty is very important since it may be a specialised trading subsidiary – consider credit support (*eg* guarantee) as appropriate. It is useful to include an express reference to the jurisdiction of incorporation of your counterparty to ensure that local law commodity issues have been addressed. Include statement that transactional 'confirmations' can overrule a master agreement.

  (ii) *Calculation of Fixed and Floating Amounts*

      (a) *Calculation*

          This is usually a straightforward provision, though terminology varies. The basic concept is a provision of a formula to allow the 'Notional Quantity' (*eg* a number of barrels) to be multiplied by the 'Fixed Price' (*ie* US$ per barrel) and/or the 'Floating Price' (*ie* US$ per barrel) to give 'Fixed Amounts' (*ie* US$ payment due) and 'Floating Amounts' (*ie* US$ payment due) respectively. Consider whether 'options' (*eg,* caps, collars and floors) should be included and, if so, which types of option?

(b) *Market Disruption to Floating Price*

Parties need to anticipate the possible disruption of the availability of the price of the underlying commodity.

(c) *Adjustments for Market Disruption*

Having determined that a Market Disruption has occurred in respect of the floating price, the parties need to agree on how adjustments are made to the floating price to take account of that disruption.

Rather than defer calculation indefinitely to the next day on which the price source is available, or revert after a specified period to the 'old' formula and method used before the disruption, some counterparties prefer to 'call a halt' and opt for termination of the transaction if the price source cannot be obtained after a suitable specified period (typically 3–5 days). The singular problem, however, with using this 'termination' approach is that, by definition, the floating price is unavailable – the accuracy of any loss calculation is therefore bound to suffer.

NB Adjustment of 'Fixed Payment Date': whichever method is chosen, remember that if floating payment is deferred, then, in order to avoid unmatched payment obligations, the corresponding fixed payment obligation should be adjusted (*ie* deferred) accordingly.

(iii) *Payment*

(a) *Frequency*

Under cash-settled commodity derivative transactions, payment dates will typically be semi-annually, quarterly or, less frequently, monthly. Up to five days is usually allowed for payment.

(b) *Currency*

Typically US$.

(c) *Netting of Payments*

There are two main types of netting, (i) payment netting; and (ii) close-out netting:

(i) *Payment Netting*

Straightforward administrative procedure – same currency payment obligations falling due on same date are netted against each other (*ie*, extinguished) and 'novated' into a single payment obligation, being the difference between those separate amounts (this can be done on an aggregate basis for all transactions under a master agreement).

(ii) *Close-Out Netting*

This is an expression used to describe settlement provisions which purport to net 'termination payments' following a default (*eg* where an executory contract is terminated prior to its scheduled termination date).

(d) *Gross-Up*

It is important that an indemnity is required of the payer for any withholding or deduction of taxes which result from a change in tax law following the execution of the agreement and which have the effect of decreasing the payee's anticipated payment. This should be coupled with a requirement on the payee to deliver and complete appropriate tax forms. Exclude taxes solely attributable to a 'connection' between the jurisdiction imposing the tax and the payee.

(e) *Default Interest*
Consider the provision of default interest at a reasonable rate (*eg*, 1 per cent over cost of funds) during any applicable grace period for late payment.

(f) *Condition Precedent*
Payment obligations should be subject to the absence of a counterparty default under the agreement.

(iv) *Representations and Warranties*
These need to address the usual due, proper and valid incorporation/ establishment issues, power and authority to conclude and perform commodity derivatives and any special representations relating to commodities unique to particular jurisdictions.

(v) *Events of Default*
These should include the usual failure to pay, insolvency/bankruptcy and breach of agreement issues but should also include counterparty cross-default (*ie* for 'borrowed money') and default under other derivative transactions. Affiliates or providers of credit support (*eg* a guarantor) should be included where appropriate. Consider automatic early termination on the occurrence of insolvency/bankruptcy.

(vi) *Termination Events*
These should include 'no-fault' events such as a change in tax law or supervening illegality. Include merger, takeover and acquisition of control protection (*ie* material creditworthiness decline following these events).

(vii) *Early Termination – Calculation of Settlement Amount*
Loss calculation may be in the form of (i) a general loss indemnity (*ie* a non-defaulting party (or the party to whom the 'Termination Event' has not occurred, as the case may be) determines its loss by reference to the cost of liquidating transactions and/or the economic cost of their replacement); or (ii) by reference to selected market makers who are asked to quote on the value of the terminated transactions. In each case include legal expenses (although this may be less sustainable for a no-fault event) and any unpaid amounts. Provide for default interest at a reasonable rate (*eg* 1 per cent over cost of funds).

(viii) *Set-Off*
Where possible, a comprehensive contractual 'set-off' provision should be included. This is a common practice in the derivative markets due to the wide range of business which a financial entity may have with its counterparty (or its affiliates) outside of the terms of the relevant agreement. For reasons discussed earlier, it is far less common in the physical markets where an agreement may be viewed in a more isolated context.

(ix) *Transfer/Assignment*
Should be drafted restrictively (*ie* no transfer without prior consent) to permit both parties to evaluate the legal and regulatory consequences of a potential new commodity derivative counterparty.

   (x)   *Notice Provisions*
       Attention details should be carefully entered to ensure that all those who 'need to know' are adequately informed (*eg* risk manager, credit officer and legal counsel) – this is frequently overlooked.

  (xi) *Governing Law and Submission to Jurisdiction*
       This discussion has been based on the choice of English governing law and submission to the jurisdiction of the English courts. Include appropriate provision for the appointment of a 'process agent' for service of legal process outside England and Wales. Waiver of immunity should be included by sovereign (or quasi-sovereign) entities.

6.3.2 Transaction Confirmation

The confirmation is intended to be a clear statement of the commercial terms of the transaction and any amendment(s) to the relevant master agreement.

   (i)   *Preamble*
       Should clearly identify the relevant master agreement and a statement incorporating its terms by reference. Where no master agreement has been executed, the parties should choose a 'fall-back' set of terms, pending negotiation in good faith of a suitable agreement.

   (ii) *Commercial Terms*
       Care should be exercised to use terms previously defined in the master agreement properly. This arrangement only works efficiently where terms are used consistently.
       The following basic commercial terms should be addressed:

     (a) **Exact legal name of counterparties** – include exact legal name of any credit support provider;

     (b) **Transaction type** – *eg* swap, option, etc;

     (c) **Trade date** – meaning the day upon which the transaction is orally concluded;

     (d) **Effective date** – meaning the first day by reference to which a floating payment begins to accrue;

     (e) **Termination date** – meaning the day upon which the last determination or calculation period ends (see below). This may not be the day that obligations terminate since the last payment may be payable after the termination date;

     (f) **Designation of fixed/floating payers** – *ie* the parties;

     (g) **Notional quantity** – meaning the number of units (*eg* barrels) which provide the multiplier for determining the parties' payment obligations. May be expressed as a total for the entire transaction or may be expressed as a set number per determination period;

     (h) **Price source** – meaning the origin of reference to obtain the floating price of the underlying commodity (*eg Platt's Oilgram*). Consider including an alternative or fall-back price source;

     (i) **Description of underlying commodity index** – meaning the index by reference to which the floating price is calculated (*eg* 'the closing price per barrel of Brent blend Crude oil, as quoted under the heading

"Spot Crude Price Assessments: International: Brent" contained in the price source'). This needs to be as precise as possible with accurate specifications. Consider including a fall-back index. 'Market disruption' language does not need to be duplicated here if already included in the master agreement. Consider whether or not any proprietary rights exist in the use of an index;

(j) **Delivery month** – *eg* July 1992;

(k) **Determination or calculation periods** – meaning the fractional period between one payment date and the next payment date (also the effective date to the first payment date). Not essential except for 'Asian-style options';

(l) **Fixed price** – used to calculate fixed price payer payment amounts. May be specified as 'fixed amounts' instead;

(m) **Payment dates** – meaning the due dates for payment (include appropriate payment date convention to deal with non-business days);

(n) **Business days** – meaning days upon which payments can be made;

(o) **Governing law** – often omitted on basis that it is already included in master agreement (which is incorporated by reference). Must be included where master agreement is not yet signed;

(p) **Calculation agent** – meaning the entity (usually one of the parties) responsible for doing the administrative calculation of the amounts owed by each party prior to each payment date under the transaction. Can include responsibility for calculation and adjustment following 'market disruption' if the parties agree. Not to be confused with the entity responsible for calculation of a 'termination amount' payable following the default of one of the parties – that is usually the function of the non-defaulting party;

(q) **Payment details** – meaning correspondent bank details for payment; and

(r) **Acknowledgement** – the confirmation may include a brief form of acknowledgement to be returned to the sender, acknowledging and agreeing to the terms of the confirmation. Most financial entities consider it prudent to follow up with a hard copy confirmation. This has the advantage of being a single written instrument, removing any potential inconsistencies which may arise as a result of an exchange of telexes and helps to ensure that the legal terms (as opposed to the commercial terms) of the confirmation have been reviewed by an appropriate authorised signatory and/or legal counsel.

Index

313